THE SHADOW OF THE SWASTIKA

The Rise of Fascism and Anti-Semitism in the Danube Basin, 1936-1939

Bela Vago

Published for the Institute of Jewish Affairs
London
1975

 Saxon House

SAXON HOUSE,
D. C. Heath Limited,
Westmead,
Farnborough, Hants, England

© The Institute of Jewish Affairs 1975

The Institute·of Jewish Affairs is grateful for the assistance of the Memorial Foundation for Jewish Culture which made the preparation of this volume possible.

The publishers gratefully acknowledge the support of the University of Haifa.

Transcripts of Crown-copyright records in the Public Record Office appear by permission of the Controller of Her Majesty's Stationery Office.

ISBN 0 347 05002 6
Library of Congress Catalog Card Number 74 — 3909

Typeset in Great Britain by
Preface Ltd., Salisbury, Wilts.,
and printed and bound in Great Britain
by Redwood Burn Limited, Trowbridge & Esher.

Contents

Note

The official name of the main right extremist party in Romania during the period covered by this book was "Totul pentru Țară" (All for the Fatherland), led by Corneliu Zelea Codreanu and subsequently by Horia Sima. This party was in no important respect different from the "Legion of Archangel Michael", or from the "Iron Guard".

The name of the main Hungarian right extremist party in the first years of our period was "Hungarist Movement", or "Hungarian National Socialist Party", later "Arrow Cross Party", led by Ferenc Szálasi. (During the last War years the party changed its name to "Arrow Cross Party – Hungarist Movement".) During the whole period the names "Iron Guard", "guardists" and "legionnaires", respectively "Arrow Cross" ("nyilaskeresztes", "nyilas") have become best known. Hence the various names have been used interchangeably.

Usage before the War spelled the name of the country as "Roumania" or "Rumania". In the last decade, English has more or less accepted the spelling "Romania", which has been adopted for this work. Quotations have been left as they were spelt at the time.

In part II (Documents) we omitted all salutations, opening sentences and closures.

Acknowledgement

I wish to express my gratitude to the Institute of Jewish Affairs (London) which commissioned this work and made possible its appearance, and to the University of Haifa for its generous subsidy.

In preparing this volume I have had the assistance of many individuals I should like to express my gratitude to Dr. S. J. Roth, Director of the Institute of Jewish Affairs, and to Dr. O. Arie, its Administrative Manager, for their friendly co-operation. I am grateful to Miss Ann Harroway for her valuable assistance in the editing of this book, and to Mr. George Schöpflin of the School of Slavonic and East European Studies (University of London) and of the B.B.C., who translated or revised the major part of the manuscript and contributed to its improvement with his valuable remarks.

PART 1

Introduction

In their researches into the growth of fascism in the inter-war period in the Danube Basin, scholars have tended mostly to depend on source material from one side only – the German archival material on the one hand and the rather sparse contemporary documentation of the extreme right-wing movements of the period.

With the release of the pre-war material of the British Foreign Office, the opportunity has arisen for the first time to observe the process from another viewpoint, a non-fascist or anti-fascist Western one, and to follow the rapid pace at which the small states of Eastern Europe were driven to the extreme right within the direct sphere of influence of Germany.

In contrast to the official German archival material, which reflects a prettified version of the situation, consonant with Berlin's *Wunschtraum,* the material at the Foreign Office presents the situation unembellished and with far-reaching objectivity. Not that all British diplomats proved to be excellent observers of events, nor was their information accurate in all cases, nor did Whitehall necessarily draw the right conclusions from the information received, but the contacts between the leading figures of British diplomatic, political and economic life with the policy makers of Eastern Europe were more sincere and more intimate, perhaps, than the contacts available to the Germans or Italians. King Carol or Admiral Horthy – or for that matter even the pro-Nazi Romanian Octavian Goga and the Hungarian pro-Nazi Béla Imrédy – spoke more freely to British officials than to German or Italian diplomats and politicians. Western observers – and this includes the French as well – had a better knowledge of the mood and political opinions of the man in the street than had the Germans. As a result of all this, the British records of policy and diplomacy – even if they are not more detailed than other sources – do provide material which reflects the realities of the pre-World War II political life of the Danubian countries more faithfully than anything else hitherto available. This concerns particularly Romanian and Hungarian ruling circles and to a lesser extent Czechs and Slovaks after Munich. The British records contain illuminating information on the covert political views of these leaders and on the real motivations of their activities, such as is not to be found in material of any other provenance.

The Foreign Office material throws light on numerous questions which have remained unresolved precisely because of the one-sided nature of the existing source material. Our aim is to assist those involved with the study of the dynamics and methods of the successes of the extreme right by publishing here a selection and interpretation of the relevant material from the Foreign Office archives.

The material in question examines little-known details of Britain's policy towards Eastern Europe and, at the same time, it also throws light on neglected aspects of the policy of appeasement. This policy was not only applied *vis-à-vis* Hitler and Mussolini, but it also had a directly harmful impact on the democratic opposition forces in Eastern Europe. With the objective of restricting the successes of the extreme right, British policy tended to support the supposed moderate right, rather than the democratic forces, with the slogan of "taking the wind out of the sails" of the extreme right, regardless of the fact that the so-called moderate right was increasingly adopting the programme of the extreme right. Critics of appeasement will find a good deal of useful ammunition in the Foreign Office material published here.

The Foreign Office archives offer a good deal of primary material for students of fascist-type movements, particularly where their objectives, character and real motive forces are concerned. At the same time, the material contains information on the connections that these movements had with Nazi Germany.

This study deals only with Romania, Hungary and Czechoslovakia — strictly speaking, regarding right radicalism, Slovakia only — among the states of the Danubian area. In the mid-1930s, particularly after 1936, the growth of right-radicalism rapidly altered the physiognomy of the political life of Romania, Hungary and Slovakia. On the eve of World War II, the Romanian Iron Guard, the Hungarian Arrow Cross and the Slovak Hlinka party were among the most radical and most widely supported right extremist mass movements in Europe.

In Romania, a wing of the extreme right gained power as early as 1937. The short-lived Goga-Cuza government was followed by the Royalist Dictatorship, inaugurated in February 1938, and this may have been more moderate than the pro-Nazi, anti-semitic National Christian regime which it replaced, temporarily checking the Iron Guard's struggle for power; but for all that, in the final analysis it was no more than a transition towards a Nazi-type dictatorship.

Immediately after Munich the fate of Slovakia evolved under the influence of both the Hlinka party's activities and those of the Third Reich. Bohemia-Moravia was likewise the subject of a shift to the right. The post-Beneš vacuum was filled by right-wing elements, which showed a much stronger inclination to collaborate with Berlin than contemporary Czechoslovak historians are prepared to concede.

There was no change of system in Hungary until 1944, but the anti-semitic legislation (zsidótörvény) of the late 1930s, coupled with the intensifying of territorial revisionism and chauvinism, created the atmosphere in which Hungary developed into a crypto-fascist state serving the Axis powers, before any other country in the area.

These three countries followed Nazi Germany most closely and most radically in their "solution" of the Jewish question. Given the fact that in Eastern Europe extreme nationalism and the extreme right were inseparably fused with anti-semitism, this study simultaneously chronicles the pre-history of the holocaust of East European Jewry. The Foreign Office archives show with great clarity how anti-semitism became a political weapon in the power struggles of the area, both in domestic and in foreign affairs.

The selective documentation in this work relates only to the right-radicalisation and to the breakthrough of anti-semitism in the three countries concerned and is no more than a small part of the available British source material. The scope of the study, which precedes the documentary part of this work, based on the British archival material, is at most a sketch. A thorough exploitation of these sources will facilitate a survey of the background of the authoritarian and totalitarian extreme right movements and systems in the Danubian area, and of the Jewish holocaust, thus offering further means to a more faithful analysis of the origins of World War II as well.

This work deals essentially with the attitude of British diplomats and observers of other governmental services on the spot towards the above-mentioned trends and developments. Obviously one has to distinguish between the diplomatic service and the Government. Consequently the material quoted and analysed here reflects first and foremost the viewpoint of British diplomats and representatives of different governmental Offices in the area, which were not always and not

5

automatically identical with the attitude of the British Government. Besides the diplomatic service, the policy-making of Great Britain was influenced by a number of factors, such as internal party policies, the attitude of the defence establishment, of the Colonial service, the influence of Jewish organisations upon governmental circles etc. "British policy", or "the British attitude" towards the uprush of the extreme right in the Danubian area and the radicalisation of anti-semitism cannot be defined without taking into account all the components of the shaping of the official policy. Nevertheless, the specific aspect and channel of policy-making presented in this work must have exerted a determinant influence upon the view adopted and the decisions taken by the Foreign Office and thus often by the Government itself. Both the importance of the diplomatic service and its intelligence, and at the same time the limitations of its influence on British policy-making, should be borne in mind when attempting to evaluate this selection of documents from the Public Record Office.

Sortie from the West European Glass-House

"... if I were to say that Britain's interests in peace are geographically limited I should be giving a false impression ...

The world has now become so small – and every day with the march of science it becomes smaller – that a spark in some sphere comparatively remote from our own interests may become a conflagration sweeping a continent or a hemisphere. We must therefore be watchful at all times and in all places ... We must neither mislead others nor be misled ourselves by any of those comfortable doctrines that we can live secure in a Western European glass-house."

(Anthony Eden, Bradford speech,
14 December, 1936)

Although British foreign policy in the mid-1930s left the walls of the West European glass-house far behind, it turned towards the small states of Eastern Europe only belatedly, and even then it was not greatly interested in them, nor did it attribute much significance to their internal developments. The prism through which the British Government observed the fate of the states of the Danube Basin was that of the forward thrust of German and to a lesser extent Italian policy. British (and French) interest in the Danube Basin intensified as the pressure of the two totalitarian powers on the area grew in the economic, political and ideological fields. But though British interest in the internal problems of Austria, Czechoslovakia, Hungary and Romania increased, this was not sufficient to lead to any action.

The starting-point of British foreign policy was that the most efficient

7

way of preventing German and Italian penetration into Eastern Europe was to impede the progress towards power of the extreme right-wing movements. To further this, British foreign policy, once Eden was in charge, sought allies in the area to break the power of local Nazi and fascist forces.

In Czechoslovakia there was no danger from extreme right subversion until the moment the Czechoslovak Republic disintegrated, but the activity of the Slovakian extreme nationalist Hlinka party did occasion some uneasiness in London at the time of the Sudeten crisis. In spite of this, no attempt was made to take any effective steps, which might have weakened the position of the Slovak extremists. Consequently, some doubt must arise that the danger represented by the Slovak clerical extremists to Czechoslovakia and beyond this, to the entire Danube Basin, remained unrecognised until the autumn of 1938.

The situation was wholly different with regard to Romania and Hungary. In both countries, the political arena could be divided into three broad trends. There was (a) the right-wing group in power, gradually weakening; (b) a heterogeneous group of democrats and the left; and finally there was (c) an equally heterogeneous extreme right, gradually gathering strength. The alternatives from the Western point of view were the following – either to support the bourgeois democratic and socialist forces, with the aim of helping them to gain power, or to support the right-wing group in power against the extreme right, even if this meant dropping the democratic forces. With few exceptions, the local representatives of British foreign policy tended to regard the latter course as preferable, on grounds of *Realpolitik*.

In Romania the right-wing National Liberal Party (NLP) had been in power since 1933. It had had to cope with a strong agrarian opposition. The National Peasant Party (NPP), democratic but strongly nationalistic, had managed to maintain its power base among the masses, despite electoral chicanery and police terror. In addition to the NPP, the small Radical Peasant Party had made its voice heard on the bourgeois left against the rightist government forces. The socialists and the extreme left offered no effective opposition to the rule of the NLP. The socialists were divided into several groups and tiny parties. The stronger of them, the Social Democratic Party, was on the right wing of the Socialist International and had failed to adopt any rigorous and uncompromising stand against the right-wing regimes of the inter-war period. The illegal Communist Party, with a membership of about 1,000, played no significant rôle in the country's political life.

8

Until 1935 the extreme right was seriously split and it was not in a position to consider taking power. Corneliu Codreanu's Iron Guard, Professor Cuza's anti-semitic League of Christian National Defence (LANC) and Octavian Goga's fascist-type party, taken together, held not more than nine per cent of the seats in parliament. However, 1936 proved to be a turning-point and it led to a rapid accession of strength by the extreme right.

The Romanian political arena — not the misleading balance of strength in parliament — was by and large divided into three equal camps. There was the ruling right-wing NLP, the extreme right and the democratic forces. As to the country's foreign policy, whereas the extreme right demanded a re-orientation towards Germany and Italy, the democrats and the ruling NLP were both predominantly Francophile, but also pursued a pro-British orientation. Whilst the democrats agreed in general with the NLP over foreign policy, the NLP, which commanded the majority of seats in parliament, was closer to the extreme right on the question of the Jews and of the national minorities. The government party was "moderately" anti-semitic, whilst the various groups of the extreme right demanded radical solutions on the German model.

From the mid-1930s on, the authoritarian King Carol began increasingly to throw his weight into day-to-day politics — externally, leaning on Britain and also France for support; internally, leaning rather towards the right than towards the democrats. In the circumstances, it was obvious that British foreign policy would regard the King and, for many years, the NLP as its allies.

Although in social structure, economic life and foreign policy, there were more divergent features and processes than similarities between Romania and Hungary, the division of political forces was strikingly alike. In Hungary in the mid-1930s the National Unity Party, headed by aggressively revisionist and "race protector" (fajvédő) politicians who enjoyed Horthy's confidence, commanded a comfortable majority of nearly 70 per cent of the seats in parliament.

The bourgeois democratic opposition to the regime was heterogeneous and ineffectual. The strongest opposition party was the Independent Smallholders' Party (ISP) which held almost 10 per cent of the seats in 1935. Representing well-to-do farmers and small landowners, it could hardly be called bourgeois and democratic. The party leader, Tibor Eckhardt, a militant counter-revolutionary and "moderate" anti-semite, was a typical representative of the Hungarian gentry. Nonetheless, the ISP differed sharply from the government in the field of foreign policy — the

9

majority of the ISP leaders were hostile to a _rapprochement_ with Germany, which, they feared, would lead to the loss of the country's independence. Instead, they advocated a policy of collaboration with the democracies of the West. Another grouping of the opposition was a Catholic, legitimist and conservative bloc, broken up into several factions, and likewise holding about 10 per cent of the seats. This grouping was also opposed to any alliance with Hitler, disagreeing with the majority on this issue of foreign policy. The leaders of both the ISP and the Catholic-conservative bloc, especially the latter, were markedly pro-British in their attitudes.

The bourgeois liberal and radical opposition, whilst also in disagreement with the government's pro-Axis policy, was equally critical of its anti-democratic domestic policies. This group held seven to eight parliamentary seats in the mid-1930s.

The socialists and the extreme left did have some influence on Hungarian political life, but this factor was regarded as non-existent for practical purposes by British foreign policy. Hungarian social democracy could look back to a rich past and carried some weight in domestic affairs. Despite the undemocratic electoral system, it was able to secure parliamentary representation throughout the era, though never more than four to six per cent of the seats. Anti-communist persecution made it impossible for the Hungarian communists to reorganise their movement after the collapse of Béla Kún's Soviet Republic in July 1919. In 1936 the party numbered at most 1,000 members.

The extreme right – the Nazi-type movements of Böszörményi, Szálasi, Hubay, Count Festetics and others – was still in its infancy, without mass support, with eight to ten seats in parliament (out of 245). The extreme right emerged for the first time as a considerable political force in Hungary in 1936. From that year on, the extreme right, and especially the movement led by Ferenc Szálasi, had reached the centre of the political stage. The growth of this grouping may have been uneven, but by 1939 it had emerged as a force with serious prospects of taking power.

Two political issues in Hungarian public life linked on a common platform the "moderate" right, the extreme right and a part of the opposition generally regarded as democratic: territorial revisionism and the question of the Jews. In practice, every political group in Hungary was revisionist and with the exception of the extreme left and bourgeois-liberal democratic circles, every party was anti-semitic. So far as the Jewish question was concerned, the ruling National Unity Party was divided only by a hair's breadth from the extreme right, whilst the leadership of the ISP, and its following, counted as "moderately" anti-semitic.

In as much as Britain supported the right-wing parties in power in

Romania and Hungary, on grounds of *Realpolitik*, it gave its seal of approval automatically to the official anti-semitic trend, operating with "legal" methods. And commensurately with the growing influence of the extreme right on the masses, British foreign policy made concessions to the anti-democratic and anti-semitic measures of the Hungarian and Romanian Government, aimed at taking the wind out of the sails of the extreme right. The Foreign Office was hardly overjoyed at this competition between the right and the extreme right, which involved an unceasing radicalisation of the right – in an authoritarian and anti-semitic direction; nonetheless, it expressed its understanding and even its approval of the process.

In 1936, as a result of international developments and of domestic events both in Romania and in Hungary, the struggle among the three principal political forces (the ruling parties, the left and the extreme right) grew more intense. Around 1936 the internal crisis, coupled with the rapid advance of nazism and fascism, resulted in a measure of polarisation in both countries. The ruling right was weakened, as were the moderate forces of the centre, whilst the extreme right – as also the extreme left – gained in strength. Financial troubles became worse in both countries and agriculture was severely depressed, mainly in Romania. In Hungary, after the death of the dictatorially-minded Gyula Gömbös, a more moderate, more cautious and less authoritarian government came to power. This government, that of Kálmán Darányi, showed less enthusiasm about a pro-German orientation than had Gömbös, the "godfather" of the Axis. The new government was incapable of coping with the economic problems which beset it, just as in Romania the Tătărescu government could find no solution to its problems. In both countries the standard of living of a large part of the population was deplorably low, the foreign debt per head of the population was among the heaviest in Europe, the middle classes were impoverished and general discontent was obviously increasing. In Hungary, as in Romania, the extreme right was the main beneficiary of this growing restiveness.

1936 was also the year when the Axis powers gained their first significant victory on the international plane, which went hand-in-hand with the growth of their influence and the intensification of their propaganda in Hungary, in Romania and even in those Slovak circles which were voicing noisy separatist and ultra-nationalist demands. All this had the consequence that in all three countries, especially in Romania and Hungary, the moderate right became more radical. It revised its political objectives and tactics, taking over many of the elements of the ideology and methods of the extreme right. These three developments – the success of the extreme right, the radicalisation of the moderate right and

11

the gradual penetration of the Danube Basin by the Axis powers – led British foreign policy to take a greater interest in the politics of these three countries from 1936 onwards. The Foreign Office was interested in more than just the question of the Sudeten Germans in Czechoslovakia and minority problems in general; it took note of extreme-right activity among the Slovaks on the one hand and the rising strength of a trend in Czech circles which favoured a *rapprochement* towards Germany. In the case of Romania and Hungary, the Foreign Office devoted particular attention to the grave developments in these countries, possibly for the first time, in 1936.

It is surprising, however, that as late as 1936, by which time numerous ominous reports were reaching London from the three Danubian capitals, the British Government should still have underestimated both the great-power ambitions of Germany and Italy in the Danubian area and also the internal transformation taking place, which eased the way of German penetration in a short period of time.

The Southern Department of the Foreign Office prepared a report for the Cabinet, which discussed German political and economic penetration at the end of February 1936. About the rising tide of fascism in Romania, the Department noted only that "Roumanian organisations of a Fascist character have, from time to time, played a certain part". With regard to German penetration and the co-operation between local extreme right-wing forces and Nazi Germany, the Foreign Office entertained harmful illusions and thereby affected the British Government as well. ". . . Germany does not appear to have made any serious attempt to influence the course of events in Roumania", stated the report, "or to have any political ambitions there".[1] Nor did the view of the Department differ concerning Hungary. "The aim of German policy appears to be not to absorb Hungary politically, but to make her economically the complement of Germany and her partners."[2]

It was only at the end of 1937 and the beginning of 1938, rather late in the day and involving rather few people, that London awoke to the fact that the internal evolution of Eastern Europe was heading rapidly towards fascism, which would lead sooner or later to their domination by Germany, not least because an efficient, organised and determined internal opposition to this was lacking. It was only then, by which time it was irremediably late, that the Foreign Office thought that rather than supporting the right, they should be supporting democratic forces in the countries exposed to German aggression. Sir Orme Sargent, writing in 1937 about the domestic upheavals in Romania, mentioned "a general trend in the Danubian countries away from parliamentary democracy", which "is being hastened by the growing fear that Germany's domination of the

12

Danubian Basin is now inevitable. If the Danubian states now begin to put on the Nazi garb, it will be because imitation is the sincerest form of flattery and because they want to ingratiate themselves in time with their future master".

Prague appeared the only fixed point in this constellation, but Sir Orme struck a realistically pessimistic note with regard to the Czechs as well. Beneš, he wrote, "may soon be standing in Prague, like the boy on the burning deck, whence all but he had fled. But will even he stand for very long, when once he feels himself completely abandoned by his Little Entente allies?" His conclusions on the tasks ahead for British policy were more sceptical: "As for us . . . the only thing which might stop [the 'German flood'] would be to put new courage into the democratic elements of Central Europe by showing them that the great democracies of the West are resolved to prevent the Nazi flood from breaking through the present weak and weakening dyke, which is Austria; and this the great democracies are definitely not prepared to do."[3]

Just over two months passed after these lines were written and the Danubian countries had their proof that the great democracies had neither the capacity nor the intention of preventing the Nazi flood from breaking through.

At the same time, Sir Alexander Cadogan's estimate of the situation was also pessimistic. "It certainly seems", he wrote on 3 January 1938, "that an authoritarian wave is beginning to surge through the countries of Central and Eastern Europe. The trend is away from 'democracy' which is represented as clogging and inefficient for dealing effectively with the successive shocks to which the world is subjected . . . We can only hope that the Western democracies may one day, by their firm action, give the lie to all the stories of this 'effeteness'." [4]

During those days, under the impact of the shocking events in Romania, Neville Chamberlain and Anthony Eden asked every British minister in South Eastern Europe for the first time for their views of the shift to the extreme right and on German penetration. Before anything else, they noted that "for some time past a trend away from parliamentary democracy has been noticeable in most of the countries of the Danubian Basin and the Balkan Peninsula (with the notable exception of Czechoslovakia). But the recent occurrences in Romania [5] may be symptomatic of a more positive development in the direction of authoritarian government on the model of Germany or Italy." The Prime Minister called the attention of the British diplomats to the fact that "if and where this tendency towards authoritarian government does exist, it is of considerable interest to know what constitutes the motive force behind it". Chamberlain enquired of British diplomats, "Is it [the trend towards

13

authoritarian government] merely due to the feeling that temporarily during the period of political and economic abnormality . . . a stronger and more efficient form of administration is needed than in a more peaceful and settled period? Or is the real impulse due to the influence of Germany's example, combined with the fear that Germany's domination in Central and South-Eastern Europe is now inevitable?" The Prime Minister also asked the diplomats for their views on whether, perhaps, the veering away from democracy and towards authoritarian regimes might be ascribed to a disposition "to fortify themselves for resistance against German encroachment" or whether this phenomenon "denotes a determination, proceeding from a conviction that German dominance is merely a matter of time, to compound with the inevitable, and by ingratiating themselves stave off the worst effects of that domination when it eventuates."[6]

There is no evidence to suggest that following on this request there was any significant shift in British foreign policy towards Central and South Eastern Europe. At most one can conclude that there was no encouragement of local democratic forces, but on the contrary, the right-wing forces in power continued to enjoy the confidence of Chamberlain, who took little interest in the Danubian states anyway; his endorsement of the rightist regimes was shared by Eden and later by Halifax.

After the *Anschluss* the Foreign Office had no illusions left about Germany's ambitions in Eastern Europe or about the internal developments in the Danubian states. A memorandum was drawn up by the Foreign Office towards the end of April 1938 on the situation in Central and South Eastern Europe. This sketched the prospects in dark colours: "[Germany] will attempt to extend her influence and make her will predominant by means of (a) the organisation of Nazi (or its equivalent in the idiom of the country concerned) cells or parties within the country itself and (b) by economic pressure." As regards the organisation of Nazi parties in the area, the author is certain that in Romania "the Iron Guard . . . constitutes the nucleus of a formidable party organised something on the lines of the Nazi and Fascist parties in Germany and Italy. In Hungary those in favour of totalitarian government represent so far only a small minority but active Nazi propaganda is being carried on with the help of German subsidies." In the Balkans "Yugoslavia and Greece are already virtually military dictatorships, and Bulgaria, though engaged in re-erecting a façade of parliamentary institutions, still enjoys what is in essence an authoritarian regime. The seed of Nazi doctrine, therefore, falls on fertile ground." As regards German economic pressure, the memorandum established that Germany already had a predominant

14

share in the trade of the area and that, following on the *Anschluss,* this share would rise.[7]

During the first half of the period under discussion, British foreign policy allowed itself illusions about German-Italian rivalry in Central and South Eastern Europe. There was some hope felt that this rivalry would act as an impediment both to the strengthening of the locally-grown extreme right and to the attainment of domination by the two totalitarian powers. Sir Orme Sargent had no doubts at the beginning of 1937 that the "Fascist Government [of Italy] are aware of the dangers of a *rapprochement* with Germany which they have chosen to negotiate" and "darkly behind the 'forest of eight million bayonets', we can discern the shadow of deep disquiet."[8] There can be no doubt as to the accuracy of the interpretation, only as to the conclusions drawn from it, which were certainly not borne out by events in the Danube Basin.

Towards the end of 1938 and the beginning of 1939, opinion in the Foreign Office was virtually unanimous that the danger represented by Nazism and Fascism to the British Empire had become the central question. A Foreign Office memorandum of early 1939 pointed out that "there is little reasonable doubt that of all the nationalism abroad at present, including Communism which in theory at least is international, none represents such an *immediate* menace as Nazism and Fascism."[9] All this, however, failed to bring about a change in the line pursued by the Foreign Office; on the contrary, it convinced a large number of politicians and diplomats that the nationalist right was the best possible ally in the Danubian area against Nazi German and Italian Fascist expansion and domination. For a considerable period of time, the view prevailed in London that the local extreme nationalist movements would unquestionably come into conflict with a Nazi Germany that was aiming at their subjection.[10]

In the late 1930s a natural concomitant of the rightward shift in the Danube Basin was the intensification of anti-semitism. Romania had a government in power with an anti-semitic programme as early as December 1937; in Hungary the first anti-Jewish laws were passed in the following year;[11] even before Munich an anti-semitic trend began to be clearly discernible in Slovakia, whilst the birth of the Slovak state in 1939 resulted in anti-Jewish legislation similar to the Nuremberg Laws.

The anti-semitic policy of "taking the wind out of the sails" of the extreme right, adopted in Romania and Hungary, had catastrophic consequences for the 1.6 million Jews living in the two countries. Although the British and French Governments frequently and successfully

15

intervened against extremist anti-Jewish measures, they too adopted the principle of "taking the wind out of the sails", whereby they accepted moderate anti-semitic measures as desirable and useful. British diplomats in Bucharest and Budapest, well intentioned and not anti-semitic, together with a number of Foreign Office officials of a similar disposition, were of the opinion that moderate anti-semitic measures would de-fuse the anti-semitism of the mass of public opinion and were, therefore, desirable from the viewpoint of the ruling right-wing governments, because in this way they would avoid being "compromised" in the eyes of the masses, which would not thereby be pushed into the arms of the extreme right solely on the issue of the Jews. British diplomacy unquestionably went much further in collaborating with the right-wing governments on this issue than did the French. It happened more than once – the interventions against the Goga-Cuza government in Romania were one instance – that the British Government tried to influence the French Government, so that Paris would not appear over-committed to the Jewish interest and thereby indirectly provide ammunition for the extreme right.

Virginio Gayda, the Italian journalist, the semi-official mouthpiece of the Fascist regime, wrote of the Danubian states in January 1938 that there existed one point of "national cohesion" among the various political groups and this was anti-semitism. There was an element of truth in this, particularly as regards Hungary and Romania. The assumption cannot be dispelled that there were British politicians and diplomats who respected this "point of national cohesion", or at least were willing to take account of it. Consequently, they were unwilling to prejudice Britain's links with those circles in the Danubian area which were simultaneously anti-semitic and anti-German, by harping too much on the Jewish issue.

The evaluation of the reports arriving from the Danubian area and their utilisation in Britain's foreign policy were considerably hindered by the inconsistencies and contradictions within the Cabinet. Whereas anxiety about the fate of Central Europe grew daily within the Foreign Office, Sir Thomas Inskip, the Minister for Co-ordination of Defence, reported to a meeting of the Cabinet shortly before Munich on the eastward thrust of Germany, ". . . we were prepared to see Germany a great people, with a rising population, and a tremendous force in the world. Nor did we propose to deny Germany a *dominating position in South Eastern Europe,* if this could be obtained by proper methods. What we objected to was the use of threats and force."[12] Halifax shared this view; to be more exact, in reality it was his view.[13]

On the one hand, British foreign policy tried to influence developments

16

in the Danubian countries in the vital interests of the Western democracies, whilst on the other, it happened frequently that senior diplomats were severely criticised in London for having attempted to influence local political factors. Presumably Eden was serious when he asserted in 1937 that "it is nations' foreign policy, not their internal policies, with which we are concerned."[14]

Two years later, after the occupation of Prague, Chamberlain openly committed himself to defend East Central Europe. At the time when he offered guarantees to Romania and Greece, he announced in the House of Commons: "What we are concerned with is to preserve our independence and when I say 'our independence' I do not only mean this country's. I mean the independence of all states which may be threatened by aggression . . ."[15] Exactly one year earlier Chamberlain thought that Britain might have some special part to play as conciliator and mediator in the European crisis and no more.[16] When Halifax succeeded Eden, he wrote to him, ". . . you have got to live with the devils whether you like them, or not . . ."[17]

It was hard to know in East Central Europe in the late 1930s whom the British regarded as "devils", in what circumstances Britain would play the rôle of conciliator and mediator and who, to what extent and in what situation, could count on Britain for the defence of their independence. Nor was it clear how far anyone could rely on London to be interested not only in their foreign policy, but also in their internal affairs, when faced with brutal intervention on the part of Germany and Italy – all the more so seeing that the connection between the internal and external policies of the Danubian states was probably never as close in the entire inter-war period as in the late 1930s. It is the complexity and contradictions of this policy which help to explain why Britain failed to play a rôle in the Danubian area, to which her great power status, moral weight and prestige would seem to have predestined her. But perhaps it is precisely this inconsistency and the multiplicity of connections – far exceeding those of Nazi Germany – which have made the primary documentation in the Foreign Office archives on the area so far-reaching and credible.

Notes

1. Memorandum prepared by O'Malley, head of the Southern Department in the Foreign Office, for Cabinet, Committee on Germany, 24 February 1936 (Doc.No.3)
2. Ibid.
3. Minutes by Sir Orme Sargent, 1 January 1938 (Doc.No.59)
4. Minutes by Sir Alexander Cadogan, 3 January 1938 (Ibid.)

5. The coming to power of the extreme right-wing Goga-Cuza government on 30 December 1937

6. Chamberlain to Hoare, 6 January 1938 (Doc.No.65)

7. F. O. Memorandum prepared by P. Nichols, 21 April 1938 (Doc.No.98)

8. Foreign Office Memorandum, prepared by Sir Orme Sargent, 11 January 1937, Public Record Office [P.R.O.], F. O. 371, R 622/188/12

9. Foreign Office Memorandum, 25 January 1939 (P.R.O., F.O. 371, N 2975/1459/38)

10. On the contrary, the Germans were convinced about the willingness of the nationalistic, rightist regimes of the area to collaborate with Nazi Germany. Wohlthat, one of Ribbentrop's top officials, in charge of economic affairs, wrote in February 1939 after a visit to Bucharest: "The political development of the national states in Southeastern Europe will follow the German pattern to an increasing extent, while the influence of the Western European democracies and the Soviet Union would be eliminated." (Documents on Germany Foreign Policy [DGFP], Series D, Vol. V, Doc.No.306)

11. The law, followed by more drastic ones, was called "the first Jewish Law", thus leaving out of consideration the real first one, the "*numerus clausus*" law of 1920.

12. P.R.O.,613,Cab.23 (95), Cabinet 38 (38), Conclusions, 14 September, 1938, p.56 (author's italics).

13. Oliver Harvey noted on 19 March: "H[alifax] told me he could quite understand German action in regard to Austria . . . There was in any case no objection to Germany having economic hegemony in Central Europe. What H. objected to was the methods employed. . ." (*The Diplomatic Diaries of Oliver Harvey, 1937—40,* ed. John Harvey, London 1970, p.121)

14. Speech in the House of Commons, 1937 (*The Eden Memoirs: Facing the Dictators,* London 1962, p.508)

15. Neville Chamberlain, *The Struggle for Peace,* London (n.d.), p.434

16. Speech at Birmingham, 8 April 1938 (Ibid., p.177)

17. The Earl of Birkenhead, *Lord Halifax. The Life of Lord Halifax,* London 1965, p.380

ROMANIA

1 Rightist Explosion

Paradoxically, Greater-Romania groaned under the burden of victory and success after the First World War. In October 1918 Romania was still a defeated party and part of its territory was under German occupation in the terms of a Brest-Litovsk kind of "peace-settlement". In the months following, however, it played the rôle of a victor on the side of the Entente in the new period.

The acquisition of Transylvania (including Maramureş, Crişana and the Banate), Bukovina and Bessarabia more than doubled the territory and population of Romania. The enlarged country could look forward to rapid development and prosperity. The integration of the new territories, however, especially the Western ones, did not go without a hitch. The Regat[1] had neither the administrative nor the cultural means to initiate new state processes. In the absence of democratic traditions and political experience, the parliamentary system was democratic only on paper. The corruption and levantine political practices were a bitter disappointment to those who had expected a modern, democratic evolution.

Equally paradoxically, national unification created a "nationality" state rather than a "national" state. In 1920 the nationalities formed around 30 per cent of the country's population. Bessarabia and the Hungarian minority in Transylvania proved to be particularly difficult problems. Bucharest was under permanent threat from Hungarian irredentism and revisionism and the Soviet state never recognised the annexation of Bessarabia. All this generated an anti-minorities psychosis and drove Romanian nationalism, in any case chauvinistic, to new extremes in which anti-revisionism, anti-communism and anti-Sovietism all figured. The roughly 800,000 Jews, a significant portion of whom lived in the newly-annexed territories and thus seemed doubly alien in the traditionally intolerant, anti-Jewish atmosphere, formed the target of a virulent anti-semitic agitation.

21

When it emerged that the expected prosperity was not to be and the country was shaken by a serious economic crisis (1918–1923), one of the by-products of which was growing intellectual unemployment, the ground proved fertile for left-extremist and right-extremist agitation. The ruling bourgeois circles sought to ward off the menace of extremism with unevenly dealt blows at right and left. They were ruthless towards the extreme left and more inclined to overlook the extreme right. The Communist Party was declared illegal in 1924 and the socialists split up into several groups and parties, exposed to constant persecution. With the exception of the 1926 elections, when the socialists won 19 seats out of 369 in the Chamber, their parliamentary representation and political influence were minimal.

On the extreme right, ultra-nationalist, anti-semitic and extremist anti-communist organisations had appeared as early as 1919,[2] but it was not until 1923 that Professor A. C. Cuza's "League of National Christian Defence" (LANC) gained national importance. It was at the head of this movement, at the side of Cuza, that Corneliu Zelea Codreanu, a student leader from Moldavia with fanatical and mystical inclinations, came to the fore. Codreanu, who soon acquired notoriety as the organiser of political murders, turned away from his master, Cuza, the monomaniac doyen of Romanian anti-semitism, accusing him of conservatism, of a lack of dynamism and of accepting the country's corrupt political system. Together with a few fellow-students, he founded the "Legion of the Archangel Michael" in 1927 and he created the Iron Guard in 1930 as the political activist section of the Legion (the two were in practice the same from the beginning).

At the centre of the political spectrum in the second half of the 1920s, only two large parties proved capable of survival, after every other bourgeois party had disintegrated or disappeared. The National Liberal Party, representing above all the interests of finance-capital and the upper bourgeoisie, was right-wing, pro-Entente and pronouncedly nationalist. The National Peasant Party, the result of the merger between the Peasant Party and the Transylvanian National Party in 1926, represented the middle peasants and the more prosperous village strata, but it also found adherents among democratically-minded intellectuals, especially in Transylvania. This party, too, was strongly nationalist and its democratic ideals existed more in its principles than in practice during its few years in power. In the period under consideration, the Liberal Party held office, with a strong parliamentary majority (from 1933 to the end of 1937).

It is next to impossible to assess the relative strengths of the political parties, seeing that the parliamentary elections hardly reflected reality. Henry L. Roberts, the author of an excellent work on modern Romania,

22

wrote of the morals of Romanian political life: "Romanian elections were notorious for their corruption, their ballot stuffing, and general unreliability as measures of public sentiment . . . In most cases elections were 'made' in advance."[3] It was against corruption and the professional "politicianism" that permeated every aspect of political life that Codreanu rebelled. He proclaimed a misty national rejuvenation and moral and spiritual "rearmament", assailing industrial development with anti-capitalist and anti-modernist slogans, idealising and exalting the peasant way of life. Codreanu promised the obliteration of the parliamentary system, the dissolution of the political parties and, first and foremost, the exclusion of the Jews from the country's life in the event that his national revolution was successful. At first he was not noticeably anti-Western in his statements on foreign policy, but after Hitler came to power he demanded that Romania take up a position alongside Nazi Germany and Fascist Italy. Codreanu gained his first parliamentary mandate only in 1931 (with 30,783 votes, a mere 1.2 per cent of all votes cast). His progress was unspectacular until the mid-1930s, but the *Capitanul* ("Captain"), with his undeniable charisma, had already become a focus of interest earlier, whilst his movement embodied terror, hooliganism and crude brutality in spite of its Christian mysticism and pietism. After it had been repeatedly banned, it re-appeared in 1934 bearing the name *Totul pentru Ţară* ("All for the Fatherland") under the nominal leadership of General Zizi Cantacuzino.

Side by side with the Iron Guard, Cuza's "League", a *par excellence* anti-semitic body, which could count on the conservative and conformist elements of the extreme right, maintained its strength but scored no significant advances. When in 1935 the League merged with Octavian Goga's extreme nationalist and anti-semitic National Agrarian Party to form the "National Christian Party", the Iron Guard came up against a serious rival. In addition to these two main forces on the extreme right, 1935 also saw the emergence of a third, though rather weaker, right-extremist group, namely the "Romanian Front" led by Alexandru Vaida-Voievod, a former Peasant Party Prime Minister. Vaida called for a *"numerus valachicus"*, a kind of *"numerus clausus"*, whereby the participation of the minorities, especially of the Jews, in the country's economic and cultural life would be restricted. Although Vaida was not ranked as an out-and-out extremist and his "Front" never represented a clearly delineated camp, his rôle unquestionably helped to weaken the moderate and democratic elements. It is worth mentioning the defection of George Brătianu from the Liberal Party in the early 1930s. His Neo-Liberal group might be termed "Fascisant", although it did not identify itself with Italian fascism or Hitlerism.

23

Whilst Codreanu promised a switch to the side of the Axis in foreign policy within 48 hours of his victory, Goga, Cuza and George Brătianu were inclined to be more cautious in cutting the traditional links with the West. Vaida was unwilling to break with the Western powers for Hitler's sake. This was the framework within which the political crisis that was to lead rapidly to the disruption of Romania's parliamentary system emerged in 1936.

The troubled year 1936 in Romania favoured the opposition National Peasant Party (NPP) on the one hand and the Iron Guard on the other (which from 1934 bore the name *Totul pentru Țară*). Early in 1936 the NPP placed the seizure of power high on the agenda. The party's impressive demonstrations in May that year in Bucharest took on an anti-fascist character and received the support of the entire left. At the same time, the NPP, supported by the left, won two parliamentary by-elections and headed the poll in the municipal elections in the capital. These results, achieved in spite of the "Liberal" government's terror, were evidence of country-wide support for the democratic forces. A large section of the bourgeoisie, increasingly apprehensive of the onslaught of foreign and domestic fascism, was moving towards a leftist radical stance. "The time was almost ripe for the National Peasant Party to come to power", reported Sir Reginald Hoare, the British Minister in Bucharest.[4]

The pro-German trend of the extreme right was opposed by a number of public figures, including Nicolae Titulescu, the Foreign Minister, Nicolae Iorga, the well-known nationalist historian and former rightist Prime Minister, Grigore Filipescu, the conservative leader and other leading figures in finance and industry.

In the summer of 1936 the extreme right, together with the National Liberal government of Gheorghe Tătărescu, mounted an offensive against the NPP of Iuliu Maniu and Mihalache and against the left as a whole. Controversies in the press, unprecedented in their ferocity, threw the country into a fever. The right-wing press, led by *Universul*, launched a vitriolic campaign against the democratic papers and those branded as Jewish[5] and urged their liquidation. Right-wing terrorist bands attacked newspaper offices, assaulted journalists and burnt the newspapers. In fact, the campaign ended with the elimination of two of the main democratic papers, *Dimineața* and *Adevĕrul*. The by-election results, the relative electoral successes of the democratic forces and the campaign against the democratic press stimulated the extreme right to a mobilisation of unprecedented intensity. Two groups of the extreme right came to the fore to lend dynamism of a kind to Romanian political life in 1936. One of these was the Iron Guard, whilst the other was the National Christian Party, led by Octavian Goga and Professor A. Cuza.

24

At the by-elections the Goga-Cuza group was the more active. Its blue-shirted Storm Troopers turned the electoral districts into bloody battle fields. The country was kept in a state of high excitement throughout 1936. It witnessed student unrest, spectacular congresses and political murders, despite the state of siege that had been instituted early in 1934.

The British diplomatic reports shed light on an unusually important and characteristic element of the activities and successes of the extreme right in 1936. Sir Reginald Hoare, who was well informed and had excellent contacts at the highest levels, had proof that the two extremist parties exploded their wave of terror at the instigation of and with the support of the government, and on occasion even acted on the initiative of the government. The very real prospects that the NPP had of taking power led the leaders of the ruling party to the conclusion that they ought to utilise the weaker extreme right terrorist groups – still incapable of taking power – against the democratic parties, which represented the greater danger. At the by-election held in January 1936 in Suceava, the government party entered no candidate, but supported the candidate of the Goga-Cuza party against the NPP. In two subsequent by-elections, at Mehedinti and Huneadoara, the National Christians – according to Hoare – were being allowed to benefit from the administrative organisation of the Liberals and received every support from the government.[6] This arose because there was no doubt that the NPP enjoyed very real support in the country, as was stressed by the British minister.

The Prime Minister and the Minister of the Interior strongly rejected charges of collaboration with the terrorists of the extreme right, but Hoare managed to buttress his case with first-hand information, despite official denials. He had a discussion with Titulescu on 26 April. The Foreign Minister, who was democratically-minded and pro-Western, spoke quite openly with the British Minister in private. He informed Hoare that he had spoken "very emphatically to the King about the folly of encouraging Hitlerist tendencies." Titulescu also told Hoare that "he had made it plain to the King that he did not cling to office but would resign rather than condone an internal policy which conflicted with Romania's affiliations in Western Europe."[7]

During a conversation with the Minister of Finance at the beginning of April, Hoare mentioned that "the mentality of the students – according to the opposition – was the result of the encouragement of the 'Iron Guard' or Nazi propaganda by members of the government." The Romanian Minister "protested with a vehemence", noted Hoare, "which would have been quite unnecessary had he not known that the charge was fully justified."[8]

25

Hoare reported anxiously in April 1936 that "the question of the spread of extremist 'right' doctrines among the youth, and particularly the students, . . . is coming rapidly to the fore, and I propose to revert to the matter in the near future."[9] Hoare reported also that some of the leaders of the ruling Liberals, Victor Iamandi for instance, disapproved of government backing for the extreme right ("it was essential to the safety of the State that no further encouragement should be given to the movements of the extreme right"). Furthermore, the British Minister reported to the Foreign Office that "there has been a growing feeling of concern in the country regarding the excesses which the right wing have been allowed to commit, *with the connivance or even the active support of the Government.*"[10] However, Hoare was not convinced that the government supported the extreme right with the approval of King Carol.

In the second half of the year, Hoare gave his account of the further shift to the right that had taken place. He noted that as a result of events in France and Spain, a trend away from the democratic parties had become discernible. "A growing number of Roumanians are beginning to look with disfavour and suspicion on the 'Front Populaire', whilst it is no exaggeration to say that the vast majority of Roumanians whom we meet prefer to see the nationalist or military elements in Spain victorious . . ."[11]

At the end of August 1936 the Tătărescu government was reconstructed, the dismissal of Titulescu being the only important change. This undoubtedly signified a move away from Romania's traditional pro-Western policies. In those tense days, Hoare again had an opportunity to gain insight into the co-operation between the Liberal leaders and the extreme right. Early in September he heard the views of Costinescu, the Minister of Labour and Health in the new Tătărescu administration, on the policies of Inculeţ, the Minister of the Interior. "M. Inculeţ had believed that he could draw the claws of the extremists of the Right by entertaining personal relations with and affording financial help to the leaders, and that he could then gradually ferment discord amongst them. His 'diplomatic' methods had evidently failed."[12]

The programme of the new Tătărescu government laid considerable emphasis on putting a stop to the extremist activity of different fascist-type organisations. This was the information given to Hoare by the new Foreign Minister, Victor Antonescu. Hoare, however, was sceptical about the new government's intentions and intimated to London that the general public did not believe that any serious attempt would be made to put an end to Nazi organisations. He wrote on 10 September, "in my view, it would be madness if the Roumanian Government hesitated any longer to put an end to Nazi organisations, the effect of which is to push

26

the National Peasant movement to the acceptance of extreme socialist ideas ..."[13] The British Minister rightly recognised that it was madness on the part of the government to fail to take action against the extremists, but his argument, that right-extremist activity would push the NPP towards the extreme left, was wholly incorrect. The leaders of the NPP were anti-communist without exception; they rejected socialist concepts of whatever type and were reluctant to co-operate with anyone who counted as leftist within the framework of a possible Popular Front. Hoare, and through him or perhaps even independently of him, the Foreign Office and thus the British Government maintained their reservations *vis-à-vis* Maniu and Mihalache and one of the unjustifiable reasons for this attitude was their fear that the NPP would shift leftwards.

It is worth adding that British political contacts with the NPP were rather few and that British diplomats in Bucharest did not build such close connections with the Romanian agrarians as the British Minister to Hungary, Sir Geoffrey Knox, did with the Hungarian Smallholders. Naturally enough, the NPP had better links with French democratic circles. It is hard to say whether it was the British or the NPP that had failed to take the initiative in establishing contact, but there is no doubt that the absence of these links was prejudicial to the cause of democratic development in Romania.

As far as Hoare's anxieties were concerned, he would have counselled the Romanian Government to break the power of the extreme right for another reason, namely, to avoid thereby any active counter-measures by the Soviet Union. This reasoning was faulty, however, since the chances of Soviet intervention at the time were minimal. In all, the British Minister's judgement of the situation was grave, because he had no great confidence in the government's determination to deal firmly with fascist-type organisations. "I expect to see gradual deterioration, tension, occasional murders, beating of Jews and trouble generally."[14] This was the first occasion – in the autumn of 1936 – on which Hoare mentioned the possibility of a royalist dictatorship, the results of which, incidentally, he judged equally pessimistically. "Perhaps we might see King Carol setting up some sort of dictatorship, which might work but which might also lead to an attempt at revolution."[15]

Afraid of upheaval, the Minister requested the Foreign Office for its consent to authorise him to speak to King Carol, in order to look for a way out. London agreed,[16] but there is no trace of any discussion between Hoare and King Carol on this subject, though on 26 September he was received in audience by the Prime Minister, Tătărescu. Hoare expressed his anxieties about the ground gained by right-extremism and anti-semitism. Tătărescu assured him that he had not the slightest intention of allowing the extreme right to get out of hand nor was extremism part of the Romanian national psychology. Concerning foreign affairs, Tătărescu stated that Germany constituted the principal threat to peace and he hoped that Italian co-operation would again be available and that "peace in Europe would be assured by an unbroken line running from London, through Paris, Rome and the Balkans to Moscow."[17]

On the day that Tătărescu made his statement to Hoare, Eden held a conversation with the Romanian Foreign Minister, Victor Antonescu, in Geneva, about the situation in Romania after the departure of Titulescu. Antonescu offered as one explanation of Titulescu's departure, among others, that he had objected to the failure of the government to take stern measures against manifestations of anti-semitism. The question of extremist movements did not arise in discussion between the two Foreign Ministers, but Antonescu's views on Italian-Romanian relations differed from those of Tătărescu. In contradiction to what Hoare had learned from the Prime Minister on the same day, Antonescu said to Eden that "the policy [of Italy] was too uncertain and too opportunist for Roumania to be able to have a close friendship with her, even if she wished to do so."[18]

In reality the Romanian Government's measures against right-extremism consisted mostly of words, whereas in its foreign policy after Titulescu's dismissal it sought closer relations firstly with Rome, and attempted to improve relations with Germany, consonant with the rightward shift internally.

In November 1936 the extremist National Christian Party scored its first major success, when it organised a vast demonstration in Bucharest. About 100,000 peasants from all over the country marched through the city, with a large number of demonstrators wearing blue shirts and swastikas. The fact of the matter was that the King had given his permission for this Nazi-type demonstration and had ensured that it could take place unmolested. So far as Carol's attitude to the extreme right was concerned at the time, it was not untypical – even if it did not wholly fit the facts – that the acting Secretary-General of the Romanian Foreign Ministry remarked to Hoare, "If King Carol had at times appeared to encourage the leaders of the right, it might well have been in the hope of thereby exerting indirect pressure on the leaders of the NPP and bringing them to a more tractable frame of mind."[19]

Towards the end of the same year Hoare drew far-reaching conclusions regarding the King's political attitude, coming close to reality, ". . . the King's heart, though perhaps not his head, inclines him towards Fascist ideas . . ."[20] This cannot be equated with charges of sympathy for Goga and Cuza, or for Codreanu, but outside observers took the view that the King was doing more than just using the fascist movements against his democratic opponents, that his own attitude was itself not far removed from fascism.

Analysts of the Romanian scene in 1936 came again and again to the view that the government party, even the King himself perhaps, was not just backing the extreme right, but that both Tătărescu and the King were deliberately using the two main fascist-type organisations against the only democratic party capable of taking power. The question remains open to this day, as to how far the Tătărescu government and King Carol were directly or indirectly responsible for the breakthrough of the extremist movements. The only comprehensive work on the Iron Guard published in post-war Romania proves the guilt of the Liberals and the King in the matter with an abundance of archival material.[21] The lack of objectivity of the authors, together with the fact that their aim was as much to discredit the NPP, makes this publication of the available British Foreign Office material all the more useful.

The Iron Guard, which outdid its main rival, the National Christian Party, in its organisation, leadership and also in terrorism, became a national political factor in 1936 only, leaving all its right-extremist competitors far behind. The first Iron Guard document which can be regarded as a milestone in the movement's history was the "Memorandum to the King, Politicians and Country", published in November 1936. Corneliu Zelea Codreanu threatened politicians responsible for an "anti-national" foreign policy with death and declared that the "Iron Guard would shoot anyone who should force them to side with bolshevism against those who defended Christian civilisation".

British diplomacy and the British press began to take an interest rather late in a movement that was operating with methods unprecedented in Romanian political life. They only did so, in fact, when it was well on the way to seizing power through terror in addition to legal means. For a long time the danger to the Romanian parliamentary system, as well as to the interests of the democratic powers in the Danube Basin, was underestimated. The rather fatuous view of Alexandru Vaida-Voievod, a former agrarian Prime Minister of Romania, who subsequently moved to the extreme right, had prevailed in judging the Iron Guard, namely, that "the children should be allowed to play", for once they were grown up, they would put away childish things and would change for the better.[22] "The children's games" played by the Iron Guard consisted, *inter alia,* of numerous political murders committed by death squads, like that of the Liberal Prime Minister, I. G. Duca, who was shot by legionnaires on 29 December 1933. They made normal teaching at the university impossible, they terrorised the country's Jewish population and tens of thousands of fanatical young men were organised into para-military formations, preparing openly to settle accounts with democracy, with the establishment qualified as corrupt. But the most important target of the Iron Guard was the left and the Jews. It is rather difficult to explain why Western opinion took little notice of the fact that the Iron Guard had close links with a large part of the Orthodox clergy, not least because in Romania, an Orthodox country *par excellence,* where the church had a dominant influence on the backward peasant masses, these connections had a special significance of their own.

Early in 1937 the Iron Guard attracted the attention of those who had until then been indifferent to it, by organising a political *coup de théâtre.* Two leading members of the movement, Ion Moța and Vasile Marin, had been killed in Spain, fighting for Franco. Two coffins were brought to Bucharest, escorted in solemn procession through the capital by legionnaires, many of whom had come in from the country in special trains, alleged to have been furnished by the government at greatly reduced rates – noted Hoare.[23] He added, further, that the funeral was attended by the Patriarch and other high dignitaries of the Church, stressing also that "the police were conspicuous by their absence". In addition, Iron Guard members appeared in uniform, disobeying government orders, *"but this they do regularly".* [24]

This was the event that opened Hoare's eyes to the strength and significance of the Iron Guard. "The Iron Guard is becoming a serious menace and must, therefore, be dealt with." He concluded his report with the words, "It is easy in a country which produces a new rumour every half an hour to fall into exaggeration, but I have a fear that, if the Government draw back now, we are at the beginning of a Nazi movement which will gather irresistible impetus, driven by a fanatical spirit similar to that which so frequently produces a tragedy in Japan."[25]

In the spring of 1937 the Tătărescu government changed its policy and began to deal more harshly with the Iron Guard. This was particularly so after the legionnaires made an attempt to assassinate the democratically-minded Rector of the University of Iași. On that occasion the government addressed a letter to the Patriarch, couched in strong terms, and appealing to the clergy "to keep clear of all political connexions".

The appearance of Codreanu's book, *For the Legionnaires,* offered Hoare an opportunity to express his opinion on the character of the movement. Transmitting a summary of Codreanu's book to the Foreign Office, he remarked, *inter alia,* in his covering letter, "It is difficult to judge from M. Codreanu's book what his own estimate is of the strength of the movement. Such strength as it has lies possibly in the astonishing vagueness of his doctrines which do little more than enjoin a nationalism of a nebulous nature."[26]

30

One of the Foreign Office specialists on the area made the following comment on Hoare's letter: "Roumania being among the number of the 'Haves', the Iron Guard movement is deprived of one of the stalking-horses of nationalism and derives its strength in the main from hatred of Jewry and of the 'politicians'. Sir Reginald Hoare draws attention to points of dissimilarity between the movement and German National Socialism. On the whole I think the resemblance is to the Croix de Feu."[27] It was indeed difficult to fit the Iron Guard into the kaleidoscope of the fascist movements of Europe and this problem continues to exercise students of fascism today.[28]

The attitude of the Tătărescu government and of the King towards the Iron Guard was unclear to Hoare during the phase when support for the movement on the part of the government and the King was tantamount to suicide. The Minister tried to make certain whether the remark made to him by Titulescu in November 1935 could still be considered valid. Titulescu had said, "Even if the King himself told you that he was going to form an Extreme Right Government, I should advise you to tell the Foreign Office that 'I don't believe it'."[29] In the meantime, M. Grigorcea, the Romanian Minister in London, tried vaguely to allay the anxieties of the Foreign Office about the Iron Guard: "The Iron Guard was not yet very formidable. It was a Fascist organisation, strongly anti-semitic." He then expressed the view that the government had not dealt with it sufficiently seriously in the past and now they were beginning to alter their attitude. "It was high time they did so, for the movement was showing itself anti-monarchist as well as anti-democratic and anti-semitic".[30]

Any judgement of the nature and policies of the Iron Guard was made more difficult by the fact that early in 1937 rumours began to circulate of a hardly credible development, namely that a *rapprochement* was coming about between Maniu, the leader of the NPP, and Codreanu. It took half a year for this *rapprochement* to evolve into a sensational electoral "non-aggression pact".

In May 1937, Hoare was received in audience by King Carol. The British Minister learned nothing from the King regarding the extreme right, but it was noteworthy that the King sought to defend the anti-semitic trend of the Tătărescu government. At the same time, he also expounded the essential distinction between his own political conception and that of Britain: "... the great difference between British and Continental thought was that Britain was more impressed by the Nazi than by the Communist danger." Hoare agreed with this view. He sought to underpin the King's argument by telling him the following, "... to illustrate the issue, I told him that my Polish colleague had recently remarked to me that as between the utterly distasteful alternatives, Poland would sooner see Czechoslovakia conquered by Germany than victoriously defended against Germany by the Soviets'. The Minister added: The King and I realise that from the Polish point of view this was fairly natural."[31]

It was only months later, in the autumn of 1937, that Hoare came to the view that the King had launched a campaign to break the Iron Guard in the interests of his personal prestige and authority. In October, Carol established a youth organisation, the Straja Țării ("Sentry of the Fatherland"). The setting up of this royalist youth organisation, wrote Hoare, "marks a further step towards the consolidation of the King's personal authority ... and I presume that he has personally decided that by this means he can steal the thunder of the Iron Guard."[32]

An Intelligence Report on Romania, prepared in July that year in Bucharest, looked at the situation realistically and foresaw the establishment of a royalist dictatorship. "A considerable body of opinion consisting of Right Parties in Roumania looks with sympathy on National Socialism in Germany. But the advent of these parties to power would by no means necessarily imply a change in Roumania's foreign policy ... If only the extremists of either side can be held firmly in check, there is no real reason why internal stability should not be maintained, all the more so, since the King has slowly but unostentatiously established for himself a position of autocracy – a regime which seems to suit this country, in its present state of political development, somewhat better than a weak and corrupt democracy."[33]

Shortly after this Report was completed, H. L. Farquhar, the British Chargé d'Affaires in Bucharest, reported on the political situation in the country, wrongly estimating the chances of the extreme right coming to power. He noted that the "Shirts" movement had been in abeyance ever since the government's firm handling of the situation, but added that "fears have been expressed in certain circles of the possible advent to power of the National Christians ... or a combination with other parties with consequent manifestations of extreme nationalism in its more obnoxious forms and a disquieting increase in German and Italian influence." Five months before Goga and Cuza came to power, the British Chargé d'Affaires could add the following comment on this: "Such an eventuality seems less likely to occur than six months ago ..."[34]

The elections were announced for December 1937. Well-informed observers had few doubts that in the event of "free" elections, even according to the Romanian interpretation of that concept, the government party would fail to win 40 per cent of the votes.[35] The failure of the Liberals would, in the circumstances, have threatened the collapse of the parliamentary system itself, seeing that neither the King nor the extreme right would have permitted the victory of the left, whilst the success of the extreme right would have led to a fascist dictatorship. It was against this background that both domestic and foreign observers were astounded by the electoral "non-aggression pact" that Maniu's NPP concluded with the Iron Guard and with George Brătianu's strongly right wing and pro-Axis faction, the so-called Neo-Liberals. Hoare's opinion of Maniu's move was devastating. "It is regrettable that one of the parties essential to the maintenance of the democratic principle should have fallen on such evil days."[36]

Despite this bitter comment, Hoare and a section of British opinion was ready to explain away the Maniu-Codreanu pact — mistakenly — by saying that, after all, it had been reached only to defeat the Liberals and the *tendency towards autocratic government.*[37]

The Liberals did, in fact, fail to gain the necessary 40 per cent of the votes. The ultimate outcome of the December 1937 elections, which took place in an atmosphere of extreme tension and violence, was to start the process which marked the end of the Romanian parliamentary system. The Liberal Party, together with a few affiliated groups, obtained 36 per cent of the votes. The NPP won almost 21 per cent, whilst the Iron Guard achieved a spectacular success with just under 16 per cent. The Liberals were not capable of forming a new administration and the NPP was prevented from doing so by the Court. The King's solution, to entrust Goga and Cuza with the formation of a minority government, was obviously intended to serve as a transition to his own personal dictatorship.

Notes

1. *Regat:* Kingdom. The notion was used to designate the pre-World War I "Old" Romanian Kingdom *(Vechiul Regat)*
2. e.g. the "Association of Christian Students" and later the short-lived "Fascia Naţională Română" under the leadership of an officer named Ştefan Tătărescu, which was a slavish imitation of the Italian Fascists.
3. *Romania, Political Problems of an Agrarian State,* New Haven, Conn. 1951.
4. P.R.O., F.O. 371, R 5293/782/37
5. The so-called Sărindari-press, after the street where *Dimineaţa, Adevărul* and *Lupta* were edited.
6. Telegram from Sir Reginald Hoare, 28 February 1936 (Doc.No.4)
7. Hoare to Eden, 27 April 1936 (Doc.No.9)
8. Hoare to Eden, 4 April 1936 (Doc.No.6)

9. Ibid.
10. Hoare to Eden, 23 April 1936 (Doc.No.8) (author's italics)
11. Hoare to Eden, 27 August 1936 (Doc.No,16)
12. Hoare to Eden, 3 September 1936 (Doc.No.17)
13. Hoare to Eden, 10 September 1936 (Doc.No.18)
14. Hoare to O'Malley, 11 September 1936 (Doc.No.19) Cf. Hoare's report about a conversation with Ostrovsky, Soviet Minister in Bucharest. (Doc.No.11)
15. Hoare to O'Malley, 11 September 1936 (Doc.No.19)
16. Telegram from the Foreign Office to Hoare, 21 September 1936 (Doc.No.20)
17. Hoare to Eden, 26 September 1936 (Doc.No.21)
18 Eden reporting on conversation with V.Antonescu, 26 September 1936 (Doc.No.22)
19. Hoare to Eden, 8 October 1936 (Doc.No.24)
20. Annual Report on Romania, 1936 (Doc.No.29)
21. Mihai Fătu and Ion Spălățelu, *Garda de Fier,* Organizație teroristă de tip fascist, Bucharest 1971. It is to be noted that the sources used in this work are still not open to foreign researchers.
22. Vaida excused Iron Guard crimes "as being merely youthful ebullience without political importance. He even appeared to suggest that the murder of M. I. G. Duca fell into the same category", wrote Hoare on 18 May 1936. (P.R.O., F.O. 371, R 3009/282/37)
23. Hoare to Eden, 24 February 1937 (Doc.No.33)
24. Ibid. (author's italics)
25. Ibid.
26. Hoare to Eden, 26 March 1937 (Doc.No.36)
27. Ibid. Minute by A. D. M. Ross, 6 April 1937
28. See *Impotriva fascismului (Against Fascism),* papers presented at a scientific session about *Fascism in Romania* held in Bucharest in March 1971 (Bucharest 1971). See also Z. Barbu, "Rumania" in: S. J. Woolf (ed.), *European Fascism,* London 1968, pp.146–66; Stephen Fischer-Galati, "Fascism in Romania" in: Peter F. Sugar (ed.), *Native Fascism in the Successor States,* Santa Barbara, California 1971, pp.112–22; F. L. Carsten, *The Rise of Fascism,* London 1967, pp.181–93; and Eugen Weber's article on the Iron Guard in: Hans Rogger and Eugen Weber (eds), *The European Right – A Historical Profile,* London 1965, pp. 520–57.
29. Telegram No. 50 of 7 November 1935. Cf. Hoare to Eden, 9 April 1937 (Doc.No.37)
30. Telegram from the Foreign Office to Hoare, 17 April 1937 (Doc.No.39)

31. Hoare to Eden, 19 May 1937 (Doc.No.40)
32. Hoare to Eden, 8 October 1937 (Doc.No.50)
33. Intelligence Report on Romania, Bucharest, 2 July 1937 (Doc.No.43)
34. Farquhar to Eden, 30 July 1937 (Doc.No.46)
35. In conformity with the electoral law of 1926, the party (or list) that obtained 40 per cent or more of the votes got 50 per cent of the seats, the remaining 50 per cent being proportionally shared by the parties that achieved 2 per cent or more of the total number of votes; the majority party also enjoyed this proportional distribution.
36. Hoare to Eden, 2 December 1937 (Doc.No.56)
37. Hoare to Eden, 3 December 1937 (Doc.No.57) (author's italics)

2 'A Hair From the Dog That Bit It': The Goga-Cuza Government

At the end of December 1937 Octavian Goga formed a government of the National Christian Party, which had won less than 10 per cent of the votes at the election. British observers in Bucharest, above all Sir Reginald Hoare himself, suspected from the first that the formation of the Goga government was a manoeuvre of the King's directed primarily against the Iron Guard. This surmise was based, among others, on a statement made to one diplomat by a Legionnaire leader, to the effect that the establishment of a National Christian government was the only thing that the Iron Guard had seriously to fear. "I therefore do not exclude the possibility that the King intends to give the country 'a hair from the dog that bit it' as the surest means of counteracting the rapid growth of the Iron Guard", cabled Hoare to London.[1]

At the Foreign Office, Sir Orme Sargent based his judgement partly on Hoare's reports and partly on information appearing in the British press. "[King Carol] has appointed M. Goga in order to steal the thunder of the Iron Guard, just as Hindenburg appointed von Papen in the hopes of out-manoeuvring Hitler. If so, the precedent is not a very encouraging one . . ."[2] Sir Orme Sargent regarded the violently anti-semitic policy of the new government as its most important element, but otherwise he regarded the Iron Guard as a greater potential danger than Goga. ". . . What is more important than Goga's probably ephemeral appearance on the political stage is the growing strength of the Iron Guard – a purely Nazi party in Roumania."[3]

Sir Alexander Cadogan took the opportunity of the Romanian events to express his thoughts on Nazi and Fascist successes and their connection with Danubian nationalism. '. . . On one point I am not clear: if these countries admire the German (or Italian) system of government, they may adopt it and we can't stop them. That is an 'ideological' point. But would

37

that make them love Germany any the more or be any more yielding to her? Neither Nazism nor Fascism . . . includes among its tenets the idea of giving away anything to any other nation. I should have thought that they were both in essence violently nationalistic. It would be logical, if Roumania went genuinely Nazi, that she should go violently Roumanian. But perhaps I am wrong."[4]

The French Government was also inclined to regard the establishment of the National Christian Party in power as a prophylactic inoculation against the greater evil of the Iron Guard.[5] It was in this connection that A. D. M. Ross noted in Whitehall that, "the efficacy of this treatment depends on the strength of the more virulent germ. It was powerless when Herr von Papen was put up to keep Herr Hitler out. But the Iron Guard cannot compare, from the point of view of strength and appeal, with the N.S.D.A.P."[6]

The policy of Goga and the King may have been determined by the need to keep the Iron Guard in check during the short lifetime of the government, but there is equally little doubt that the Iron Guard threat was used by the Goga government as a pretext for introducing extremist measures, above all, anti-semitic ones. Istrate Micescu, the new Romanian Foreign Minister, tried to convince Hoare of this: "Something must be done lest the Iron Guard prevail". That something concerned moves against the Jews. Hoare had a "long and rambling" conversation with Goga on 5 January, about which he reported on the same day, "[the Prime Minister] is convinced that he must make an attempt to accomplish something, not only because he is a prisoner of his past, but because he believes rightly or wrongly that the only way to defeat the Iron Guard is to steal its thunder, in which a considerable element is, of course, antisemitism . . ."[7]

The manoeuvrings of the Goga government *vis-à-vis* the Iron Guard were correctly interpreted by A. D. M. Ross in London, who noted that "M. Micescu's preoccupation is evidently to take the wind out of the Iron Guard's sails. There will be reprisals not only against Jews but against the 'corrupt' members of the bureaucracy who have given the Jews a leg up."[8] P. Nichols's analysis was deeper: "It looks very much as though the present Roumanian Government were going to use the Iron Guard as a threat with which to blackmail foreign Powers into acquiescing in a policy which is in itself reprehensible. But the whole position still remains somewhat obscure, and more particularly the part played by the King and likely to be played by the King in the future."[9]

Chamberlain, the British Prime Minister, agreed with the suggestion that King Carol's objective in calling Goga to power might be to combat "the infection of the Iron Guard movement by injections of a similar but less virulent germ". Nevertheless, according to Chamberlain, one would have to reckon with the establishment of an authoritarian regime along fascist or Nazi lines in Romania.[10]

The Goga-Cuza cabinet dissolved parliament (which had not assembled as yet) and called for new elections for early 1938, but these were never held. The month of January in Romania was characterised by economic panic, principally the result of the anti-Jewish measures, by British and French pressure on the government — either to bring it down or to have it moderate its policies — and by a desperate inter-party struggle.

The advent to power of the Goga government took both the country and the National Christian Party itself by surprise, so that it was unable to cope with the crisis. Its flustered measures, the excesses of the "Blue-shirts", the dilettantism of the new and untried senior officials, often without any administrative or political experience, and the economic and financial troubles all combined to create a catastrophic situation. The chaos was intensified by the instability within the various parties. Some well-known personalities of the National Peasant Party went over to Goga. Armand Călinescu, an outstanding figure in the NPP and former deputy minister, received the important portfolio of the Ministry of the Interior in the Goga cabinet. General Antonescu, later to be the dictator of Romania and close to the Iron Guard in 1938, became Minister of Defence. There was uncertainty in foreign policy too. The Foreign Minister, Istrate Micescu, an extremist anti-semite,[11] was well disposed towards the Axis, but he was anxious about the country's independence from Nazi Germany and was reluctant to stir up a hornet's nest in Romania by reversing the two-decades-old pro-Western orientation in foreign policy. Paradoxically, the Iron Guard was the main rival of the National Christian Party on the threshold of the new elections. For his part, Codreanu had no great hopes of the elections, but he feared the worst for his movement, the institution of a royal dictatorship. In the second week of January, he issued a statement, threatening those who were trying to drive the Crown to a dictatorship, which, in his opinion, would have been a disaster.

Hoare was received by the King on 19 January and on that occasion he had the opportunity to hear the King's views on the Iron Guard. The King "was quite clear, that it [the Iron Guard] must be combated and that *the only* way to do so was to adopt part of its programme. To use force against it and so create martyrs was not the way to handle the situation, though if force became unavoidable, he would not hesitate to use it."[12] Romanian political life was caught up in a vicious circle and the policy of both the government and the King was unremittingly radicalised in an undemocratic, unparliamentary and anti-semitic direction. The moderate

39

right, the extreme right and the King were running in the race and in the heat of it the moderates became ever more extremist, taking over more and more of the slogans and the programme of the extreme right, in order to steal the thunder of the Iron Guard. Nonetheless, Goga and Micescu were unwilling to call their rule "fascist" and totalitarian and attempted thereby to ensure for themselves the support of the moderate right, side by side with that of the extremists.[13]

By the end of January fear of the advent to power by the Iron Guard on the part of the moderate right, including members of the Goga government, was so widespread that the institution of a royal dictatorship was seen as the only way out. One such member of the Goga government, the Minister of Air and Marine, was a close confidant of Hoare's.[14]

A Memorandum was prepared in the Foreign Office at the end of January 1938, dealing with the political situation in Romania. It concentrated on two problems: the chances of the Iron Guard coming to power and the establishment of a royal dictatorship. The first problem was linked directly to the question of the Jews. "From our point of view, the advent of the Iron Guard to power is a development which we would wish most earnestly to avoid, because it is pledged to ally itself with the Berlin-Rome axis . . . If, therefore, it is true that the present government must put forward a fairly strongly anti-Semitic programme, if they are to beat the Iron Guard, then this is possibly the lesser evil of the two."[15]

Not that the Foreign Office showed any great enthusiasm over the alternative of the royal dictatorship. "The formation of another dictatorship would not suit His Majesty's Government for many reasons: it might also mean the disappearance of Parliamentary Government in Roumania for a very long time."[16] The only solution which was favoured in London was a non-party government and this was the viewpoint represented by Eden. His views were summed up extremely cautiously in the Memorandum: "[the Secretary of State] had been turning the situation over in his mind and though, of course, he had no wish whatever to intervene in what was a matter of internal Roumanian politics, he wondered whether at this moment a non-party Government might not serve Roumanian and European interests best, always assuming that the present Government did not, as he hoped they would, obtain sufficient support at the polls to enable them to carry on in power . . ."[17]

By the end of January, Sir Reginald Hoare had come out unequivocally for British intervention with King Carol. His main reason was that Goga could not put an end to the anti-semitic agitation that was raging and, further, that there would be no possible alternative government that could secure a majority in the new parliament, in which case fresh elections would be a culminating catastrophe, only serving to strengthen the Iron

Guard. "I think effort will be made to convince the King that suspension of Parliament is the only solution", he concluded. [18] In the same telegram, he stated that it had been put to him, "that genuine dictatorship would be . . . preferable to a 'bastard' one which has grown up under the late Government". Hoare added that he agreed with this view. [19] There was a constant exchange of telegrams between Hoare and Eden in the last days of the Goga government. Eden proposed that Hoare should try to convince the King of the advantages of the postponement of elections, but Hoare was opposed to this. There was, in fact, a conflict of opinion between London and the British Legation in Bucharest regarding intervention with the King. Hoare wanted to moderate the tone of Western protests about the Jewish question, whilst the Foreign Office considered that in other fields than the Jewish question the British minister was over-dramatising the situation and that he was alarmist regarding the information he sent to London. The whole debate was academic, seeing that the fate of the regime had already been decided by then and the King was determined to institute a personal dictatorship. Nonetheless, one of Hoare's observations at the end of January is worth noting: "The dominant factor, in my opinion, remains the King's conviction of the value of the British connexion . . ." [20] This was no exaggeration. It was strengthened by the fact that several Romanian politicians, hostile to the extreme right, secretly asked the British Government to intervene, suggesting that Hoare be instructed to establish personal contact with the King. Lord Cranborne, the British delegate to the League of Nations, was told by Prince Antoine Bibesco, his Romanian opposite number, that he thought it would be of great assistance if Sir Reginald could speak to King Carol, Romania being a semi-dictatorship, and a personal approach of this kind might, therefore, be of use. [21]

At the beginning of February, the British Cabinet discussed the Romanian situation, taking Eden's report as a starting point. Essentially, the British Government was concerned with the question of the minorities, rather than with that of the Jews, though without bringing any change in existing policy. The question of the Jews was seen as the main tactical problem. Intervention was deemed necessary, but it was also recognised that excessive interference might prejudice the position of the King and the moderates and could serve as a pretext to the Iron Guard and extremists in Goga's camp for demands for further radicalisation and a break with the West.

Sir Orme Sargent and Sir Alexander Cadogan both disapproved of what they regarded as too much interference by Hoare in Romania's internal affairs, and Eden was also to some extent against it. They had in mind especially Hoare's proposal to have the elections postponed and to set up

41

a non-party government. "A minister gets on to very dangerous ground once he begins to express opinions in matters of internal politics in an independent country," noted Sir Orme. [22]

Quite a number of contemporary observers stressed the "social revolutionary" character of the Iron Guard, albeit less frequently and in a less categoric manner than in the case of the Arrow Cross. In his report submitted in the summer of 1940 to the Foreign Office, Hugh Seton-Watson remarked that among the young generation some were Guardists "because they were social revolutionaries, wishing to free the poor classes from 'Jewish exploitation'."

Statements by a number of leading Romanian personalities during the 1938 winter crisis regarding the alleged permeation of the Iron Guard by communist elements are also noteworthy. Shortly before the fall of the Goga government, the Minister of the Interior, Armand Călinescu, affirmed during a conversation with Hoare that Codreanu's party contained many "strange" elements and that "there was not a shadow of doubt that since the Communist party had been illegal . . . the vast majority of its members professed Iron Guard sympathies." [23] Brătianu, the leader of the Liberals, thought that in many respects it was hard to distinguish the electoral campaign of the Iron Guard from communism. [24]

The information that Hoare had on this subject from General Antonescu after the fall of the Goga government is both interesting and valuable. "The General . . . told me that he had spoken very seriously to M. Codreanu about the presence of communists in his movement. The reply had been that they were all converted, and the General had said that this was nonsense, as it had not been a matter of individual adhesions, but of whole groups joining with their organisations intact . . ." [25] This comment of Antonescu's is all the more significant, because in January 1941, after the abortive *coup d'état* of the Iron Guard, one of the main accusations made by the dictator against the Iron Guard was that the movement had been penetrated by communism.

In our view these assertions do not fit the facts, for they greatly over-simplify the thesis of the convergence and the mutual inter-dependence of the two extremist movements. It should be noted, however, that the Hungarian Arrow Cross movement was the subject of similar charges made by the democratic parties and the moderate right. It cannot be denied, on the other hand, that there was a certain oscillation between extreme right and extreme left among dissatisfied and otherwise extremist *déclassé* elements. The Iron Guard drew a good deal of support from the large industrial plants and transport undertakings in Bucharest, whilst the Arrow Cross found many recruits in the working class quarters of Greater Budapest.

42

After World War II there was a large influx of right extremists into the Communist Parties of both countries. This did not mean, however, that in the late 1930s the vast majority of Communist Party members in Romania and Hungary professed Iron Guard or Arrow Cross sympathies and the assertion cannot be applied under any circumstances to the few who were convinced communists.

On 10 February King Carol put an end to the violent inter-party altercations and to the growing pre-electoral tension. He dismissed Goga and installed Miron Cristea, the Orthodox Patriarch, at the head of a non-party government. Political parties were dissolved and a new Constitution was drawn up. Thus began the royal dictatorship which came to an end early in September 1940 with the dismemberment of Greater Romania, when General Antonescu and the Iron Guard took power in a "national-legionnaire" dictatorship.

There is a wealth of information in the Foreign Office archives analysing the change of regime in Romania. It was almost universally accepted, in Romania and in the West, that the fall of Goga had been brought about first and foremost by a British *démarche* to King Carol. [26] German documents do not corroborate this assertion and there is no evidence to substantiate this from British sources. Nonetheless British and French pressure undoubtedly played an enormous rôle in bringing about the decision of the King and of his right-wing advisers. Surprisingly, German sources reflect an ambiguous and contradictory but quite balanced view about British and French rôles in Goga's overthrow. [27]

The National Christian Party gave the King no trouble. In practice it accepted dissolution without opposition. The similarly right-extremist Frontul Românesc ("Romanian Front"), an insignificant group led by Vaida-Voievod, which had fought the election on a common platform with the Liberals, likewise proved to be no obstacle, not least because Vaida supported the King from the very beginning of the crisis. The Iron Guard, for its part, was actually dissolved by Codreanu. This temporary disconnection of the movement went through smoothly, not only by giving the appearance of self-dissolution, but also, as Hoare correctly assessed, because "the people were wearied to death of politicians and graft." [28] Hence the general reaction was one of relief that the crisis which had threatened civil war was over and that the nightmare of a regime based on nothing other than terror was dispelled. The first right-extremist, anti-semitic, pro-German and pro-Italian experiment in Romania had failed dismally after 44 days.

great pt.

Notes

1. Telegram from Hoare, 29 December 1937 (Doc.No.59)
2. Minutes by Sir Orme Sargent, 1 January 1938 (Ibid.)
3. Ibid.
4. Minutes by Sir Alexander Cadogan, 3 January 1938 (Ibid.)
5. See Telegram No.1. Saving from Sir Eric Phipps (Paris), 1 January 1938 (Doc.No.62, Minutes)
6. Minutes by A. D. M. Ross, 3 January 1938 (Doc.No.62)
7. Telegram from Hoare, 5 January 1938 (Doc.No.64)
8. Minutes by A. D. M. Ross, 6 January 1938 (Doc.No.63)
9. Minutes by P. Nichols, 6 January 1938 (Ibid.)
10. Chamberlain to Hoare, 6 January 1938 (Doc.No.65)
11. Characteristic of misinformation of some Foreign Office officials about Danubian affairs is the following note by Harvey: "New Rumanian Minister of Foreign Affairs, Micescu . . . makes a bad impression. Although *obviously a Jew* [author's italics], he is in a Government with strong anti-Semite programme; he, however, is at pains to assure us that the Government for all their violent words will take no serious *action* against Jews." (Harvey, op.cit., Geneva, 26–28 January 1938, pp.79–80)
12. Hoare to Eden, 19 January 1938 (Doc.No.69)
13. It is significant that even the Cominform was confused in "classifying" the Goga-Cuza regime, branding it fascist, but later stating that this judgement was wrong, the Government being "only" pro-Fascist (International Press Correspondence [INPRECORR], Vol.18, Nos.1,2,3,4)
14. Telegram from Hoare, 24 January 1938 (Doc.No.72)
15. Foreign Office Memorandum on the political situation in Romania, 24 January 1938 (Doc.No.73)
16. Ibid.
17. Ibid.
18. Telegram from Hoare, 24 January 1938 (Doc.No.74)
19. Ibid.
20. Telegram from Hoare, 28 January 1938 (Doc.No.75)
21. Record of an interview between Lord Cranborne and Prince Antoine Bibesco, Geneva, 31 January 1938 (Doc.No.77)
22. Minutes by Sir Orme Sargent and a remark by Sir Alexander Cadogan, 10 February 1938 (Doc.No.83)
23. Hoare to Eden, 7 February 1938 (Doc.No.84)
24. Telegram from Hoare, 5 February 1938 (Doc.No.83)
25. Hoare to Eden, 24 February 1938 (Doc.No.91)
26. Foreign Office Memorandum, 21 February 1938 (Doc.No.89)

27. The first German reaction came the day after King Carol's taking over: "...influences from France and England, and perhaps also America, in the score of the Jewish question probably also played a role [in Goga's fall]." (DGFP, Series D, Vol. V, Doc. No. 170) Later on the *Auswärtiges Amt* pointed out that "the position of the Goga government was made still more difficult, if not crucially so, by the intervention of France and England..." and stressed the fact — quite correctly — that "the consequences of Goga's fight for anti-Semitism were not the sole reason for his downfall." (DGFP, Series D, Vol. V, Doc. No. 179, Berlin, 9 March 1938)

28. Hoare to Eden, 24 February 1938 (Doc. No. 91)

3 The Royalist Dictatorship

One of the controversial problems about the inter-war history of Romania is that of the character of the royalist dictatorship of King Carol, from 1938–40. The opinions of contemporary commentators and post-war historians are strongly divided on this question. To some, King Carol was a fascist-type dictator and a political adventurer; others regarded him as an autocrat, whose only objective in liquidating Romania's parliamentary system was to save the country from anarchy. The extreme right considered Carol to have been the hireling of the Jews and an agent of the Western democracies, whilst the democratic opposition in Romania thought him a disciple of authoritarianism with no time for the concepts of Western democracy, who was much attracted by Italian fascism and the Nazi *Führerprinzip,* who had exacerbated the question of the Jews and who bargained unscrupulously with the extreme right, including the Iron Guard. The problem to be considered here is not so much that of Carol's personality, but what rôle he and his regime played in the transition to fascism. In other words, the question is whether or not his dictatorship – for his regime was clearly more than just authoritarian – slowed down or speeded up the advent to power of the Iron Guard and of the military dictatorship of 1940. And a corollary of this problem is how far Carol's experiment helped to bring about Romania's decline to the status of a Nazi satellite.

In view of the fact that for two decades Romania was an important constituent part of the Western alliance system, on which the security of Europe and particularly that of Eastern Europe depended, the measure of responsibility to be borne by those, Carol included, who helped to undermine that system is not insignificant. Or did Carol, perhaps, have no choice in the face of German pressure and the Soviet danger, having been abandoned by the West?

47

These questions might not be answered satisfactorily by the material in the Foreign Office, but the information in these archives does bring one closer to a solution of the problem and to a correct interpretation of Romania's situation on the eve of World War II.

Sir Reginald Hoare saw from the outset that Carol's dictatorship was not the logical outcome of a purposive policy pursued by him. It was, rather, the institution of a "bloodless revolution" in order that the King might save the country from economic disaster and from a state of affairs leading potentially to civil war. One of the reasons which led to the royalist *coup d'état* was Carol's fear of the Iron Guard, suggested Hoare, in whose opinion Carol's determination to meet the Iron Guard threat could be dated back to the spring of 1937.[1]

Hoare did not underwrite the views of those, like the Liberals and the NPP, according to which the King was working "with diabolical skill to break up the two big parties and thus automatically to create such an excess of demagogy as to render drastic change inevitable." He believed, at most, that the King had been striving towards the establishment of an autocracy, but he did not consider as proved the charge that the King had conspired deliberately to set up his dictatorship.[2] What Hoare had heard from the King shortly after the *coup d'état* carried more weight than alternative interpretations. Carol told Hoare that "he had for some time past been anxious to bring about a modification of the Constitution and the establishment of parliamentary life on a corporative basis". But it could not be concluded from this, according to Hoare, "that he worked for the political impasse . . . and deliberately faced the very real risks of internal disorders".[3] As Hoare saw it, however surprising it might sound, the King would have been prepared to allow parliamentary life to continue, had not Maniu been determined to extract from him conditions, involving even his private life, which were quite unacceptable.[4] Hoare was also convinced of the fact that the King would have been ready to introduce modifications in the system by constitutional means. According to this interpretation, Maniu's stubbornness and anti-royalist obstruction were among the reasons for the royalist dictatorship. Even if this hypothesis is entirely rejected, it still provides a good insight into Maniu's image among British diplomats in Bucharest and into the efforts made by them to give Carol the benefit of the doubt regardless.

In March 1938 Hoare wrote, "as regards the future . . . if the present experiment proves a failure, I should be inclined to say that a National Peasant revolution, which would mean the substitution of a strictly controlled King Mihail for an autocratic King Carol, would be more likely than the establishment of an Iron Guard dictatorship, though the issue would, of course, be greatly influenced by general developments in Europe".[5]

Having considered Hoare's views on the matter, A. D. M. Noble in the Foreign Office came to the conclusion that the background of the changes in Romania was not the German factor, but that they had originated primarily from domestic causes, from the discontent with the corruption and inefficiency of the politicians. He added that he saw the trend as having been towards an autocratic dictatorship and not towards a totalitarian dictatorship, because Romania's difficulties sprang from maladministration rather than from a clash of ideologies.[6]

After the royalist *coup d'état,* Carol was successful in re-establishing relative stability in political and economic life. A non-party government, headed by the Patriarch, Miron Cristea, a man of much prestige and extreme anti-semitic views, was installed to run the country. It was made up of experts and of politicians who had deserted their own parties to side with the King, among them Armand Călinescu. Later the King reorganised Cristea's government, giving a more important rôle to dissident Liberals and NPP members. Within a few months, economic conditions returned more or less to normal. The Jewish question was being handled less severely and the new administration held the reins of power very firmly. The first pre-condition of this was to wind up the Iron Guard and this was carried out ruthlessly by the King, with the help of Călinescu. Shortly after Codreanu's announcement of the dissolution of the Iron Guard (22 February), the legionnaires gave clear proof that they were only suppressed but not destroyed; they did so by various subversive acts. In mid-April Călinescu had Codreanu arrested and he was sentenced to six months' imprisonment after a short trial. Parallel with this, the majority of the leadership of the Legion was arrested and in May Codreanu was tried again, this time for treason. In addition to the liquidation of the Iron Guard, the objective of the trial was to demonstrate German involvement in the Guard's activities. Carol began thereby, albeit in a covert fashion, to play a dangerous game against Hitler too. Codreanu was given ten years and it looked as though the elimination of the Iron Guard had been achieved. However, the Iron Guard continued to inspire student unrest, anti-semitic outbreaks and political assass-inations and there were rumours in the autumn that a rising of the Guard was imminent.

Carol could not fail to respond to this if he wanted to preserve his line of policy and his power. At the end of November he returned to Romania from a trip to Germany and Britain. He had held discussions with Hitler on Romania's external and domestic problems.[7] He was on his way home

49

when, undoubtedly on his orders, Călinescu had Codreanu and twelve of his companions shot on 30 November. Hoare wrote in his Annual Report that "horror was soon followed by a sense of finality and relief, for there is no lack of oriental fatalism in Roumania, although life itself may be somewhat less cheap than in some other Balkan countries".[8]

Having rid himself of his right extremist opponents, Carol set up a unified political organisation at the end of the year, called the National Renaissance Front, which Hoare described as "a political organism of corporative structure and totalitarian complexion".[9] In the final analysis, although Hoare may have perceived "totalitarian" features in the make-up of the King's regime, he was inclined to see it as "authoritarian". He did not use the expression "royalist dictatorship" then or later.

In the meantime German economic penetration accompanied the Nazi political and "cultural" activity in Romania. In 1937 Germany absorbed 61.2 per cent of Romania's maize exports and in 1938, after the *Anschluss,* 26.5 per cent of Romanian exports were despatched to the Reich. The December 1938 economic agreement between Germany and Romania, and all the more the March 1939 economic treaty, followed by the so-called Waffen-Öl pact of 1940, had most adverse repercussions on Romania's economic and political position by deepening its dependence on the Reich.

It was only in the summer of 1938 that the British Government began, uncertainly and hesitantly, to initiate measures which would somehow impede German economic penetration of the Danube Basin.

At a Cabinet meeting on 1 June 1938, Halifax proposed steps to counter German political, economic and commercial influence in Central and South Eastern Europe.[10] He reiterated these on 15 June, with the result that the government set up an Inter-Departmental Committee under the chairmanship of Sir Frederick Leith-Ross, with the task of mapping out these counter-measures.[11]

The decision to send commercial missions to Romania and Greece was taken rather late in February 1939. Although Halifax was convinced that "from the psychological point of view . . . this proposal was of considerable importance", he had his misgivings, suggesting that the missions should only be despatched if concrete results could be assured.[12] A few days after the occupation of Prague, at its meeting of 18 March 1939, the Cabinet still failed to decide on the implementation of the counter-measures. Oliver Stanley, the President of the Board of Trade, "reminded his colleagues that the Cabinet had decided . . . that this mission should not be despatched until he had been able to inform the German Government of our intentions during the course of his visit to Berlin, which had now been postponed." In the end, the decision was that

50

Halifax should consult Romania before sending and announcing the mission.[13] In this way, as a result of the long drawn out delay, the British missed the opportunity to implement effective economic counter-measures.[14]

In March 1939 Miron Cristea died and Călinescu was his successor as Prime Minister. This led directly to a new and bloody settling of accounts between the King and the Iron Guard. On 21 September, Horia Sima — who had taken over from Codreanu — had Călinescu murdered by legionnaire fanatics. The murder of the Prime Minister was followed by severe retaliation. The Minister of the Interior of Argeșeanu's interim government, General Gabriel Marinescu, a reliable royalist, directed the purge and a high proportion of the élite of the Legion fell victim to the cleaning up. Prominent members of the Iron Guard in every county were shot without trial and their bodies were exhibited publicly with the inscription, "this is the fate of traitors". Only a few of the leaders escaped abroad, primarily to Germany, among them Horia Sima. Those of the leaders who survived the executions were interned.[15]

To all appearances, Carol had rid himself of the Iron Guard and at the outbreak of the war he could continue the consolidation of his rule undisturbed. He had time to establish a single party, the Party of the Nation, to which he successfully attached the bulk of the country's political figures.

The outbreak of the war did, however, distract attention from domestic events and the revisionist territorial demands of Romania's neighbours came to the forefront. In the latter half of 1939 and the first half of 1940, Romania found itself in a situation of the gravest tension. Carol tried to unite behind him nationalists of whatever hue with the slogan, "the country is in danger". In May 1940, his representatives established contact with Sima in Germany and negotiations for reconciliation were opened. On 26 June 1940, the Soviet ultimatum signifying the end of Greater Romania indirectly brought about the fatal move to fascism. The King signed an amnesty in favour of the Iron Guard in late June and Sima called on his followers to join the Party of the Nation. The pro-fascist and pro-Nazi Gigurtu government took office on 4 July. Its first moves were to renounce the Franco-British guarantees, to leave the League of Nations, to join the Axis formally and to introduce anti-Jewish legislation of the Nuremberg type. The development that would have been thought impossible a year earlier, the offer of portfolios to the Iron Guard by Gigurtu, also transpired and, in fact, two leading members of the Guard — Sima himself for a few days — joined Carol's government.

The territorial and domestic disintegration of Greater Romania could not be halted. Shortly after the Soviet occupation of Bessarabia and

Northern Bucovina, the Second Vienna Diktat (30 August 1940) attached Northern Transylvania to Hungary, and in September Romania ceded Southern Dobrudja to Bulgaria after bilateral negotiations. Carol's regime could not survive this collapse. General Antonescu and Horia Sima took over on 6 September 1940. They jointly ruled over the so-called "National-Legionnaire State", a brutal regime of terror, until the end of January 1941. The abortive armed rebellion mounted by the Iron Guard against Antonescu once more led to the dissolution of the "Legion", and this time, paradoxically enough, by Antonescu himself, an admirer of Codreanu and a long-time Iron Guard fellow-traveller.

As far as Great Britain's responsibility for Romania's fate is concerned, it is worth considering Maniu again. In the decade before the collapse, as the leader of the strongest democratic opposition party, it was he who sought most consistently to prevent the coming to power of one dictatorship after another and the decline of Romania to German vassalage. Maniu was the strictest critic of the two Western democracies, especially of Britain, for their failure to defend actively Romania's independence and democratic system. His criticism, quoted below, might have been exaggerated, seeing that it was voiced in the autumn of 1940 when the Transylvanian peasant leader, always a nationalist, was particularly depressed by the collapse of Greater Romania, the loss of Northern Transylvania and the seizure of power by the Iron Guard. His words, reported to the Foreign Office by Sir Reginald Hoare, are nonetheless noteworthy: "In the past both we and the French had failed lamentably, firstly in leaving the field open to German penetration both economic and commercial, and cultural, but our prime mistake had been the support of King Carol."[16] Despite his bitterness, Maniu manifested a strong desire for British support and "went on to tell me that he felt convinced that Great Britain would play a major part in the reorganisation of South Eastern Europe and she should now start interesting herself in Romanian problems."[17] Sir Reginald's reaction is typical of the standpoint of British diplomacy. Whilst conceding that Maniu had a moral prestige that no other Romanian statesman could rival, Sir Reginald wrote nonetheless, "he is very negative" and "I continue to believe that he is not capable of anything constructive."[18]

To complete the picture, it should be noted that Maniu's stock stood no higher in London at a later stage, when he warned the British Government before Yalta of the Soviet Union's true intentions in Romania. When eventually the Western powers did decide to support Maniu, in 1945 and 1946, their intervention was too late and in vain. Maniu did not survive the dissolution of his party and the Sovietisation of his country by much. He died cut off from the outside world in a labour camp in Maramureș.

52

Notes

1. Hoare to Halifax, 11 March 1938 (Doc.No.94)
2. Ibid.
3. Ibid.
4. Ibid.
5. Ibid.
6. Minutes by A. D. M. Noble, 23 March 1938 (Ibid.) On the contrary, Gafencu later assured Germany that the Romanian development "was intended to follow lines similar to National Socialism and Fascism". (Either Gafencu was not sincere, or Fabricius interpreted in his own way Gafencu's words.) (Fabricius to the Foreign Ministry, Bucharest, 2 February 1939, DGFP, Series D,Vol.V,Doc.No.280)
7. DGFP, Series D,Vol.V,Doc.No.254 and Annex to No.257
8. Annual Report on Romania, 1938 (Doc.No.136)
9. Ibid.
10. P.R.O.,Cab.27(38)6
11. Ibid., Cab.28(38)1
12. Ibid., Cab.3.(39)4
13. Ibid., Cab.12(39)4
14. About Lord Lloyd's and Lord Sempill's missions of no consequence see *inter alia* P.R.O.,F.O. 371, R 8152/223/37, R 8195/223/37 and R 8196/223/37, respectively R 959/959/37 and R 960/959/37.
15. About King Carol's policy towards the Iron Guard H. Seton-Watson opines that the King "had used the Iron Guard to terrorise Roumanian democrats, giving its leaders material help and police protection in their work of perverting the idealism of the younger generation into mere worship of bloodshed and bestiality. Then, when the Guard had captured the imagination of the masses, and was no longer content to be a tool of others, he . . . massacred its leaders." (Hugh Seton-Watson, *Eastern Europe Between the Wars, 1918–1941* Cambridge 1946, pp.209–10.)
16. For similar early reproaches we quote M. Constantinescu, Minister of National Economy, who "expressed [in 1938] his feelings of alarm and disappointment at the failure of H.M.G. to take proper economic interest in Roumania." (Farquhar to the Foreign Office, P.R.O.,F.O. 371, 7515/223/37)
17. Sir Reginald Hoare to the Foreign Office, Bucharest, 11 November 1940 (P.R.O.,F.O. 371, R 85/79/37)
18. Ibid.

53

4 The Obsession of the 'Jewish Leprosy'

"The Jewish leprosy spreads like eczema over the whole country."
  (Octavian Goga, national poet and later Prime Minister of Romania, on 9 November 1936)

"Failure to react and to escape from [the Jewish] danger would be the mark of a cowardly and indolent people and would be tantamount to digging one's own grave."

"Defence [against the Jews] was a national and patriotic duty and was not antisemitism."
  (Miron Cristea, Patriarch and later Prime Minister of Romania, in an article in Universul, *20 August 1937)*

Romanian Jewry, numbering around 800,000,[1] was very heterogeneous, in terms of cultural background, language and political experience. The Jews of the Regat obtained their full emancipation only in 1923. The bulk of them was concentrated in Moldavia and Bucharest and tended to be petit bourgeois. At the first census more than half of them gave Yiddish as their mother tongue and were outside the limits of Romanian culture.

The absolute majority of the roughly 200,000 Jews in Transylvania spoke Hungarian; they were on a higher cultural level than the Jews of the Regat, as well as having a higher standard of living. The Jews of the Bukovina spoke German, whilst those of Bessarabia gave Russian as their second language after Yiddish. In this way, traditional Romanian anti-semitism found a new target for its anti-Jewish agitation. Over and above the customary economic pretexts there were objections that about half the Jews of the enlarged country served foreign cultures and foreign interests and were one of the instruments of revisionism. The formula *Jew-Communist* was used of the whole of Romanian Jewry, but it was applied particularly against the Bessarabian Jews by the anti-semitic camp. "When I say Communist, I mean Jew", wrote Corneliu Zelea Codreanu.[2] He considered the destruction of "Jewish Communism" as the primary objective of the Iron Guard and preached that the struggle of the Legion, waged against democracy, was aimed at averting the Jewish peril.[3]

Anti-capitalist and anti-plutocratic slogans served Codreanu and other extreme-right leaders in their anti-semitic and anti-democratic struggle, as they considered democracy a servant of international Jewish high finance.[4] Thus they equated the Left, Communism, capitalism and plutocracy with the Jews.

A. C. Cuza, Octavian Goga, Vaida-Voievod and even Nicolae Iorga contrasted nationalism with the Jewish left, equating "true" nationalism with anti-semitism.

In inter-war Romania every government and virtually every party was nationalist, and Nationalism in Romania meant the same as anti-semitism.[5] Just about every Romanian Government pursued a policy of anti-semitism and differences were marginal. The Liberals in power in the 1930s instituted a policy of "moderate" anti-semitism, but the concept of "moderation" varied from politician to politician and more than once individual ministers were more extremist in their policies and practice than the Government itself.

If one were to establish a scale of anti-semitism, it could be said that the moderately anti-semitic National Liberal Party had Vaida-Voievod's extreme nationalist *Frontul Românesc* to its right; Goga and Cuza were further to the right still and the most radical of all was the Iron Guard. Characteristic of the image formed by foreign observers about the feelings of the Romanian right wing towards their Jewish fellow-citizens is the remark of Sir Reginald Hoare made at the end of the thirties: the parties of the Right are professional anti-semites.

On the Left certain NPP leaders did occasionally come out against anti-semitism in public, but the agrarians too had their own anti-semites. In the last years of the decade, even the NPP officially accepted the justification of some anti-Jewish measures, whilst the insignificant radical and socialist political forces to the left of the National Peasant Party protested uselessly against "legal" persecution of the Jews.

In spite of the anti-Jewish policy of most of Romania's parties, even of the moderate rightist parties, it was in no respect surprising that the bulk of Romanian Jews did not give their support to either the extreme left or even the left in general.[6] Towards the end of the 1920s the Jewish Party of Romania came to be set up, comprising Zionist and Jewish-national minded elements, especially from the newly-annexed territories. In the elections in 1931 and 1932, the Jewish Party gained about half of the Jewish vote. The other half, and at other elections an absolute majority, was divided among other parties.

In contrast to the *Jewish Left-anti-Jewish Right* cliché, the moderate Right, despite its xenophobia and chauvinism, did not close its political organisations to the Jews. The National Liberal Party ran several times for the elections in an electoral pact with the greatest organisation of Romanian Jewry, the Union of Romanian Jews (UER). Besides the Liberals, a number of other rightist parties − such as Marshal Averescu's People's Party − also counted upon Jewish votes. Quite naturally, Maniu's and Mihalache's National Peasant Party, the largest allegedly democratic party, enjoyed a large Jewish support. Even the Hungarian Party in Transylvania, with its mainly gentry and aristocratic leadership, enjoyed the support of a not inconsiderable proportion of Transylvanian Jews. Thus the Jews of Romania faced an ever more intense anti-semitic agitation politically and organisationally divided.

There is a wealth of material in the Foreign Office archives concerning the question of the Jews in the Danube Basin. In view of the fact that the penetration of Nazi German propaganda was not confined to right extremist channels, but also involved specifically anti-semitic groups, London paid considerable attention to the nature of the Jewish question, regarding it as an important aspect of German penetration. The Foreign Office was also concerned with the question of Jews because British and Western Jewish circles in general, together with liberal non-Jewish political factors, exercised constant pressure on the British Government, to induce it to wield its influence against the persecution of Jews in Eastern Europe. This was particularly noticeable *vis-à-vis* Romania from the events of 1937 right up to the outbreak of war.

In conversations with British diplomats in Bucharest it was an agreed fact that the Romanians were by definition anti-semitic, a point that was made by Tătărescu, the Prime Minister, by Victor Antonescu, the Foreign Minister, and by others.

The question of the Jews played a greater rôle in the by-elections of 1936 than ever before in Romania. In addition to the anti-semitism of the National Christian Party, Vaida-Voievod's *Frontul Românesc* proclaimed that its chief aim was to "assure the position of the Roumanian element" by the repression of the minorities and the elimination of the Jews. In 1936 the Tătărescu government was still relatively moderate in its handling of the Jewish question. The Prime Minister defined the distinction between the policy of the Liberals and of the extreme right by saying that the nationalism of the latter was expressed by aggressive

57

means, whereas that of the Liberals took into account that a quarter of Romania's population was made up of minorities, so that a policy of conciliation was pursued (on paper) towards them all, the Jews included.

The summer of 1936 proved to be the turning-point in bringing about a general anti-semitic agitation. There were three main events leading to this anti-semitic explosion – the campaign against the so-called Jewish press, the "de-Judaisation" of the Bar, and the communist trials. In the course of that summer, as already mentioned, the militant right extremist paper *Universul*, with the co-operation of the entire extreme right, launched a Nazi-type nationalist and anti-semitic campaign against the great democratic papers, branded as "Jewish". In fact, the campaign was successful not only in eliminating the leading democratic papers, but also in creating such an atmosphere of terror that it was taking a risk even to be seen reading a democratic paper publicly. The word "Judeo" was attached invariably not only to "bolshevik" and "socialist", but also to "democratic". The extremist press, from *Universul* to the Stürmer-type *Porunca Vremii* and the Iron Guard *Buna Vestire*, urged on the liquidation of the "Judeo-bolshevik" and "Judeo-democratic" papers, without meeting the slightest obstacle from the government.

The persecution of Jewish lawyers was directed by Istrate Micescu, the president of the Bucharest Bar and later Foreign Minister in the Goga-Cuza government. Thanks to the passivity of the government, the extreme right was successful in eliminating virtually every Jewish lawyer from the Bucharest Bar and in introducing a *numerus clausus* in other associations throughout the country. The trials of the communists, in which the Jewess Ana Pauker was the principal accused, provided further opportunity for noisy anti-semitic agitation.

Despite the repeated proclamations of a state of siege and the censorship, as well as the reassurances offered by the Tătărescu government, the anti-semitic campaign continued unhindered. A banquet on the occasion of the twentieth anniversary of *Universul*, held in Bucharest in October 1936, was typical of the atmosphere. Sir Reginald Hoare regarded the banquet as a political event because *Universul*, owned and edited by the pro-fascist Stelian Popescu, propagated highly anti-semitic views (Hoare's expression). The proceedings were opened by the Patriarch Miron Cristea, and Popescu was then congratulated by Octavian Goga for his action in checking the tide of "parasites who had swarmed into the country".

Congratulatory speeches were made by representatives of military, cultural and educational organisations, by school teachers and pupils, by the Orthodox clergy and public functionaries. Stelian Popescu was presented with a high decoration at the ceremony on behalf of King Carol.[7]

58

After the event Hoare asked Virgil Madgearu, one of the leaders of the NPP, "whether a foreign journalist would have been justified, in reporting these proceedings, if he had headed his article 'Patriarchal Benediction of the Anti-Semitic Movement in Roumania'." Madgearu replied that such a headline "would have been justified by the bald facts, but essentially it would have been misleading, though it was true that anti-semitism was making headway among the Orthodox clergy."[8]

The huge demonstration organised by the National Christian Party early in November 1936 in Bucharest, with over 100,000 participants, provided another opportunity for anti-semitic outbursts. "Down with the Jews" was the most frequently heard slogan and in his speech Goga, the party leader, demanded a ruthless struggle against the "Jewish leprosy" which "spreads like eczema over the whole country."[9]

Hoare wrote in his Annual Report that "the only minority which had real cause for complaint in 1936 was that of the Jews ... there is no doubt that anti-semitic feeling was on the increase ... and all sorts of petty discriminations were practised against the Jews ... Nearly all prominent officials and politicians (with the exception, of course, of the Right Wing parties) were prepared to admit privately the unfortunate effects of anti-semitism, but professed themselves unable, public opinion being what it was, to take any active measure ..."[10] – a realistic and pessimistic account.

Hoare listed in his report some of the causes of the increase in anti-semitism. In addition to the "rise of imitators of Hitler", he thought that "patriotic" students were being led to believe that Jewish competition ought to be circumscribed. "This led to constant agitation for proportional ethnic admission to the universities and sporadic beatings of Jews." Since the word "Jew" was synonymous with "communist" in the propaganda of the extreme right, this too led to an intensification of anti-semitism, given that Romania lived in constant anxiety about the Soviet Union.[11]

As mentioned, the Goga-Cuza party was pre-eminent in anti-Jewish agitation in the election campaign; but it was the Iron Guard that took the lion's share in organising anti-semitic outbreaks and press campaigns. As early as 1936 the puppet president of the "Totul pentru Țară" party, General Zizi Cantacuzino-Grănicerul, envisaged the only solution of the Jewish question: the extermination of the Jews.[12]

A frequently repeated anti-Jewish slogan in 1936 was "down with Madame Lupescu". This line of agitation too was encouraged by the Iron Guard, which sought to direct its anti-semitic smear campaign in such a way as to link it with Carol and his Jewish mistress. Hoare was right when he wrote that "the success of the Guard's extreme nationalism found its natural counterpart in the growth of anti-semitism. . ."[13]

59

It emerges from the Foreign Office archives that the question of the Jews began to arise in conversation between the British diplomats and the King only from 1937 onwards. Carol's comments contribute to clearing up the fairly controversial question of the extent to which he approved of or opposed "official" anti-semitism. In May 1937 Carol declared to Hoare that the country should be rid of a proportion of its Jews, specifically those who were not legally Romanian citizens. "There was [said the King] no doubt that a considerable number of Jewish immigrants obtained Roumanian citizenship by fraud" and he "was not sure that it might not become necessary to turn them out of the country." The King saw emigration to Palestine as one way out, whereby the pressure of "a most difficult problem" might be eased.[14] In connection with the possibility of revising citizenship, Hoare remarked "I made a wry face and said that I felt that any such decision would give rise to much administrative abuse..."[15] (It is to be noted in Hoare's favour that he missed no opportunity of speaking out for moderation over the Jewish question in his conversations with the King and members of the government.)

In the summer of 1937, probably as a result of the anti-semitic agitation preceding the autumn elections, as well as of interventions by Jewish organisations in Britain, the Foreign Office prepared a Memorandum on the Jewish question. This Memorandum estimated the number of Jews in Romania at between 800,000 and 1,000,000. (The "moderate" anti-semites were willing to increase the official figure of 800,000 to the one million mark; Goga and the Iron Guard, as well as Nazi German propaganda, estimated the number of Jews at two million and at times "demonstrated" even higher figures.)[16] According to the Memorandum, "competition between Jews and 'ethnic' Roumanians is keen, especially in the legal profession and in small retail business".[17] After listing the causes of the rise of anti-semitism, as noted in other documents, the Memorandum concluded that the most important incident in the anti-semitic campaign up to July 1937 was "the tabling of a draft law which would have discriminated against the employment of members of the minorities . . . to the extent of fixing a compulsory minimum of 75 per cent of employees of so-called 'ethnic' Roumanian origin".[18] The Memorandum also mentioned meetings and resolutions calling for the institution of a *numerus clausus* or *numerus nullus* in the liberal professions and then turned to the involvement of Jewish organisations in Britain. "The Foreign Office are frequently approached by the Secretary of the Joint Foreign Committee . . . who asks for the latest information on the trend of anti-semitism in Roumania. By arrangement between the Department[19] and H.M. Legation at Bucharest, these enquiries are forwarded to H.M. Minister who furnishes his observations at his discretion."[20]

Miron Cristea, the Patriarch, and his anti-semitic activities were kept under observation by the Foreign Office even before the head of the Orthodox Church became Prime Minister. The reason for this was the visit paid by the Patriarch to Britain in 1936 and the contacts he made with leading figures of the Church of England, including the Archbishop of Canterbury. On the one hand, Jewish organisations objected to these close links with a noted anti-semite like the Patriarch and on the other the British government and church circles were themselves anxious to see the problem clearly. Only a few extracts are included from among the numerous Foreign Office documents on this topic in this collection. Although the Patriarch tried hard not to give the impression of being an active extremist while in London, reports dealing with him leave no doubt that he was one of the vociferous spokesmen of Romanian anti-semitism.[21] Hoare's view of Cristea's anti-semitism was that it was "partly at any rate prompted by desire for popularity". Regarding British interventions aimed at moderation, especially where the Archbishop of Canterbury was concerned, Hoare wrote that Miron Cristea "is like every one else in Roumania anxious to stand well with us and would therefore accept a brotherly remonstrance from the Archbishop. . ."[22] The Patriarch may well have accepted these "brotherly remonstrances", but did nothing to stop his anti-semitic incitement, a fact on which there was complete agreement between government and ecclesiastical circles in London.

Interest in the Foreign Office in the question of the Jews intensified as the 1937 elections approached, but it was the advent to power of the Goga-Cuza government which occasioned the extraordinary attention devoted by London to the subject, even in the months after the fall of Goga. Apart from the material on the persecution of the Jews in Germany, the documentation in the Foreign Office with the most thorough and complete analysis of the Jewish question concerns Romania.

And when Hoare wrote that he did not exclude the possibility that the King intended to give the country "a hair from the dog that bit it" as the surest means of counteracting the rapid growth of the Iron Guard, he contemplated the likelihood that the King would let loose a full scale anti-semitic campaign. It was in this connection that Sir Reginald Hoare made his first comment with undertones of appeasement about it. "For the moment, my main anxiety is lest the French press aggravate the situation by denouncing betrayal [of the West] possibly under the influence of Jews who are naturally dismayed."[23] The Goga-Cuza government was the lesser of two evils, as Hoare saw it, so that it was wrong to attack and alienate it, and thereby create new difficulties for it, from purely Jewish considerations.

Sir Orme Sargent may have noted that Goga's first acts as Prime

Minister had been violently anti-semitic – in effect, the only ostensible policy in the first days of his administration – but for all that, he could not accept that King Carol would have much sympathy for violent anti-semitism ("with Mme. Lupescu still the power behind the throne"). "It may, therefore, be supposed, that the King will try to keep Goga's persecuting activities within bounds . . . But having once allowed the ball to start rolling, he may not be able to stop it", he added with justification. [24]

There is a great deal of published material available on the international interventions against Goga's persecutions, so that this collection is confined to hitherto unpublished primary material. In a discussion described as "very frank", at the beginning of January 1938, Istrate Micescu expounded to Hoare that "the Jews have morally vitiated the minority treaty by enlisting outside support for a minority which consistently refused to be loyal to the state". Hoare's reaction to this appears in retrospect to be astonishing: "As you are aware, I have some sympathy with this view. . .", and though he may have counselled moderation, it did not make much of an impact on his views. Hoare warned Micescu that there would be trouble for Romania at Geneva unless it acted with circumspection, but Micescu replied that the "government must proceed with its measures or play straight into the hands of the Iron Guard." [25]

On the same day, Hoare had a conversation with Goga as well and had to hear the Prime Minister's stereotyped arguments for the persecution of the Jews, ". . . something must be done, lest the Iron Guard prevail". [26] Hoare took Goga's anti-Jewish preparations seriously, not only because "he is a prisoner of his past, but because he believes rightly or wrongly that [the] only way to defeat the Iron Guard is to steal its thunder, in which [a] considerable element is of course anti-Semitism. . ." [27] Goga threatened half a million Jews with dispossession and expulsion from Romania and the British Government was seriously concerned with this threat, curiously, on the ground that a mass expulsion of Jews from Romania would envenom the situation in Palestine. Consequently, the British Government's interest was, first and foremost, to dissuade Goga from the mass expulsion, in order that it might not be constrained to allow mass emigration to Palestine.

The question of Jewish emigration to Palestine and British restrictions on emigration kept both British diplomats and the government occupied during the life of the Goga government. Hoare wrote to E. M. B. Ingram, Counsellor in the Foreign Office, on this issue, "I am inclined to think that if we could arrange a 'symbolical' absorption of Jews from here into some part of the Empire it would have a good effect both on nationalistic

62

Roumanian opinion and on the Jews. . ."[28] As far as possible solutions were concerned, as to where Jews might emigrate, he put forward the idea of British Guiana "as a possible home for the Assyrians"[29] — a suggestion not entirely free from cynicism. In any event, he proposed to London that some effort should be made to find another safety valve, seeing that immigration to Palestine was quite out of the question. Hoare stressed the serious value which such an effort would have and added that if no action were taken, "an unpleasant explosion" might well become unavoidable.[30]

There were some Foreign Office officials who felt that if Britain were to show any inclination towards accepting Jews from Romania, it would have a negative effect, in as much as Romanian anti-semites "would only be the more encouraged to clamour for the ejection of more Jews".[31] Others took a different line. G. W. Rendell considered that Britain was "under a strong moral obligation to do something for the Jews within the Dominion or Colonial Empire, and that it would be quite possible to do it if the question were faced frankly and courageously".[32] Rendell saw the difficulty of the problem in the British Government's Palestine policy. "It has been difficult for the Eastern Department to raise the question hitherto, without drawing a red herring across the track of the far more immediate and dangerous problem of Palestine . . . Too many interests and prejudices would be likely to come into play if the question of doing something for the Jews within the Empire were raised at this stage . . ."[33]

Hoare was in daily contact with Goga or with members of his government and there is also good evidence that the leaders of the Jewish community in Romania provided him with regular confidential information, both as regards what was taking place in the country and on the discussions between the Jewish organisations and the government. Likewise, it is clear that Hoare warned Goga several times of the harmful consequences that anti-semitic excesses were likely to have on Romania's contacts with the West. Furthermore, he put constant pressure on the King, letting him know that there would be no question of his planned tour of Britain if he could not end the persecution of the Jews in Romania.[34] In spite of this, Hoare advised London repeatedly against doing anything that might precipitate the downfall of the Goga government and he went out of his way to maintain friendly relations with it. Hoare disapproved of the firm steps taken by the French and American Governments[35] and he even regarded some of Eden's proposals as excessively strong.[36]

The British and French Governments tried to co-ordinate their actions in Bucharest, with the objective of preventing the Goga-Cuza government from taking any irreversible steps against the Jews. However, the co-ordination also involved efforts by London to stop Paris from intervening too strongly in favour of the Jews. Hoare probably played the decisive rôle in this. It emerges from one Foreign Office minute (by Sir Orme Sargent) that the British informed Cambon, the French Ambassador in London, about Hoare's very strongly-worded warning, that in dealing with Romania the dangers to be avoided were "(a) weakening the position of the King, (b) badgering the Roumanian Government to an extent which would give [them] and the Iron Guard the election cry for foreign interference".[37]

Hoare discussed the question of the Jews with the King in the second half of January and the King defended the anti-semitic policies of the government on various opportunistic grounds. "Some measures must be taken to relieve the pressure", the King asserted. He thought it necessary that a proportion of the Jews be made to emigrate and in his opinion "The ideal thing would ... be an independent Jewish state and he regretted that His Majesty's Government had not originally tackled the Palestine problem from that aspect."[38]

British diplomacy was also active in Geneva, at the League of Nations, in attempting to moderate Goga. The Romanian response, mostly as transmitted on behalf of Micescu, was as a rule that anti-Jewish measures were made necessary not only because of the Iron Guard, but also in the interests of the Jews themselves. This was the price that the Jews had to pay to avoid having the Iron Guard in power, which would have meant a complete catastrophe for them, ran this line of argument.[39]

London was not deceived by Micescu's disingenuousness and in the final analysis, the policy of the Foreign Office towards the problem of the Jewish persecutions in Romania was one of embarrassment. On the one hand, the British press and public opinion expected firm intervention by the government and this was the line taken by France as well; on the other hand, Sir Reginald Hoare and quite a few other Foreign Office officials counselled caution and moderation. "You should leave M. Goga under no illusion", wrote Eden to Hoare, "as to the reaction on British public opinion if a wave of anti-semitism is encouraged either by the measures or the propaganda of the Roumanian Government. .."[40] At the same time, London made it quite clear that the British and French Governments differed on the question of the Jews in Romania and Eden was all the time "conscious of the danger of saying anything which could be interpreted or exploited as interference in Roumanian internal affairs".[41]

On the last day of the Goga government in power, 9 February, Micescu first objected to the excessive sensitivity of the French Government regarding the Jews and then threatened Hoare that "if anything could drive Roumania into the German camp ... it would be the impression that [Britain's] only interest in Roumania was the Jewish question". On the same day, Goga received Hoare and when the latter brought up the acts of brutality committed against the Jews, Goga "deplored them", but said that "nationalism which here was bound to be anti-foreign semi-officially could not be dispensed in strictly medical doses". Goga promised, however, that he would try and stop the ill-treatment of the Jews.[42]

The days of the Goga government were numbered anyway, quite independently of London's somehow not wholly unambiguous attitude. There was a general realisation in early February in Romania that the country was moving towards a grave crisis and Goga's persecution of the Jews was declared ever more widely to have been "folly".[43] The leaders of the dissolved political parties, Dinu Brătianu among them, besieged the King with memoranda to change the situation, which, in their view, had evolved into a crisis not only as a result of the Iron Guard's campaign, but also because of the government's anti-semitic propaganda.[44]

Notes

1. According to the 1930 census the number of persons of Jewish faith was 725,318 (just above 4 per cent of the total population).
2. Corneliu Zelea Codreanu, *Pentru Legionari*, Bucuresti 1936, p.352
3. Ibid., pp.385-6.
4. Ibid., p.387. Cf. *Cărticica Şefului de cuib (The Booklet of the Chief of the Nest)*, Bucureşti, s.a., pp.62–3
5. "The Jew had been the whipping-boy for all but a few nationalists" (Stephen Fischer-Galati, "Romanian Nationalism", in: Peter F. Sugar and Ivo J. Lederer (eds), *Nationalism in Eastern Europe*, Seattle and London 1969, p.392)
6. See the present author's "The Jewish Vote in Romania between the Two World Wars" (in: *The Jewish Journal of Sociology* Volume XIV, No.2, December 1972, pp.229–44)
7. Hoare to Eden, 17 October 1936 (Doc.No.25)
8. Ibid.
9. Hoare to Eden, 9 November 1936 (Doc.No.28)
10. Annual Report on Romania, 1936 (Doc.No.29)
11. Ibid.
12. Hoare to Eden, 26 September 1936 (Doc.No.21)
13. Annual Report on Romania, 1937 (Doc.No.61)
14. Hoare to Eden, 19 May 1937 (Doc.No.40)
15. Ibid.
16. The number of persons registered as Jews was 756,930 in 1930 (i.e. 4.2 per cent), and may not have exceeded the 800,000 mark in 1939.
17. Foreign Office Memorandum, 7 July 1937 (Doc.No.44)

18. The draft law was pronounced illegal by the Legislative Council and was dropped.
19. i.e. the Southern Department of the Foreign Office
20. Foreign Office Memorandum, 7 July 1937 (Doc.No.44)
21. See Documents Nos.49, 51, and 52.
22. Telegram from Hoare, 12 October 1937 (Doc.No.52)
23 Telegram from Hoare, 29 December 1937 (Doc.No.59)
24. Minutes by Sir Orme Sargent, 1 January 1938 (Ibid.)
25. Telegram from Hoare, 4 January 1938 (Doc.No.63), already qoted in another context
26. Ibid.
27. Telegram from Hoare, 5 January 1938 (Doc.No.64)
28. Hoare to Ingram, 11 January 1938 (Doc.No.66)
29. Ibid.
30. Ibid.
31. Minutes by A. D. M. Ross, 19 January 1938 (Ibid.)
32. Minutes by G. W. Rendell, 21 January 1938 (Ibid.)
33. Ibid.
34. Telegram from Hoare, 17 January 1938 (Doc.No.68)
35. Telegram from Hoare, 5 January 1938 (Doc.No.64) Cf.Telegram from Hoare, 17 January 1938 (Doc.No.68)
36. Ibid.
37. Minutes by Sir Orme Sargent, 3 February 1938 (Doc.No.81)
38. Hoare to Eden, 19 January 1938 (Doc.No.69)
39. Letter from Walters to Stevenson, Geneva, 19 January 1938 (Doc.No.70)
40. Foreign Office telegram to Hoare, 4 February 1938 (Doc.No.82)
41. Ibid. The Germans had no doubts about the difference between the French and the British interventions on behalf of the Jews. A Memorandum by the Foreign Ministry (9 March 1938) noted that "in much milder form [than the French Minister in Bucharest] the British Minister. . .also took up the Jewish question. . ." (DGFP, Series D, Vol.V, Doc.No.179)
42. Telegram from Hoare, 9 February 1938 (Doc.No.85)
43. Telegram from Hoare, 5 February 1938 (Doc.No.83)
44. Ibid.

5 The Jewish Policy of the Royalist Dictatorship

The fall of the Goga government may have come as a great relief to Romanian Jewry and was received with great satisfaction by all those concerned with the fate of the Jews of Romania, but for all that there was no great change in official policy towards the Jews thereafter. The most extremist and most senseless of the measures instituted under Goga were cancelled — among them, for instance, the decree forbidding Jews to employ as domestics Christian women under the age of 40 — but Miron Cristea's government was reluctant to return to the *status quo ante* regarding the question of the Jews. "No change of policy was officially proclaimed", stated the Annual Report on Romania prepared by the British Legation in Bucharest but "it became obvious that the more stringent Jewish measures would be allowed to lapse or would not be applied with excessive severity . . ."[1]

The Foreign Office brought up the further evolution of the anti-semitic course in connection with King Carol's planned visit to London. On 14 February, a mere three days after the fall of the Goga government, Cadogan cabled Hoare: "if the new government modifies the anti-Semitic policies of its predecessors . . . there would be no longer any reason why the Royal visit should not take place."[2] Somewhat later, the Foreign Office instructed Hoare to speak to the King about his policy towards the Jews. "You should inform His Majesty that you have been instructed to have a frank talk with him regarding the forthcoming State visit . . . in the event of His Majesty's new Government continuing the anti-Semitic measures of their predecessor there can be little doubt but that British opinion will be aroused . . . If His Majesty can give you an assurance that his new Government will not proceed with any anti-Semitic measures, and will do their best to suppress persecution of the Jews then there is reason to believe that the visit could take place . . ."[3]

The Foreign Office had no wish to make Carol's position in Romania more difficult; it was convinced, after all, that he was "on the whole the best element in a very unstable situation". On the other hand, it saw the visit as a certain failure "unless it can be made reasonably apparent to the British public that anti-Semitic measures have been damped down . . ."[4] As a rule, when the Foreign Office intervened against the persecution of the Jews in Romania, it did so on the grounds that Romania was breaking its obligations under the Minorities Treaty. This was the international juridical basis on which Britain (and France) protested. British public opinion, however, would have had very little knowledge of the Minorities Treaty and its pressure on the government sprang from its dislike of Nazi-type oppression and from sympathy for the underdog. This mood was general in Britain and the Foreign Office had to take it into account, even when it might have pursued different policies looking at global foreign interests or what were perceived as such interests.

The new regime in Romania followed essentially the same policies towards the Jews as the Goga government had done, but "proceeded more gradually".[5] At an audience granted to Hoare by King Carol, the King proved unwilling to make any fundamental concessions regarding the anti-Jewish measures. "Replacement of the Jews must and would continue",[6] he declared and again remarked to the British Minister that "there was some danger lest we [the British and the French] create [an] impression that [the] only interest we took in Roumania was in the Jews. ."[7] (Sir Reginald Hoare was certainly eager to avoid such an impression.)[8]

On 17 February Hoare was received by the new Prime Minister, the Patriarch Miron Cristea. The Patriarch spoke only of the Jewish question and in a tone that astonished even the British minister who was prepared for anything. "[The Patriarch] unfortunately believes that the Jews have almost literally sucked the blood of the Roumanians and that a drastic remedy must be found."[9] He promised, though, that the rights of "genuinely established" Jews would be respected, but after the revision of the citizenship of the Jews, his Government would probably appeal to the League of Nations "to find a solution, i.e. a home for those who had no right to be in Roumania."[10] He suggested that the British set up an "impartial" enquiry into the question of the Romanian Jews.

There was a fruitless and quite irrelevant debate in the Foreign Office at this time, as to whether it would be possible to co-operate with an Iron Guard that "could be weaned away from its affection for the Rome-Berlin Axis and from its violent anti-Semitism" and, further, whether "if someone else were to pay the Iron Guard, they would change their tune".[11] This tended to be the level of speculation about Romania's

68

future policy towards the Jews, too. Sir Orme Sargent added a laconic and gloomy comment to the debate, "Roumania is bound to go Nazi, and that will automatically settle the Jewish question".[12]

In mid-April Hoare had a talk with the Romanian Foreign Minister, Petrescu-Comnen, who regarded the solution of the Jewish question as being of great significance. His suggestion was international action aimed at resettling a part of Central European Jewry. He thought this task not only urgent, but also of world-wide importance. He also had talks along these lines with the American minister in Bucharest, with the consent of the King.[13] Comnen also proposed that Romania be granted an international loan with which the resettlement of the Jews somewhere in the British Empire "in a real national home" would be made possible.[14] Comnen warned Hoare that for countries with "an excessive percentage of Jewish population, such as Roumania and Poland, there could be no real peace, and there was danger of serious trouble . . ." unless the Jews were resettled. Hoare was himself inclined to be pessimistic and he urged London that it should indeed support a small measure of emigration. If the Miron Cristea government failed to make "even a beginning of a solution of the Jewish problem", then, he feared, in a not too distant future "serious trouble from the Iron Guard is to be expected". Even in the second month of the royalist dictatorship, Hoare saw the Romanian Jewish question as one that "is almost certain to become . . . acute". He urged the Romanian Government, therefore, not to reject his proposals lightly.[15]

The question of the Jews remained on the agenda of the League of Nations, which was a serious blow to the new Romanian regime's self-esteem. Petrescu-Comnen requested the British Government not to keep harping on the Jewish question at Geneva and not to make life more difficult for Bucharest, seeing that the "Roumanian Government were still engaged in critical struggle with a dangerous movement of [the] extreme right and in that struggle [the] Jewish issue played an important . . . part".[16] The royalist dictatorship kept repeating its reasoning that a policy of limited anti-semitism was advisable, as a weapon and protection against the Iron Guard. Carol was convinced of the value of this policy as a lightning conductor, and, perhaps, he regarded it as justified, regardless of the fact that it would do more than just restrict the participation of Jews in the country's economic life and exclude them from its intellectual life – it would also aim at massive emigration, amounting in practice to deportation.

In May 1938 the British Cabinet again considered the question of the Jews in Romania, though without any specific motive. Halifax reported on the question and, essentially, the conclusion of the Cabinet was that it would be advisable to debate the question in an international framework, at the League of Nations in Geneva.[17]

Towards the end of 1938 the question became acute once more. Acts of violence left the Jewish community in a state of tension. One of the reasons for the outbreak was the recrudescence of the Iron Guard, but according to Comnen "there could not be the slightest doubt that recent German excesses against the Jews[18] had given a strong fillip to anti-Semitism here". In his view, the government had instituted energetic measures to prevent violence, but the only way out was still to have the Jews emigrate and Bucharest repeatedly urged the British Government to do something concrete in the problem of a "national home" for the Jews, regarding this as "more and more urgent".[19]

Summarising the events of the year 1938, the British Legation in Bucharest came to the comforting conclusion, contrary to previous evaluations, that "anti-Semitism, particularly after the suppression of the Iron Guard, ceased to be an actual problem".[20]

The major developments in Central Europe lessened Foreign Office interest in Romania. During the months before Munich there was a decline in the amount of material devoted to Romania and by 1939 little attention was paid to internal developments there, including the Jewish question. There were no dramatic changes in Romania in the year of the outbreak of war, so that the decline in interest was justified.

The royalist government continued to regard the Jewish question as grave, but it was not prepared to accept any intervention by outside powers in its handling of it and it was also opposed to the League of Nations concerning itself with the problem. "Considering the difficulties which are brought up by anti-Semitic propaganda and the importance of the Jewish problem in Roumania", according to a Romanian note to the British Government, "the Roumanian Government would very much appreciate it if the Minority Section of the League would not attempt to raise any such question, rendering more difficult the task our Government is following . . ."[21]

The League of Nations did, in fact, take the question of the Jews in Romania off its agenda, seeing that a completely new situation had arisen in international relations with the occupation of Prague, which made the question of Romanian Jewry rather insignificant. The international Jewish organisations, however, did not abandon the struggle and Rabbi Perlzweig, one of the leaders of British Jewry (Chairman of the British Section of the World Jewish Congress), included Romania in his tour of South Eastern Europe in the summer of 1939, with approval of the Foreign Office. Perlzweig was received by the Romanian Prime Minister, Călinescu, with Hoare present. There are some passages in the record of the conversation reflecting the policies of the royalist dictatorship. According to Călinescu, "neither he nor his government was anti-Semitic. Their suppression of the Iron Guard . . . had been of great benefit to the Jews. But they had to take certain elements in the life of the country into account . . . certain measures had to be taken 'pour calmer l'opinion publique'. But it had all been carried through deliberately in a spirit of moderation."[22] Perlzweig had Călinescu's promise that the worst wrongs would be remedied and the latter expressed his agreement in principle to allow Romanian Jews the right to organise and set up a representative committee. The Prime Minister showed himself not unwilling to continue collaboration with the Jewish organisations to lower tension.

After the murder of Călinescu, the Argeşeanu and then Tătărescu governments did nothing to change the *status quo.* The position of the Jews neither improved nor deteriorated and a mood of "profound pessimism" prevailed among them.[23] The catastrophic turning-point came in 1940, as the predictable concomitant of the total chaos and the advent to power of the Iron Guard following the dissolution of Greater Romania.

King Carol's dictatorship brought a measure of relief to the life of Romania's 800,000 Jews by putting an end to the terror spread by the "Blue-shirts" storm-troopers and by holding the Iron Guard in check. However, his regime followed a policy of "moderate" anti-semitism and applied a discriminatory policy against the Jews in every sphere of economic, social and cultural life.

The severity of the regime's anti-Jewish line remained to the last dependent upon international developments on the one hand, and upon the impact of diverse domestic forces on the other. As German pressure mounted and Carol and his entourage became more convinced that continuing Romania's Western orientation would be impracticable, official anti-semitism assumed a sharper and fiercer aspect.

Opinions are highly divided regarding Carol's Jewish policy. From the wide range of contradictory opinions, King Carol's image emerges in numerous forms varying from the anti-German, "Jewish-hireling" king, to the fascist-minded, anti-semitic politician.

Carol II was not an avowed anti-semite. Nevertheless, in the Jewish question he tended to yield to Germany and to the internal anti-semitic front even if this was not justifiable by external or internal necessity. It was precisely on this point that Carol sought to win the goodwill of Germany and to make his regime acceptable to the domestic right wing. In the last analysis King Carol's regime not only preceded the holocaust of Romanian Jewry but paved the way for it as well.[24]

71

Notes

1. Annual Report for 1938, Romania (Doc.No.136)
2. Telegram to Hoare, 14 February 1938 Doc.No.86, Enclosure
3. F.O. Telegram to Hoare, 16 February 1938 (Doc.No.88)
4. Ibid.
5. Foreign Office Memorandum, 21 February 1938 (Doc.No.89)
6. Sir Reginald's reply was somehow surprising: "I thought educated opinion would have regarded [the replacement of Jews] as a perfectly reasonable one if taken nineteen years ago. Now it would be regarded as a submission to popular clamour which could yield no practical results." Telegram from Hoare, 23 February 1938 (Doc.No.90)
7. Ibid.
8. A. D. M. Ross remarked in March 1938 that Hoare "rightly deprecates any attempt to constitute H.M.G. as the protector, official or unofficial, of Roumanian Jewry." (Doc.No.91,Minutes)
9. Hoare to Eden, 24 February 1938 (Doc.No.91)
10. Ibid.
11. Minute by A. D. M. Ross, 7 March 1938 (Ibid.)
12. Remark by Sir Orme Sargent, 11 March 1938 (Ibid.)
13. Gunther, the U.S. Minister in Bucharest, reported Comnen's request to Washington for favourable consideration.
14. Hoare to Halifax, 14 April 1938 (Doc.No.97)
15. Ibid.
16. Telegram from Hoare, 28 April 1938 (Doc.No.101)
17. Cabinet meeting, Conclusions, 4 May 1938 (Doc.No.102)
18. Comnen was referring to the "Kristallnacht" of 9 November 1938.
19. Telegram from Hoare, 8 December 1938 (Doc.No.130)
20. Annual Report for 1938, Romania (Doc.No.136)
21. R. Florescu, Counsellor of the Romanian Legation in London, to the Foreign Office, 7 March 1939
22. Record of conversation between Călinescu and Perlzweig (Enclosure to Doc.No.160 of 15 June 1939)
23. Hoare to Halifax, 15 June 1939 (Doc.No.160)
24. Cf. the present author's "The Jewish Policy of the Monarchist Dictatorship in Rumania" (in: *Zion*, 1964, I, pp.133—51)

CZECHOSLOVAKIA

1 Breaches in Democracy

"Czechoslovakia is a solid, indestructible lighthouse of democracy and of quiet, progressive evolution to ever higher grades of social, economic and national justice in Central Europe; a country which, in these present days of convulsion, will unyieldingly abide by the middle path of development between the extreme Left and the extreme Right . . ."

(Edvard Beneš, speech at Liberec, 19 August 1936)

In the one or two years preceding Munich, Czechoslovakia was generally regarded as the only democracy in Central Europe, in isolation, completely surrounded by authoritarian and totalitarian regimes. The Czech leaders too considered their country the only really successful democracy east of the Rhine. They invariably rejected in their speeches all the methods of violence in internal policy, the suppression of personal liberties and of free expression, even if their actions at times belied their words.

British diplomats in Prague tended to depict in somewhat darker colours this idealised state of affairs of the mid-1930s in Czechoslovakia — above all, Sir Joseph Addison, then R. H. Hadow, with less ill-will, and finally B. C. Newton, who strove most of all towards objectivity. Regarding the Sudeten German question, the view of both the Legation in Prague, and of Whitehall as well, was that the Czech political arena included strongly rightist intolerant elements. A Minute prepared early in 1936 expressed serious reservations about the right-wing opposition to Masaryk and Beneš, and did not spare the Beneš regime much either. "On the one side, Czech extremist fascism strengthened itself [in 1934] — as though the policy of the Government itself throughout 1933 had not been of a sufficiently fascist type – by the formation of the Opposition *'National Alliance'*."[1] The development of the Slovak nationalist movement was also kept under observation by London and as early as the beginning of 1936 it was described as "dangerous".

The power relations of the political parties in the Republic and the composition of the coalition governments in the thirties did not justify the forebodings about a development in the direction of the right and towards intolerant Czech nationalism. No fewer than seven parties co-operated in the coalition formed after the May 1935 elections (the Czechoslovak Agrarians, the Social Democrats, the National Socialists,[2] the Catholic Party, the Traders' Party, as well as the German Social Democrats and the German Agrarians). As compared with the 1929 elections the Agrarians, the Traders and the Social Democrats strengthened their positions. As a matter of course the two democratic German parties suffered a severe setback.

In the opposition camp the Communists scored considerable gains, achieving on the whole 100,000 more votes than Beneš's National Socialists. The fascists had to content themselves with a mere 167,000 votes (out of a total of 8,231,412), and with six deputies out of 300 in the National Assembly. Consequently there was no indication of a slipping towards the right of Czechoslovak political life. An official British analysis made in 1936 of the trends in the Czechoslovak parties labels the Catholic party only as "slightly chauvinistic", while in the ranks of the opposition Czech parties (i.e. not among the German and Slovak ones), it only mentions the "National Alliance" as being "slightly chauvinistic".

As compared to the situation in 1929 a considerable shift towards the extreme right occurred only in the ranks of the Sudeten Germans and the Slovaks. Quite paradoxically, Henlein's party became the country's largest single party (polling 1,249,000 votes). Hlinka's People's Party scored 564,273 votes, as compared to 425,052 votes in 1929 (the overall number of votes polled in the country had increased from 1929 to 1935 by about 11 per cent, while the number of votes obtained by the Hlinka party went up by 31 per cent).

The coalition parties, mostly democratic of a Western standard, controlled 166 mandates out of a total of 300 – so that the absolute majority of the voters could not have been accused of an anti-democratic and chauvinistic attitude.

It is beyond any doubt that the above mentioned conclusion of the Foreign Office Minute regarding the fascist character of the Prague Government's policy, was completely unfounded and misleading.

In the summer of 1936 Hadow, who succeeded Addison as British Minister in Prague, was afraid of the strengthening of an extremist nationalist trend among the Czechs, including the ruling parties (with Minister of Defence Machnik as the leader of the nationalists) and he complained, "how blind are Beneš's extremist followers, in this bitter racial struggle."[3] British diplomats tended to regard the greatest Czech political party, the Agrarian Party, with distrust, not only holding it to be rightist and nationalist, but also fearing that the Party was looking for means of *rapprochement* with the Third Reich. Rudolf Beran, the Agrarian leader, may have denied rumours of Agrarian sympathy for Hitlerism,[4] but according to Addison the opinion was widespread in Czechoslovakia that the Agrarian Party "wishes to come to terms with Germany, if only it can find a way to do so without being pilloried . . . as a betrayer of Czech independence . . ."[5]

Hadow, together with Charles Bentinck, a senior diplomat at the Legation, were primarily interested in whether a strengthening of the right was to be expected in Czechoslovakia and whether that would bring with it a possible turn towards Germany. They devoted their attention principally to the Agrarian Party, which they saw capable of such a turn as early as 1936. The anti-communist conservative wing of the Agrarians would have been happy to see more friendliness towards Germany and less co-operation with the Soviet Union. According to Hadow, the middle classes, who ruled Czechoslovakia, were uncomfortably aware that there was little room for an independent Czechoslovakia, should either German National Socialism or communism come to prevail. As they were quite clear on the fact that the rivalry between these two extremes was the main issue in Europe, "resignation rather than hope . . . is increasingly the order of the day in Prague . . ."[6]

In the autumn of 1936, the Agrarian Party went over to the offensive against the left and threatened to break up the coalition, in the event of its demands remaining unfulfilled. These demands included the repression of "proletarian ideas" and the cessation of attempts to form a Popular Front. The right in Czechoslovakia increased its pressure on Beneš to loosen his connections with the Soviet Union and, no doubt as a result of this pressure, he did become more careful in his relations with Moscow. "He has informed me," wrote Bentinck, "of his intention to steer 'a middle course between fascism and communism'."[7] As regards fascist sympathies in the midst of the rightist circles, Bentinck reported a persistent rumour that the Agrarian Party was strengthening ties with Italy and, further, that "a mild flirtation" between the Agrarians and Germany could be perceived. Bentinck did not exclude the possibility that, counting on the fascist states gaining the upper hand in the Danube Basin, "the more far-sighted of the Agrarians . . . [would] wish to keep one foot in this camp".[8] During the course of 1937, the number of reports to

London that "there exists a strong movement among the Right-wing Agrarians in favour of closer relationships with Berlin . . ." multiplied.[9]

The early objections raised against the Agrarians and particularly against the Beran wing proved only partly justified. It is beyond all doubt that the Agrarian party did have a strong right wing; neither is there any doubt as to the rightist views of Beran, whose collaboration in the post-Munich period did not in the least surprise those who knew him well. It is likewise obvious that the Czech fascists, who in the mid-thirties had also made use of indirect means in their struggle, "were working chiefly through the Czech Agrarian Party . . ."[10] Yet what is indeed astonishing in the analyses of the British diplomatic circles is the fact that they judged Beran with his followers and Beneš by the same standard, as if there had been a common denominator between them. Thereby they not only deprived Beneš of Western backing against the Beran-like rightists, but indirectly denigrated him and the Czech democracy, undermining Beneš's credit in the Western world.

Addison, extremely critical of the Beneš government, was probably incapable of understanding all the implications of the Sudeten question and he plied London with the most severe judgements on Czech democracy. "Czechoslovakia presents to the outside world the semblance of a bulwark of democracy, freedom and liberty, whereas it is in fact a 'Polizeistaat', similar to other states where arbitrary rule prevails . . ."[11] In his opinion the Czechoslovak Government's attitude to the minorities question was highly undemocratic and he objected to "anti-German" measures in the Sudetenland. He held the Czechs to be "ultra-chauvinistic" and wrote to Eden that "there is no semblance of 'decent democracy' as yet". His opinion of Beneš was equally devastating: "He is ruthless in his internal policy and suppresses political opponents . . ."[12] It is not easy to show what impact these exaggerated and extreme judgements had on London, but it must be considered probable that they caused a good deal of harm and helped to pave some of the way leading to Munich.[13] Kamil Krofta, Beneš's Foreign Minister, was quite right when he complained that "the British Legation at Prague were notoriously out of touch and out of sympathy with the Czecho-Slovak Government."[14]

Bentinck, like Addison, belonged to the school of thought that had no faith in the viability of the Czechoslovak State and as early as 1936 and 1937, they were advising the Foreign Office to dispel any illusions that might exist in Prague about the future. As Bentinck wrote, "I venture to deprecate 'a formula of reassuring nature'. The sooner the disagreeable and dangerous facts are realised, squarely faced and a remedy honestly sought, the better for all concerned".[15] The reference was to the need for persuading Prague to make serious concessions to the Sudeten Germans.

In 1936 legislation known as "national preparedness" or "national defence" was passed and it met with no sympathy in British diplomatic circles. Because of this law, Hadow saw no further justification for Czechoslovakia to claim to be "a democratic island in a sea of authoritarianism".[16] He proposed to the Foreign Office directly that Beneš should be threatened with the withdrawal of Britain's moral support unless he abandoned a course of "racial, linguistic and political discrimination".[17]

Reports from Prague on the position of the Slovaks and Ruthenes were equally critical of the government and were inclined to regard claims of national discrimination by the Hlinka party and Ruthene nationalists as justified.

In 1937, the debate in Prague about Czechoslovakia's foreign policy orientation grew embittered and the right wing of the Agrarians was charged with "selling the country to Germany".[18] That year, a more active right wing had come into existence and it created the preconditions for a collaborationist leadership among the Czechs.[19]

Until Munich there was practically neither a significant Czech extreme right nor a fascist movement, which might have exerted a real influence upon the country's life. Under Czechoslovakia's particular circumstances even the reaction brought about in the wake of the 1929–33 world crisis had a strengthening effect on the left, instead of the right, as was the case in the other countries of central and Eastern Europe. The fact nevertheless remains that "in an interwar Europe generally on the move toward the right and peculiarly receptive to fascism, even the Czechs were not entirely immune to its appeal".[20]

In the early twenties certain small fascist organisations started making their appearance on Czechoslovakian soil. Anti-German, anti-Hungarian, anti-Polish and in every case anti-semitic, as well as anti-socialist and anti-communist motives gave rise to extreme nationalistic, fascist-type organisations. Thus in 1925 the National Fascist Community (NOF) was formed which, achieving notoriety for its vociferous demagogy and its glorification of brute force, was strikingly out of place in the democratic and tolerant atmosphere of the Czechoslovak political arena. The late twenties and early thirties also witnessed the emergence of various fascist-type organisations and movements. They were headed by former right-wing leaders of the disintegrating National Democratic Party, the extremist veterans of the Czech Legion, the militant elements of agrarian radicalism and some discontented bourgeois politicians. Only two of these leaders could be regarded as national figures, General Rudolf Gajda and Jiri Stribrny. The former, a well known senior officer of the Legion, became Army Chief of Staff in 1926, but was soon dismissed from the

Army and degraded for dishonesty and corruption.[21] Stribrny, an ex-National Socialist (Czechoslovak) politician, stood at the head of an extreme right opposition group. His *rapprochement* with Gajda was mainly due to his hatred for the *"Hrad"* ("Castle"), that is the Masaryk-Beneš group, and he joined forces with the adventurer ex-General in 1929. In 1934, the ephemeral National Union came into being, a fascist coalition, supported financially by influential Czech banking circles.

The Czech fascists, who prior to 1938 were mainly under the influence of Italian Fascism, failed to emerge as a significant political factor. This failure may be ascribed to several local characteristics, partly anchored in the Czech past and partly accounted for by the inter-war economic and social development of the prospering Republic, enjoying more internal stability than other countries in the area. A thorough scrutiny of these circumstances would reach beyond the limited scope of this work.

In the pre-Munich period the fascists achieved their first and only relative success in the May 1935 elections, when – as already mentioned – they polled 167,000 votes (2 per cent of the overall votes), managing to assure six seats in the Chamber of Deputies.

The Czech fascists are but sporadically and incidentally mentioned in the British documents up to the autumn of 1938. On the eve of Munich, following the shift to the right, the interest of British observers and of the Foreign Office concentrated around the "respectable" bourgeois right, and first and foremost around the right-wing Agrarians. It is undeniable that the Agrarians were radicalising rightwards as Munich approached.

At the head of the Party's right wing, Beran took great steps in the direction of collaboration with the Germans in the first half of 1938. The fact that, after the collapse of Czechoslovakia, there were former politicians (like Beran) who were willing to collaborate, came as a surprise only to those whose knowledge of Czechoslovak political life was superficial and who had idealised Czech democracy. The above-mentioned British diplomats evidently did not belong to those circles who were surprised by Czechoslovak developments at the end of 1938. On the other hand, it has to be said against them that their picture of the shortcomings of the Beneš democracy was too dark, that they over-dramatised the chauvinism of the Czechs in relation to the minorities and that long before Munich they had shaken confidence not only in the viability of the Czechoslovak state, but also in the honesty of the Beneš regime. At the same time, they almost ignored the existence of other forces professing right extremist ideas – for example the radical wing of the Slovak autonomists which, on the pretext of remedying the grievances of the minorities, were working for the disruption of Czechoslovak democracy and were in the final analysis serving the interests of Nazi Germany.

Apart from sporadic notes, the Foreign Office had no detailed information on right extremist organisations in Slovakia. One of the first thorough reports on Slovakia was submitted by Newton in May 1938. At that time Newton did not believe that the Hlinka nationalists were capable of open treachery to the Czechoslovak state, but he remarked that "Slovakia has a new, nationally conscious and under-employed intelligentsia", which, under Hlinka's leadership, could be a serious danger. "The possibility of Slovak defection — even if it is no more than a possibility — should perhaps be taken into account".[22] As British diplomats had no direct contacts with Slovak autonomist leaders, the Foreign Office, presumably, had formed no clear picture until Munich as to how far extreme nationalist Slovaks were prepared to go in their striving for independence and as to how far the Hlinka movement was dependent on Nazi Germany by that date.

Notes
1. Foreign Office Minute, 20 February 1936 (Doc.No.2) (The National Alliance was a loose coalition of anti-Beneš, strongly anti-communist and nationalistic groupings, which achieved 456,353 votes in 1935, gaining 17 seats in the National Assembly.)
2. The name of the Czechoslovak National Socialist party had no connection of any kind with that of Hitler's National Socialists.
3. Hadow to O'Malley, 9 June 1936 (Doc.No.13)
4. Addison to Eden, 3 August 1936 (Doc.No.14)
5. Ibid.
6. Hadow to Eden, 28 September 1936 (Doc.No.23)
7. Bentinck to Eden, 7 November 1936 (Doc.No.27)
8. Ibid.
9. See e.g. Hadow's report to Eden, 3 August 1937 (Doc.No.47)
10. Joseph F. Zacek, "Czechoslovak Fascism" (in: Peter F. Sugar (ed.), *Native Fascism in the Successor States,* Santa Barbara, California 1971, p.61)
11. Addison to Eden, 25 August 1936 (Doc.No.15)
12. Ibid.
13. R. H. Hadow depicted Czechoslovak Parliament as "an impotent debating club during its short sittings." (Hadow to O'Malley, Prague, 28 February 1936, F.O. 371, R 1317/32/12)
14. F.O. 371, R 4398/125/67 (Foreign Office Minute, 21 July 1936)
15. Telegram from Bentinck, 5 January 1937 (Doc.No.30)
16. Memorandum on Czechoslovakia by Hadow, 2 February 1937 (Doc.No.31)
17. Ibid.

18. Hadow to Eden, 10 August 1937 (Doc.No.48)
19. About the controversial secret conversations, of no importance and of no consequence, between Nazi emissaries (Albrecht Haushofer and Graf zu Trautmannsdorf) and the Beneš administration see G. L. Weinberg's article in the *Journal of Central European Affairs,* January 1960.
20. Zacek, op.cit.,p.57
21. "M. Gajda is a gangster of the worst sort, judging by the account of him in 'Personalities' [in the annual report of the British Legation in Prague about Czechoslovak public figures]", wrote one of the senior officials of the Foreign Office in March 1939. (P.R.O.,F.O. 371,C 2566/7/12)
22. Newton to Halifax, 16 May 1938 (Doc.No.104)

2 'Authoritarian Democracy' in Czechia

After Munich, the British diplomatic reports faithfully reflected the surprising fact that the disappearance of the Beneš system resulted in much less frustration, regret or demoralisation than might have been expected. (On 5 October 1938 Beneš resigned; the caretaker government was led by General Syrový, but the leading personality from the beginning was Rudolf Beran, the rightist Agrarian leader. Beneš's successor was Emil Hacha, President of the Supreme Administrative Court, elected on 30 November.) As Newton reported in October 1938: "The ordinary peasant [does not feel] greatly affected by the recent upheavals. . .and his chief feeling is probably one of relief that he was not called upon to spill his blood. I am not suggesting that he would not have done his duty, if called upon to do so, but. . .he had no great use for the politicians of the past régime, whom he regarded largely as a band of robbers feathering their own work. . ."[1] Newton's view of the dominant Czech party, the Agrarians, was unfavourable. The Agrarians "have always been renowned for political opportunism. . . It may safely be assumed that they stand today for co-operation with Germany and have persuaded a majority in the Government that that is the only possible policy."[2] He was equally severe on the behaviour of Beneš's National Socialist party (or at any rate its two leading papers) which "turned pro-German almost overnight".[3]

In the final analysis, what took place in Czechoslovakia was something which had seemed inconceivable in the West in the summer of 1938 – a significant part of public opinion had moved rightwards, thereby abruptly denying the values of twenty years of democracy. "The authoritarian trend is clearly visible and, as the left is discredited and German influence an obvious if unpleasant necessity, it means a drift to the Right and not the Left form of authoritarianism."[4] In the Foreign Office, R. G. A. Etherington-Smith drew the correct if distressing conclusion, "the main tendency seems clear, i.e. a steady trend towards national-socialism."[5]

Reports prepared in the late autumn of 1938 underpin the views of these British diplomats that there was a tendency to attribute to the "short-sighted and selfish policy of the parties. . . a considerable share of the blame for the country's . . . misfortunes", and that the opinion was widely held, at all political levels, that the former party system needed radical reform. As for what system the masses would have preferred to see, Newton quoted *Venkov,* the organ of the Agrarian Party. The paper demanded the formation of a national party on a wide basis, which would create a corporative-type "authoritative and disciplined democracy".[6] At the same time, it was noted that signs of Czech anti-semitism, let alone Slovak, were on the increase. Nowhere in the diplomatic source material is there any reference to the possibility of Czech resistance, whereas there is much evidence of willingness to collaborate, thus illustrating the rapidly advancing rightward radicalisation and the growing resentment against the country's democratic past. In this atmosphere, Newton's reflections on the Masaryk-Beneš system could hardly have been very favourable: the democratic system had not been a "wholly unmixed blessing", it was not free of corruption and nepotism and the multi-party system, as well as the civil service, left much to be desired.[7]

Newton not only found a rapid rightward shift among the Czechs, but he also remarked that things were going, at a greater remove, in a fascist direction. "Economic measures are being taken of an increasingly authoritarian nature. There are some who suggest that the Czechs are going fascist as hard as they can, in order to spite the French and the English, against whom their bitterness has little abated."[8] Newton's observation that towards the end of 1938 and the beginning of 1939 the Czechs gave themselves over to resignation and opportunism, as well as his report of their sudden conversion, seem rather demoralising in retrospect. Newton appeared ready to understand the reasons which, in his opinion, would naturally have led the Czechs to change their political outlook: ". . . it seems clear that they have no option now but to do Germany's bidding . . . Secondly, the paths of democracy have led them but to the grave, and it is only natural that they should turn elsewhere in their efforts at reconstruction". Among other explanations, he mentioned the Czechs' historical experience, and that they "were accustomed for three hundred years to a very different system, and a tradition of authoritative rule dies hard".[9] The need for change, he felt, could not have been doubted or that the Czechs were seeking it on the authoritarian right. In the Foreign Office, too, the view prevailed that, "as the . . . democratic régime and its leaders are so clearly discredited. . .and drastic remedies will be needed, evolution towards an authoritarian régime seems inevitable".[10] But where were the people who could implement it, asked Newton rhetorically. Was there anyone who could not have seen that the days of

84

the Czecho-Slovak state were numbered and that no change of system would help?

Among those putting the new system into effect, Beran, who followed General Syrový as Prime Minister in December 1938, was alone in having played a major rôle in the past. It was he who demanded the establishment of a party of national unity and the institution of a national regime, with the slogan of "authoritative democracy". The notion had been prepared to head a "national regeneration". The notion "authoritative democracy" seems to have been thrown into the political arena by Beran and his rightist Agrarian followers. They claimed that the country was demanding this "recipe for salvation" which at the same time "doesn't mean totalitarianism".[11] Beran as Prime Minister moved towards a system assuring "national purity" in a "Christian spirit" under extremist nationalist slogans. By mid-November the "Party of National Unity" that he demanded had been set up. It was formed by the Agrarians, the Traders' Party, the National Alliance Party, the Clerical Party and the so-called National League. Although the new Unity Party could count on fewer than half the deputies who had been in parliament under Beneš, it cannot be overlooked that there were over 100 deputies who were ready to back the new regime. Beran regularly declared that the Czechs had no intention of copying foreign systems – meaning Nazi Germany and Fascist Italy – but the tendency to take over the ideas and methods of these systems was certainly not absent. (It should be noted that General Gajda also joined the Unity Party.)

From the second half of November onwards, that is, from the creation of the Unity Party, the process taking Czechoslovakia towards the extreme right speeded up. Newton noted at the end of 1938 that the Czechs were more pliable than they might have appeared at first sight. "It is disillusioning to see how low the stock of Dr. Benes and even Dr. Masaryk has fallen in the country to which they devoted their lives and energies . . . "[12] In practice, Beran's Czecho-Slovak state became a vassal of Hitler's and with this knowledge a debate continued in the Foreign Office as to whether it was worth supporting such a state and whether it should still be treated as independent. Sir Orme Sargent wondered "what purpose will be served by our guaranteeing this vassal state. . ."[13] But there were at the same time some voices raised which did not deny Britain's share of guilt in what had happened both to and in Czecho-Slovakia. As F. K. Roberts remarked, "It is true that Czechoslovakia is now a 'vassal state'. But we are at least partly responsible for that. And though it is true that there is nothing now left to guarantee, the argument that we should now recede from our promise does not lie well in *our* mouths. It would come better from the enslaved."[14]

On 14 December 1938 the Czech Chamber of Deputies approved the government's Full Powers legislation and this created the opening for Beran to reconstruct the truncated state along authoritarian lines without an opposition. In addition to the Unity Party, he relied on the so-called "Young Unity Movement", which had been set up in the autumn, having taken over many of the features of the *Hitlerjungend* and the *Balilla*. British observers regarded it as a sort of ginger group, but they did not underestimate the dangers inherent in the movement, and they noted, further, that within the movement, a small minority fascist group possessed by reason of its radical views an importance out of all proportion to its size. [15]

The question of the Jews took up a good deal of Beran's time and it must be noted in the Czechs' favour that, despite strong German pressure, they did not go to extremes in this field.

The Beran government tried to save what it could in Slovakia and Ruthenia, making great efforts to defeat separatism in the two areas. Ultimately, Beran did not attempt to employ extremist methods and his government did not overstep the boundaries of authoritarianism, taking on neither a totalitarian nor a dictatorial character. The political colouring of Prague on the threshold of German occupation was strongly rightist, but not fascist.

In vain did various fascist groups attempt to fill the void created in the wake of the disappearance of the Beneš regime. The most active group of the fascist camp was the Nazi *"Vlajka"* ("Banner"), followed by the blatantly anti-semitic "Action for National Restoration". Gajda was prominent among the leaders this time too. The post-Munich governments, including Beran's relatively moderate rightist cabinet, energetically and effectively repelled all the fascist attempts to seize power, rejecting at the same time the fascists' proposals for collaboration. In November 1938 the Syrový government arrested some of the *"Vlajka"* leaders and disbanded the main fascist organisations. Beran's authorities managed to frustrate Gajda's *coup*-attempt just a few hours before the German occupation of Prague.

Gajda could not count upon the unequivocal support of the Germans, just as later on in Bucharest and in Budapest, the Iron Guard and the Arrow Cross respectively failed to enjoy the backing of the German Government against Antonescu and Horthy. Disregarding their ideological considerations, the Germans preferred not to become involved in adventures with the fascist movements, largely made up of *Lumpen*-elements, under the leadership of unreliable and dubious figures. The Nazi authorities rated Gajda as "morally inferior" and an opportunist[16] and dropped him definitively at the end of March 1939, together with the rest of the extreme right leaders who were regarded as *"Offiziere ohne*

Mannschaft" [17] In their stead their choice for partners fell on the collaborationists belonging to the Establishment, like Hacha, Beran and Chvalkovsky. Prague was the "birthplace" of a long-lasting German policy which preferred the moderate right, inclined to collaboration, capable of securing "order" and normal economic life, to the irresponsible, adventurous extremists, albeit closer to them ideologically. This feature was duly assessed by the British observers, but they were not in a position to draw any far-reaching conclusions from this first link in the chain. [18]

Only sporadic first-hand information from Prague could reach London following the German occupation. If we raise the problem of the quality and the reliability of the information that the British Government was fed by its diplomatic service in the last pre-war years, the answer seems to be far from satisfying. Alongside of a great deal of material based on precise observation and accurate information, the reports are not free from distorted and erroneous evaluations, and demoralising, defeatist conclusions. All this must have played a considerable part in the elaboration and pursuit of the policy of appeasement related to Czechoslovakia. The shortcomings and failures of the Foreign Office regarding its evaluation may have had an indirect share in the eventual disappearance of the state which was termed by one of the Foreign Office officials in 1936 as "little more than a geographical expression, and not a very good one at that." [19]

Notes

1. Newton to Strang, 22 October 1938 (Doc.No.114)
2. Ibid.
3. Ibid. Cf. Newton to Halifax, 1 November 1938, (P.R.O.,F.O,371, C 13469/2475/12)
4. See Doc.No.114
5. Ibid., Minutes, 31 October 1938. Cf. George Kennan's reports from Prague. In December 1938 he reports about "disapproval of democracy", "distrust and alienation of the labor element", "Catholic piety", "moderate and decorous anti-Semitism". (George F. Kennan, *From Prague After Munich. Diplomatic Papers, 1938–1940,* Princeton, New Jersey 1968, p.9)
6. Newton to Halifax, 26 October 1938 (Doc.No.116)
7. Newton to Halifax, 1 November 1938 (Doc.No.118)
8. Ibid
9. Ibid.
10. Minutes by J. K. Roberts, 11 November 1938. (Ibid.) Cf. Kennan on this process: "every feature of liberalism and democracy...was hopelessly and irretrievably discredited." (Letter from Prague, 8 December 1938, Kennan, op.cit., p.7)

11. See Newton to Halifax, 3 November 1938, P.R.O.,F.O. 371, C 13602/2475/12, and Troutbeck to Strang, 8 November 1938 (Doc.No.121)
12. Newton to Halifax, 8 December 1938 (Doc.No.131) According to the American Czech historian Vojtech Mastny, "Like the French under Pétain in 1940, the Czechs in 1939, haunted by the memory of their imperfect democracy, were prepared to accept the paternalism of the Hacha regime. They welcomed its program of political concentration in the name of national unity." (Vojtech Mastny, *The Czechs Under Nazi Rule. The Failure of National Resistance, 1939–1942,* N.Y. and London 1971, p.62)
13. Minutes by Sir Orme Sargent, 16 December 1938 (Doc.No.131)
14. Minutes by F. K. Roberts, 23 December 1938 (Ibid.)
15. Newton to Strang, 12 January 1939 (Doc.No.140)
16. Quoted by Detlef Brandes, *Die Tschechen unter Deutschen Protektorat,* Oldenburg und München 1969, pp.26–27. "Gajda's policy is basically anti-German", opined Heincke, the German Chargé d'Affaires in Prague on the eve of the German occupation. (DGFP, Series D.Vol.VI, Doc.No.203)
17. Brandes, op.cit., p.45 About the Nazi reluctance to consider Czech fascist leaders suitable as collaborators, see Mastny, op.cit., pp.57–60.
18. Troutbeck expected even two weeks before the occupation of Prague a shooting ahead of Gajda. (Troutbeck's report on Czech party life, 27 February 1939, P.R.O.,F.O. 371 C 2510/7/12)
19. P.R.O.,F.O. 371, R 839/188/12

3 'Clerical-Fascism' in Slovakia

Extreme nationalism in Slovakia attracted interest in the West fairly late, not much before Munich, and British diplomacy proved no exception. The Czech problem that held the political stage in the mid-1930s was the Sudeten question, followed by the Hungarian minority and Hungarian revisionist demands against Czechoslovakia. The future of Czechoslovakia was overshadowed not only by pressure from the Third Reich, but also from Hungary, which showed much more concern with Czechoslovakia than with either of the other two successor states (Romania and Jugoslavia). As early as 1936, Hitler advised Hungary to concentrate its efforts against Czechoslovakia and he assured Budapest of his backing. Precisely because of this twofold pressure and because Hungarian demands affected Slovakia, extreme Slovak nationalism, as a force aimed at the disruption of the Czechoslovak state, did not enjoy mass support. However shortsighted Slovak nationalist leaders may have been, they could not have weakened the state to the point of collapse, since they saw clearly that Nazi Germany and Horthy Hungary would draw the benefits. A further reason why little notice was taken of extremist nationalist activities among the Slovaks in the West during the two or three years preceding Munich was that these activities represented no great danger for the unity of the state. Another reason may have been that a fair number of Slovaks held leading positions in Prague, among them Milan Hodža, who was Beneš's Prime Minister for years. Here and there objections were voiced in Western diplomatic circles regarding Prague's policy towards Slovakia, occasionally some sympathy was expressed for Slovak grievances, but by and large, the Hlinka movement and the entire extremist nationalist camp around it emerged unobserved, in spite of the fact that it became ceaselessly more and more radical. In early 1938 secret talks had already taken place between Hlinka's representatives and Hitler and the outlines of an anti-Czech front, composed of Henlein and the leaders of the equally Nazi-oriented German minority in Slovakia, could already be seen, without the West being aware of the explosive potential of this extremist factor. At the time when Sir Joseph Addison and Hadow were feeding the Foreign Office with reports highly critical of Beneš's democracy, the growth of Slovak separatism and pro-Nazi organisations rated hardly a mention in their writings.

In fact, it was only from the beginning of 1937 that the Foreign Office started to express interest in Slovakia and even then, it was more from the angle of national equality and autonomist demands, rather than the fact that the Hlinka movement was evolving to be a new disturbing factor in the Danube Basin as a potential ally of Berlin's. It is possible, too, that the Czechoslovak Minister in London, Jan Masaryk, may have played a rôle in devaluing the question, since there is no trace of his having drawn anyone's attention to the dangers of extreme nationalism in Slovakia, despite the fact that he was always listened to with respect in London. As far as we are aware, the British press likewise took no notice of this aspect of Czechoslovak politics until 1937.

In 1937, there were a few sporadic reports coming in from Prague about Slovak extremism. Newton reported in March that the Hlinka deputies had launched anti-semitic attacks in parliament upon "the increasing Jewish penetration of Slovakia". He submitted his first detailed report on the political situation in Slovakia and the rôle of the Hlinka party to Eden in October that year, but without attributing any particular significance to Slovak extremism.[1] The qualitative leap in Whitehall came about in the spring of 1938. Newton wrote one of his first detailed accounts of some disquieting features of Slovak nationalism. He took note for the first time of the possibility that Slovak nationalists might have started on the road to "defection", although he was unconvinced that the Slovak majority also supported this "treachery" against the republic.[2]

Actually, up to 1938, Hlinka's People's Party was but one of the Slovak parties, far from representing the bulk of the Slovak population, and it could be labelled as autonomist rather than separatist. Even though the separatist and Fascist-Nazi oriented wing in the party, controlled by radical, mostly young elements, gathered strength in the mid-thirties, on the whole there is no justification for calling the party separatist, or fascist prior to 1938. At least until the summer of 1938 the clerical, conservative, autonomist leaders had the upper hand over the separatist extremists headed by Vojtech (Béla) Tuka, Ferdinand Ďurčansky, Alexander Mach and others. As concerns the strength of the party, it should be borne in mind that in 1929 it won only 18 seats in the Chamber of Deputies, while at the same time the Slovak Agrarians, faithful to the Czechoslovak idea, secured 12 seats, the Social Democrats 4, and quite a few more mandates were divided between other parties and groups. Although the Slovak "Autonomist Bloc" formed around the Hlinka party won 22 mandates in 1935, the People's Party remaining the largest single Slovak party, not even then did it enjoy the backing of the absolute majority of the Slovaks.

There is no clear evidence that might indicate that the conservative leadership may have conducted a disruptive policy as early as the mid-thirties, aiming at the demolition of the Republic. Thus, the British observers are by no means to blame for their failure to perceive in this party, prior to Munich, those anti-Czech and anti-democratic splitting forces which eventually were to compel even the formerly moderate elements to become mercenaries of the Germans. Yet on the other hand we cannot disregard the fact that the severely critical attitude of the British diplomats towards the Beneš regime, which overlooked the growing fascist tendencies of the Slovak extremist nationalism, could only have presented the British Government with an unbalanced picture of the Czechoslovak political reality. Addison, for instance, may have achieved such an effect in London: he accused Beneš unjustifiably of a ruthless internal policy and of the suppression of his political opponents and termed the Czechs "ultra-chauvinistic", denying the existence of a "decent [Czech] democracy",[3] while at the same time failing to register the strengthening of anti-democratic, pro-fascist and pro-Nazi disruptive forces in the Slovak anti-Beneš camp.

It took Munich for the Slovak People's Party, led by Jozef Tiso, after the death of Hlinka, to reach the forefront of the Foreign Office's interest. Shortly after Munich, Newton reported that the Slovak People's Party "is going ahead on fascist lines far more openly and obviously than the central Government". He regretted that the Slovak Catholic leadership completely excluded Slovak Protestants from power, for he regarded them as the most "civilised" people in Slovakia and the most inclined to co-operate with the Czechs. On that occasion his report on Slovak nationalism was realistic and pessimistic: "I fear we must look forward to a period of very crude Slovak nationalism ..."[4] A few days later, the information he was sending London was alarmist. He reported that the Tiso group was building up a corporate system and pursuing an extremist anti-left and anti-Jewish campaign: "Fascist ideals and practices seem clearly to be the order of the day in the new Slovakia, to which must be added a primitive clericalism ..."[5] At the same time, P. M. Troutbeck, the British Chargé d'Affaires in Prague, was adopting a similar tone in describing Slovak events: "The Slovaks are being as Slovak as ever. They have now invented the original slogan 'One God, one Party, one Nation' ". The information available to the British remained surprisingly scanty at the time and Troutbeck was inquiring at the Ministry of Foreign Affairs in Prague as to "precisely what the Hlinka Guard[6] amounted to". "I received no very clear reply. The idea is of course copied from Germany."[7] Later he reported that German influence was making headway in Slovakia. "Everything indeed points in that direction. The members of the new Slovak Government are mostly very young men to whom the pomp and circumstance of Nazi display make a strong appeal. . ."[8]

After Munich, Slovakia went through a very rapid internal transformation. In reality, power was in the hands of Tiso and his associates – not of Prague – and the Slovaks made their own arrangements in Bratislava, quite independently of the Czechs. The only functioning political organisation was the Hlinka party – other parties were obliged to join the "Party of Slovak Unity", which in effect meant Tiso's Slovak People's Party. The elimination of Czechs from the administration was carried through at a rapid pace and politically Slovakia underwent a radical transformation.

Towards the end of 1938, Newton's account of extremist anti-Czech feeling and anti-semitism among the Slovaks was distinctly gloomy. He wrote that the new slogan was "Slovakia for the Slovaks, Palestine for the Jews, the Danube for the Czechs". The Slovaks were turning with growing alacrity to German methods, which they were using to build Slovakia on the Nazi model and "the first concentration camp will soon be open. The Hlinka Guard struts about in its new black uniform, which is remarkably similar to that of the Reich SS."[9] He expressed his surprise that Nazi persecution of the Catholics did nothing to diminish the pro-German enthusiasm of the Slovak Catholic Party and he gave his account also of the first steps taken in Carpatho-Ruthenia to set up separatist, fascist-type organisations, one of the signs of which was the setting up of "Sič"-formations resembling the S.A.[10]

In his Annual Report, Newton gave some indication that he suspected that the Catholic extremists would try to secure Slovakia's separate status with German backing.[11] From the beginning of 1939, the reports of the British consul in Bratislava, P. Pares, on Slovak developments, came thick and fast through Prague to London. Pares reported early in February that Slovakia was over the first early post-Munich months, which had been riotous and undisciplined and the situation was calmer. It emerges from the reports that the consul did not regard the Slovak leaders as having sold out completely to the Germans, but that the most extreme elements of the Hlinka Guard, like Murgaš, the chief of staff, "continue to be fascinated by the . . . Reich".[12] Later, he regarded the Slovak system as having retained some moderation. He sought to underpin this view by citing Šaňo Mach, the chief of the propaganda bureau, who had come out

92

against extremists, who "want to be more Catholic than the Pope only in order to create chaos and disorder". [13] As Pares saw it, on the basis of his talks with Mach, there was a moderate wing in the Tiso government, including Mach himself, which was opposed to the extremists, amongst them Ferdinand Ďurčansky, having wholly sold out to the Germans. His reports were not entirely accurate, however, particularly where Mach's connections were concerned. Whilst Pares described Mach as a moderate, who was ready to confront right extremism, Newton, in a report written on the same day, remarked that Mach has made "embarrassing proposals", in consequence of which he was constrained to leave the government; he proposed severance from the League of Nations, accession to the anti-Comintern pact and the expulsion of all Czechs from Slovakia. [14]

The British Minister in Prague regarded Professor Vojtech (Béla) Tuka, the honorary head of the Hlinka Guard and subsequently Prime Minister, as a dangerous extremist, whom the Slovak Government unfortunately had no intention of pushing into the background. He thought Tuka's speeches irresponsible and felt that Mach and Tuka were tarred with the same brush. Newton regarded the view of the Italian consul in Bratislava as definitive, on whether the Bratislava Government was moderate or extremist: the Italian consul "was inclined to be sceptical as to the reality of a moderate and extreme section of Slovak opinion and to think that all the Slovak leaders were pretty well hand in glove, a moderate or extremist being put up to speak as the occasion demanded". [15] Troutbeck stressed in his reports that the Tiso government was reforming Slovakia's cultural, spiritual and educational life in a Christian and conservative way, whilst Pares observed that the new Slovakia was being transformed into a corporate state. [16] In spite of this, he thought that the Hlinka party could not be identified with National Socialism and that Tiso's "purely Christian ideology" would save him from falling into a Nazi and fascist ideology. [17]

The events of 15 March 1939 and the proclamation of an independent Slovakia were followed by some fruitless speculation in British diplomatic circles, as to whether the new Slovak system was moderate or right extremist along Nazi and fascist lines. Interest focussed on Karol Sidor, who was thought by British diplomats to be a pan-Slav and a leader with the potential for breaking German influence. After the first three or four months of the life of the independent Slovak state, this speculation on the character of the regime and its foreign policy orientation was abandoned. Quite a few British experts were convinced that every factor in Slovakia had "bowed to the inevitable" and what happened thereafter no longer depended on Bratislava but on Berlin.

As far as the controversy about the character of "independent" Slovakia was concerned, which has been termed "Clerical-Fascist" by quite a few scholars in the fore-front of the post-war literature on the subject, there are a number of documents worthy of mention in the Foreign Office archives proving the uncertainty and confusion in this capital question among contemporary Slovak politicians themselves. British diplomats in Budapest held confidential talks with two senior Slovak officials in mid-November 1939. According to these two Slovaks, the Bratislava system was "authoritarian on a democratic basis", the Hlinka party was not identical with the government "and might become less so in the future"; they considered the introduction of dictatorship to be inconceivable and they regarded German interference as negligible. The British diplomat who noted the discussion himself considered that the Slovaks "do in effect appear to have a large measure of economic independence". [18]

After the outbreak of war, Bruce Lockhart, who knew Central Europe well, prepared a Memorandum about Slovakia for the Foreign Office. He thought the creation of the "independent" state to have been the consequence of a German diktat, but he did not deny that a considerable number of Slovaks welcomed that step, "mainly through their own short-sightedness and the mistakes of the Czechs both before and after Munich . . ." The author of the Memorandum was inclined to see a turning-point in Slovakia in the course of July 1939. Until then, "autonomy" – or rather "independence" – had been an endurable sham. From July onwards, disillusionment on account of German control was rapid and complete. "The Slovak peasant realised that he had been sold to Germany, and turned against his so-called autonomous Government which now exercises its functions solely at the bidding of its German masters, and with the support of German bayonets." [19] The German authorities had abandoned co-operation as a policy, and left in being only the machinery of a puppet Slovak Government, with the help of which they exploited the country ruthlessly. Political administration was harsher than in the Czech Protectorate, wrote Bruce Lockhart, and economic conditions were worse. One of the author's Slovak informants, General Viest, declared that 90 per cent of the Slovak population and the army "sigh for the old days under the Czechoslovak Republic." General Viest held Tiso to be "fundamentally a genuine, although misguided patriot", whilst he branded Tuka and Ďurčansky as "gangster traitors".

According to Bruce Lockhart, the situation in Slovakia at the time the reports were written (October 1939) was characterised, inter alia as follows: (a) there was discontent with German domination; (b) the Slovak intelligentsia and the Slovak Evangelicals (20 per cent of the population) were solidly opposed to the existing regime and were in active subterranean revolt (this was completely without foundation) and (c) the majority of the Slovak Catholic clergy was opposed to the autonomous government. Like many of his British colleagues, he was moved to admit that the "Slovaks are politically immature" and, although there were serious objections to open British support for the Slovak cause, he saw nevertheless one aspect of the Slovak situation, to which he drew the attention of the Foreign Office, namely, that Slovakia belonged to that group of states (with Ruthenia and perhaps also Bulgaria) which were most exposed and most likely to succumb to the process of sovietisation. "Never perhaps in history has the ground in South-Eastern Europe been so favourable as it is now to Russian penetration". It was from this point of view that he would have approved British and French encouragement to Slovakia. [20]

On the eve of the outbreak of World War II, a good deal of thought was given in London to the working out of a position on Slovakia. "They are a primitive and irresponsible people, quite incapable of managing their own affairs", maintained a Foreign Office memorandum of 1st September on the Czech Lands and Slovakia. "The question whether we should include the Slovaks in our war aims on the same terms as proposed for the Czechs depends on whether we may assume that they are keenly resentful of German rule. Likely though that is to be the case, we have no direct evidence of it . . ." [21]

This lack of trust towards the Slovak regime could not have been dispelled, not least because Slovakia joined in Hitler's war and a *de jure* state of war was declared between Slovakia and the two Western democracies. But the lack of trust towards the Slovak people remained as well and there was no change in this until the final phase of the war, when the Slovak uprising broke out in August-September 1944.

It is an open question how readily and how far Tiso and his group served Nazi Germany, and it is equally debatable whether "Clerical-Fascism" adequately describes the character of the Tiso system. Slovak rightist émigrés tend to deny the fascist character of the Hlinka movement and even of the Tiso regime. A few Western historians likewise advocate an apologetic and whitewashing approach towards Tiso. The strongly biased G. L. Oddo asserts that "Tiso. . .was never a Nazi, or even a pro-Nazi. He was first and always a devoted Slovak autonomist, a Christian democrat, who was forced by circumstances completely outside his control to cooperate with Berlin. . ." [22]

In the opinion of some impartial and severe critics of the Slovak state, the People's Party "might better be labelled conservative-nationalist or reactionary-nationalist than 'clerico-fascist'." [23] Yet others in the latter category have no doubts that, after 1935, Hlinka and Tiso "inclined more and more toward Fascism", and that already before Munich "some fascist elements" did show up in the People's Party, which served as "the broad basis of fascist developments", and that after the establishment of the Slovak state the regime became "truly fascistic". [24]

The past Slovak opponents of the Hlinka-Tiso party, such as Jozef Lettrich,[25] the former leader of the democratic Slovak Agrarians, or communist historians of the pre-Dubček era, like F. Kavka,[26] regard the People's Party of the mid-thirties, and of course Tiso's regime, as typically fascist and totalitarian. The expression "Clerical-Fascism", labelling the character of the 1939–45 period, is quite frequent in today's literature.[27]

Already in the very first days of the Tiso government in the Czecho-Slovak Republic, it became manifest that the Slovak regime was extreme right, extreme nationalist, anti-democratic, anti-communist and anti-semitic, displaying fascist tendencies and rapidly switching over in the course of 1939 to a totalitarian, fascist system. The roots of this regime, which most certainly enjoyed the confidence and the support of large masses of the Slovak people, go back well beyond October 1938, to a time when the movement's real tendencies went almost unnoticed by British and other Western observers. Nevertheless, and in spite of failures of interpretation and evaluation, in the controversy about the character of the Tiso regime, the British sources are a valuable help, proving the validity of our view expressed above.

Notes

1. Telegram, 11 March 1937 (P.R.O., F.O. 371, R 1842/217/12); report to Eden, 20 October 1937 (Ibid., R 7198/154/12)
2. Newton to Halifax, 16 May 1938 (Doc.No.104)
3. Addison to Eden, Prague, 25 August 1936 (Doc.No.15)
4. Newton to Strang, 22 October 1938 (Doc.No.114)
5. Newton to Halifax, 1 November 1938 (Doc.No.118)
6. The Hlinka Guard, set up in the autumn of 1938, was the radical, pro-German paramilitary organisation of the Hlinka party.
7. Troutbeck to Strang, 8 November 1938 (Doc.No.121)
8. Troutbeck to Halifax, 15 November 1938 (Doc.No.124)
9. Newton to Halifax, 8 December 1938 (Doc.No.131)
10. Ibid.
11. Annual Report for 1938, Czechoslovakia (Doc.No.135)
12. Memorandum on Slovakia by P. Pares, 3 February 1939 (Doc.No.145)
13. Telegram from Pares, 12 February 1939 (Doc.No.148)
14. Newton to Halifax, 14 February 1939 (Doc.No.152)
15. Ibid.
16. Troutbeck to Halifax, 22 February 1939 (Doc.No.153)

17. Pares to the British Legation in Prague, 27 February 1939 (Doc.No.154)
18. Record of a conversation between the staff of the British Legation in Budapest and members of a Slovak trade delegation, 14 November 1939 (Doc.No.164)
19. Memorandum by Bruce Lockhart on Situation in Slovakia, 10 October 1939; transmitted by the British Consulate in Bratislava (P.R.O., F.O. 371, C 16390/7/12)
20. Ibid.
21. Foreign Office Memorandum on the British attitude towards Czechia and Slovakia as soon as war breaks out with Germany, 1 September 1939 (P.R.O., F.O. 371, C 13304/7/12)
22. Gilbert L. Oddo, *Slovakia and Its People*, New York 1960, p.266
23. Zacek, op.cit., p.59
24. Jan Havranek, "Fascism in Czechoslovakia" (in: Peter F. Sugar (ed.) *Native Fascism in the Successor States*, Santa Barbara, California 1971, p.52)
25. Jozef Lettrich, *History of Modern Slovakia*, New York 1955
26. F. Kavka, *An Outline of Czechoslovak History*, Prague 1960
27. "... the expression 'Clerical Fascism' best defined the character of Hlinka's party and its leadership during the Second World War." (Yeshayahu Yelinek, "Bohemia-Moravia, Slovakia and the Third Reich During the Second World War", in: *East European Quarterly*, Vol. III, No.2. June 1969, p.236)

4 The Dispersal of a Legend

In inter-war Europe a belief took root that Czechoslovakia was not only the sole non-Western country where, because the system was democratic, there was no anti-semitism, but also because the Czech people itself was not anti-semitic. When the Jewish question came to the fore in Czechoslovakia, in the mid-1930s, the causes of this were sought exclusively in two areas – Nazi propaganda among the Germans of Czechoslovakia and the agitation of the Catholic Slovak People's Party. It was accepted as a fact that there were no anti-semitic manifestations of any kind in the Czech Lands. This was true in so far as there was no anti-Jewish discrimination on the part of the various governments following one another and popular anti-semitism was barely perceptible – Slovakia and to a lesser extent Ruthenia excluded. The Foreign Office material does show, however, how suitably the ground had been prepared for the absorption of the anti-semitic poison even among the Czechs, as soon as the objective circumstances of an anti-semitic explosion had come about. The material also shows how many people there were, shaped by the Beneš years, who joined the ranks of anti-semitic demagoguery in 1938–39. Equally, it is quite clear from the above-mentioned material that there were political parties, the Agrarian Party for example, which nurtured anti-Jewish sentiments. As against this, the anti-semitic agitation of a few, insignificant fascist groups does not deserve mention.

One of the first reports with a bearing on the Jewish question reached London in May 1937. It was a report on Carpatho-Ruthenia, prepared by a local man, a Czech translator at the British Legation. This Memorandum observed that in 1919 the Ruthenes received the Czechs as "liberators" from the Hungarian yoke and from "Jewish profiteering", but they had become disillusioned, because their territory had not been granted autonomy and because there had been a policy of "Czechisation". All this had badly shaken confidence in the Czechs, whose policy "very often depends on Jews, and even on Hungarians".[1]

Essentially, the British diplomatic missions received sporadic reports on a mood of anti-semitism exclusively from southern and south-eastern areas, but there was no Jewish problem in these parts of the country, either in Slovakia or even in Carpatho-Ruthenia — though these two areas were the least developed in the Czechoslovak Republic and had a much higher proportion of Jews than the northern and north-western areas. (The Czechoslovak Constitution acknowledged Judaism both as a religion and as a nationality. According to the 1930 census 356,830 citizens regarded themselves as Jewish by religion and only 204,800 as Jewish by nationality. About 156,000 Jews, that is 44 per cent of Czechoslovak Jewry, were concentrated in Slovakia and in Ruthenia.)

1938 proved to be the fateful year, which brought a complete change to the life of the Jews in the Republic. Munich and the rightward shift in the *Hradčany* were still far away, but British reports on Czech anti-semitism could be found, including anti-semitism of long standing. Hadow noted in the margin of some diplomatic correspondence in July 1938, "With regard to the remark . . . that 'there is no anti-Semitic feeling among the Czechs", this is quite incorrect. Mr. Short [one of the informants of the British Minister in Riga] talked to the Jews of Prague whose constant complaint is that they are disliked by both sides: by the German-speaking (Henlein) minority as anti-Germans, by the Czechs as 'Germans' because they speak and use that language for business purposes, support the German (and not the Czech) opera . . . and must — in order to live — trade with Germany."[2] Hadow saw other reasons for antipathy towards the Jews: "Their gradual 'occupation' of such professions as medicine, law . . . and their hold over business have — as in Vienna — earned them the most unfortunate dislike of Czech and Sudeten students alike."[3] Hadow had no doubts about the existence of popular anti-semitism among the Czechs. "In fact in Czechoslovakia . . . there is a deep-seated *popular* prejudice against [the Jews] due largely to their success and 'encroachment' upon restricted fields of activity . . . The Czechoslovak Government does not . . . discriminate against them as elsewhere; but they [the Jews] are not liked by the Agrarian or 'National Alliance' political parties. . ."[4]

Soon after Syrový and later Beran and his associates came to power, the British reports gave a very full account of anti-Jewish activity within the government and of the outburst of an anti-Jewish mood among the people.[5] It emerges from the British material that this anti-Jewish feeling burst out in the despair of the collapse, quite independently of German pressure and the constraints on the government. By the end of October it

100

was known in London that the Czech Government was preparing to restrict the activities of Jews and it was noted that "a new point we shall have to keep an eye on is the likelihood of anti-Jewish legislation".[6]

The fate of the Jews expelled from the occupied Sudetenland posed a major problem for the Prague authorities. The government tried to prevent Jewish refugees or expellees from settling in the truncated country and Prague requested British intervention in Berlin to ask Berlin to stop the German authorities from dumping Jews into what remained of Czechoslovakia.[7] Newton regarded this request as justified, not least because he saw a political danger in the growth of the Jewish population in the Czech Lands, fearing a strengthening of anti-semitism, fed by Czech broadcasts from Germany.[8] Newton sensed a growing wave of anti-semitism in the Czech Lands, and he noted a recent resolution passed by the Sokol, the national youth organisation set up in the Beneš era: "The Jewish question should on national and social grounds be so resolved that those who have immigrated into the country since 1914 should return to their original homes". The remainder were to be incorporated into the nation's social structure in proportion to their number.[9]

By the end of October, the reports were speaking not merely of an anti-semitic trend, but of the first anti-semitic street demonstrations in Prague.[10] The Memorandum prepared for the Foreign Office in November marks the gloomy state of reality — which probably few people among the circle of Western Czechophiles would have found plausible. "There is no doubt that feeling [in the Czech Lands] at the present moment is extremely anti-Semitic and the Jews are much frightened. . ." London reckoned with the possibility of a "wholesale expulsion of the Jews," amounting to 150,000 to 250,000 people.[11] (In post-Munich Czecho-Slovakia the number of Jews decreased to 251,000 constituting a bare 2.5 per cent of the population. According to the outdated 1930 census, more than 105,000 persons of Jewish faith must have remained on the territories annexed by Germany and Hungary.) No more than three weeks after Munich, Newton informed the Foreign Office that "feeling against the Jews is on the increase not only in Slovakia, where the Slovak People's Party have long been making party capital out of it, but also in Bohemia which has sometimes been regarded as a kind of haven for the chosen race."[12] A remark not entirely devoid of irony.

R. J. Stopford, the British Government Representative for Refugees, sent first-hand reports on the views of Foreign Minister and former Czechoslovak Minister in Rome, Chvalkovsky, known for his anti-semitic views. According to Chvalkovsky, "The Jewish problem must be settled. Although the Germans were pressing for action to be taken against the Jews, there must be no pogroms before January or February", he declared with unparalleled cynicism, "as nothing must be done to interfere with the possibility of obtaining a further Anglo-French loan." On the other hand, Chvalkovsky hoped that in the meantime all the Jews would decide that they would have to emigrate.[13]

Troutbeck found these statements by Chvalkovsky "disturbing", together with the position of the Jews in general. He did not object to the desire of the Czecho-Slovak Government to avoid increasing their Jewish population and accepted restrictions on the number of Jews in the various professions, "but a deliberate policy of driving the Jews to the wall" was more than he could stomach. "A virulent and new-born anti-Semitism in Czechoslovakia would indeed be an unfortunate offshoot of the policy of appeasement inaugurated at Munich",[14] wrote Troutbeck, thus putting his finger on an ineluctable concomitant of the policy of appeasement, a point, incidentally, which has eluded scholars working on the subject to this day.

Czecho-Slovakia was given a £10 million loan in connection with the detachment of the Sudetenland and the consequent convulsions, with the primary objective of easing the refugee problem. (Czechs fled in their hundred-thousands to the truncated Czech lands from the Sudetenland, from Southern Slovakia – returned in November to Hungary – from rump-Slovakia, from Cieszyn and from Carpatho-Ruthenia as well.) The British Government attempted to restrain Prague from anti-Jewish discrimination by means of this £10 million loan and by the prospect of further loans. "We must do what we can to extract assurances from the Czechs in connexion with these negotiations that they will abstain from anti-Jewish measures", proposed a Foreign Office official.[15]

The question of the loan occupied the British Government for weeks. The problem was complicated by the conviction that "the new Czechoslovak Government will be Nazi in spirit and is likely to pursue anti-Semitic measures".[16] The Foreign Office tried to extract assurances that the Jewish question would be handled humanely and that the money would be used exclusively for the refugees. The Czechs were told that any further financial favours "depend upon Czech policies, particularly as regards the Jews and refugees".[17] All this could do little to change Czech policies, not least because the possibilities for manoeuvring open to Prague had disappeared. William Strang was absolutely correct when he told the Treasury that "we are asking the Czechs to promise something which it is certain as anything can be that they will not be in a position to fulfil."[18]

Sir Orme Sargent was more than just sceptical about the Czechs being able to keep their word and stop the persecution of the Jews against the promise of a British loan. He was opposed even to £2 million being granted to the Czechs more or less "as a bribe" not to introduce

102

anti-semitic legislation. "...It is surely unfair even to ask the Czechoslovak Government to give such an undertaking and to accompany it with a bribe of £2 million . . . they will naturally be tempted to give the undertaking, pocket the money, and then proceed to argue, quite truthfully, that they were unable to honour the undertaking. . ."[19]

There is mention made of the views of Hacha, the Czecho-Slovak President, on the Jewish issue. The elderly President, whose rôle was purely nominal, regarded the Jewish question as less critical in the Czech Lands than in Slovakia, for instance, on account of the relatively small number of Jews, but he did admit that "a way must be found to limit the rôle of the Jews. . ."[20] This "way" was difficult to find because of German pressure. "The Czechs . . . find themselves between two fires, being urged by the Germans to destroy the Jews and by ourselves to protect them", wrote Newton, "I fear there is little doubt which advice will be more strongly heeded, nor in which direction the sentiments of the Czechs themselves are now turning." Newton reported on anti-semitic manifestations among the Czechs, including anti-Jewish activities by students. The helplessness of the situation was illustrated by a remark, quoted by Newton, made to one of the people at the Legation, by a "decent-minded" Czech: "We were never in our history anti-Semitic, but the world is forcing us to become so."[21]

Courageous and sober voices were, in fact, raised against the wave of anti-semitism in the Czech parliament right up to the German occupation,[22] and there were no drastic anti-Jewish measures or atrocities on the German model initiated by Syrový's or Beran's government.

In concrete terms, the Jews "were suffering from all sorts of restrictions arising not from any legislation, but from police regulations and other forms of practical obstruction". Nevertheless, quite independently of any German interference, the Czech local authorities were busily putting into effect various anti-Jewish measures, which had not been sanctioned by parliament but were the result of their own arbitrary actions.[23] While the Prague Government was reassuring the West that the anti-semitic movement in the Czech Lands was merely "an irresponsible undercurrent" and that "restrictions" might have to be imposed, but there was no question of "persecution",[24] British sources bore out the anti-semitic atmosphere among the Czechs[25] and the Jewish community faced the future in a mood of panic. Their fears were justified by the fact that "the German Government had been doing everything to foment anti-Jewish movements by their broadcasts and had criticised Beran for not going far enough" — according to a Treasury report.[26] The Foreign Office made strenuous efforts to stop the Czechs from taking extreme anti-Jewish steps, but it was recognised that Beran's government, "with the best will in the world, was not capable of withstanding the intensifying German demands." ("Clearly the Czechs will find great difficulty in avoiding anti-Jewish measures, but they have hitherto put up a good fight", noted Roberts in the Foreign Office.)[27]

The British Legation in Prague mooted the question of "how far anti-Jewish measures are being forced upon the Czechs and how far the Czechs are merely alleging German pressure as an excuse for taking action which they themselves desire".[28] From the Foreign Office archives, one can conclude that the Beran government tried to reduce the proportion of Jews in the country's economic life and exclude them from its intellectual life, still within a legal framework and without employing brutal methods. It also emerges with complete clarity that in the two to three months before the occupation, Beran was forced to radicalise his policy towards the Jews on account of German pressure. But it is beyond debate that a wave of popular anti-semitism had begun, that Beran and a good many of his associates held anti-semitic views and that on the facts themselves, a large part of the Czech population could not be absolved from the responsibility for the persecution of the Jews that did take place prior to the occupation.[29] Not only Chvalkovsky, but Beran also assured Berlin about the willingness to carry out anti-Jewish measures,[30] and actually the Czech Government exploited anti-semitic agitation for its own purposes — according even to German sources.[31]

The quite frequent British interventions with the Prague Government on behalf of the Jews are relevant both to the British view on the future of the Jews and to the Czech reaction to these steps.

Chvalkovsky and senior officials in the new Prague administration were in general responsive to the British interventions and usually tended to shift the responsibility for anti-Jewish measures upon the Germans.[32] On the other hand they were eager to reassure London that "the Czechs were determined not to follow German anti-Semitic ideas".[33] Even a few days before the German occupation Chvalkovsky stated to Newton that the Czechs evaded action against Jews and justified themselves with the Germans by maintaining that the Jewish question was an international problem, in regard to which the Prague Government proposed to pursue the same policy as Romania and Poland.[34]

It is worth mentioning that a tendency of a certain self-reassurance prevailed in the Foreign Office; even though they did not foresee a rosy future for the Jews, neither were they apprehensive of Nuremberg-like persecutions. This relatively optimistic assessment was upheld by a similar French view. The British Ambassador in Paris, Sir E. Phipps, reported on 10 December 1938 that the French Government's information "did not cause them any anxiety with regard to Jews in Czechoslovakia."[35]

The persecutions that took place after the establishment of the Protectorate could not be listed as a Czech responsibility, but it is not without interest that the British diplomatic material does contain information, sporadic certainly, about anti-semitic measures taken on Czech initiative, after 15 March 1939. Thus the British mission in Prague (only a Vice-Consulate by that stage) reported in August 1939 that the Budejovice branch of the National Union Party had issued an order "in the interest of cooperation with the German nation", which resembled the Nuremberg laws, for instance, that "social intercourse between Czechs and Jews, both in public and in private, is considered to be undesirable and compromising".[36]

As to Czech anti-semitism in general, and to that of the post-Munich period and after the German occupation in particular, opinions have been much divided on the question up to this day. The condemnatory British view of the alleged Czech anti-semitism was questioned by Czech émigrés as early as 1940–41. Thus, an official publication of the Beneš government in exile quoted Coulondre, former French Ambassador in Berlin: "In its great majority . . . the Czech nation, even after Munich, maintained a decent attitude and accepted anti-Semitic measures merely as one of the sad necessities which had befallen the Republic".[37]

Nor is there any doubt that Czech collaborators assisted the Nazi occupiers against the Jews. But after the setting up of the Protectorate, the fate of the Jews of the Czech Lands was exclusively in the hands of the Germans and it would be quite useless to insist on trying to apportion responsibility between Czechs and Germans regarding the fate of the Jews of Bohemia-Moravia after 15 March 1939.

We do not think we will be distorting the historical truth if we supplement the image of Czech anti-semitism, as reflected in our documents, with some characteristic post-war fact-finding evidence. A public opinion poll drawn up in Czechoslovakia in 1947 revealed that although the majority of Czechs (67.2 per cent) did not bear a grudge against any particular religious belief, dislike of Jews (15.9 per cent) remained far and away the strongest popular prejudice.[38]

Notes

1. Memorandum on the Autonomy of Subcarpathian Russia prepared by T. H. Kadlčik, 20 May 1937 (Doc.No.41)
2. Remarks by Hadow on P. W. Scarlett's letter from Riga, 14 July 1938 (Doc.No.106)
3. Ibid.
4. Ibid.

5. e.g. R. J. Stopford's Memorandum, 14 November 1938 (Doc.No.122) and Troutbeck to Halifax, Prague, 21 February 1939, P.R.O., F.O. 371, C 2333/7/12

6. Newton to Strang, 22 October 1938; Minutes by R. Spear Hudson, 2 November 1938 (Doc.No.114)

7. Telegram from Newton, 22 October 1938 (Doc.No.115)

8. The British Government did in fact protest to Berlin on the basis of the Munich agreement against the expulsion of the Jews (F.O. Telegram to Sir Neville Henderson, 26 October 1938)

9. Newton to Halifax, 26 October, 1938 (Doc.No.117)

10. Newton to Halifax, 1 November 1938 (Doc.No.118)

11. Memorandum by R. J. Stopford, 14 November 1938 (Doc.No.122) Reports about anti-semitism in Czechoslovakia mentioned in P.R.O., F.O. 371, C 395/3/12, 6 January 1939 (Doc.No.139)

12. Newton to Halifax, 26 October 1938 (Doc.No.117)

13. Record of a conversation between Count Kinsky and R. J. Stopford, 14 November 1938 (Enclosure to Doc.No.124)

14. Troutbeck to Halifax, 15 November 1938 (Doc.No.125)

15. Letter from Makins to Waley, 26 November 1938 (Enclosure to P.R.O., F.O. 371, C 1437/118896/12)

16. Minutes by R. M. Makins, 24 November 1938 (Enclosure to Doc.No.125)

17. Telegram from Newton, 5 December 1938; Minutes by J. K. Roberts, 7 December 1938 (Doc.No.128)

18. Minutes by W. Strang, 5 January 1939 (Doc.No.138) (See Chvalkovsky's complaint in Berlin about British conditions for the protection of the Jews in connection with the £10 million loan in: DGFP, Series D, Vol.IV, Doc.No.159, Berlin, 23 January 1939.)

19. Minutes by Sir Orme Sargent, 5 January 1939 (Ibid.)

20. Newton to Halifax, 5 December 1938 (Doc.No.129)

21. Newton to Halifax, 8 December 1938 (Doc.No.131)

22. Newton to Halifax, 20 December 1938 (Doc.No.132)

23. Foreign Office Memorandum, 4 January 1939 (Doc.No.137) For reports on anti-Jewish measures and anti-Jewish feeling see P.R.O., F.O. 371, C 16068/1667/62 and C 16001/1667/62 (December 1938). For Newton's pessimistic prognoses see C 14418/11896/12.

24. Ibid. Beran stated in December 1938 that the Jewish question would have to be solved, but the "attitude of the State to those Jews who had long been resident in the Republic's territory and who had 'a positive attitude' to the needs of the State . . . would not be hostile." (P.R.O., F.O. 371, C 15719/2475/12)

25. Minutes by Gladwyn Jebb (Central Department), 6 January 1939 (Doc.No.139)
26. Record of conversation between Sir Frederick Leith Ross and Dr. Pospisil, 12 January 1939 (Doc.No.141)
27. Minutes by J. K. Roberts, 26 January 1939 (Doc.No.143)
28. Troutbeck to Halifax, 9 February 1939 (Doc.No.146)
29. Kennan did not confirm the existence of popular anti-semitism in Czechia prior to the occupation: "The mass of the people appear simply to have very little interest in anti-Semitism." (Kennan, op.cit., p.45. [Prague, 17 February 1939])
30. Political Archives of the German Foreign Minister, Bonn, Pol.IV. 449, Tschechoslovakei 36, 13 December 1938
31. "The fact that by their anti-Jewish activity Gajda's followers often diverted the effects of the anti-German feeling among the population is convenient for the (Czech) Government at present". (The German Chargé d'Affaires in Prague to the Foreign Ministry, 13 March 1939, DGFP, Series D, Vol.IV, Doc.No.203)
32. About shifting responsibility solely upon the Germans see C 466/3/12 (6 January 1939)
33. F.O. Minute by J. K. Roberts (quoting Mr. Slaby, a personal friend of Beran) P.R.O., F.O. 371, C 698/3/12 (17 January 1939). On other interventions on behalf of Czechoslovak Jews see among other documents C 42/3/12, C 43/3/12; for anti-Jewish measures causing concern in London see among other papers C 15068/1667/62.
34. Newton's telegram to the F.O., 10 March 1939 (Doc.No.156)
35. F.O. Memorandum by J. K. Roberts, 4 January 1939 (Doc.No.137)
36. British Vice-Consulate (Prague) to the Foreign Office, 4 August 1939 (Doc.No.161)
37. Two years of German Oppression in Czechoslovakia. Czechoslovak Ministry of Foreign Affairs, Department of Information (London) 1941, p.80.
38. J. Lion in *Svobodne slovo*, 4 December 1966, p.5, quoted by W. Oschlies, "Phases and Faces of Czech Antisemitism" (in: *The Wiener Library Bulletin*, 1970/71, Vol.XXIV,No.2,p.23)

5 The Slovak 'Clerical Anti-Semitism'

Slovak émigré literature continues to insist tenaciously that Tiso was not anti-semitic and that even the genuine Slovak anti-semites were moderates, who excluded any "physical" solution from their policies and acted as a moderating factor on German anti-Jewish persecution in Slovakia.[1] British archival material provides some valuable illumination on this question as well.

The anti-Jewish mood of Slovakia during the twenty years of the Republic was palpable throughout, and it was so in somewhat unusual circumstances, in that this was under the influence of the Catholics, or strictly speaking a part of the Catholic clergy. The history of Slovak nationalism during the inter-war period is closely linked with the fortunes of Andrej Hlinka's People's Party. And in as much as the Hlinka movement was chauvinist and anti-semitic, Slovak nationalist ideology as a whole included within it the concept of anti-semitism. The reasons for this Slovak anti-semitism are complex. In part, it is explained by the backwardness and to some extent xenophobia of the Slovaks. Until 1918, under Hungarian rule, in the eyes of the Slovaks the Magyarised and urbanised Jewish bourgeoisie and the fairly extensive Jewish tenantry were a foreign and exploiting element. The Slovak nationalist semi-intelligentsia saw a factor of Magyarisation in the Jews. The Catholic clergy, with its enormous influence over the peasantry, led the autonomist, anti-Prague chauvinist movement and was generally anti-semitic. Already in the early years of the Republic, a large part of Slovak Jewry was accused of looking towards Prague, of serving Czech interests primarily, to the detriment of Slovak efforts. (At the same time, the German-speaking Jews of the Czech Lands were accused by Czech nationalists of propagating German culture.)

It was fairly natural that until the Sudeten crisis the question of Slovak

109

Jews did not attract much interest in Whitehall. Information bearing on the Jews and Slovak anti-semitism is to be found rather late in the British diplomatic papers. Here and there, prior to 1938, one can find reports[5] that Slovak nationalists made anti-semitic sounding speeches in the Prague parliament, but the first reports of any value started to reach London from Prague and Bratislava only in mid-1938. Thus, for instance, Newton was told, on the basis of information supplied by Sidor's circle, that the Hlinka group objected to the fact that the financial power of the Jews was great and accused them of not being "averse from lending a hand to Hungarian intrigues."[2] This accusation was, of course, quite untenable, given that it was only a very small proportion of the Jews in Slovakia that regarded itself as Hungarian, quite apart from the fact that the anti-semitic policies pursued by Budapest made the charge implausible. According to Newton, the Jews of Slovakia were anxious about the future, many of them believing the Czechoslovak state to be doomed and that a political change would bring the Slovak anti-semites to power.

By the time of the September crisis, the Slovak autonomists were pursuing a vociferous anti-semitic campaign and after Munich, a policy of anti-semitism was inaugurated almost automatically. Whereas the British entertained some hopes with regard to the Czech Lands that financial aid and traditional influence would moderate Beran's policy towards the Jews, there were no such hopes with regard to Tiso. From the first moment on — after Munich — official statements from Bratislava were far more extremist in their anti-semitism than government and other political circles in Prague. In the very first days, Sidor and many others published violent anti-Jewish articles, made inflammatory speeches, demanding that "the country must be swept clean and the Aryan clause proclaimed".[3] On 5 November, the Tiso government announced measures affecting a very large number of Jews, on the ground that this would be a punishment for hostile Jewish elements "which had worked against the State, particularly at the time of the negotiations with Hungary".[4] It does not emerge from British reports how far British diplomats recognised the impossibility of this accusation.

On the basis of information supplied by Stopford, Troutbeck reported in mid-November that "an unpleasant feature of the new regime in Slovakia is the strong anti-Semitic trend". He also noted incidents of anti-Jewish hooliganism and the expulsion of thousands of Jews to Hungarian territory, from where the Hungarians drove the wretched, terrorised crowds back to the no-man's-land between the two countries.[5] Several papers dealt in detail with the anti-Jewish terror in Slovakia and with the fate of the refugees and expellees. The question of the persecution of the Jews in Slovakia was brought up at the end of 1938 in

110

the Prague parliament by moderate Czech deputies, on the ground that the foreign repercussions of this persecution were unfavourable and might prejudice the country's foreign trading contacts. A deputy of the Slovak Unity Party rose in defence of the policy of Bratislava, adopting the kind of tone associated with Göbbels, declaring that "the time had passed when Jews could clothe their egoistic capitalism in the red garments of Marxist internationalism and provoke a class war." And so far as the future was concerned, the Jews "would now have either to subordinate themselves to the national community or disappear . . ."[6] The almost permanent state of disorder in Slovakia made anti-Jewish excesses practically a daily occurrence, nonetheless there is no indication that London attempted to restrain Bratislava directly. Reasons of protocol – the Tiso government was not recognised – or political and diplomatic reasons or that the situation was recognised for what it was too late, plus the fact that the British Legation had contacts mainly with the Czechs in Prague, all help to explain why the British Government had failed to intervene in Bratislava.

Some sporadic information did reach London on the reaction of the Jews of Slovakia. Pares reported, for instance, that ". . . the considerable migration of Jewish capital from Slovak to Prague banks is reckoned a serious source of weakness to the Slovak financial position . . . In anticipation of discriminatory measures the Jews in Slovakia are endeavouring to emigrate. The extent of this movement can be particularly well assessed at a British Consulate where numerous callers enquire every day regarding immigration into the British dominions and colonies."[7] Pares saw Tiso as a "level-headed" man, worried about the future of Slovakia, who disapproved of the excesses committed against the Jews, above all because of the economic consequences. Tiso's "references to the Jewish problem are not radical and though he says he intends to arrange a final solution of it he will see that this is carried out without damaging Slovak economic interests."[8] Pares described Tiso as a moderate in several of his reports. He cites an interview given by Tiso to a Jewish journalist in which he said that the solution of the Jewish question would be "just, social and humane. Emigrant Jews would either be sent home to their own countries or would be assigned a place of residence [in Slovakia]."[9]

Pares paid special attention to active anti-semitism on the part of the Catholic clergy. In one of his reports, he quotes Rudolf Mikuš, Provincial of the Jesuit Order in Slovakia, at length, to the effect that the Catholic Church was in favour of a rapid solution of the Jewish question. Mikuš recommended the complete exclusion of the Jews from public and commercial life "to limit their evil moral and material influence". He insisted, nevertheless, Pares added, that the solution must be just.[10] Mikuš

111

incidentally supported the conversion of Jews and was ready to regard baptised Jews as non-Jewish.

In mid-February, Pares had a long discussion with Šano Mach, who took great pains to convince him that the treatment of Jews in the refugee camps was humane, and explained that the government did not expect to solve the Jewish question immediately. But Mach declared that "public opinion in the villages, always strongly anti-Semitic and in recent months fanned by fiery speeches and newspaper articles, is. . . complaining that the government is proceeding too slowly in the solution of the Jewish problem." He asserted that the Hlinka Guard was recommending to the government that something had to be done to allay the rising discontent over the slow and mild treatment of the Jewish question.[11] Pares added the following comment on Mach's complaints: "since the Hlinka Guard are themselves responsibile for the increase in anti-semitic feeling, it is rather odd that they should now lay the blame on the people. However . . . it is just possible that after shouting themselves hoarse for several months the Hlinka Guard are genuinely perturbed to find that somebody has been listening to them."[12] From the viewpoint of the post-war polemics over responsibility and guilt, and in the knowledge that at present Ďurčansky is directing Slovak anti-communist agitation in Munich, it is not without interest that according to Mach, Ďurčansky was "responsible for a great deal of the anti-semitic agitation, on account of his daily denunciations. . ."[13] Mach also told Pares that the inflammatory Slovak-language broadcasts from Vienna "are said to be controlled by Ďurčansky".

In early spring, Pares saw a general easing up in the handling of the Jewish question. "The active anti-Semitism of the early days of November had been only rarely repeated", he wrote, underlining the following sentence in his long and detailed account, "the manner in which the Jewish question is to be solved will apparently be quite moderate . . . Dr. Tiso declared that Slovakia will not imitate any other country, but in evolving her own plan must consider the consequences for her national life."[14] There is a good deal of evidence in the British papers that Tiso, although having no experience in economics, was extremely careful lest a drastic "solution" of the Jewish question might bring about too great a dislocation in the Slovak national economy, which in any event was in a crisis situation.

The establishment of the independent Slovak state inevitably meant a turning-point in the Jewish issue. On 18 April, the Jewish Law appeared, with its curious contradictions — to which attention was drawn by British reports. The Law was relatively "mild", in the judgement of the reports, but Pares noted that the "likelihood that further laws will be passed must

112

create a feeling of insecurity among the Jews. . ." The tendency among the Jews to opt for emigration would not be stopped, thought Pares, rightly guessing that the Jewish question would inevitably become critical in the spring months in the Nazi-satellite state. Later, when the Jewish question reached its "final solution" phase, British diplomacy no longer had direct on-the-spot information at its disposal. Nonetheless, the documentation which closes with the autumn of 1939 leaves one in no doubt whatever that it was not just extremists of the Ďurčansky type, who regarded the situation as ripe for a "final solution", without the need for any duress on the part of the Germans to have this accepted by the people. "Moderates" like Tiso and other anti-semites with a human face had also come to the same conclusion.[15]

Notes

1. e.g. Milan Stanislao Durica, *La Slovacchia e le sue relazioni politiche con la Germania, 1938–1945,* I, Padova 1964. Idem, *Die slovakische Politik im Lichte der Staatslehre Tisos,* Bonn 1967. Joseph A. Mikuš, *Slovakia. A Political History: 1918–1950,* Milwaukee, Wisconsin 1963. Cf. François d'Orcival, *Le Danube était noir. La cause de la Slovaquie indépendante,* Paris 1968, pp.214–28.
2. Newton to Halifax, 16 May 1938 (Doc.No.104)
3. Newton to Halifax, 1 November 1938 (Doc.No.118)
4. Troutbeck to Strang, 8 November 1938 (Doc.No.121)
5. Troutbeck to Halifax, 15 November 1938 (Doc.No.124)
6. Newton to Halifax, 20 December 1938 (Doc.No.132)
7. Memorandum by Pares, 3 February 1939 (Doc.No.145)
8. Ibid.
9. Pares to Troutbeck, 10 February 1939 (Doc.No.147) On Tiso's moderate policy towards the Jews see also Troutbeck to Halifax, 22 February 1939. (Doc.No.153)
10. See Doc.No.145. Cf. Kennan, op.cit., pp.51–2. (Despatch from 17 February 1939)
11. Pares to Troutbeck, 14 February 1939 (Doc.No.151)
12. Ibid.
13. Ibid.
14. Pares to the British Legation in Prague, 27 February 1939 (Doc.No.154)
15. Tiso stated in the early days of the Slovak state that "the new social and business order can be established only when we shall completely uproot the Jews from our national life." Tuka and Mach "were calling . . . for the final and definite solution of the Jewish problem." (Lettrich, op.cit., p.181)

1 The Gentry Establishment Against the Nazi 'Parvenus'

The disintegration of Greater Hungary after the First World War was accompanied by greater convulsions and led to more radical changes than in the other defeated countries. The revolution of October 1918 made the creation of the first genuinely democratic system possible. Unfortunately, Count Mihály Károlyi's republic was not willing to accept the territorial sacrifices demanded by the Entente, its policy towards the nationalities had failed and it was incapable of standing up to left-extremist pressure. On 21 March 1919, a coalition of communists and left Social Democrats, led by Béla Kún, proclaimed the Hungarian Republic of Soviets; from the very beginning it was vulnerable to the concentric attacks of its internal and external enemies. The attempted bolshevisation of the country was not very successful, the peasantry turned against the regime, counter-revolutionary organisations were launched at Arad, Vienna and Szeged, counter-governments were formed and a "national" army was set up – all these with the effective help of the Entente. When it became clear that the Red Army was incapable of preventing the country's territorial disintegration and was unable to withstand the advance of the Romanian army on Budapest, the leaders of the Republic gave up the struggle and most of them fled abroad in the last days of July 1919. After a few days of temporary administration by trade union leaders, the old ruling class and the officers' corps, which had been set aside in the interim, began their counter-governments were formed and a "national" army was set up – all truncated country, which were ratified by the Treaty of Trianon in 1920, had emerged. Hungary lost more than two-thirds of its territory and 63.3 per cent of its population.

The beginnings of right-extremist organisation were, in fact, identical with counter-revolutionary organisation and the construction of the Horthy system. The reaction following the two revolutions and the months of the White Terror proved to be fertile soil for the burgeoning of anti-democratic and ultra-nationalist organisations. Over and above the counter-revolutionary attitudes of the aristocracy, the gentry and the upper bourgeoisie, the most explosive and most dynamic groups in society began to organise on a right-extremist basis. The officers' corps, the greater part of the student body, the thousands of unemployed former officials of the oversized pre-war administration, the refugees streaming into the truncated country from the lost territories and generally all those who found themselves socially downgraded as a result of the two revolutions and of the collapse, sought a way out of the economic and social crisis on the extreme right. Various racial, Christian, extreme nationalist, anti-semitic, militarist, irredentist and revisionist organisations were formed among officers, former combattants and students[1] and some of these were soon transformed into political movements and parties. The trend was halted in the second half of 1921. In the summer of that year Count István Bethlen came to office and initiated the moderate and sober policies which characterised the period of consolidation that bears his name. Apart from the communist party, which was banned from the fall of the Republic of Soviets until the end of the Second World War, every other political force was allowed to appear on the political arena. An individual variant of liberalism prevailed during the ten years or so that the conservative Bethlen held office. Although the undemocratic electoral system safeguarded the authoritarian rule of the government party (the Christian National Union, later the Party of Unity) and numerous administrative regulations placed restrictions on the opposition, nonetheless it tolerated a broad spectrum of oppositional activity, from the legitimists (who sought a Habsburg restoration), the bourgeois liberals to the agrarians and Social Democrats. (The country's second largest party was the Smallholders, which represented the well-to-do peasantry and certain gentry and bourgeois categories, and was led in the 1930s by Tibor Eckhardt, a former counter-revolutionary, but nonetheless it counted as a left-wing party given the peculiar Hungarian situation.)

The right-extremist organisations of the early 1920s, which generally did not demand any radical social reforms and accepted the Horthy system, declined in strength and impetus towards the end of the Bethlen era and some of them were absorbed into the system. Various fascist and Nazi types of radical movements and parties arose in their place in the early 1930s. The earliest of these worth a mention was the Hungarian National Socialist Workers' Party of Zoltán Böszörményi, a former student leader. The movement, founded in 1931, known as the "Scythe

118

Cross" — Böszörményi chose crossed scythes as his emblem — based itself mainly on the agrarian proletariat, but its anti-liberal, anti-communist and anti-semitic slogans, its programme demanding radical land reform and its hopelessly confused ideology found no great echo. The organisation of a still-born peasant rebellion in 1936 put an end to Böszörményi's movement.

One or two urban Nazi-type organisations had more of an impact in the early 1930s. Zoltán Meskó founded his Hungarian Hitlerist movement in 1932. In the following year he adopted the arrow cross as his emblem instead of the swastika and exchanged brown shirts for green. In 1933 Count Festetics came on the scene with his National Socialist party, paralleling Meskó, and this was rapidly succeeded by one rival Nazi organisation after another. However, Gyula Gömbös's government (1932–1936) was not favourable to the Arrow Cross. The former counter-revolutionary leader and devotee of Italian Fascism was, it is true, a disappointment to those who expected radical reforms and the establishment of an anti-semitic and anti-liberal dictatorship, but his prestige was sufficient to attract the bulk of the extremists in the establishment to him. At the 1935 elections only two or three deputies were elected on the Arrow Cross list to a Chamber of 245. The situation changed in favour of Nazi-type organisations after the death of Gömbös (October 1936), the international successes of both Italy and Germany and the growing strength of Nazi propaganda and subversive activity.

The mid-1930s saw the emergence of Ferenc Szálasi on the extreme right in Hungary. Szálasi, a former staff officer, founded his Party of National Will with a handful of supporters in 1935. Initially, its anti-semitic, anti-capitalist and ultra-nationalist slogans, complemented by a social-demagogic programme demanding land reform and a rise in the workers' standard of living, made little impact on the masses. Szálasi's efforts to gain a mandate proved unsuccessful. But his agitation was considered dangerous by the Darányi government and he was twice arrested in 1937. In the meantime, Szálasi's small party merged with László Endre's Nazi organisation to form the National Socialist Hungarian Party-Hungarist Movement in October 1937 and this attracted several small groups on the extreme right to itself. By 1938 it had become the government party's most serious and most dangerous rival. At the forefront of the Party's social propaganda stood demands for the radical transformation of agrarian conditions and this could hardly have remained without response in the land of "the three million beggars".[2] In the 20th year of Horthy's rule the peasantry that formed 95 per cent of the agrarian population owned a mere 37 per cent of the land and the landless peasants and agrarian labourers or those who were unable to provide

119

adequately for themselves from their dwarf holdings genuinely did fluctuate around three million – or one-third of the country's population. But it would be an error to place too much faith in the social radicalism of the Arrow Cross. The majority of its leaders were not radical in socio-economic questions and belonged to the ruling classes. It was only among the less influential leaders that there were petty bourgeois and lumpenproletarian elements who did perhaps seriously believe in the need for overturning the existing social order.

Towards the mid-1930s British diplomacy began to take an interest in the extreme right in Hungary for the first time and especially in Szálasi's movement.

Of all the Danubian countries in which the extreme right gained power, Hungary was the last. Paradoxically, until the outbreak of World War II, the extreme right gave less cause for concern in Hungary than, for example, in Romania, despite the fact – or perhaps because of it – that Hungary had been the first country in the area in which a rightist, anti-semitic, semi-authoritarian regime had struck roots.

Britain was less involved economically in Hungary than in either Czechoslovakia or Romania. Similarly, so far as Trianon was concerned, British policy until Munich tended to side rather with Czechoslovakia and Romania. Nevertheless, British public life cultivated closer relations with Hungary than with Romania and the Foreign Office had at its disposal sources of information in Budapest which embraced virtually all the shades of opinion represented by both the ruling circles and the opposition. A fortunate chance that contributed to London's accurate and lavish up-to-date information about goings-on in Hungary was the presence in Budapest of Sir Geoffrey Knox, an outstanding observer and an adroit diplomat, who managed to build up and foster a widespread network of connections and enjoyed the confidence of personalities over the entire political spectrum from right to left. Knox, a former representative of the League of Nations in the Saar, was anti-Nazi and the Hungarian Nazis launched a press campaign against him, quite unprecedented in Hungarian diplomatic life. Nevertheless, Knox remained in Hungary up to the outbreak of war and was trusted by Horthy, as well as by quite a few personalities of both the ruling party and the opposition.

Whilst the allegedly moderate Hungarian right, which in the 1930s wielded power without any challenge, was more radical than the Romanian rightist ruling party (the National Liberals) up to 1936 the extreme right was more fragmented and weaker than that of Romania. The year 1937 witnessed no fewer than six right extremist movements and organisations in competition. Likewise, in contrast to Hlinka's, Goga's or Codreanu's movements, Hungarian national socialism was to become a real mass movement with a large following only in the late 1930s.

120

In late 1936, after the death of the ambitious Gyula Gömbös, the balanced policy and moderation of his successor, Kálmán Darányi, inaugurated a period of greater tranquillity in internal politics. The removal of Gömbös's more violent adherents from the forefront of political life checked the likelihood of a drastic change towards extremism by the government.[3]

Similarly, after Gömbös, Hungary's movement towards Germany seemed to come to a halt. In April 1936 Knox was a witness to some anti-German outbursts during a conversation with Kálmán Kánya, Minister for Foreign Affairs, and at an audience with Admiral Horthy. Kánya "wondered how long this universal madness in Germany could last", whilst Horthy emphasised that "he was not Germanophile . . . he disliked the [German] people, their manners and their eternal refrain of 'Deutsch' and 'Deutschland' ". At the same time, Horthy had "nothing but admiration for Hitler's gesture in tearing up the Treaty of Locarno."[4]

In their domestic policies, the ruling aristocrat and gentry circles not only mistrusted the local Nazi movements, which made lavish use of anti-capitalist phraseology, but also kept German Nazi ideas at arm's length.

Notwithstanding Darányi's and Kánya's cautious foreign policy, Hungarian revisionism drew ever closer to Hitler's and Mussolini's objectives in Central Europe, while at the same time it skilfully exploited German-Italian rivalry in the Danube Basin. Knox reported in May 1936: "It is felt [in Hungary] that, so long as the two 'Fascist' States to some extent balance one another, the smaller Powers are still free to go their own traditional way, but, if once they were united, the attraction of their political system would be irresistible . . . The thoughts of many were expressed by a member of the Government party who . . . summed up the situation [i.e. the Italian victory in Abyssinia and the repudiation of the Locarno Treaties] as the triumph of the great Fascist Powers . . . over the great capitalist democracies . . ."[5] Knox felt it was London's task and an important one at that, to bring about some change in Hungarian public opinion, which was showing more and more anti-democratic and pro-fascist sympathies. In his view, "the superficial minds" who formed the majority discerned nothing of the great principles of personal liberty and national strength that lie behind the free expression of opinion. The majority contrasted the "ruthless efficiency of dictatorships . . . with what they see, or think to see, in the great democracies – in France a fog of petty squabbles of party ideology and in England a public opinion clamorous, idealistic, ill-informed, imposing its influence on the most delicate decisions of foreign policy." Consequently, he believed that "It would give much encouragement to those abroad who support the cause of free institutions and . . . a policy of peace, if some of our greater organs

121

of opinion, notably, *The Times*, could descend from the heights of conscious rectitude . . . and deal, in a manner comprehensible to others less happily endowed, with the brutal realities and dangers which have to be faced in this troubled world."[6]

Becoming aware of the intensification of Nazi propaganda in 1936, Knox did not in the least underestimate its impact upon broad Hungarian circles and did not discount the assumption that some semi-official organs were receiving financial support from Germany.[7] Reports dating from the second half of the same year were already full of the British Minister's suspicions that Germany had succeeded in enlisting agents even in government circles.

A. Gascoigne, the Chargé d'Affaires in Budapest, also reported on the increasing efficiency of Nazi propaganda: "I learn from a reliable source that, while the National Socialist party in Hungary is at present not particularly flourishing, financial assistance from Germany continues to be given to the development of German propaganda in Hungary."

Whereas in 1936 the Hungarian national socialist movements were still in their infancy and on the defensive, the extremist elements of the government party, as for instance the vociferously ambitious Béla Marton, or Béla Imrédy, who was already flirting with the extreme right, took their first steps in the direction of setting up a new grouping which was to have been located somewhere in the middle between the Nazis and the government party. As to the German danger, Imrédy had by then moved quite some distance from Darányi's cautious policy, but was far from willing to relinquish Hungary to Hitler, as he was to become a few years later. In November 1936, Imrédy, then governor of the Hungarian National Bank, assured Ashton-Gwatkin, "There is no danger of Hungary slipping into the position of economic dependence upon Germany, in which some other South European countries had recently found themselves . . ." Concerning Hitler, Imrédy was inclined to think that "there was something in Hitler's claim to be a bulwark against communism . . . He knew that in England we are not disposed to take this danger very seriously; but in Hungary they had personal experience of it and were inclined to feel some gratitude to Hitler on this account", reported Ashton-Gwatkin.[8]

By early 1937, the Arrow Cross already figures as a competitor to the ruling Party of National Unity. Darányi made his first statement to the effect that his party was resolved to take up arms against the Hungarian Nazis. On 13 February, he issued a communiqué announcing that his party would fight not only against the extreme left, but against the Arrow Cross as well. At the same time he admitted that "there were some shades of difference" within the ruling party, which had a bearing upon relations with the extreme right and with Germany.

122

During the talks on the implications of Nazi propaganda in Hungary, Baron Bessenyei, the acting Political Director of the Ministry for Foreign Affairs, informed Gascoigne that "the Hungarian Government were not particularly disturbed by this propaganda, as they did not believe that the Magyar mentality and temperament provided fertile soil for the planting of such a creed . . ." At about the same time, incidentally, Romanian ruling circles were comforting themselves with a similar rationalisation regarding Nazi propaganda. "The Hungarian was far too fond of his personal liberty to become enamoured with the 'Prussian' principles of national socialism", declared Bessenyei and then added the remark that Budapest would make a point of intervening in Berlin in order to dissuade the Germans from attempting to spread their "gospel" in Hungary. All in all, Gascoigne thought that the Darányi government was "more perturbed regarding the national-socialist activities . . . than was admitted . . . by Baron Bessenyey."[9]

The first major incident caused by the extreme right in Hungary took place in early March 1937. But even then, the disturbances could be attributed more to adventurists on the right wing of the Party of National Unity — i.e. to what had been Gömbös's entourage — than to the Arrow Cross. A tiny group headed by two P.N.U. deputies (Marton and Mecsér) were brewing plans for a *coup d'état* with the assistance of a few of the *nyilas* (the Arrow Cross). Thus it was not a proper attempt at a coup, but its initial phase of planning only. However, the event offered adequate opportunity for the democratic opposition and for the diplomats of Western powers to be on the look-out for the activities of the extreme right. The fact was that the extremists were agitating in the countryside "by exploiting . . . the economic distress of the agricultural labourer", enjoying Germany's propagandistic and also financial support.[10]

Knox presented an analysis prepared by a senior Hungarian intelligence officer on Nazi activity in Hungary. "Ever since the death of General Gömbös, Hitlerism had lost ground among the better classes and it was in order to make good this lost ground that the importers of Hitlerism had turned to the lower orders . . . as the most promising field for their activities. Sixty per cent of the present day followers of Hungarian Hitlerism were the people who . . . followed Béla Kún."[11] This evaluation must, of course, have been exaggerated, but the emphasis on the proletarian character of the Hungarian Nazi movements and their permeation by former communist elements seems to be a recurrent motif in Knox's reports. Even when writing about German agitation, Knox's attention was mainly attracted by the specific situation of the Hungarian proletariat. He considered that the Germans were exploiting the unsatisfactory conditions of both the agricultural and the industrial labour force, and the poor prospects open to educated youth.[12] He personally regarded social reform as the most appropriate means of defence against extremist doctrines and kept a watchful eye on Hungarian developments from this point of view as well.

Knox estimated that the government had no illusions about the danger of Nazi propaganda and realised that a Nazi regime would be only the first step towards the eventual incorporation of Hungary in the Reich.[13] After all, despite the closest connections between Hungary and Germany, Knox believed that Hungary had not bound itself "body and soul" to Germany and that the present government was determined to maintain the country's independence.

Knox did not underestimate the right extremist danger, although on the surface there was no significant *nyilas* activity in the first months of 1937. "The Hungarian Government is to-day faced with an internal problem of some magnitude – that of the extreme right wing which it inherited from General Gömbös and which is now leaning on Germany and, in alliance with the local Nazi parties, assumes a monopoly of patriotism and exploits the economic distress of the rural population", wrote Knox in April 1937.[14]

It is worth mentioning that Knox was drawing a distinction between the "Hungarian extreme right" and "the national socialist groups in Hungary". The distinction becomes paramount if we keep in mind that among the right extremists in Hungary there were some obviously anti-German elements, who endeavoured to achieve a regime which was to remain Hungarian in character and was to safeguard its independence from Germany. In this context, the following remark by Sir Orme Sargent on one of Knox's reports is of interest: ". . . I think it is all to the good that it should be known in Danubian states that we are not going to acquiesce silently in the establishment of an Italo-German protectorate, and that we have ideas of our own as to how the Danubian States ought to defend their independence.[15] It is pertinent to note on this point that those British politicians who strove to prevent Hungary's *rapprochement* with Germany by means of backing Hungarian revisionism were labelled as irresponsible by Knox.[16]

A conversation took place in July 1937 between Gascoigne and Baron Apor, Secretary General in the Ministry for Foreign Affairs, about the "dissemination of national-socialism in Hungary and pan-German propaganda". Apor's rationalisation turned on the argument of "Hungarian temperament", often voiced in official circles: ". . . the government and the major portion of public opinion . . . are averse to the importation into their country of an ideology which is not compatible with the Magyar temperament". Baron Apor referred to one of Interior Minister Széll's statements to the effect that the government would act firmly against the "turbulent and fanatical extremists" as soon as they discovered disquieting symptoms.[17] Later, the Minister of the Interior pledged again that the government was in complete readiness to act against the "foolish plans" of the extremists on both sides, and by the end of October 1937 the first severe sentence was passed against three leaders of a National-Socialist group on a charge of subversive conspiracy.[18] At the same time, the press attaché of the British Legation was most confidentially notified by the chief of the political police that in the near future the police would take drastic measures against extremist agitation.[19] However, fascist or Nazi-type activity was a fact which was to be taken into account, even if there was no reason to overrate its significance in 1937, Knox warned.

As time passed, Knox became more and more preoccupied with the communist-like character of the Hungarian extreme right and its activities. In a letter to Sir Orme Sargent, quoting Hungarian sources, he stressed that the German Nazis exploited "the deplorable situation of much of the agricultural population in Hungary by preaching to them, in the Nazi interest, ideas which differ in little or nothing from the gospel of Béla Kún . . ."[20] Knox, also using the argument according to which the "temperament" of the Hungarian people was opposed to Nazism, and stressing the absence of competent leadership in the extreme right camp, did not fear the development of a serious Nazi movement. Nevertheless, he warned London that "the ground is propitious [for the extreme right] as the poverty of the labouring classes is extreme."[21]

The sentencing of fascist leaders to prison at the end of 1937 offered Knox an opportunity to express his views on the character of the fascist and Nazi-type movements in Hungary. In October, sentence was passed on Böszörményi, leader of one of the Nazi groups, for conspiracy against the state, followed a month later by the indictment of the future *nyilas* dictator, Ferenc Szálasi, who was sentenced to ten months of "state imprisonment" on charges that he had participated in activities which "might prove disastrous to the nation".

In Knox's opinion, Böszörményi was no more than "a harmless fanatic, who endeavoured to persuade a crowd of uneducated peasants to join him in an attempt to overthrow the Government". Böszörményi had no followers among the intelligentsia, nor any support from influential quarters. On the other hand, Knox saw in Szálasi, "the most dangerous of the Nazi agitators in Hungary. He is a popular swashbuckler with a brilliant war record and ready eloquence; he is also a virulent anti-Semite and is believed to enjoy the sympathy, if not the support, of exalted quarters."[22] In his Annual Report for 1937, he mentioned Szálasi as the

125

only leader on the extreme right to have achieved some significance and who was reputed to be a good organiser and a forceful speaker.[23] A few months later, Gascoigne sent information about Szálasi's qualities as a popular leader. Count Mycielski, the Polish Chargé d'Affaires in Budapest, who knew Szálasi well, told Gascoigne that whilst he found him "fairly practical in his outlook, [he] did not consider that he had the makings of a *Führer* either physically or mentally. He did not think that he possessed the attributes which are necessary for a leader."[24]

Knox found the situation in Hungary identical with that in Romania, where the rightist ruling élite considered the extreme right a potential weapon against the democratic parties; in both countries, the ruling rightist parties, or at least their extremist wings, made use of the extremist movements against the agrarian and bourgeois democratic opposition parties. In both countries, legal proceedings had been instituted by the authorities against certain leaders of the extreme right. Some extremist groups were banned and their press was harassed, whilst at the same time the Hungarian *nyilas*, the Romanian legionnaires and Goga's "Blue-shirts" managed to find protectors, financial sponsors and even backers in the most elevated government circles.

According to Knox, there was a growing tide of opinion in Hungary which held that the indulgence shown by the government towards extreme right movements was inspired by the sympathy that was tacitly extended to them by the Regent, by officers of his household, by some of the senior military commanders and by the right wing of the government party.[25] In his Annual Report for 1937, Knox emphasised that in spite of its promises, the government had not taken active measures to suppress the Nazi movement and reiterated his assertion that one of the reasons for the government's "lethargy" towards the Nazis should be sought in the attitude of Horthy, who as "a violent anti-Semite" sympathised with them.[26]

Knox, uncertain and in two minds at the time, was not expecting dangerous and dramatic developments in the Nazi movement in the immediate future. Like the majority of Hungarian politicians, he accepted the frequently voiced assumption that national socialism could not constitute a grave menace in Hungary, because it was "incompatible with the national temperament and traditions". However, he sounded a cautious warning that "the extreme poverty of the working classes, the preponderance of Jews, and the wide extension of German propaganda" rendered the soil "by no means unfruitful to Nazi doctrines."[27] He admitted that national socialist ideas were widespread in Hungary and Nazi slogans "find a ready echo among the labouring classes . . . and among the educated youth who see in the future little prospect of settled employment".[28]

126

In answer to Chamberlain's and Eden's telegram, inviting observations by the heads of the diplomatic missions in the Danubian capitals on the trend towards authoritarianism in Central and South Eastern Europe,[29] Knox despatched a report expressing his mixed feelings on the issue – illusions built upon romanticism, alternating with accurate, shrewd observations. He considered the Hungarian constitutional past a safe guarantee against a seizure of power by the extreme right. "The Crown of St. Stephen and the Golden Bull, the Hungarian National Charter of 1222 . . . are likely to oppose a formidable moral barrier to any attempt to set up an authoritarian regime." He had no doubts – "at least not for the present" – that the great majority in Hungary remained in favour of a constitutional government. Nevertheless, he added a cautious warning that no fewer than six extremist movements exercised a considerable appeal among industrial and agricultural workers.

In addition, Knox was also concerned about extremism among the country's youth. "The promise of spoliation of Jews . . . arouses new hopes" among young people, who were afraid of the prospect of intellectual unemployment. More politically-minded young people were attracted by "the possibilities inherent in an authoritarian régime, of rapid action and radical solutions, the ease with which public opinion is formed and guided and the seemingly infinite spending power which appears, under this system, to be the corollary of national bankruptcy."[30]

It appears from a private letter of Knox's that Count István Bethlen, a conservative with whom he maintained friendly relations, shared his belief that the remedy against the extreme right in Hungary could only be social reform.[31] The British minister saw right extremist activity in Hungary primarily as a social problem and whenever he reported on the Hungarists or on other Nazi organisations he did not fail to make a point of the utter destitution of the agrarian and industrial proletariat, which thus constituted a most fertile soil for the flourishing of Nazi movements. Nevertheless, Knox, who by 1938 was becoming more and more pessimistic, was concerned not so much about the growing strength of extremism at the grass-roots, but rather about the ground gained by Nazism in the ruling circles and among personalities controlling parliamentary life. These new Nazis were neither proletarian nor young intellectuals who had arisen from the poor peasantry, dreading a future without hope.

Prime Minister Kálmán Darányi was numbered among those who were determined to stem the advance of the Nazi movements.[32] One of his arguments against them was identical with that used about the Iron Guard by the Romanian Minister of the Interior, Armand Călinescu, in conversation with Sir Reginald Hoare at much the same time. In a speech delivered in Györ in early March 1938, Darányi sounded a strong warning with ominous undertones: "It must not be forgotten . . . that Communism was often proved to conceal its subversive movements under cloaks of a democratic, liberal or even Nazi character. Such masked movements would not be tolerated and none of Bolshevism's 'piratical standards' would be respected."[33]

This identification of communism with nazism and fascism was intended to serve mainly tactical aims. It was certainly easier for the anti-Nazi rightist leadership to attack the extreme right by means of anti-communist slogans, than doing it overtly, in a straightforward manner. By the end of the 1930s, this identification was increasingly seen in the West as a mere pretext, because nazism and not communism was regarded as the main danger. Arguments similar to those put forward by Darányi and Călinescu were deemed by Western observers to be no more than a tactical device and assertions about the communists concealing their activities under "a green shirt" were rightly disregarded as mere bluff. However, one of the main objectives of the democratic West was to weaken the extreme right in Central Europe and the arguments used by the moderate right to defeat the extreme right were of secondary importance. That was why identifications of the kind made by Darányi or Călinescu were not objected to by the democratic opposition in the Danubian countries. In the late 1930s, very few people realised how small the gap between the two extremes actually was in the eyes of the masses; how conspicuous the resemblance between the power politics and methods of the two systems was and how close to the Molotov-Ribbentrop Pact the two totalitarian powers stood. Nevertheless, it was not only diplomats, but also Western experts familiar with Danubian problems who were willing to accept as fact the presumption that, *faute de mieux* and lacking any form of legal activity, a good many communists operated through and with the extreme right. Royall Tylor, the British financial expert, suggested that many communists in Hungary "find in the Nazi doctrine enough to their liking to make them willing to join forces and to improve the new opportunities for agitation conferred on them by a label which is not taboo".[34]

The alleged socialist character of the Arrow Cross and the swelling of its ranks by discontented social elements, including industrial and agricultural proletarians, among them communists, preoccupied Knox and other British observers throughout the whole period under review.

Knox thought that in 1938 and 1939 the *nyilas* movement was probably the strongest political force in Hungary both among the skilled workers and in certain districts even among the peasants. He explained this by "social causes", namely by the fact that "it had been for years impossible safely to express any dissatisfaction with the regime without risking a long term of imprisonment for 'bolshevism'. Yet there existed a large amount of latent rebellious feeling which found a chance of expressing itself when Nazism came into power."[35] Knox reported that Hitler's "social achievements of revolutionary order" like disregard of class distinctions, high wages and the *"Kraft durch Freude"* organisation were "admired" in Hungary. The German Nazi regime ably exploited these feelings and led some of them into genuinely pro-German channels, "but others of the poorer *nyilas* followers were simply and solely interested in social reform, irrespective of the quarter whence it came. A large number of them were identical with the old Communists of 1919."[36]

Professor C. A. Macartney, whose political assessments about Hungary were influential with the Foreign Office, also shared the view of those observers who held that the lower strata of Hungarian society were attracted by the prospects of radical social reforms in case of a Nazi takeover. In one of his Memoranda submitted to the Foreign Office in 1938, Macartney stressed the fact that "a considerable number of the poorer classes believe that only a Nazi system can give them the social reforms which they desire."[37]

As it was already pointed out in connection with the Iron Guard, I would not agree to exaggerated conclusions concerning the fluid and sometimes even imperceptible dividing line between communists in Romania and in Hungary and the Legionnaires or the Hungarist Nazis. Nor do I believe in communist-minded masses seeking the fulfilment of the aims of the proletarian revolution in the framework of the two fascist organisations. However, I would draw attention to the attractive force of their "social revolutionary" programme upon the destitute masses. In the light of the post-war controversy about the social character and composition of the two movements and especially regarding the appeal of the Arrow Cross to industrial and agrarian proletarians, the contemporary opinions discussed above might contribute towards the crystallisation of a conclusion based more on facts than on present day conjectures.

Notes

1. e.g. the racialist *Etelköz* Association, the *Turul* Association, and Gyula Gömbös's anti-semitic Racialist Party.
2. *Three Million Beggars* – the title of a much discussed book by György Oláh (*Három millió koldus*, Miskolc 1928)
3. Knox to Eden, 7 December 1936 (P.R.O., F.O. 371, R 7456/470/21)
4. Knox to Eden, 9 April 1936 (Doc.No.7)
5. Knox to Eden, 9 May 1936 (Doc.No.10)
6. Ibid.
7. Knox to Eden, 23 May 1936 (Doc.No.12)

8. Memorandum by F. Ashton-Gwatkin, 7 November 1936 (Doc.No.26)
9. Gascoigne to Eden, 26 February 1937 (Doc.No.34)
10. Knox to Eden, 11 March 1937 (Doc.No.35)
11. Ibid.
12. Ibid.
13. Ibid.
14. Knox to Eden, 16 April 1937 (Doc.No.38)
15. Minute by Sargent, 4 May 1937 (Ibid.)
16. Knox to Eden (Ibid.)
17. Gascoigne to Eden, 16 July 1937 (Doc.No.45)
18. Knox to Eden, 20 October 1937 (Doc.No.54)
19. Knox to Sargent, 4 November 1937 (Doc.No.55)
20. Ibid.
21. Ibid.
22. Knox to Eden, 4 December 1937 (Doc.No.58)
23. Annual Report for 1937, Hungary (Doc.No.60)
24. Gascoigne to Nichols, 20 August 1938 (Doc.No.109)
25. Knox to Eden, 4 December 1937 (Doc.No.58)
26. Annual Report for 1937, Hungary (Doc.No.60)
27. Doc.No.58
28. Doc.No.60
29. Foreign Office, 6 January 1938 (Doc.No.65)
30. Knox to Eden, 13 January 1938 (Doc.No.67)
31. Knox to Ingram, 12 February 1938 (Doc.No.87)
32. It is worth mentioning that the *nyilas* leaders saw Darányi's attitude in a different light. They asserted that he tried "honestly" to help Szálasi, and that after his resignation there followed a "period of reaction", that is an anti-*nyilas* policy. (The National Archives of the U.S., Microcopy T–973/5, 000739)
33. Knox to Halifax, 10 March 1938 (Doc.No.93)
34. Memorandum by Royall Tylor, 14 May 1938 (Doc.No.103)
35. Memorandum by Knox, February 1940 (P.R.O., F.O. 371, C 734/734/21)
36. Ibid.
37. Memorandum by C. A. Macartney (P.R.O., F.O. 371, C 12627/2319/12)

2 The Arrow Cross Bid for Power

The year 1938 witnessed a sequence of events on the internal political front in Hungary which was likely to undermine the optimism of British diplomats who regarded the Hungarian "spirit" and "temperament" as insurmountable obstacles in the way of the Nazi movements. László Endre, who as Under-secretary of the Interior was later to be among the chief executors of the liquidation of Hungarian Jewry in 1944, and who temporarily joined forces with Szálasi in 1937, had already achieved notoriety for his Nazi views and his virulent anti-semitism in the early 1930s. In February 1938, he was elected to be deputy Lord-Lieutenant ("alispán") of the County of Pest. At a dinner given in honour of this occasion, the Speaker of the Lower House, Sandor Sztranyavszky, delivered a speech. Sir Geoffrey who was present thought it worth quoting excerpts for London's benefit. Sztranyavszky declared that the assumption that right extremism had been smuggled in from abroad was untenable. On the contrary, "it was deeply rooted in the soul of the Hungarian people, and it was the ideas of liberalism, democracy, and freemasonry which had been imported".[1] Sztranyavszky went on to say that the "future of the nation was bound up with the Hungarian right extremist policy. The success of this policy was extending over the whole world and could not be restrained by any power . . ." Knox added the laconic comment: "These utterances appear strange in the mouth of a Speaker . . ."[2]

They must have appeared strange indeed, all the more so, since the self-same government, that of Sztranyavszky's and Hóman's own party, was simultaneously clamping down on the Hungarists, raiding the party's premises, confiscating its documents and arresting quite a few of its members – among them Szálasi, who had only recently been released from arrest, pending appeal against his sentences.

131

In one of his letters, Knox had expressed the belief that the Hungarians would remain faithful to their constitutional parliamentary system, "albeit of the feudal complexion, traditional in this curiously unmodern country."[3] What was indeed true in this assumption was the fact that Hungary was a curiously unmodern state, in whose parliament the Social Democrats shared a bench with the representatives of the semi-feudal legitimist aristocracy or gentry, whilst elsewhere in the Danubian area, Social Democratic parties had long ceased to exist. Equally, Jewish deputies were allowed to voice their fears of the Nazi peril, whilst *nyilas* deputies predicted their annihilation.[4] It was not in the least surprising in this context that one representative of the government should have glorified the Nazi future, whilst another should have signed the warrant of arrest of Nazi leaders accused of planning just such a Nazi future for Hungary.

The impact of the *Anschluss* on the Nazi movements in Hungary was immediate. At the end of March, a by-election was won by Kálmán Hubay, one of the *nyilas* leaders, with a considerable majority. British observers attributed this victory mainly to the *Anschluss*. Gascoigne, the British Chargé d'Affaires, stated that the *Anschluss* had acted as a powerful stimulant, but expected its effects to be ephemeral.[5] Both Knox and Gascoigne believed that, over and above the impact of German successes, Hungary's social conditions accounted for the Nazi victories in the early months of 1938. "There is a substantial amount of poverty . . . in the industrial, agricultural, and professional spheres . . . It is not perhaps surprising . . . that many members of the middle and lower strata of the population should be impressed, generally with the efficiency of German methods", wrote Gascoigne to Halifax.[6] As time passed, the image of the right extremist movements of the Danubian area presented by British diplomatic reports became more and more one of social revolutionary movements, *par excellence.* They were seen as aiming to solve the problems of the destitute agrarian and industrial proletariat, of the pauperised peasants, and of the petty bourgeoisie as well.

While pointing out the scarcity of information available about the internal organisation and the genuine aims of the extremist movements, Gascoigne reported that the *nyilas* programme consisted of the following: (a) the complete eradication of the Jewish element from Hungary's financial, economic, cultural and public life; (b) agrarian reforms; (c) the redistribution of capital; and (d) intensive economic development of the country on German lines.[7] Some of Gascoigne's and Knox's information about the Arrow Cross was furnished by F. G. Redward, the Press Attaché, who had been for many years a "close personal friend of Major Szálasi's chief lieutenant".[8] It was on this source that Gascoigne based his

132

assertion that the Hungarian Nazis rejected any idea of domination by Hitler's Germany and were striving to set up a regime that would remain Hungarian in character. As to the future, Gascoigne, cautious in his prognostications, outlined the possibilities of the policy of "taking the wind out of the sails" of the extreme right. ". . . The Prime Minister's policy of dealing with the extremists will be to endeavour to clip their wings by the gradual adoption, by constitutional means, of a programme similar but substantially less drastic than their own."[9] This amounted to just two fields: social reform and the Jewish question. Whereas only some insignificant measures were initiated by Darányi in the field of social reform, preparations were begun for the first Jewish Law (*zsidótörvény*) along German lines.[10]

Knox's reports in the spring of 1938 were rather depressing. He was complaining that "the obscurity veiling the internal situation in Hungary has by no means lightened" and that "the trend towards national socialist doctrine among the public and more particularly in the army becomes more marked . . ."[11] This was the period when Knox came to realise that among the Nazi groups, Szálasi's Arrow Cross had the best prospects. "I notice for the first time [at the end of April] the somewhat ominous symptom that public attention is beginning to concentrate on a particular one of the half dozen groups which represent this ideology and on a particular leader — Szálasi."[12]

As regards the government's policy, Knox noted that, on the one hand, Darányi and Horthy had not fulfilled their promises to suppress subversive activities (Szálasi, though under house arrest, was able to carry on with his agitation "with the same energy and with a more romantic background than before"), whilst on the other hand, the government "seems to be bent on placating the right wing by stealing the thunders of the extremists and re-emitting them as stage noises."[13] Such a policy was certainly not likely to inspire Knox with much confidence, as by then he could well have had the not too encouraging precedents of Papen and Goga in mind.

It is worth taking a look at the differences that arose between Knox and officials at the Foreign Office about the question of whether Germany was or was not supporting the Hungarian Nazi movements. Concerning Berlin's policy towards Romanian extreme right movements and their dependence on Nazi Germany, even after the war, Sir Reginald Hoare still believed that the Iron Guard "was not directed by Germany."[14] Knox held similar views regarding the Arrow Cross. His argument was that "it is natural enough that the Germans should not wish to indispose a Hungarian Government which appears to be sufficiently subservient to them, by any encouragement of a subversive movement . . ."[15] A. D. M. Ross in the Foreign Office was of a different opinion: "Germany can perfectly well countenance and encourage the spread of Hungarian Nazism and at the same time prevent it from discomfiting the subservient Government at Budapest."[16]

In the spring of 1938 Montagu Norman, the Governor of the Bank of England, visited Budapest, where he had talks with, among others, Béla Imrédy, then Governor of the Hungarian National Bank. His impressions made it possible for Halifax and his advisers to obtain a more comprehensive picture about the trend of Hungarian political life. "The young men of Hungary, and not only those without employment, are infected, to an overwhelming majority, with National Socialist and notably anti-Jewish ideas. More serious still, these ideas are rampant among the officers."[17] He was not convinced of the existence of German support and held to the belief that "with or without German support, the movement exists, and . . . it is fast gaining in momentum."[18]

The British reports of the period contain numerous references to the *nyilas* gaining ground in the Army. Albeit, in the late 1930s, this concerned mostly less senior officers, it became evident before long that one of the decisive factors influencing Hungary's plunge into the war in 1941, as well as its wartime attitude, could be attributed to the penetration of the general staff by the Arrow Cross — quite apart from the fact that a number of senior officers, colonels and generals had direct connections with the German Nazis, Henrik Werth, the Chief of the General Staff, General Ruszkay and General Rácz among them. A recurrent feature of Montagu Norman's report was the extent of extreme right activity in the officer corps, against which the government failed to take any energetic measures. ". . . Officers guilty of observations perilously approaching high treason have been told not to be naughty boys"[19] — and this and nothing more was the price that had to be paid for their affiliation with the Arrow Cross. Montagu Norman suggested to the Hungarians that they should make a firm start in eradicating politics from the Army and make it clear to the country's youth that their way would sooner or later lead to certain destruction. However, he did not see Darányi as a forceful leader who could fire men with enthusiasm and who could "set the wheels of the machine turning again".[20] In Montagu Norman's eyes there was only one man suitable for the post — Béla Imrédy. Less than one year was to pass before Imrédy himself provided the most conclusive evidence of Montagu Norman's error.

At about the same time, in the spring of 1938, the political situation in Hungary was described in a report by another financial expert, Royall Tylor, already quoted, who had been the financial advisor of the League of Nations on Hungary. He noted that public opinion in Hungary was nearly unanimous in considering a break with the past as a necessary

134

precondition of progress and that the main obstacle to progress was to be found in the conservatism of the ruling party and the ruling circles. Dissatisfied elements, the extremists, believed that "fidelity to the Hungarian Parliamentary tradition" was "a fatal handicap" to quick and efficient action. "At present an active, confident and irresponsible minority is agitating for a Nazi solution", wrote Royall Tylor, but that minority was increasingly gaining ground.[21]

The Darányi government fell in May 1938. The new government was formed by Béla Imrédy, with the main objective of weakening the position of the extremists by implementing radical reform measures. Police action was ineffective by the second half of 1938. "With long impunity, with tacit and even sometimes overt encouragement from above ... National-Socialism has spread widely in the Army and even in the Police force, so that to send Major Szálasi and his compeers to penal servitude might no longer offer a solution ..." wrote Knox.[22]

In the summer of 1938, Count Alexander Festetics's Nazi movement merged with Szálasi's Arrow Cross, thus increasing the *nyilas* camp to some 90,000 registered followers. which made it into a considerable force.

Meanwhile, in the aftermath of the Sudeten crisis, the hour had struck for a partial fulfilment of Hungary's revisionist aspirations. Attention centred on Czechoslovakia, and internal affairs were forgotten in Hungary, at least temporarily.

During the first months of Imrédy's rule, it was assumed in the British diplomatic circles that the Prime Minister was "relentlessly" pushing on with his economic, financial and cultural reforms, with the aim of "exterminating the National-Socialist disease".[23]

Stephen Horthy, the elder son of the Regent, admitted in a conversation in Berlin to F. N. Mason-MacFarlane, the British Military Attaché in Germany, that the Nazi upsurge in Hungary had assumed serious proportions, but for all that, he was confident that Imrédy would act firmly against it.[24] Some experts on Hungary in London regarded Imrédy's appointment as an ideal solution in the confrontation with the Arrow Cross. In the opinion of Sir Arthur Salter, Imrédy and Count Pál Teleki were probably the best bulwarks against Nazism in Hungary.[25]

Yet at the time of Munich, it was expected of Imrédy that he should represent his revisionist successes in such a way as to lessen the influence of the *nyilas*. Sir Arthur was expressing the view of numerous experts when he said that he felt it essential "that if Nazism were to be prevented in Hungary ... the ... Government should be enabled to show a reasonable ... success in foreign policy, viz. in the minority question in Slovakia and Ruthenia."[26] This view was shared by Professor C. A. Macartney, the most eminent British expert on Hungary.[27] British

135

financial, economic and intellectual circles were advising the Foreign Office "to take a little more friendly interest in the question of Hungarian claims" with a view to strengthening Imrédy against the *nyilas*. [28] A. D. Noble, a Foreign Office expert on Hungary, suggested that "it is worth our while to do what . . . we can to help M. Imrédy to retain some slight freedom of manoeuvre if only because Hungary may . . . form the battleground in a clash of German and Italian interests . . ." [29] In the tense days of the Czechoslovak crisis, the Foreign Office judged it opportune to lend Imrédy a helping hand in clamping down on Szálasi, otherwise his movement (the Arrow Cross) "weak or strong, will be a formidable weapon in German hands . . ." [30]

In the autumn of 1938, there were rumours — spread by the Hungarian Government, according to Knox — that Germany was intending to overrun Hungary. By this form of blackmail, Imrédy tried to exert pressure on Britain to gain economic and financial concessions — again, in Knox's opinion. The belief persisted in Britain that in the event of massive subventions being granted to Hungary, it would be possible to avoid the establishment of a Nazi regime there and Hungary could remain outside the German orbit. Knox did not accept this thesis. He advised London to let British economic policy be governed solely by considerations of mutual benefit, free of all political factors. And as to the possibility of Hungary staying outside the German orbit or acting as an obstacle in the way of German expansion to the south-east, Knox concurred in Ciano's comparison "of the single strand of wire in front of an elephant". [31]

The Foreign Office disagreed with Knox on one point, namely, that any effort on Hungary would be wasted, because Hungary could not be saved for the West anyway. Noble held that Imrédy, with all his faults and weaknesses, deserved British support. Contrary to Knox, he wrote, "extreme Governments may come to birth at least partly because foreign powers fail to give encouragement and support to moderate regimes . . ." [32] P. Nichols remarked, in disapproval of Knox's defeatism, that "a kind of surface logic seems to have a fatal attraction for Sir G. Knox." [33]

The fate of Hungary was causing greater concern in the Foreign Office than that of Romania. King Carol's regime was believed to be relatively stable, whereas in Hungary, seizure of power by the extreme right was envisaged as more likely on account of the far stronger German pressure on Hungary than on Romania. In the autumn of 1938, a memorandum was drawn up for the Foreign Office by John Keyser, a friend of Count Teleki's, following on a trip to Hungary. Keyser wrote of a *nyilas* "social revolution" and was convinced that all social classes were demanding such a revolution. Restiveness and general discontent sprang from the absence of any solution to social problems. The more extemist sections of society looked towards Germany as the land of milk and honey.[34] Keyser estimated, however, that the bulk of the extreme right was not in favour of pro-German Nazism, as "nationalism and individualism are far too strongly developed in the Hungarian character to permit a wholesale submission to foreign ideas and rule." Keyser had no fears of an impending Nazi take-over, because of bad organisation, the rivalry among different Nazi factions and the absence of competent leaders — Szálasi's and Hubay's "mouths are full of words which probably neither they nor certainly anyone in Hungary really understands."

In Keyser's estimate, the army was reckoned to be 80–90 per cent Nazi and pro-German and he regarded this as a major cause for concern. He was fully justified in concluding that Imrédy's "programme of 'taking the wind out of the sails' of the extremists is somewhat dangerous, for it may play straight into their hands".[35] Keyser's report (not a particularly good one, incidentally, and full of contradictions) aroused comment in the Foreign Office. Noble thought the Nazi movement still weak on account of the absence of effective leadership, but potentially strong, because "it appeals to a large class of young people who are dissatisfied". He expected that a remedy would be found in Imrédy's pushing through a comprehensive programme of social reform and dealing firmly with extremists."[36]

Reviewing the events of 1938, Knox again stated that the main cause of the Nazi upsurge was not so much German influence, but rather "the very low standard of wages and of living" that "must tend to make men seek a remedy in extremist doctrines, and since any 'leftward' agitation has been ruthlessly and effectively suppressed . . . the forces of discontent inevitably tend to the extreme Right".[37]

Remarkably, Count János Eszterházy, the leader of the Hungarian minority in Czechoslovakia, told Lieutenant-Colonel H.C.T. Strange, the British Military Attaché in Prague, that it was dissatisfaction among the peasants and young people that explained why Nazism was gaining ground so rapidly in Hungary. "The land . . . would have to be more fairly distributed and that would probably come about under a Nazi régime. There would also be less unemployment and better markets for produce . . ."[38]

Thus it would appear that to most observers the extreme right had become a significant political factor primarily because of the emphasis it placed on unsolved social problems and because it was the only outlet for social discontent with the prescription of the extreme left.

The beginning of 1939 brought with it a disconcerting development for those experts who had for years been expecting Imrédy to act as the

137

obstacle to nazism. The Prime Minister, holding the mandate of a moderate right-wing party, inaugurated a new movement, called the "Hungarian Life Movement", with an out-spokenly right extremist programme. ". . . The movement appears designed as a bowdlerised edition of the Nazi and Fascist parties", reported Knox, disappointed.[39] The explanation, that Imrédy's real aim might have been to defeat the Nazis by a "home made" extremist party under his control, was not discarded in Hungary. As Knox put it, "it is hoped that [Imrédy's Movement] will be successful in rallying substantial numbers of the masses to the Government side, and thus weaken the ranks of Hungarian National-Socialists . . ."[40] The competition between the extremists and the so-called moderates was under way and the latter, just as in Romania, were taking over more and more of the programme and methods of the former. Imrédy exceeded all previous limits in this direction, so that it was hardly surprising that in 1945 he should have finished up on Szálasi's side. Gascoigne realised – albeit rather late in the day – that Imrédy had "annexed a large part of [the Hungarists'] programme", had moved away from the parliamentary system and had "assumed a number of the personal characteristics of the modern dictator."[41]

Imrédy was toppled in February 1939. Paradoxically, one of the factors leading to the downfall of this anti-semitic Prime Minister was the purported "discovery" of a partly Jewish ancestry. His successor was Count Pál Teleki, Professor of Geography and a public figure of great prestige. He had been actively involved in the counter-revolution after World War I on the side of Horthy and, although a convinced anti-semite, he was regarded as a moderate rightist and an avowed opponent of the Hungarian Nazis. Certainly, his first measure was to outlaw the Hungarists, a step for which the bombing of the largest synagogue in Budapest, in the *Dohány utca,* furnished the immediate pretext. Teleki labelled the Hungarists "a centre of illegal and anti-constitutional action" and they, in turn, accepted suppression without resistance – the more so, given that some of the party's leaders were in prison. Teleki then proceeded to merge the ruling Party of National Unity with Imrédy's Hungarian Life Movement. The new party was given the name of Hungarian Life Party. Thus in a matter of days, at the end of February 1939, Teleki weeded out, or at least appeared to have done, both Szálasi and Imrédy from Hungarian political life – and he had done this with the consent of the Regent. Teleki had made these moves in order to prevent the country from falling under German domination. The scion of one of the oldest Transylvanian aristocratic families, he must also have been impelled by feelings of class superiority, in his determination to destroy movements which were mobilising the lower classes by intoning a social revolutionary phraseology.

Regarding Horthy's rôle in all this, some conclusions can be drawn from various contradictory statements made by him and from some equally contradictory opinions about him. Knox pointed out that although the Regent had used "forceful enough" language against extreme right agitation in a broadcast made in April 1933, "the general public was not reassured and the belief persisted . . . that the Regent himself and members of his immediate entourage sympathised inwardly with the [Hungarist] movement."[42] On the other hand, the Regent disclosed his pro-British sympathies on quite a few occasions and permitted himself anti-German outbursts in front of Western diplomats. In March 1939, shortly before the annexation of Carpatho-Ruthenia, he complained to Knox of "Germany's 'betrayal' of Hungary", and pointed out that this had had the result of entirely extinguishing "any sparks of Nazism that there had been in the Honvéd".[43]

Following the fusion of Imrédy's movement with the government party, the former Prime Minister moved openly towards the extreme right. "There has been something almost pathological in Imredy's decline". The atmosphere created by Imrédy had been "clearly a mixture of innate German mysticism and inbred Hungarian romance", and not a good one, in Knox's view. "Though I have had great liking for him personally and much respect for his intelligence I can now only hope, for Hungary's sake, that he and his white stag[44] will remain in the wilderness."[45]

In May Teleki dissolved parliament and held new elections. The British Legation in Budapest was realistic enough not to have drawn any far-reaching conclusions from the repeated proscriptions of Szálasi's movement. The "situation deserves closely watching. It is possible that, as happened . . . when the same party was dissolved in 1938 . . . the extremist organization may rear its head again under some different guise",[46] wrote Gascoigne. As was to have been expected, the Arrow Cross did participate in the elections, this time under the name of the Hungarian Arrow Cross Party. Contrary to predictions, that the Hungarists had not recovered from the action taken against them by Teleki,[47] the Arrow Cross won 42 mandates and about 20 per cent of the votes cast. This was to have been the high water mark attained by Szálasi. British diplomats interpreted the success of the Arrow Cross mainly as a reflection of public impatience with the slow progress of social reform legislation. One of the conclusions drawn by O'Malley was that there was no need to fear imminent German domination, because the extremists themselves opposed it and "many of the Hungarist candidates spoke openly against a German ascendancy". He added that it was "regrettable" (?) that many of the Arrow Cross deputies elected were "mostly persons who neither deserve nor enjoy the personal respect of their countrymen".[48]

It was the Soviet-German Pact that helped Teleki indirectly to rally public opinion behind him against the *nyilas* at a time when it seemed likely that their star was on the ascendant. The Hungarian Minister in London, G. Barcza, described the impact of the Molotov-Ribbentrop Pact on Hungarian political life in realistic terms. "The signature of the . . . Treaty had completely demoralised the Hungarian Nazi Party. . . . [The *nyilas*] were now so weakened and so disorganised that they no longer constituted any danger . . . and the possibility of their being able to organise a *coup d'état* . . . might now be ruled out."[49]

The outbreak of World War II found the Teleki government in a secure position. Territorial gains – the annexation of Carpatho-Ruthenia – had helped to consolidate Teleki's rule. Hitler himself was not eager to encourage the seizure of power by such unreliable and dangerous types as the Arrow Cross, whose power base lay among the populace.[50] Although Teleki refused to join Hitler's war against Poland, he was considered a loyal ally of the Axis, so that it was only reasonable on Berlin's part to abstain from interfering in Hungarian internal affairs. As to the Arrow Cross, which found itself losing its power gradually during the early years of the war, it was to play the rôle of being the Reich's army of reserve until October 1944, when at long last – though too late – its hour struck. It is worth noting, however, that the political atmosphere under Teleki was in no way that of a *détente* and that from April 1941 onwards – after Teleki had committed suicide – László Bárdossy's government took on an overtly extremist character.[51] This manifested itself most strikingly in Bárdossy's Jewish policy.

Notes

1. Knox to Halifax, 27 February 1938 (Doc.No.92)
2. Ibid. The dinner was attended by, among others, Minister of Education Bálint Hóman, the pro-Nazi and anti-semitic historian.
3. Knox to Eden, 13 January (Doc.No.67)
4. Cf. Seton-Watson's opinion: "It is a strange fact that Hungary, where Reaction and Terror were introduced earlier, and where the people had fewer rights and liberties, retained longer than any other Eastern European State remnants of Liberalism." (H. Seton-Watson, op.cit., p.197)
5. Gascoigne to Halifax, 11 April 1938 (Doc.No.96)
6. Ibid.
7. Ibid.
8. Ibid.
9. Ibid.

10. The Germans were quite satisfied with Daranyi and did not press towards an Arrow Cross take-over of power. Erdmannsdorff, the German Minister in Budapest, stated, "[Hitler] is supposed to have said to ... Seyss-Inquart that he much preferred the present Hungarian Government to a National Socialist Government. He was probably thinking of the ... lack of leadership in the right-radical movements here, which are very much at odds with each other." (Erdmannsdorff from Budapest, 21 April 1938. DGFP, Series D, Vol.V, Doc.No.195)
11. Knox to Halifax, 24 April 1938 (Doc.No.99)
12. Ibid.
13. Ibid.
14. "The Iron Guard was not directed [in 1937] by Germany and remained a pre-Nazi formation" in: *La Roumanie indépendante*, 25 December 1947 (Quoted by Eugen Weber in: Hans Rogger and Eugen Weber (eds), *The European Right. A Historical Profile*, London 1965, p.554)
15. Knox to Halifax, 24 April 1938 (Doc.No.99)
16. Minutes by A. D. M. Ross, 29 April 1938 (Ibid.)
17. Norman to Halifax, 26 April 1938 (Doc.No.100)
18. Ibid.
19. Ibid.
20. Ibid.
21. Memorandum by Royall Tylor, 14 May 1938 (Doc.No.103)
22. Knox to Halifax, 21 May 1938 (Doc.No.105)
23. Gascoigne to Halifax, 15 August 1938 (Doc.No.107)
24. Henderson to Halifax, 26 August 1938 (Doc.No.111)
25. Minutes by I. Mallet, 12 October 1938 (Doc.No.112) Cf. C. A. Macartney: "... Imrédy owed his appointment largely to the belief that he was Liberal and 'Western' in his outlook and would act as a barrier against the extreme Right." (C. A. Macartney, *October Fifteenth. A History of Modern Hungary, 1929–1945*, I, Edinburgh 1961, p.220)
26. Minutes by Mallet, 12 October 1938 (Doc.No.112)
27. Memorandum by C. A. Macartney on "The Hungarian Question", 12 October 1938 (P.R.O., F.O. 371, C 12627/2319/12)
28. Foreign Office Minutes, 17 October 1938 (Doc.No.113)
29. Ibid.
30. Minutes by Noble, 14 November 1938 (Doc.No.119)
31. Knox to Halifax, 5 November 1938 (Doc.No.120)
32. Minutes by Noble, 24 November 1938 (Ibid.)
33. Minutes by Nichols, 25 November 1938 (Ibid.)

34. Memorandum by John Keyser, October 1938 (Doc.No.126)
35. Ibid.
36. Minutes by Noble, 28 November 1938 (Doc.No.127)
37. Annual Report for Hungary, 1938 (Doc.No.134)
38. Newton to Halifax, 15 August 1938 (Doc.No.108)
39. Telegram from Knox, No.1 Saving, Budapest, 11 January 1939 (P.R.O., F.O. 371, C 612/166/21)
40. Knox to Halifax, 27 January 1939 (Doc.No.144)
41. Gascoigne to Halifax, 27 February 1939 (Doc.No.155)
42. Annual Report for 1938, Hungary (Doc.No.134)
43. Knox to Sargent, 13 March 1939 (Doc.No.157)
44. One of the "Turanian" symbols used by Imrédy's movement.
45. Doc.No.157
46. Gascoigne to Halifax, 27 February 1939 (Doc.No.155)
47. Gascoigne to Halifax, 6 May 1939 (Doc.No.158)
48. O'Malley to Halifax, 1 June 1939 (Doc.No.159)
49. Minute by Sargent, 26 August 1939 (Doc.No.163)
50. The "Arrow Cross" enjoyed in effect the financial and propagandistic support of different Nazi agencies. Protesting against the German support to the "Hungarists", Teleki and Csáky assured Hitler and Ribbentrop that "the Hungarian Government, from the German point of view [was] absolutely reliable" therefore such a German policy not only "much annoyed [the Hungarian] Government and public opinion, but was also senseless." (DGFP, Series D, Vol.VI, Docs.Nos.300 and 436)
51. According to László Szenczei, a leftist Transylvanian publicist and author of several historical works, up to the end of the thirties "the menace of Hungarian Fascism had played the part of a catalyst in Romania's trend towards the Right; afterwards [after the Legionnaire seizure of power in 1940] Romanian Fascism assumed the same rôle in relation to Hungarian politics." (Szenczei László, *A magyarok és a románok [Hungarians and Romanians]*, Budapest 1943. The reciprocal "catalyst" rôle of Hungarian and Romanian Fascism should not be overlooked by scholars searching the motive forces of the extreme right in the two countries.

3 Pioneering in European Anti-Semitism

"For a development and growth of antisemitism in Hungary, there was no need of a German example or influence. On the contrary, there is probably no country in which the situation would be more propitious for anti-semitism."

(Count Pál Teleki in a letter to
Mr. John Keyser, 13 February 1939)

During the Hitler-Horthy meeting of May 1943 at Klessheim the Führer is said to have angrily denounced Hungarian "softness' towards the Jews. The offended Horthy referred to his regime's anti-Jewish record; he dwelt on Hungary's "pioneer" rôle in the history of modern European anti-semitism.

Even Miklós Kállay, the moderate and anti-Nazi Prime Minister in 1942-44, often recalled Hungary's unassailable record in the van of European anti-semitism and reminded the Germans that Hungarians needed no lesson in anti-semitism from the Nazis.

The 500,000[1] or so Jews of Trianon Hungary were more homogeneous and assimilated than those of Romania and Czechoslovakia. In contrast to the latter two countries Hungarian Jewry was not capable of establishing an autonomous political organisation of its own. There were no plans at all to found a "National Jewish Party" or a religious party in the inter-war years and the Zionist movement was weaker in Hungary than anywhere else in Central and Eastern Europe. The Jewish vote split two ways: it went to the Social Democrats and to the bourgeois liberal and radical parties. The Smallholders received the support of a small fraction of the Jewish voters, whilst a minute proportion of the Jewish vote, from the upper reaches of the well-to-do classes, went to the government party

143

during Bethlen's Prime Ministership. Paradoxically, it was precisely the most assimilated Jewish community in the Danube Basin and the one which stood furthest from any organisation on a Jewish national basis that had to suffer the earliest post-First World War pogroms and anti-Jewish legislation. The fact that there was a very substantial proportion of Jews in the leaderships of the two revolutions, above all of the Hungarian Soviet Republic, coupled with a kind of Hungarian-Jewish *Dolchstoss* myth, precipitated an extreme wave of anti-semitism in the first phase of the counter-revolution, such as was without parallel in the rest of Europe with the exception of the Ukraine during the civil war. Excluding the Social Democrats and small bourgeois liberal groupings, there was no political party in Hungary in the early 1920s that did not in practice incorporate anti-semitism in its programme.

The calmer atmosphere of consolidation under Bethlen merely blunted the edge of anti-semitic agitation and organisation, but did not end the anti-Jewish attitudes that permeated the widest circles of Hungarian society. They came to the fore again in a virulent form in the early 1930s.

Hungary's early anti-semitic policies and the acute state of the question in the mid-1930s, together with the early anti-Jewish legislation, explain why British circles followed the Jewish question in Hungary with such unusual attention. A contributory factor was the conviction in London that the Jewish question in Hungary was one of the central issues which would decide the struggle between the moderate right and the extreme right and that, in turn, would influence the future of German penetration into Hungary. There is some British material from an early date, in 1936, bearing out the interpretation that both Horthy and the ruling "moderates" and in some instances anti-German circles as well were extreme anti-semites. After the war, Horthy rejected charges made against him that he was anti-semitic,[2] yet such excellent observers as Sir Geoffrey Knox, the British Minister, regarded him as obsessively anti-semitic. The Regent often spoke very sincerely to Knox and described the Jews on one occasion "as a virus spreading through the world".[3] Kálmán Kánya, Foreign Minister of Hungary before Csáky, who was no friend of Nazi Germany in the least, was so much a prisoner of his anti-semitic sentiments that once when discussing the possibility of a Soviet-Yugoslav or Soviet-Bulgarian *rapprochement* with Knox, he remarked that he could not imagine Yugoslavia or Bulgaria coquetting with "ce sale Juif" Litvinov.[4] Count István Bethlen enjoyed the highest prestige and reputation of any Hungarian politician in the 1930s. During and after the Gömbös era he was in opposition on a conservative "Christian-national" and to some extent anti-German basis. Bethlen did not count as an anti-semite; nevertheless, he too was of the opinion that the Jewish problem and land reform were the two mines lying dormant, which anybody without a conscience could explode at any time, so that he regarded their solution as urgently necessary.[5]

After the death of Gömbös, in the summer of 1936, the government party – the Party of National Unity – was reorganised. On Jewish affairs it followed the line of its predecessor, the Christian National Party. This line, unbroken since 1920, was identical with the so-called "Christian Course", which in practice meant a policy of "race protection", anti-semitism, anti-democratism and extremist nationalism. The majority of the party leaders were not of Nazi inclination – indeed there were some anti-Germans among them. But in one question there was no difference of opinion between Berlin and the ruling party in Hungary in the 1930s and this was hostility to the Jews. Although the position of the Jews was much better in Hungary than in Nazi Germany, it would have been hard to distinguish the anti-semitism of the ruling circles in Hungary from that of the Hungarian national socialists. This applies particularly to Marton and Mecsér, deputies of the majority party (which they later left), who formed an identifiably Nazi group within the government party, with close connections linking them to Berlin.

Any anti-semitic propaganda by Berlin was superfluous in Hungary, yet in this field Nazi activists were busy in Hungary. Knox noted early in 1937 that systematic and effective Nazi propaganda intensified indigenous anti-semitism,[6] and that German agents were active on the same task among the German minority in Hungary. Both Knox and Gascoigne raised the question of the Jews with members of the government and leaders of the opposition. Knox himself felt the blindness of anti-Jewish hatred when he became the target of attacks by Hungarian Nazi papers at the behest of Germany. Although he had no Jewish connections whatever, he was branded a Jew and a freemason by the extremist press.[7]

Knox and his fellow diplomats started paying attention to the Arrow Cross anti-semitic agitation only fairly late in the day – until the end of 1937 they saw no serious danger in the Nazi-type organisation that was going on. So far as the Jews were concerned, the generally held view among the diplomats was that anti-semitism did exist in Hungary, officially too – the government party and the National Socialists were both anti-semitic and Horthy was "violently anti-semitic"[8] – but there was no ground for anxiety for intervention (as in Romania), seeing that the position of the Jews in economic and cultural life, as well as from the legal point of view, was acceptable. In retrospect, there is no need to quarrel with this standpoint. Despite the humiliations and the anti-semitic abuse, the Jews could play an important rôle in the world of the press,

145

films, theatre and literature, in fact a more important one than their proportion suggested. Apart from humiliation and molestations, they faced no serious obstacles in commercial or industrial activities either. The situation changed completely during 1938 and the radicalisation of the Jewish question is faithfully reflected in the British diplomatic reports. Furthermore, they shed light on the deeper causes of this radicalisation, on the complexity of its roots in domestic and foreign affairs, and on the weight and importance British diplomacy attached to Hungary's Jewish problem.

In explaining the relative successes of the right extremist movements, Knox mentioned the appeal that "the promise of spoliation of the Jews" had in a society with a "deplorably low standard of living".[9] This was particularly so where the government party itself created an atmosphere hostile to "Jewish capital" by its agitation. Did Hungarian Jewry have at its disposal the kind of economic power which might have justified the anti-Jewish, anti-capitalist campaign of demagogy promoted by the right and extreme right? Surprisingly, Gascoigne gave a categorical "yes" to this question: "... the bulk of the private commercial and financial enterprises ... are in the hands of the Jews. Statistics show that some 75 per cent of the business houses, banks, etc. of Pest are owned and staffed by Jews ..." (basing himself on statistical data which were clearly the inventions of Nazi fantasy and the inaccuracy of which it was not difficult to demonstrate.)[10] In a letter written to Eden in a fairly personal tone, Gascoigne stated early in 1938, "During the past two years the feeling ... against the Jews has been inflamed by the sedulous anti-Semitic propaganda put about by the extremist organisations. Moreover, there is no doubt that considerable indirect pressure is exerted by the Hungarian authorities to induce Jewish firms to employ Christians in preference to their co-religionists ..."[11]

Public opinion held up Count István Bethlen as the typical instance of the Jewish policy of the moderates. Bethlen, Gascoigne wrote, "deprecated the methods employed by Nazi Germany to eradicate the Jews, and suggested that a solution might be found by the introduction of a progressive programme designed to assist Christians to win back their position in the economic sphere."[12] Gascoigne's views and standpoint did not differ from that of Bethlen. "Those hotheads in the ranks of the extremists who are in favour of drastic action against the Jews similar to that adopted by the German Nazis, would do well to take Count Bethlen's counsel to heart. For any change in the existing situation must be brought about very gradually since ... there is no class in Hungary to-day capable of replacing the Jews in ... commercial and industrial life ..."[13]

Bruce Lockhart, Advisor to the Hungarian National Bank, had a discussion with Imrédy, then President of the National Bank, on the forthcoming Jewish Laws. What is interesting about this is that Bruce Lockhart understood and approved the anti-Jewish bill. The view held by Foreign Office officials about the legislation was quite different: "at present the Jews occupy a predominant position in commerce and the intellectual professions, because they are abler than the Hungarians, who incline to disinterest themselves in such things . . . It may be true that the law under consideration is better than the iniquitous system in force in Germany, but that does not make it anything but a wicked law." The writer of the minute, Noble, did not think that Darányi, the Hungarian Prime Minister, would take the wind out of the sails of the extreme right with this Law. He was afraid that Darányi would be replaced by someone more extremist and that the legislation then being prepared would be followed by more severe enactments. "I fear this is the beginning and not the end of a drive against the Jews in Hungary. . ."[14] As a matter of fact, Noble's prophecy did not spring from any extraordinary pessimism. A second Jewish Law was passed in Hungary before the outbreak of the war and it was, of course, more radical than the first. It is worth noting too that the Budapest Legation agreed with the note on the preparation of the Jewish Law sent by Bruce Lockhart, who maintained friendly relations with Imrédy.

Knox regarded it as a sign of the times that candidates at by-elections, coming forward with an extremist programme, should be successful, or that a senior official, known for his fanatical hatred of the Jews, should be appointed to the number two position in the administration of Pest county. British diplomatic reports reflected faithfully the fact that it was ever more frequent for government figures to stand up openly in support of violently anti-semitic individuals. Nor is there any omission in the reports of the growing anxiety of the Jewish community or of their turning more and more often to the British, in the hope that Britain would act as a brake on Hungarian anti-semitism. The material in the Foreign Office archives does not convince one that these complaints were listened to in London; quite in contrast to the readiness with which the British Government intervened in Bucharest against the persecution of the Jews.

By March 1938 the propaganda of the Arrow Cross had become ever more strident – demanding "the complete eradication of the Jewish element from every area of the country's life in the shortest possible time". Both Knox and Gascoigne reported that on account of that and because the first Jewish Law was about to be introduced, "the unrest amongst the Jews . . . had amounted almost to a state of panic . . ."[15] British observers tended to regard anti-semitism as the main factor which led the Hungarian middle and lower classes into the ranks of the Arrow

147

Cross. "Herein lay the chief strength of the Nyilas Movement, for there is always a great latent anti-Semitism in Hungary and large sections of the population only wait for the chance to express it", wrote Knox at the beginning of 1940.[16]

In the spring and summer of 1938, under the strong pressure of the local Nazis, the Hungarian Government vied with them to win the support of the extremist masses, taking over more and more the slogans of the Nazis with regard to the Jews. "It is too early to forecast whether this new orientation of Hungary's internal policy" – that is, social reforms and anti-semitic legislation – "will have the effect of stemming the tide of extremism. At any rate", wrote Gascoigne, "something concrete is now being done to counter it [extremism], although it still remains to be seen whether the 'New Deal' and the anti-Jewish measures contemplated will go far enough to satisfy the predatory exigencies of the Nazis."[17]

The tabling of the bill to restrict the normal activities of the Jews, exactly at the time of the *Anschluss,* only contributed to further unrest and instability in Hungary and weakened the position of the government, according to Knox.[18] The Foreign Office was itself pessimistic about the future of the Hungarian Government in competition with the propaganda put out by local Nazis and by Berlin. "The Hungarian Government's policy against the Nazis . . . is proving ineffective. But even an effective policy against the Nazis would not release Hungary from the German embrace . . ." wrote A. D. M. Ross.[19] Montagu Norman, quoted in an earlier chapter, was also inclined to be pessimistic about Hungary's political future and the fate of the Jews. He was of the view that the overwhelming majority of Hungary's youth was "infected . . . with National Socialist and notably anti-Jewish ideas."[20] Astonishingly and not very convincingly, he suggested that the Jews themselves favoured some mild anti-Jewish restrictions in order to avoid more drastic measures later. The Jews "would have welcomed, and indeed many of the more far-sighted, on the principle of half a loaf being better than no bread, actually solicited the sacrifices imposed upon them by the economic programme and even by the anti-Jewish Law, had those measures been accompanied by firm action on the part of the Government to put a stop to extremist agitation."[21] However, the government took no steps worthy of mention to curb extremism. Montagu Norman, gravely mistaken, regarded Imrédy as a suitable person to do this, and added the curious and wholly untenable opinion of Imrédy that Eckhardt and the Jews were "supporting him to death".[22] Reports similar to this contributed to the favourable light in which Imrédy was seen in London right up to the beginning of 1939.

Another British financial expert, Royall Tylor, the League of Nations financial adviser to the Hungarian Government, thought that one of the reasons for the discontent in Hungary was precisely the reluctance and the fear of the government to deal with the Jewish question.[23] He was not very hopeful that the reform measures initiated by the government – the capital levy and the anti-Jewish legislation among them – would bring the expected result, that is, the confidence of the masses in the government. The government's position could not be held because of its ambivalent measures. It could not have succeeded in simultaneously promoting anti-Jewish slogans and fighting them, or rather, their original propagators. Quite apart from that, Knox's opinion was that the task of suppressing extremist and extreme anti-semitic agitation "was beyond either the powers or the will of the Darányi Government."[24]

One of the first steps taken by Imrédy's government, formed in May 1938, was to push the so-called First Jewish Law through the Upper House, taking up the struggle against Szálasi at the same time. The anti-Jewish atmosphere in the country did not decline and this could hardly have been one of Imrédy's objectives in any event. Gascoigne reported in August that year that anti-semitism was on the increase, "but this is not as yet conducted as a racial question".[25]

The growth of anti-semitism in the second half of 1938 was the direct consequence of Imrédy's Machiavellian policies. Knox saw through it all quite clearly: ". . . the new steps foreshadowed against the Jews . . . are generally said to have been brought to the fore, because the Prime Minister did not feel himself strong enough to carry through a reasonable measure of agrarian reform and hoped to divert public attention in this manner."[26] Knox thought it would have been useful for the British press to speak out against Imrédy's anti-Jewish measures, because he knew that the Hungarian Government was sensitive towards British opinion and was afraid of the reaction in the City. But, asked Knox, on what papers could one have relied, adding that the Budapest correspondent of *The Times* – a former Hungarian diplomat and currently editor of the *Pester Lloyd* – was entirely servile to the Axis.[27] Once again, the mood in the Foreign Office was one of helpless pessimism: "There is a considerable danger of an anti-Jewish hunt in Hungary; whether remarks about it in the British press would really help, it is difficult to say . . . I can't help feeling that if the Hungarians are such fools as to attack the Jews, no press warning will deter them", remarked Noble.[28] P. Nichols, on the other hand, shared Knox's view and suggested that it would be useful "to pass the hint on to *The Times* and perhaps the *Daily Telegraph* as well"[29] Ingram, however, was sceptical about putting the press on to this issue, whereas Bramwell, who was highly pessimistic about the future of Hungarian Jewry, feared that the mobilisation of the press would achieve

149

the opposite aim. "I fear action ... might serve merely to increase [anti-semitism] without assisting the Jews ..."[30]

We have already quoted Virginio Gayda, according to whom the binding cement in the nationalism of South Eastern Europe was anti-semitism. In the opinion of British observers, it was exactly this shared anti-semitism that linked the various groups of the right and the extreme right, and in fact, the anti-semitic platform united all the extremist movements, not least because hatred of the Jews was becoming "increasingly fierce" by the end of 1938.[31] The speedy radicalisation of Imrédy's policy towards the Jews came as a surprise to the British diplomats in Budapest and Knox sent telegrams to London full of anxiety. The Jewish Bill, he wrote, "as an instrument of persecution goes far beyond the existing law which already violates principles of Article 58 of the Treaty of Trianon". He saw no check after Imrédy and felt that the Hungarian anti-Jewish legislation could have repercussions throughout the whole of South Eastern Europe. In the circumstances, he saw the situation as an opportunity for British intervention, as had happened in Romania, and this was all the more justified, seeing that Great Britain had the right, possibly even the duty, to intervene against a violation of the Treaty of Trianon, to which it was a signatory. The only trouble was that Knox felt that a possible British intervention would be fruitless, indeed, even harmful. He could not exclude the possibility that Hungary would use the intervention as a pretext for leaving the League of Nations. Hence he proposed indirect action, which would have more chance of success. He made concrete proposals on this to London, adding the analysis, "the Hungarian has never shown the capacity nor the inclination to occupy the positions from which the Jew is being ousted. The result is that the Jew will be replaced ... by the Magyarised German." Then he concluded, "I consider that our influence on Hungary by precept and example has sunk to nothing; our 'nuisance value', however, both in the financial domain and as one of the principal factors of world opinion is very great. The present is, I think, an occasion on which we should use it."[32] But what would have been the right course of action for the British Government to have taken, when not even the Chancery of the British Legation in Budapest agreed with Knox on the tactics?[33]

Imrédy fell in February 1939, a few weeks after he had formed the right extremist movement christened "The Hungarian Life". Opinions are still divided over the immediate causes of his fall and the available documentation is insufficient for clarification of the question. In all probability, an important rôle was played by his extremist anti-Jewish policies on the one hand and by the campaign waged against him by Szálasi on account of Imrédy's alleged Jewish ancestry on the other.[34] It is possible that he was removed by Horthy, as the Regent himself claimed after the war, because his anti-Jewish plans were held to be excessive. However, Horthy's rôle precisely concerning the Jewish policy was more than ambiguous. Knox had the opportunity of speaking several times to Horthy early in 1939 and over a brief period of time, he twice informed London of the Regent's anti-semitic remarks, even in conversations when he would give himself over to violent outbursts against Hitler and Germany.[35]

The bombing of the synagogue in *Dohány-utca* on 3 February 1939 – the work of the Arrow Cross – aroused public opinion to such a degree that Horthy could well have considered the moment an opportune one for ridding himself of Imrédy, whom he regarded as a difficult, dictatorial type of man. Nor did it help Imrédy that he introduced a state of emergency after the bombing as a move against the Hungarists.

At the end of February, Imrédy's place was taken by Count Pál Teleki, who had not the least intention of changing his predecessor's Jewish policy.[36] Teleki was a convinced anti-semite. John Keyser, who was a personal friend of Teleki's, wrote critically to him of the Jewish Bill. Teleki replied in a letter written a few days before his nomination as Prime Minister, in which he expounded his anti-semitic views. The letter, which reached the Foreign Office through Butler and became the subject of study and argument, is an important document on the anti-semitism of the Hungarian gentry.

Teleki regarded as natural the flaring up of anti-semitism in a country "where anti-semitism is age-old as a feeling". The Hungarians had no need of a German example or of German influence, because anti-semitism existed in Hungary anyway and was justified. He accepted that some outside influence had been at work, but only some, because in his view, Hungarian anti-semitism was not a copy of German anti-semitism and "it will . . . never grow to such cruelty . . ." As far as he was concerned, the Jews represented a catastrophic danger. The middle classes and the aristocracy were intoxicated with Jewish ideas and morality, he complained, and unless an urgent and radical change could be effected in excluding Jewish influence, "it would cost the life of the Hungarian people . . . My only fear is that it is too late." Teleki saw four great dangers which had menaced the Hungarian land and its people – the Mongols, the Turks, the Jews and the Germans. The Mongols had represented the smallest danger, and the damage caused by the Turks was, likewise, not irreparable. By implication, Teleki's conclusion was that the Jews and the Germans were the most dangerous enemies of the Hungarian people. From his various activities, it was not difficult to guess that Teleki placed the Jews in the first place on his list.[37]

151

The Foreign Office did not find Teleki's thesis convincing and one official, R. L. Speaight, repudiated it point by point.

In considering Teleki's policy towards the Jews, it is worth looking chronologically at one or two fairly striking items of information in the British reports. In his introductory speech to the Lower House of Parliament, on 22 February 1939, when listing the principal points of his government's programme, Teleki began by saying that he intended to persevere with the Jewish Law (whilst modifying it in some respects). He dissolved parliament at the beginning of May and called for new elections. It was not by chance that the last action of the outgoing parliament was to pass the Jewish Law. From that moment on, the position of Hungarian Jewry deteriorated constantly, leading to further Jewish legislation and to the introduction of compulsory labour service. Later, shortly after the re-annexation of Northern Transylvania by Hungary in 1940, Teleki's government became responsible for the first expulsions of Jews, then for the first deportations, which ended up as extermination in formerly Polish territory.

There was a brief moment when Teleki came to power when Hungarian Jewry hoped for relaxations. At the end of 1939, Teleki dissolved the Hungarist Party on the grounds that Szálasi's group had been responsible for the bombing of the *Dohány-utca* synagogue. However, the dissolution did not achieve its aim and at the elections, at the end of May, the Arrow Cross Party increased its representation in parliament from 7 seats to 42,[38] out of a total of 260. Although the strength of the Hungarian National Socialists declined in the next year or two, the position of Hungarian Jews was not affected by this fluctuation. Szálasi's movement would have had little to object to in the Jewish policy pursued by Teleki and by his successor, Bárdossy.[39]

Anti-semitism, as a very important argument among Hungarians in joining or opposing external forces, was stressed by British diplomats in Budapest in connection with the outbreak of World War II. They thought that the majority of the Hungarians did not want a German victory because of the fear that "Hungary would be politically and economically at Germany's mercy, and would be reduced to the rank of a piece of *Lebensraum* — for a particularly unattractive species of *Leben*. The only advantage which anyone in Hungary anticipates from a German victory . . . is the continuance of a comparatively Jew-free life. The importance of this feeling must not be underestimated", warned the British Minister in Budapest and his collaborators the Foreign Office. "[Anti-semitism] is particularly strong among the younger and middle-aged men who have now stepped into the posts left vacant through the Jewish Law and are at present enjoying good incomes and prospects." As

152

to the Nazi pressure and influence on Hungarian public opinion after the outbreak of the war, they again and again underlined that "the easiest and most effective, as it is the commonest card of German propaganda is to threaten Hungary with a return of the Jews if the Western Powers win."[40]

For the sake of completing the story, it should be remembered that apart from the Jews deported to Kamenec Podolsk and those who fell victim to the bloodbath in the Bačka – a total of 20,000 souls, until the spring of 1942 – as well as those who perished in labour service on the Eastern front, the bulk of Hungarian Jewry escaped extermination until the German occupation of Hungary on 19 March 1944. This, perhaps, was the only fact that might have vindicated those British diplomats and politicians, who, whilst they regarded Hungary as a "hopeless case" from the Jewish point of view, still had faith in that "Hungary of the gentry" which, as Teleki wrote in 1939, would never allow itself the cruelties of German anti-semitism.

Notes

1. The number of persons of Jewish faith was 473,355 in 1920 (i.e. 5.92 per cent), 444,567 in 1930 (5.1 per cent) and 725,007 in 1941 (4.94 per cent), after the successive annexation of former Czechoslovak, Romanian and Yugoslav territories.
2. Admiral Nicholas Horthy, *Memoirs*, London 1956, pp.174–5, 219–20.
3. Admiral Horthy "spoke to me . . . on world politics with the transparent sincerity and simplicity which are so much his own, but, as always, under the influence of his three dominant obsessions, Jews, Communists and peace treaties." (Knox to Eden, 9 April 1936, Doc.No.7)
4. Ibid.
5. Miklós Szinai and László Szücs (eds), *The Confidential Papers of Admiral Horthy*, Budapest 1965, p.115.
6. Knox to Eden, 13 January 1938 (Doc.No.67)
7. Gascoigne to Eden, 19 January 1938 (Doc.No.71)
8. Ibid.
9. Knox to Eden, 13 January 1938 (Doc.No.67)
10. Gascoigne to Eden, 19 January 1938 (Doc.No.71)
11. Ibid.
12. Ibid.
13. Ibid.
14. Minutes by A. M. Noble, 22 April 1938 (Doc.No.95)
15. Knox (Gascoigne) to Halifax, 11 April 1938 (Doc.No.96)
16. P.R.O., F.O. 371, C 734/734/21

17. Gascoigne to Halifax, 11 April 1938 (Doc.No.96)
18. Knox to Halifax, 24 April 1938 (Doc.No.99)
19. Minutes by A. D. M. Ross, 29 April 1938 (Ibid.)
20. Norman to Halifax, 26 April 1938 (Doc.No.100)
21. Ibid.
22. Ibid.
23. Memorandum by Royall Tylor, 14 May 1938 (Doc.No.103)
24. Knox to Halifax, 21 May 1938 (Doc.No.105)
25. Gascoigne to Halifax, 15 August 1938 (Doc.No.107)
26. Knox to Ingram, 15 November 1938 (Doc.No.123)
27. Ibid.
28. Minutes by Noble, 26 November 1938 (Ibid.)
29. Remark by P. Nichols, 28 November 1938 (Ibid.)
30. Remarks by Ingram and Bramwell, 28 November 1938 (Ibid.)
31. Memorandum from John Keyser, October 1938 (Doc.No.126)
32. Telegram from Knox, 24 December 1938 (Doc.No.133)
33. See remark by Speaight, 9 January 1939 (Ibid.)
34. His opponents demonstrated that one of his great-great-grandparents was Jewish. This "charge" is likewise unclarified.
35. See e.g. Knox to Sargent, 12 January 1939 (Doc.No.142)
36. Teleki's "handling of the highly controversial and difficult question of the anti-Jewish legislation was, at least, tactful and correct." (Gascoigne to Halifax, 6 May 1939, Doc.No.158)
37. Letter from Pál Teleki to J. A. Keyser, Budapest, 13 February 1939 (Doc.No.150)
38. Together with "independent" Nazis the number of deputies belonging to the Arrow Cross Front amounted to 49.
39. Szálasi's anti-semitism is one of the controversial problems of the history of the Hungarian extreme right. In Macartney's opinion Szálasi was not an extreme anti-semite: ". . . there is no sign of the pathological Jew-hatred of a Hitler, a Streicher, or an Endre . . . He does not want to torment [Jews], only to be rid of them. . ." (C. A. Macartney, op.cit.,I,p.165)
40. P.R.O., F.O. 371, C 734/734/21

Those Who Lost their Way

We do not believe that a new generation will learn from the errors of their fathers. Each generation will repeat the errors of its predecessors and cap them with new ones. The Bourbons were not the only ones of whom it can be said that they learned nothing and remembered nothing. We do not believe that much purpose would be served in depicting a past age by offering better and wiser courses of political action.

Nor is it the task of the historian to judge those who acted in circumstances which posterity can no longer feel or imagine. But the situation is not quite the same in the case of those who explore the recent past, the active participants and heroes, the beneficiaries and victims of which are still with us and the human and material losses of which are shouldered by the youngest generation. It is hard to expect objectivity from any historian, but it is impossible to demand an uncommitted, neutral and uninvolved approach from one whose generation lived through, suffered and now tries to overcome the greatest tempest of all times, with all its convulsions and consequent transformations. And in spite of that, the purpose of this study and of this collection of documents is neither to judge nor to instruct.

Beneš wrote in 1939 that very severe criticism could and should be passed on the practice, procedure, means and methods of the European democracies. Towards the end of the war, he held the view that the failure of democracy was first and foremost the failure of its leaders. The democracies had become bankrupt not because the democratic system was itself bad, but essentially because its leaders had been inept, weak and incompetent. Was Beneš right in this? Would the world have looked different if leaders of a different stamp had been in charge of the democracies? Does the greatest responsibility really fall on those who led the democracies in the 1930s? But, if so, where are those who chose the

155

leaders, who approved of them and accepted them? Where are the crowds that demonstrated spontaneously at Le Bourget on Daladier's return from Munich? Where are the masses of the Danube Basin who flocked in their millions to support an inhuman and anti-human system? Can the leaders of the greater and smaller democracies be held responsible for them too? Beneš, deserted and embittered in emigration, does not offer a fully satisfactory explanation.

The development towards right extremism and extreme anti-semitism in the Danube Basin in the late thirties, with all its fatal implications, was not an objectively, necessarily prevailing process. Fascism, or nazism, was not the only alternative in Slovakia, Romania or Hungary. There existed a real basis for stemming such a development. Internal anti-Nazi forces, including nationalist and even strongly rightist but anti-German factors, supported by the Western democracies might have constituted a feasible alternative. However, its chances were underestimated both by the local anti-Nazi elements and their Western allies. Lack of confidence in resisting the Nazi trend prevailed not only in Prague, Budapest and Bucharest, but in London and Paris as well. Demoralisation and opportunism paralysed and frustrated the anti-Nazi camp. Hugh Seton-Watson's grim assertion in connection with events in Central Europe in the late sixties may hold true for the late thirties as well: "That the last fifty years have seen a failure and decline of Europe is a well-worn cliché. What is so alarming is that the knowledge of this tragic process seems to paralyse the will to resist and arrest it."[1]

As to the rôle of those involved in the events in the area who drifted along with the tide, may we evoke the remarkable public appearance of a leading Hungarian intellectual. In 1943, when Hungary had long been a satellite of Hitler's, when the Hungarian army had bled to death on the Eastern front somewhere along the Don, it was still possible to publish independent views in Budapest, albeit cautiously. It was then that Gyula Szekfü, the greatest Hungarian historian of his time, published a series of articles in the democratic paper *Magyar Nemzet*. Szekfü had begun his career on the extreme right, but had moved to support democracy and resistance by the end of the war. His series of articles was given the title "Somewhere we have lost our way".

Szekfü's generation had, in fact, lost its way and not just Hungary. But who could say where? One can speculate and reconstruct the mosaic, one can try and look at things a little more clearly and a little more understandingly in puzzling out why the greater part of the European generation had lost its way, involving itself and others in tragedy.

Were there any signposts at all in the labyrinths of the 1930s? And if so, could they not be read? And did the West, one wonders, do its part to stem the flood? And, again, did it do enough to set its face resolutely against compromise? Could the stampede that cost the lives of a million-and-a-half sons of the three Danubian nations and the lives of eight-hundred-thousand Jews of the area have been avoided?

It is hardly likely that there are unambiguous and universally acceptable answers to these questions. What can be stated, however, is that today one can offer a more accurate answer to the question why the peoples of the Danube Basin lost their way, than Gyula Szekfü and his contemporaries could. And it is clearer today, how and to what extent the West, whose ideals served as a beacon to generations in the Danube Basin, failed in its historic task and vocation. The archival evidence of the most significant Western factor of the era, Great Britain, can offer some assistance in illuminating the problems tackled with such self-torment by Gyula Szekfü and his fellow soul-searchers.

Note
1. Hugh Seton-Watson, "Central European Flash-back" (in: *Encounter,* July 1969, p.68)

List of Documents

1. Sir R. Hoare to A. Eden (Bucharest, 29 January 1936)
2. Foreign Office Minute on the German minority in Czechoslovakia (20 February 1936)
3. Cabinet meeting. Memorandum on German expansion in Central and South-Eastern Europe (24 February 1936)
4. Sir R. Hoare to A. Eden (Bucharest, 28 February 1936)
5. Sir R. Hoare to A. Eden (Bucharest, 13 March 1936)
6. Sir R. Hoare to A. Eden (Bucharest, 4 April 1936)
7. Sir G. Knox to A. Eden (Budapest, 9 April 1936)
8. Sir R. Hoare to A. Eden (Bucharest, 23 April 1936)
9. Sir R. Hoare to A. Eden (Bucharest, 27 April 1936)
10. Sir G. Knox to A. Eden (Budapest, 9 May 1936)
11. Sir R. Hoare to A. Eden (Bucharest, 18 May 1936)
12. Sir G. Knox to A. Eden (23 May 1923)
13. R. H. Hadow to O. St. C. O'Malley (Prague, 9 June 1936) 14.
14. Sir J. Addison to A. Eden (Prague, 3 August 1936)
15. Sir J. Addison to A. Eden (Prague, 25 August 1936)
16. Sir R. Hoare to A. Eden (Bucharest, 27 August 1936)
17. Sir R. Hoare to A. Eden (Bucharest, 3 September 1936)
18. Sir R. Hoare to A. Eden (Bucharest, 10 September 1936)
19. Sir R. Hoare to O. St. C. O'Malley (Bucharest, 11 September 1936)
20. Foreign Office telegram to Sir R. Hoare (21 September 1936)
21. Sir R. Hoare to A. Eden (Bucharest, 26 September 1936)
22. Report by A. Eden on a conversation with V. Antonescu, Romanian Foreign Minister (Geneva, 26 September 1936)
23. R. H. Hadow to A. Eden (Prague, 28 September 1936)
24. Sir R. Hoare to A. Eden (Bucharest, 8 October 1936)
25. Sir R. Hoare to A. Eden (Bucharest, 17 October 1936)

26. Memorandum by F. Ashton-Gwatkin on a conversation with Béla Imrédy, Governor of the Hungarian National Bank (Foreign Office, 7 November 1936)
27. C. M. Bentinck to A. Eden (Prague, 7 November 1936)
28. Sir R. Hoare to A. Eden (Bucharest, 9 November 1936)
29. Annual Report, 1936, Romania (Bucharest, 12 February 1937)
30. C. M. Bentinck to the Foreign Office (Prague, 5 January 1937)
31. Memorandum by R. H. Hadow on Czechoslovakia (Prague, 2 February 1937)
32. Sir R. Hoare to the Foreign Office (Bucharest, 22 February 1937)
33. Sir R. Hoare to A. Eden (Bucharest, 24 February 1937)
34. A. D. F. Gascoigne to A. Eden (Budapest, 26 February 1937)
35. Sir G. Knox to A. Eden (Budapest, 11 March 1937)
36. Sir R. Hoare to A. Eden (Bucharest, 26 March 1937)
37. Sir R. Hoare to A. Eden (Bucharest, 9 April 1937)
38. Sir G. Knox to A. Eden (Budapest, 16 April 1937)
39. Foreign Office telegram to Sir R. Hoare (17 April 1937)
40. Sir R. Hoare to A. Eden (Bucharest, 19 May 1937)
41. Memorandum by T. H. Kadlčik on Autonomy of **Subcarp**athian Russia: (Prague, 20 May 1937)
42. B. C. Newton to A. Eden (Prague, 8 June 1937)
43. Intelligence Report on Romania (Bucharest, 2 July 1937)
44. Foreign Office Memorandum on Jews in Romania (7 July 1937)
45. A. D. F. Gascoigne to A. Eden (Budapest, 16 July 1937)
46. H. L. Farquhar to A. Eden (Bucharest, 30 July 1937)
47. R. H. Hadow to A. Eden (Prague, 3 August 1937)
48. R. H. Hadow to A. Eden (Prague, 10 August 1937)
49. Foreign Office telegram to Sir R. Hoare (5 October 1937)
50. Sir R. Hoare to A. Eden (Bucharest, 8 October 1937)
51. Sir R. Hoare to the Foreign Office (Bucharest, 12 October 1937)
52. Sir R. Hoare to the Foreign Office (Bucharest, 12 October 1937)
53. Sir R. Hoare to A. Eden (Bucharest, 20 October 1937)
54. Sir G. Knox to A. Eden (Budapest, 20 October 1937)
55. Sir G. Knox to Sir O. Sargent (Budapest, 4 November 1937)
56. Sir R. Hoare to A. Eden (Bucharest, 2 December 1937)
57. Sir R. Hoare to A. Eden (Bucharest, 3 December 1937)
58. Sir G. Knox to A. Eden (Budapest, 4 December 1937)
59. Sir R. Hoare to the Foreign Office (Bucharest, 29 December 1937)
60. Annual Report, 1937, Hungary (Budapest, 1 January 1938)
61. Annual Report, 1937, Romania
62. Minutes by A. D. M. Ross (Foreign Office, 3 January 1938)
63. Sir R. Hoare to the Foreign Office (Bucharest, 4 January 1938)
64. Sir R. Hoare to the Foreign Office (Bucharest, 5 January 1938)

65. N. Chamberlain to Sir R. Hoare (6 January 1938)
66. Sir R. Hoare to E. M. B. Ingram (Bucharest, 11 January 1938)
67. Sir G. Knox to A. Eden (Budapest, 13 January 1938)
68. Sir R. Hoare to the Foreign Office (Bucharest, 17 January 1938)
69. Sir R. Hoare to A. Eden (Bucharest, 19 January 1938)
70. Frank Walters to R. C. S. Stevenson (Geneva, 19 January 1938)
71. A. D. F. Gascoigne to A. Eden (Budapest, 19 January 1938)
72. Sir R. Hoare to the Foreign Office (Bucharest, 24 January 1938)
73. Foreign Office Memorandum on political situation in Romania (24 January 1938)
74. Sir R. Hoare to the Foreign Office (Bucharest, 24 January 1938)
75. Sir R. Hoare to the Foreign Office (Bucharest, 28 January 1938)
76. British Delegation (Geneva) to Sir R. Hoare (Geneva, 29 January 1938)
77. Record of an interview of Lord Cranborne with Prince A. Bibesco (Geneva, 31 January 1938)
78. Record of a conversation between A. Eden and the French Ambassador in London (Foreign Office, 1 February 1938)
79. Sir R. Hoare to the Foreign Office (Bucharest, 1 February 1938)
80. Cabinet Meeting, Conclusions, Romania (2 February 1938)
81. Minutes by Sir O. Sargent on a conversation with the French Ambassador in London (Foreign Office, 3 February 1938)
82. Foreign Office telegram to Sir R. Hoare (4 February 1938)
83. Sir R. Hoare to the Foreign Office (Bucharest, 5 February 1938)
84. Sir R. Hoare to A. Eden (Bucharest, 7 February 1938)
85. Sir R. Hoare to the Foreign Office (Bucharest, 9 February 1938)
86. Sir R. Hoare to the Foreign Office (Bucharest, 11 February 1938)
87. Sir G. Knox to E. M. B. Ingram (Budapest, 12 February 1938)
88. Foreign Office telegram to Sir R. Hoare (16 February 1938)
89. Foreign Office Memorandum on political situation in Romania (21 February 1938)
90. Sir R. Hoare to the Foreign Office (Bucharest, 23 February 1938)
91. Sir R. Hoare to A. Eden (Bucharest, 24 Feburary 1938)
92. Sir G. Knox to Lord Halifax (Budapest, 27 February 1938)
93. Sir G. Knox to Lord Halifax (Budapest, 10 March 1938)
94. Sir R. Hoare to Lord Halifax (Bucharest, 11 March 1938)
95. British Legation in Budapest to the Foreign Office (Budapest, 9 April 1938)
96. A. D. F. Gascoigne to Lord Halifax (Budapest, 11 April 1938)
97. Sir R. Hoare to Lord Halifax (Bucharest, 14 April 1938)
98. Foreign Office Memorandum on political situation in Central and South Eastern Europe (21 April 1938)
99. Sir G. Knox to Lord Halifax (Budapest, 24 April 1938)

British Documents on the Danubian Area (1936-1939)

No.1

Sir R. Hoare to A. Eden
No.33 (R 670/282/37)

BUCHAREST, *January 29, 1936*

I have the honour to report that some partial elections which have been taking place in Roumania have been the cause of considerable discussion in the press owing to the violence of the electioneering methods adopted.
2. The National Christian Party seem to have been chiefly responsible for this violence. At an election at Suceava the "blue-shirts" of Monsieur Goga and Monsieur Cuza, who correspond more or less to the Nazi Storm Troopers in Germany, were said to have used revolvers and other arms in dealing with their political opponents. Whether it was due to this intimidation or not, the National Christian candidate was duly elected.
3. The National Christian party's blue-shirts caused considerable annoyance to the National Peasant Party, the victims of these tactics, who alone were putting up a candidate against the National Christians. In order to give their candidate a fair chance the National Peasants decided, in view of the next partial election, to create a body of so-called "Peasant Guards" who were to meet violence with violence. Disorderly scenes have already taken place between the rival private armies at a meeting in Turnu Severin, not far from Mehedinti, and considerable nervousness is being felt that the conflict between the National Christians and National Peasants may assume still more formidable dimensions if the present electioneering methods are not prohibited.

167

No.2,

Foreign Office Minute
The German Minority in Czechoslovakia
(R 971/971/12)

FOREIGN OFFICE, *February 20, 1936*
(Printed April 8, 1936)

(Excerpts)

The causes of Herr Henlein's appearance were . . . similar to those which brought Herr Hitler to the front in Germany. In Czechoslovakia the German minority had not merely suffered in the crisis, but suffered disproportionately; as in Germany, discontent with the old political parties was rife. They had failed in all their attempts to gain real equality of rights for the German minority. The situation was becoming more desperate every day. Herr Hitler's success in Germany was an inspiration; but direct imitation had already been proved impossible by the fate of the National Socialist party in Czechoslovakia. Herr Henlein was sure of the moral support of Germany. It has never yet been proved that he received direct material support from her.

The year 1934 clarified the issue. On the one side, Czech extremist fascism strengthened itself – as though the policy of the Government itself throughout 1936 had not been of a sufficiently fascist type – by formation of the Opposition "National Alliance". The alliance was Chauvinist. It was opposed to all concessions to minorities, and to the comparatively liberal policy of President Masaryk and M. Benes. At the other extreme, the Communists were closely supervised by the Government police. Their efforts to form a united front with the Socialists failed, but they received reinforcements in the shape of German refugees. . .

In May 1935 the Sudetendeutsche "Partei" won a greater success at the polls than any except the most optimistic had forecast. The 1,249,530 votes cast for Herr Henlein's party gave them forty-four seats in the Chamber of Deputies; the next largest party vote – 73,000 less – gave the Czechoslovak Agrarians forty-five, owing to some vagary of the Czechoslovak electoral system . . . The next largest party in the Chamber of Deputies was the Czechoslovak Social Democrats with thirty-eight mandates; the Communists won thirty. The three other German parties registered a total of 605,122 votes and twenty-two seats. Of these the German Social Democrats and Agrarians, with sixteen seats between them,

168

belong to the Government coalition, and have each a representative in the Cabinet. The German Christian Socialists with six seats belong to the Opposition. Thus Herr Henlein's party won 66 per cent of the total German vote or 15 per cent of all votes cast . . . This success was great enough to produce the fantastic situation of the Communists offering their help "against German imperialism" to a party (the Social Democrats) forming part of a Coalition including the conservative Agrarians. The opposition between the German Social Democrats and the Sudeten-deutsche party in Parliament has been very bitter. On the Coalition side difficulties have been great. The election left the old Coalition with a total of 149 seats out of 300 in place of the old majority. It was, therefore, necessary to negotiate with the Czechoslovak Traders' party (seventeen seats) and the dangerous Slovak Nationalist party of M. Hlinka (twenty-two seats). Both stood out for the most advantageous terms possible, and the negotiations with M. Hlinka finally failed. . .

No.3

Cabinet, Committee on Germany
German expansion, political and economic, in Central and
South-Eastern Europe
(Prepared by O. St. C. O'Malley, head of the Southern Department
in the Foreign Office)
(G. (36) 6)

FOREIGN OFFICE, *February 24th, 1936*

(Excerpts)

[Roumania]

Political opinion in Roumania seems to be fairly equally divided into two parties, one of which remains faithful to the alliance with France, and wishes to bolster this up by an alliance with the Soviet Union, while the other aims at a rapprochement with Germany . . . the opposition (M. Titulescu) to which King Carol himself is supposed to lean, was strong enough to prevent M. Titulescu concluding a pact with the Soviet Union last summer. . .

Roumanian organisations of a Fascist character have, from time to time, played a certain part. But Germany does not appear to have made any serious attempt to influence the course of events in Roumania, or to have any political ambitions there.

[Hungary]

. . . has no desire to see Germany dominate the Danube Basin, and this would incline her to lean towards Italy. On the other hand, she is conscious that Germany may prove, in the future, a far more powerful friend than Italy . . . The aim of German policy appears to be not to absorb Hungary politically, but to make her economically the complement of Germany and her partners.

170

No.4

Sir R. Hoare to A. Eden
No. 70 (R 1297/282/37)

BUCHAREST, *February 28, 1936*

(Excerpts)

[In the partial elections in Mehedinti and Hunedoara]... the election campaign was characterised by considerable violence.

In the early stages, when the National Christian "blue-shirts" were created, the Government complained that they had not enough police available to prevent disorders and Monsieur Tatarescu made a statement to the effect that no law existed under which the Government could act. However, the creation of the rival forces, the "Peasant Guards", apparently changed the situation. . .

[Mihalache told Hoare that] his party's success was due solely to the vigorous measures they had been forced to take in order to compel the Government to curb their opponents' terrorism. . .

It is known that the National Christians were being allowed to benefit by the Liberals' administrative organisation and received every support from the Government. In these circumstances, and especially in a country like Roumania where the Government in power disposes of considerable resources to influence elections, the success of the National Peasants must be regarded as a striking proof of the Party's strength and powers of resistance. No effort has been spared to split the Party, to which the King is notoriously hostile, and attempts are always being made to find or create a successor for the Liberals outside the ranks of the National Peasants, but recent events seem to indicate that the National Peasant Party enjoys real support in the country.

Sir R. Hoare to A. Eden
No. 90 (33/12/36)
(R 1637/282/37)

BUCHAREST, *March 13, 1936*

(Excerpts)

With reference to my telegram No.5 Saving of March 13th, regarding prolongation by the Roumanian Government of the existing state of siege and of the censorship . . . I have the honour to report that the debate on the subject which took place in the Chamber of Deputies on March 12th was marked by the unanimity of all opposition parties in attacking the Government's action.

2.   Amongst the arguments adduced by the opposition spokesmen were that . . . the Government were quite insincere in that they had protected the Iron Guard and other "right" extremists; that the state of siege was used merely to mask the Government's material and moral weakness; and that if the international situation was really as grave as had been painted, the dangers arising out of it could only be met by a free nation, not one enslaved by censorship and state of siege.

3.   The Minister of the Interior, Monsieur Inculetz, in replying to these criticisms declared that "conditions in Roumania were just as serious today as when the state of siege was instituted at the beginning of 1934." The opposition, he said, could not or would not understand that the Government had interpreted these measures in a purely preventive spirit. The state of siege did not affect those citizens whose consciences were clear; and as for the censorship, the press had been given the fullest liberty. Accusations in this respect put forward by the opposition were based on the vaguest generalities. It was true that 28 papers both of the Left and of the Right had been suspended; but only because their written programmes showed that they were dangerous to the fundamental institutions of the State.

4.   Continuing, Monsieur Inculetz denied vigorously that the Government had come to any agreements with parties of the Right, with whom they had nothing in common. On the contrary they had fought with all their power against that movement, from the moment when they had dissolved the Iron Guard; just as they had fought and would continue to fight against the "Left" movement. The Government by these measures had been able to give the country "two years of complete tranquillity and order"; and they would continue to take whatever measures they thought best to prevent annual revolutions. . .

No.6

Sir R. Hoare to A. Eden
(R 2175/282/37)

BUCHAREST, *April 4, 1936*

[Reports on the destroying by Iron Guard members of
monument of the former Prime Minister Duca]

(Excerpts)

3.   As far as I can ascertain the statement made by the Ministry of
Interior that the monument was untouched is a complete falsehood.

4.   My original informant, a Liberal Deputy, brother-in-law and devoted
follower and friend of Monsieur Duca, states categorically that the facts
are as reported in my telegram above-mentioned, and the "Times"
correspondent here is equally positive. The question of the spread of
extremist "right" doctrines amongst the youth, and particularly the
students, of the country is coming rapidly to the fore, and I propose to
revert to the matter in the near future.

5.   I happened to be seeing the Minister of Finance yesterday, and before
getting down to business I remarked that this incident at Sinaia was a
nasty matter. He agreed and said that he had heard that there had been a
collision between the students and a detachment of troops at 3 o'clock in
the morning. When I observed that the opponents of the Government
maintained that the mentality of the students was a result of the
encouragement of "Iron Guard" or Nazi propaganda by members of the
Government, he protested with a vehemence which would have been quite
unnecessary had he not known that the charge was fully justified.

No. 7

Sir G. Knox to A. Eden
No. 39 (R 2315/84/21)

BUDAPEST, *April 9, 1936*

[Reports on a conversation with M. Kánya, Minister for Foreign Affairs, and audience with Admiral Horthy.]

(Excerpts)

... [the Foreign Minister] said that Herr Hitler, by his outbursts (in connection with the denouncing of the Locarno Treaty), has burnt his boats; he could now see no hope of a reasonable compromise, and he wondered how long this universal madness in Germany could last. . .
2. M. de Kánya went on to tell me that before the war he had had the most lively fear of the pan-Slav menace . . . Now, however, he could no longer believe in its existence. Nor could he, by any stretch of his imagination, see Yugoslavia or Bulgaria coquetting with "ce sale Juif" Litvinov. The implication of this remark is clear, seeing that the eternal theme of German propaganda here is pan-Slav encirclement of Hungary. . .
8. [Admiral Horthy] spoke to me at some length on world politics with the transparent sincerity and simplicity which are so much his own, but, as always, under the influence of his three dominant obsessions, Jews, Communists, and peace treaties.

The first he described as a virus spreading through the world, and spoke of recent acts of sabotage in naval dockyards as the normal and natural consequence of the admission of Jewish refugees to England. . . He said that he was not Germanophile. . . He disliked the [German] people, their manners and their eternal refrain of "Deutsch" and "Deutschland", but he had nothing but admiration for Hitler's gesture in tearing up the treaty of Locarno which had been imposed on Germany. . .

Sir R. Hoare to A. Eden
No. 128 (R 2468/282/37)

BUCHAREST, *April 23, 1936*

I HAVE the honour to report that the last week has been marked by considerable party activity in Roumania.

2.   On the 16th April an interesting speech was delivered by M. Junian at a meeting of the Executive Committee of the Radical Peasant Party at Târgul Jiu. "The Roumanian Front," he said, "and the National Christian party propose to realise a nationalist policy by assuring the position of the Roumanian element in all places of responsibility. But have we not Roumanian elements in places of responsibility to-day? This is not at all the root of the trouble; indeed, in Goij* (the district in which he was speaking) we have neither Jewish bankers nor Jewish industrialists, yet suffering is greater than anywhere else", M. Junian went on to maintain that the real reason for this misery was that certain limited interests had been protected at the expense of the producing classes, namely, the peasants. The worst possible policy, particularly in the present state of Europe, was to encourage hostility between different elements in the same country on the ground of national or racial differences.

3.   On the 17th April a meeting of the local organisation of the National Peasants party was held at Câmpu-Lung, at which M. Mihalache delivered a bitter attack against the Government. He particularly censured the Government's encouragement of the disorderly elements of the Right wing, and M. Tatarescu's cowardice in sheltering himself behind the throne instead of sheltering the throne. M. Mihalache's speech closed with a warning that the party was prepared for immediate mobilisation, whether this would be to take over the government of the country or to overthrow the existing Government. They proposed to hold in May the great demonstration which had been arranged for the 14th November last year. . ., quite apart from whether or not the party was in power.

4.   On the 19th April a meeting of important Moldavian Liberals – Deputies, Prefects and Mayors – was held at Piatra Neamtz. The chief speaker was M. Victor Iamandi, who paid a warm tribute to Ion Duca, and proceeded to give a long historical account of the Liberals' dealings with the Iron Guard. The elements which had formed the Iron Guard, he said,

*Correctly: Gorj.

still existed, and it was a mistaken policy to allow them to form a new organisation under another name, viz.: "All for the Country"; it was essential to the safety of the State that no further encouragement should be given to the movements of the extreme Right, and this view was now fully endorsed by M. Tatarescu. Other speeches were in the same strain, and a resolution proposed by M. Manolescu Strunga was enthusiastically passed, by which the meeting agreed to urge the Government to take decisive steps to prevent false nationalism and anarchic disorders.

5.   The attitude of the Moldavian Liberals, which has been welcomed in most sections of the press, is of considerable interest. There has been a growing feeling of concern in the country regarding the excesses which the right wing have been allowed to commit, with the connivance or even the active support of the Government. This feeling, aroused by the Mehedinti elections. . ., has been brought to a head by the recent student disorders, and particularly by the desecration of the Duca monument at Sinaia. A rumour has even been current that M. Titulescu addressed a protest to the Government from Geneva, saying that their internal policy made it impossible for him to carry out the foreign policy which was essential for Roumania's interests. When I saw the Secretary-General of the Ministry for Foreign Affairs the other day I enquired about this rumour, and was informed that there was no truth in it whatever. Nevertheless, its existence is symptomatic, and is no doubt based on the principle of the wish being father to the thought.

7.   On the 23rd April, on the occasion of the unveiling of a memorial to Ion Duca at Ploeshti, M. Tatarescu, after a short laudatory address in M. Duca's honour, delivered a speech which had been eagerly awaited for some time as it was thought that he would take the opportunity to define the Government's attitude to the parties of the extreme Right. . . .

8.   After outlining the Government's forthcoming activities, M. Tatarescu turned to the present political situation. The Government's task was rendered difficult, he said, by a malicious campaign which represented them as supporting, directly or indirectly, the parties of the Right and tolerating or encouraging the excesses for which some of these parties had been responsible. The time had come to destroy this legend. Between the Government and the parties of the Right there was nothing in common; there was nothing but abysses, abysses of conception and abysses of method. The parties of the Right were characterized particularly by a nationalism expressed by aggressive means; the Government, however, could not forget that Roumania was a State which, although national, included in its population 25 per cent of minority elements, towards which a policy of conciliation must be adopted by guaranteeing them the

use of their language and their faith and free development within the framework of the laws.

9.   Criticisms that the Government had failed to repress the excesses of the Right were entirely without foundation. It had been amply proved in parliamentary debates that transgressions, whether of the Right or the Left, were suitably punished by the law. This campaign of bad faith was particularly marked in the discussions about the disorders at the recent Students' Congress of Targul-Mures. The congress was to have been a manifestation of real student elements, but it had degenerated into a political congress accompanied by a number of disorders transgressing the rules of university discipline and the penal laws. The only conclusions that could be drawn from this were that the youth of the country were riddled with politics, and that those who were responsible for their spiritual welfare must make every effort to change this unhappy state of affairs.

No.9

Sir R. Hoare to A. Eden
No. 134 (R 2434/282/37)

BUCHAREST, *April 27, 1936*

(Excerpts)

In continuation of my despatch No. 128 of April 23rd regarding the internal situation, I have the honour to report that Mr. Titulescu told me yesterday that he had spoke very emphatically to the King about the folly of encouraging Hitlerist tendencies. He personally was delighted to serve a Sovereign, but he would most certainly not serve a Führer or a Duce. He had bluntly asked the King to look at the position in Germany and Italy and to decide whether under a dictatorship a Sovereign could hope to play a part which King Carol plays to-day. Furthermore, it would be wise to reflect that if the extreme right received undue encouragement, the extreme left was most unlikely to remain passive.

2.   M. Titulescu went on to say that he had reminded the King of the circumstances in which he had agreed to accept the portfolio of Foreign Affairs. . . and he evidently wished me to understand that he had made it plain to the King that he did not cling to office but would resign rather than condone an internal policy which conflicted with Roumania's affiliations in Western Europe. The King appears to have taken this homily in excellent part and, if M. Titulescu is right, the crisis is over.

No.10

Sir G. Knox to A. Eden
No.51 (R 2476/2745/21)

BUDAPEST, *May 9, 1936*

(Excerpts)

5. Under the strong impression of this new military prestige* and looking with increasing anxiety to the internal situation of Austria and to the "Anschluss" looming nearer, Hungary has an added incentive to lean more towards Italy in that she feels that Rome can now lend, in case of need, solid military support and, in contrast to Germany, bodes no ultimate threat to her national independence. For the moment, however, her attention is fixed on England and on the steps which His Majesty's Government will now take to decide their future relations with Italy – and, with these perhaps, the fate of Europe. Sir Austen Chamberlain's speech in Parliament on the 6th May has aroused the keenest interest, and the hope is widely expressed that his warning will be heeded and that England will do nothing which would drive Italy into the arms of Germany.

6. Besides those who dread the strategic consequences of such a union – the absorption of Austria in a solid wedge across Europe, with Hungary and the other States to the eastward condemned to vassalage, and the Western Powers reduced to impotence by the establishment of Germany on the Mediterranean – there are many here who fear or hope that it would also bring the general triumph of dictatorship over democracy. It is felt that, so long as the two "Fascist" States to some extent balance one another, the smaller Powers are still free to go their own traditional way, but, if once they were united, the attraction of their political system would be irresistible. To observers here this force of attraction already appears very great. The thoughts of many were expressed by a member of the Government party who on the 8th May in the Lower House summed up the situation as the triumph of the great Fascist Powers, Italy and Germany, over the great capitalist democracies, England and France. It is perhaps not surprising that superficial minds, who, here as elsewhere, form the majority, and who discern nothing of the great principles of personal liberty and national strength that lie behind the free expression of opinion, contrast the ruthless efficiency of

* The conquest of Abyssinia.

179

dictatorships backed by the unanimity of a public perfectly schooled to applaud with what they see, or think they see, in the great democracies – in France a fog of petty squabbles of party ideology and in England a public opinion clamorous, idealistic and ill-informed, imposing its influence on the most delicate decisions of foreign policy. It would give much encouragement to those abroad who support the cause of free institutions and their concomitant, a policy of peace, if some of our greater organs of opinion, notably, the *Times*, could descend from the heights of conscious rectitude to which only the Anglo-Saxon can aspire and deal, in a manner comprehensible to others less happily endowed, with the brutal realities and dangers which have to be faced in this troubled world.

No.11

Sir R. Hoare to A. Eden
No.173 (R 3111/282/37)

BUCHAREST, *May 18, 1936*

(Excerpts)

At the parade on the 10th May the Soviet Minister, to whom I have never been more than courteous, was insistent that I should lunch with him tête-à-tête, and I did so yesterday.

He began by talking about the activities of the extreme Right, which he knew as a fact utterly disgusted some of the members of the Government and many of the "éminences grises" of the party. He had told them plainly that in his opinion the Soviet Government was happy to see Roumania on the Dniestr, but would be quite unwilling to see a dependency of Germany there within easy striking of Odessa and the industrial and agricultural wealth of the Ukraine. In the circumstances he was relieved at the removal of M. Titeano and had congratulated M. Inculetz on having got rid of his Under Secretary. I asked how M. Inculetz had received these congratulations, and he replied that M. Inculetz did not answer — "he never did". I further asked whether he had talked to M. Tatarescu about these matters, and the reply was in the negative, the manner in which it was given making it plain that to do so would, in M. Ostrovski's opinion, which I share, be a waste of time. M. Ostrovski throughout abstained from mentioning the King, but there was no doubt that he regarded the King as solely responsible for a situation which obviously preoccupied him.

M. Ostrovski went on to speak rather bitterly of the administration of justice as affording conclusive evidence of a prejudice in favour of extremism of the Right; the students responsible for the disgraceful episode at Sinaia station (see my telegram No. 41 of April 3rd last) had got off with a month, whereas it had been sufficient to dub Constantinescu-Jas* a Communist in order to secure a sentence of over two years, (my Savingram No. 8 of April 1st last). I interpolated that the charge was at least true, but even this M. Ostrovski denied, saying that Constantinescu, (sic) only offence was that he had publicly stated at Kishinev that it was wrong to kill Jews on purely racial grounds. . .

* Correctly: Iaşi

Sir G. Knox to A. Eden
No.57 (R 3115/84/21)

BUDAPEST, *May 23, 1936*

In paragraph 3 of my despatch No. 50 (41/18/36) of the 7th instant, I had the honour to refer to the development of German propaganda in Hungary. While it is naturally difficult to obtain any detailed information on this subject, the Opposition press is wont to publish from time to time reports of the activities of National Socialist agents in the more remote country districts and in those inhabitated by Swabians. Moreover it is a matter of common knowledge that the energies of the German News Agency, and of a number of permanent press correspondents which is out of all proportion to the "news-value" of Hungary, are directed far more to the dissemination than to the collection of news.

2.   Last week an incident occurred in the Chamber during the debates on the budget estimates, when a Socialist deputy affirmed that one of the Government's organs, the "Uj Magyarság", was receiving financial support from the German Government, and was actively engaged in furthering Nazi propaganda throughout the country. A photographic copy of a letter bearing the signature of a member of the Lower House connected with that newspaper and addressed to the German Telegraph Bureau, asking for financial support to enable them to contend against the powerful Jewish press, was produced in support of this accusation. Although it seems likely that the document on which the charge is based will be proved to be a forgery, it is nevertheless universally believed in Hungary that this paper is heavily subsidized by the German Government.

3.   This intensification of German propaganda does not pass without some reaction: both in Parliament and in the Opposition press attacks on the policy of the Hungarian Government towards Germany and National Socialism are becoming more frequent. . .

No.13

Letter from R. H. Hadow to O.St.C. O'Malley
(R 3417/32/12)

PRAGUE, *June 9, 1936*

(Excerpts)

. . .Jan Masaryk, thoroughly frightened by the growth in England of feeling against Czechoslovak treatment of the Sudetendeutsche, lectured me last week on the danger of exaggeration in a manner that made me feel he suspected this Legation . . . What he told me also showed that he sees the danger of the Czechoslovak Government's present policy but has failed to pour water into their wine and is even being accused of being "too easy going" not to say "pro-German"!

Both he and Benes said independently that the President "was doing all he could to win over the Sudetendeutsche". Although for the moment the extremist Czechs led by Machnik – if not also the "left wing" of his own party – hold the field, I give the President credit for seeing how blind are his extremist followers, in this bitter racial-struggle, to anything but immediate gains and party advantage.

Moreover Hodza and his Agrarians are undoubtedly sulking in their tents; their followers being afraid of "Russia's growing ascendency over Benes". Consequently I feel Benes would not altogether be sorry to be able to warn his hot-heads that Great Britain insisted upon fairer distribution of this country's loaves and fishes. . .

No.14

Sir J. Addison to A. Eden
No.162 (R 4743/32/12)

PRAGUE, *August 3, 1936*

(Excerpts)

7. . . . the treatment of minorities, which Dr. Benes had — despite article 14 of the Treaty of Saint-Germain — skilfully piloted out of reach of foreign inquisitiveness, threatens — at the very moment when Henlein's awkward Sudetendeutsche party looked like being "liquidated" — to become one of international concern; and the attitude of the Czech Agrarians towards the Government's anti-German and pan-Slav panacea for existing ills is one of considerable doubt.

8. Dr. Beran, leader and main director of the Czech Agrarian party, has, is true, hastened, in an interview given to the *Petit Journal,* to deny the rumour of Agrarian sympathy for Hitlerism. The Henlein movement, he declares, is "chance product. . .a conglomerate of divergent elements. . .a two-faced hydra" doomed to early disappearance and which the Agrarian party would fight as one man. But, despite these protestations, there persists an obstinate belief that the Agrarian party of Czechoslovakia wishes to come to terms with Germany if only it can find a way so to do without being pilloried by other Czech parties as a betrayer of Czech independence and power. . .

22. . . . The Jewish-owned section of the press has several times, almost tearfully, urged upon both sides the desirability of some such Czech-German accommodation, without which Jewry, in this land, sees itself doomed to early extinction. But Slav pride and apparently irradicable racial antagonisms seemingly stand between this "honourable accommodation" and its fulfilment. . .

(For the Minister signed R. H. Hadow)

No.15

Sir J. Addison to A. Eden
No.175 (R 5216/32/12)

PRAGUE, *August 25, 1936*

(Excerpts)

24. . . Czechoslovakia presents to the outside world the semblance of a bulwark of democracy, freedom and liberty, whereas it is in fact a "Polizeistaat" similar to other states where arbitrary rule prevails. . .

43. [Dr. Benes] is ruthless in his internal policy and suppresses political opponents by the methods which I have described. . .

44. . . Czechs are ultra-chauvinistic and there is no semblance of "decent democracy" as yet.

No.16

Sir R. Hoare to A. Eden
(R 5252/282/37)

BUCHAREST, *August 27, 1936*

(Excerpts)

[Reports on a speech by the National Peasant Party leader V. Madgearu who blamed Premier Tatarescu and the Minister of the Interior for encouraging Fascists and comments that] "Majority in Cabinet [are] insisting on repressive measures against the extremist organisation of the Right, whilst Tatarescu, the Minister of Interior and others assert that such measures are not warranted by the facts. . .

6. The presence of M. Maniu (at the head of the National Peasant Party), with his violent prejudices against the King, and of Dr. Lupu, whose orientation is considered to be too much towards the Left, acts as a stumbling block to real cohesion, whilst the elimination of these two leaders with their followers would split the party. These views were generally confirmed by the Director General of the Ministry for Foreign Affairs in my conversation with him shortly after my return from leave.

7. But although the National Peasant Party seem at the moment to be on the front page of the news, there are signs that the extremist organisations of the Right are indulging in their usual optimism. The swing to the left in France and the civil war in Spain have undoubtedly caused many to join their ranks. A growing number of Roumanians are beginning to look with disfavour and suspicion on the "Front Populaire", whilst it is no exaggeration to say that the vast majority of the Roumanians whom we meet prefer to see the nationalist or military elements in Spain victorious, rather than disorderly rabble of anarchists, communists, cut-throats and jail-birds who, they are told, represent the properly constituted Government of that country. For the moment, however, I doubt whether their immediate return to power is any more probable than it has been for the last 2 or 3 years, and I foresee no immediate political crisis, although prophecy is perhaps somewhat dangerous in this country."

No.17

Sir R. Hoare to A. Eden
No.270 (R 5293/282/37)

BUCHAREST, *September 3, 1936*

(Excerpts)

I HAVE had the honour to inform you by telegram of the bare facts of the dramatic resignation of the Tatarescu Government and of its reconstitution within the space of an hour or two with practically the same personnel but without the participation of M. Titulescu and his henchman, M. Savel Radulescu. I have also forwarded to you the explanation of this manoeuvre published by the President of the Council of Ministers. . .

2. I had an appointment at Constantsa with Dr. Costinescu, late Minister of Industry and Commerce and now once again Minister of Labour and Health, on the day after the news was published. His Excellency told me that there had been four factors in the situation: M. Inculetz, Minister of the Interior; M. Pop, Minister of Justice; Dr. Angelescu, Minister of Education, and M. Titulescu.

3. To take them in order — the King had informed the Government that definite and decisive steps must be taken to deal with the internal situation, which, though certainly not menacing, was gradually becoming a decided nuisance. M. Inculetz had believed that he could draw the claws of the extremists of the Right by entertaining personal relations with and affording financial help to the leaders, and that he could then gradually ferment discord amongst them. His "diplomatic" methods had evidently failed. That being so, he was clearly not the man to take a firm line and he had, therefore, been superseded; he would remain a member of the Cabinet and as a sop he had been appointed Vice-President of the Council, a designation which meant absolutely nothing at all. . .

No.18

Sir R. Hoare to A. Eden
No.277 (R 5485/282/37)

BUCHAREST, *September 10, 1936*

IN the new Government's programme, of which a copy was enclosed in my despatch No. 269 of the 31st August, considerable emphasis was laid on the intention to put a stop to the various movements symbolised by the wearing of different coloured shirts and to the indiscipline among students, and since then prominence has been given in the press to conferences between the Minister of the Interior and the prefects, and other advertisements of the fact that the Government is really in earnest.

2. I mentioned the matter to the Minister for Foreign Affairs yesterday and enquired whether it was really intended to act with firmness and impartiality. He replied with great seriousness that I should have no doubts on this score.

3. On the other hand, I am told that the general public believes that so far as the Nazi organisations are concerned no serious attempt will be made to put an end to their activities. It is difficult to avoid scepticism, especially on referring to my despatch No. 175 of the 21st May, in which I reported M. Savel Radulescu to have told me "that he was pretty sure that we should hear little for some time to come of student agitation now that the Government had shown a readiness to handle it with firmness".

4. In my view, it would be madness if the Roumanian Government hesitated any longer to put an end to Nazi organisations, the effect of which is to push the National Peasant movement to the acceptance of extreme socialist ideas, and will also lead to active counter-measures by the Soviet Government. I have, in fact, little doubt that my Soviet colleague's statement reported in the enclosure to my above-mentioned despatch of the 21st May — "the Soviet Government was happy to see Roumania on the Dniester, but would be quite unwilling to see a dependency of Germany there" — was a serious exposition of the views held in Moscow.

No. 19

Letter from Sir R. Hoare to O. St. C. O'Malley
(R 5519/282/37)

BUCHAREST, *September 11, 1936*

(Excerpts)

A despatch reaches you by this bag which shows that I have no great confidence in the Gov[ernmen]t's determination to deal firmly with the shirt movement. If they don't, I expect to see gradual deterioration – not a civil war as in Spain, but tension, occasional murders, beating of Jews and trouble generally, and then perhaps we might see King Carol setting up some sort of dictatorship, which might work but which might also lead to an attempt of revolution.

I propose to ask for an audience fairly soon and feel rather disposed to tell him that I hope he will encourage the Gov[ernmen]t to take a firm and impartial line with the shirts. I don't think Carol would like it but I am inclined to think it would be a good thing to do.

You might send me a short tel[egram] after reading my despatch, authorizing me, if you think fit, to speak to Carol if I think it desirable to do so.

(Minutes)

Rather a gloomy forecast of developments in Roumania.

It w[oul]d be very foolish of King Carol to make Roumania a dictatorship which w[oul]d inevitably become a satellite of Germany and therefore at loggerheads with Russia. Roumania would do much better to stick to her Little Entente policy and retain Russian goodwill. . .

N. J. A. Cheetham 18/9

No.20

Copy of a telegram from the Foreign Office to Sir R. Hoare
No. 102
(R 5485/282/37)

FOREIGN OFFICE, *September 21, 1936*

Your despatch No.277 (Sept.10th. Wearing of party shirts in Roumania. Possibility of royal dictatorship).

You may use your discretion in speaking to the King as suggested in your letter to Mr. O'Malley of Sept. 11th. But you should of course avoid the appearance of doing so officially or under instructions; and suitable opening will therefore either have to present itself or be tactfully created.

No. 21

Sir R. Hoare to A. Eden
No.291 (R 5760/282/37)

BUCHAREST, *September 26, 1936*

WITH reference to my despatches Nos. 270 and 277 of the 3rd and 10th September respectively, I have the honour to report that, in the course of conversation with the Prime Minister this morning, I endeavoured, without any great success, to obtain from him a detailed, as opposed to a general, explanation of the reasons for the expulsion of M. Titulescu from the Government. .,. .

5. This reference to internal politics led me to speak of the activities of the parties of the Right, and I received a glib assurance that M. Tatarescu had undressed the wearers of the green, blue and other coloured shirts. He was a little disconcerted when I told him that General Cantacuzène, the head of the Green Shirt movement, had received Mr. Reed, the Balkan correspondent of the Times, at headquarters almost within a stone's throw of the Legation, and had declaimed for about half an hour on the necessity of exterminating the 1 million Jews who are citizens of this country, and that during the interview young men dressed in his green shirts passed in and out of the building. I went on to say that I had an impression that extremism of the Right was gaining ground and that I thought there was a growing tendency to regard anti-Semitism and anti-communism as identical terms. To my mind this was dangerous from every point of view, the more so as it was to be expected that the Soviet Government would not remain passive spectators of such a development. I continued the attack by referring to the recent trial of five men who had taken part on the 5th July in a minor disturbance, in the course of which they had shouted: "Down with fascism — we demand the release of Anna Pauker!" and had burnt a few copies of the Universul. For this crime they had been sentenced for ten years' imprisonment. I had the impression that disorders, if they could be dubbed communistic, were treated with infinitely greater severity than if perpetrated by Right wing extremists. If I was right, this was an unhealthy state of affairs. M. Tatarescu admitted the truth of most of this indictment, which I, of course, uttered in an entirely friendly manner. Roumanians were anti-Communistic and anti-Semitic, and a breach of the peace by a patriotic, if unwise, young student was regarded by judges, as well as by the public, as a matter of minor importance; similar action by Communists was certainly treated with far greater severity. At the same time, he assured me that there was

191

not the slightest intention on his part of allowing the Right to get out of hand, nor was extremism in the national psychology. He had inherited the Iron Guard as a legacy from the National Peasants, who had tolerated its existence, and he had dissolved it when that inheritance cost his party the life of M. Duca. I interpolated that the Iron Guard had come to life again under the transparent guise of the "All for the Country." His Excellency then admitted that, while M. Inculetz was at the Ministry of the Interior, there had, perhaps, been a lack of wisdom or of firmness in dealing with these matters. They would now be handled with firmness, but also with tact, and under the admirable system of compulsory labour which he would introduce during the autumn session the patriotic fervour which was now finding a vent for its energies in undesirable channels would be disciplined and directed to the welfare of the country.

6.   With regard to the general situation in Europe, M. Tatarescu stated that geographical conditions made bolshevism a danger for Roumania, and any rare manifestations of that spirit must be severely repressed. At the same time, Germany constituted to-day the principal threat to peace. He therefore earnestly hoped that Italian co-operation would again become available and that peace in Europe would be assured by an unbroken line running from London, through Paris, Rome and the Balkans to Moscow.

*A. Eden reporting on conversation with
V. Antonescu, Rumanian Foreign Minister
(in Geneva, September 26th 1936)
(R 5754/1330/37)*

BRITISH DELEGATION,
GENEVA, *September 26, 1936*

(Excerpts)

[Antonescu explains the causes of Titulescu's dismissal.] "These considerations included difficult relations between M. Titulescu and the Prime Minister due to the former's insistence that the Government were not firm enough to deal with certain anti-Jewish elements. . . M. Antonescu repudiated any suggestion that Roumanian policy was leaning any more towards Germany. It was, however, unfortunately true that there were considerable anti-Jewish elements among the younger generation in Roumania. This was due to the fact that the majority of the population in the towns in Transylvania, Bessarabia and Bukovina was Jewish. Being the more intelligent and more hardworking of the population they were apt to absorb the better posts in the professional services. This caused resentment among Roumanians, which sentiment was no doubt supported by the German minority. . .These factors, however, had no effect whatever on Roumanian foreign policy, for his Government realised perfectly well that Germany was not going to come to Roumania's rescue if she were ever in difficulties with Hungary. Nor had Roumania any intention of going beyond strictly correct relations with Italy. The policy of the latter country was too uncertain and opportunist for Roumania to be able to have a close friendship with her, even if she wished to do so."

Remarks by McDermott

We know that in general the exclusion of M. Titulescu means a move to the Right in both home and foreign policy; but we cannot yet tell the extent of this move. . . (September 30th 1938).

No.23

R. H. Hadow to A. Eden
No.200 (R 5841/32/12)

PRAGUE, *September 28, 1936*

(Excerpts)

3.   On 26th September a leader of the Agrarian Party made a speech which. . . has been interpreted in Prague as a demand on the part of its Conservative wing for a revision of this country's foreign policy in the direction of more friendliness towards Germany and, above all, less cooperation with Soviet Russia. . .

4.   To the middle classes who rule Czechoslovakia at present the European issue is now one of National-Socialism versus Communism; and they are uncomfortably aware that there is little room for an independent bourgeois Czechoslovakia should either of these systems of Government prevail. Resignation rather than hope is therefore increasingly the order of the day in Prague; while Communist and National-Socialist propaganda strive for mastery among the lower classes Dr. Benes valiantly pursues his inscrutable but realist policies for the defence of his country.

No.24

Sir R. Hoare to A. Eden
No. 301 (33/87/36)
(R 6090/282/37)

BUCHAREST, *October 8, 1936*

(Excerpts)

I have the honour to report that the press has given considerable prominence to a recent speech by Marshal Averesco in which he spoke strongly against extremism, whether from the Right or from the Left, and laid special stress on the impropriety of identifying anti-communism with anti-semitism, which he declared to have nothing whatsoever in common. . . .

2. I mentioned this speech yesterday to M. Grigorcea, Roumanian Minister at Budapest and temporary Acting-Secretary-General at the Ministry of Foreign Affairs, and I asked him whether any special importance was to be attached to it. He replied that if I intended to ask whether the Marshal was likely to be called upon to form a Government in the near future, he thought such a development was improbable. . . It was deplorable, he said, that M. Maniu persisted in a campaign directed personally against the King, but the matter had become a complete obsession with him and nothing that his friends or colleagues could say had the slightest effect. I asked why they did not drop him and received the reply which I expected, that his influence in Transylvania was too great, as in the old days of the Austrian Empire M. Maniu had been preeminently the leader of the Roumanian national movement. The truth of the matter was that M. Maniu had for so many years conducted an active or passive campaign of opposition against Hungary that opposition of an entirely unconstructive character had become second nature to him. N. Grigorcea went on to say that he did not believe that in any circumstances the King would call the extreme Right to office, and he made the interesting suggestion that if King Carol had at times appeared to encourage the leaders of the Right, it might well have been in the hope of thereby exerting an indirect pressure on the leaders of the National Peasant Party and bringing them to a more tractable frame of mind.

3. As the conversation had turned in this direction, I said that stories were frequently current to the effect that German money was poured into the pockets of the leaders of the Right extremists. I was quite prepared to

believe that German money was spent in maintaining the "Deutschtum" of the Saxon citizens of this country, but I found it difficult to believe that MM. Vaida, Cuza, Goga, General Cantacuzène etc. accepted German subsidies in support of their movements. M. Grigorcea replied that he felt sure that neither M. Vaida nor General Cantacuzène would touch such subsidies in any shape or form. He was not so certain about the other two gentlemen I had mentioned, but even in their case any subventions they might receive would be by very indirect means.

No.25

Sir R. Hoare to A. Eden
No. 314 (33/92/36)
(R 6370/282/37)

BUCHAREST, *October 17, 1936*

(Excerpts)

I have the honour to report that the 20th anniversary of M. Stelian Popescu's directorship of the "Universul", possibly the most important Bucharest newspaper, has recently been celebrated by many congratulations of which wearisome pages are published daily in his paper, and finally by a grandiose demonstration held in his honour at Bucharest on October 11th. As M. Popescu is also founder and president of the anti-Revisionist League and as the "Universul" holds highly anti-Semitic views, the demonstration had certain political aspects.

2.   The proceedings were opened by a religious service held by the Patriarch, who after the service delivered a short complimentary address. He was followed by Professor Octavian Goga, one of the leaders of the National Christian Party, who complimented M. Popescu fulsomely not only for his defence of the country's frontiers by means of the anti-Revisionist League, but also for his action in checking the tide of "parasites who had swarmed into the country from Lemberg and other places, shedding their Jewish names and adopting the ancient names of Roumania". Innumerable speeches followed from the representatives of various organisations: military, journalistic, secondary schools, Orthodox Roumanian Women, school teachers and pupils, Orthodox clergy, public functionaries, cultural societies and many others. ,. .

5.   . . . . it appears that M. Popescu enjoys support in high quarters as he has been presented by his Sovereign with the Order of Premilitary Preparation, First Class.

6.   I found myself sitting next to M. Madgearu, the Secretary General of the National Peasant Party, at a club luncheon a day or two later, and I asked him whether a foreign journalist would have been justified, in reporting these proceedings, if he had headed his article: "Patriarchal Benediction of the Anti-Semitic Movement in Roumania". M. Madgearu replied that such a caption would have been justified by the bald facts, but essentially it would have been misleading, though it was true that anti-semitism was making headway among the Orthodox clergy. In his view, the demonstration was really of no great importance; it had had two

197

purposes, the first being M. Stelian Popescu's desire for advertisement and for the restoration of his prestige which had suffered during his paper's controversy with the "Dimineatza" in the summer. . . this purpose had no doubt been achieved. The second was that of the various leaders of the parties of the Right who had wished to show that there was an essential unity of purpose between them. . . .

No.26

*Memorandum by F. Ashton-Gwatkin
on conversation with Mr. Béla Imrédy,
Governor of the Hungarian National Bank
(R 6766/15/21)*

FOREIGN OFFICE, *November 7, 1936*

(Excerpts)

There is no danger. . . M. Imrédy said, of Hungary slipping into the
position of economic dependence upon Germany, in which some other
South European countries had recently found themselves. He believed,
however, that this surrender to Germany was a passing and temporary
phase, and that the countries concerned had already realised the danger of
it and were taking counter-measures, i.e. by limiting exports to
Germany. . .
   [Imrédy] was inclined to think that there was something in Hitler's
claim to be a bulwark against communism in Europe. He knew that in
England we are not disposed to take this danger very seriously; but in
Hungary they had personal experience of it and were inclined to feel some
gratitude to Hitler on this account.

No. 27

C. M. Bentinck to A. Eden
No. 224 (R 6716/70/12)

PRAGUE, *November 7, 1936*

(Excerpts)

10. For, on the very day on which the Prague communiqué already mentioned was being prepared, the Czechoslovak Agrarian party, which formed the present Coalition Government, has more members in the Cabinet and in Parliament than any other party, and has hitherto had its own way in most internal matters, came out – in the Committee on Foreign Relations – with demands for—

(1) An end to the recent secrecy and narrow control (by Dr. Benes) of foreign policy.

(2) Formation of a bloc of peace-loving States from the Baltic to the Black Sea.

(3) Friendlier relations with Poland.

(4) Strict neutrality in the event of a war between Germany and Soviet Russia.

(5) Cessation of attacks in Czechoslovakia upon the parties opposed to "a dictatorship of the proletariat" and of insinuations that such parties (and particularly the Agrarian party itself) must be "friendly to Hitlerian ideology".

(6) Repression of the proletarian ideas which had permeated even the Social Democratic party (which is part of the Coalition and supports Dr. Benes).

(7) Cessation of attempts to form a "Popular Front" in Czechoslovakia and thus to drive the Agrarian party out of the Coalition.

11. By attacking his henchman, Dr. Krofta, the Agrarian party thus led a direct attack upon Dr. Benes's recent foreign policy; including in their demands items which warned the President clearly enough that their followers in the countryside were against his alleged toleration, or encouragement, of a "proletarian ideology" akin to that of Moscow.

12. As has often been the case in Czechoslovakia, this high-principled attack has petered out – so far as the principals are concerned – under a gentle rain of somewhat materialistic concessions to Agrarian demands for a larger share of the profits of various State monopolies; for shelving of

some inconvenient plans for a fresh land reform; and for other pickings from the common flesh-pot. But in the minds of the rank and file of middle-class village and country supporters of the Coalition persists an uneasy fear of Moscow which has undoubtedly been instrumental in giving Dr. Benes the first rebuff to his foreign and domestic policy that observers in Prague can call to memory.

13.   Of the Soviet reaction to this attack I have no precise information; but it is clear that in future Dr. Benes will have to be more careful than of late in his relations with Moscow, and already he has informed me... of his intention to steer "a middle course between fascism and communism".

14.   As regards fascism I can only record – for what it is worth – a persistent rumour that the Agrarian party is now strengthening existing ties between itself and Italy. Of its mild flirtations with Germany you have been informed in previous despatches, and to-day there are many in Prague who believe that Rome will soon have a common policy with Berlin in the Danube Basin. Conscious of the weakness of their position should this anti-Soviet block of Fascist States (including in their minds both Austria and Hungary) come into being, the more far-sighted of the Agrarians no doubt wish to keep one foot in this camp. Meantime, as will be remembered from this Legation's despatches on Dr. Hodza's Danube plan, the latter is trying to extract some material benefit from inclusion of the Rome Protocol countries in his economic Danube Basin schemes.

No.28

Sir R. Hoare to A. Eden
No. 342 (33/94/36)
(R 7134/282/37)

BUCHAREST, *November 9, 1936*

(Excerpts)

I have the honour to report that a vast demonstration was held yesterday in Bucharest by the National Christian Party. It is believed that about 100,000 peasants came from all parts of the country to attend the demonstration, and the march past before M. Goga and M. Cuza, who greeted their supporters with the Hitler salute, lasted about 6 hours. The proceedings were entirely orderly and although one or two demonstrators were arrested for leaving the permitted lines of the march, no disturbances whatever took place. The leaders were all clad in blue shirts, and both they and a large number of their following wore swastika arm-bands or badges.

2.   After the march-past the two leaders of the Party addressed their enormous audience in the Velodrom. After a warm tribute to M. Cuza, M. Goga said a few words about the internal policy of the Party, which practically boiled down to: "Down with the Jews". ("The Jewish leprosy", he said, "spreads like eczema over the whole country".) He then turned to foreign politics. Public opinion, he said, in Roumania was deeply pained by the words spoken recently by Mussolini regarding "mutilated Hungary". He had every respect for the personality of the Duce whom he considered a great figure in contemporary history, but his conception of Hungary was profoundly mistaken. It was not a case of injustice having been done to Hungary but of justice having been done to Roumania. . . .

No.29

Annual Report, 1936,
Roumania.
Sir R. Hoare to A. Eden
No. 61 (R 1159/1159/37)

BUCHAREST, *February 12, 1937*

(Excerpts)

128.   . . . While the hopes of the National Peasants decreased, those of the Right parties, the National Christian party of M. Goga and M. Cuza and the Roumanian Front of M. Vaida-Voevod, grew sensibly greater. It was generally assumed that the King favoured a political orientation more towards the Right, and the Liberal Government, though denying that they were doing so, undoubtedly used their influence to discriminate against the National Peasants and in favour of the Right whenever occasion offered. Nevertheless, although the Right parties certainly increased their influence, they were unable to attain unity among themselves. . .

137.   In January a partial election took place at Suceava, and during the campaign the National Christian party had the country patrolled by armed bands of "blueshirts", who created a considerable disorder, but succeeded in winning the election. . . (In partial elections at Mehedinti and Hunedoara) the National Peasants won both elections, in spite of the fact that the Government had allowed the National Christian party to make use of the Liberals' organisation for election purposes. . .

139.   At the beginning of April popular indignation was aroused by the news that a monument to Ion Duca in Sinaia station had been desecrated by a party of extremist students. . . All mention of the occurrence was suppressed by the censor. . . Such was the storm of criticism aroused that M. Tatarescu decided to dismiss M. Titeanu, Under-Secretary of State for the Interior. . . and in May the students arrested at Sinaia were condemned by the Brasov court-martial. . . These measures did something to lessen public disapproval, but the weakness of the authorities in dealing with the Iron Guard could not be disguised, especially when reports began to circulate that the leader of the Students' Union. . . was presented by the King with 100,000 lei, and that at the (Tg.Mures) congress the extremist students had formed themselves into "death squads" for the purpose of eliminating undesirable individuals such as Mme. Lupescu and Mm. Mihalache, Lupu and Maniu. . .

140.   Nervousness at the failure of the authorities to deal effectively with the extremism of the Right was illustrated by a meeting of important Moldavian Liberals. . .when. . .M. Iamandi declared that it was a mistake to allow the Iron Guard's activity to continue. . . he added that the Prime Minister now fully realised that it was essential for the safety of the State that no further encouragement should be given to the movements of the extreme Right. . .M. Titulescu informed His Majesty's Minister (in April) that he had spoken emphatically to the King about the dangers of encouraging Hitlerist tendencies in Roumania, and had warned His Majesty that undue favouring of the Right would lead to unrest on the Left. . .

143.   . . .on the 5th November, Corneliu Codreanu, the Iron Guard leader, addressed a memorandum to the "King, Politicians and Country", in which he demanded that all who conducted Roumania's foreign policy or expressed opinions about it, not excluding the King and the Royal family, should answer for the line they adopted with their heads. The memorandum went on to state that the Iron Guard would shoot anyone who should force them to side with bolshevism against those who defended Christian civilisation, condemned the insults Roumania had offered Italy and the policy of M. Titulescu in this respect, and expressed unbounded horror of judaism and freemasonry. . .

144.   Certain concessions to public opinion were, nevertheless, made by the authorities in dealing with extreme activities. . .His Majesty's Minister was assured on several occasions by M. Tatarescu, by the Minister for Foreign Affairs and by responsible officials that it was the firm intention of the Government to put an end to all political excesses and to stop the wearing of party shirts. Nevertheless, . . . a vast demonstration organised in Bucharest by the National Christian party was distinguished by the blue shirts and swastikas of its leaders. . .It is, therefore, not surprising that the general public are not very certain how sincere these intentions are, especially as the King's heart, though perhaps not his head, inclines him towards Fascist ideas. . .

150.   The only minority which had real cause for complaint in 1936 was that of the Jews. No particularly flagrant cases of unjust treatment were brought to the public notice. . . but there is no doubt that anti-Semitic feeling was on the increase in Roumania, and all sorts of petty discriminations were practised against the Jews. . . Nearly all prominent officials and politicians (with the exception, of course, of the Right Wing parties) were prepared to admit privately the unfortunate effects of anti-semitism, but professed themselves unable, public opinion being what it was, to take any active measure. . .

151.   . . . Anti-semitism was on the increase owing to the rise of imitators

of Hitler, and "patriotic" Roumanian students were being led to believe that Jewish competition ought, in their own interest and in that of their country, to be circumscribed. This led to constant agitation for proportional ethnic admission to the universities and sporadic beatings of Jews.

152. Roumania being a country which lives in constant anxiety of the Soviet Russia on her border, the growing tendency to treat the term "Jew" as synonymous with "Communist" has done much to increase anti-semitism. Incidents such as the *Universul-Dimineata* dispute. . . and all trials of Communists in 1936 were responsible for savage verbal attacks against the Jews and occasionally for actual physical assaults.

Telegram from Ch. Bentinck to the Foreign Office
No.1. (Saving)
(R 133/133/12)

PRAGUE, *January 5, 1937*

(Excerpts)

In my opinion the only chance of security for this country lives in an agreement with Germany. No such agreement will be possible until situation of German minorities has undergone radical improvement. Any extension of agreement between this country and Soviet Union will only antagonise Germany still further and further endanger European situation. In the event of Germany being provoked to action, neither Soviet Union nor Little Entente would be able to save Czechoslovakia.

I venture to deprecate "a formula of reassuring nature". The sooner the disagreeable and dangerous facts are realised, squarely faced and a remedy honestly sought, the better for all concerned.

Minutes

[Benes] is also actuated by the knowledge that when Germans, Slovaks, Poles, Ruthenes and Hungarians are lumped together the Czech element is actually the minority in the Czechoslovak state, and that concessions to the Sudetic Germans would inevitably entail concessions to the other non-Czech elements which would place the continued existence of the Republic itself in grave danger.

O'MALLEY, January 8, 1937

Memorandum on Czechoslovakia
by R. H. Hadow
No.23 (R 839/188/12)

PRAGUE, *February 2, 1937*

(Excerpts)

In these circumstances it is hardly surprising that Constitutional Government should, to a considerable extent, have been replaced in 1936 by measures of National preparedness or Defence. . .which may be said to invalidate Czechoslovakia's claim to be "A democratic Island in a sea of Authoritarianism". For in the Sudetendeutsche and other Minority districts personal liberty, the right of the courts, conditions of employment, liberty of movement or domicile and other Constitutional rights of the Czechoslovak citizens are to be nullified by such enactments as to justify the statement that these areas are now almost wholly under a new military and police rule, without adequate redress to those who fall foul of local Czech autocracy.

Of this change democratic countries could not but take note. . .

It is. . .permissible to ask whether he [Benes] would not manage to trim his sails to the prevailing wind if told. . .that continuance of the moral support of Great Britain for Czechoslovakia – which in this Government's eyes is a paramount factor in ensuring the Republic's continued existence – depends upon concrete proof that the Czechoslovak Government will begin forthwith to sweep away all racial, linguistic, or political discrimination between one race of Czechoslovak citizens and another and to restore to the Minorities Constitutional liberties such as alone would justify Czechoslovakia's claim to be a democracy. . .

No.32

Telegram from Sir Reginald Hoare to the Foreign Office
No.14 (R 1246/162/37)

BUCHAREST, *February 22, 1937*

(Excerpts)

The King was. . .much incensed at Manifesto* and it has been said that but for insistent representations from his Ministers he would have taken severe measures. It is therefore possible that recent demonstration** having decided him to deal with Iron Guard he may think complication resulting from "affront to national dignity" would facilitate his task. My belief is that action against Iron Guard is overdue and that unless it is taken this organization will soon be serious menace. From internal aspect it may be good tactics, if action is really about to be taken, to be unyielding over diplomatic incident and endeavour to convince public opinion that Iron Guard has thriven on foreign support. I do not see that practical results of diplomatic conflict*** with Germany and Italy would be very serious and I therefore propose simply to watch events.

*Manifesto of the Iron Guard
**Mass demonstrations in connection with the burial of Moța and Marin in Bucharest
***Funeral of Moța and Marin were attended by the Ministers of Germany and Italy in Bucharest

No. 33

Sir R. Hoare to A. Eden
No. 92 (12/20/37)
(R 1484/162/37)

BUCHAREST, *February 24, 1937*

(Excerpts)

. . . . there have been somewhat dramatic developments in connection with the "Iron Guard" movement (as a less cumbrous term, I propose to use it in future instead of the alias, "all for the country".)

2.   Some weeks ago, a good deal of publicity was given to the fact that seven of these young men had left for Spain to fight (alongside the Germans) for Christianity. Two of them were killed and their coffins have recently been escorted home via Germany by their companions. It is said that the funeral party was received at Berlin with special honours, which were also accorded throughout the passage through Roumania to Bucharest, where it arrived on February 11th. The two coffins were then escorted in solemn procession through the town by large numbers of adherents of the Iron Guard movement, many of whom had come from the country in special trains alleged to have been furnished by the Government at greatly reduced rates. The actual funeral took place on February 13th and was attended by the Patriarch and other high dignitaries of the Church. On both occasions the organisation of the traffic was controlled by about 2,000 Iron Guardists in their green shirt uniform, and I am assured that they performed their task with great efficiency. The police were conspicuous by their entire absence.

3.   By appearing in uniform the Iron Guard of course disobeyed Government orders, but this they do regularly. . . and it was therefore simply a matter of degree, and I imagine that nothing more would have been heard of the matter had the Italian and German Ministers, the newly arrived Portuguese Chargé d'Affaires. . . and the ex-Spanish Minister. . . not attended the funeral ceremony.

4.   In the result, the Government felt bound to take this participation of foreign diplomatic representatives in an internal political demonstration with the utmost seriousness, and in reply to a question which he answered in his capacity as Acting Minister for Foreign Affairs. . . the President of the Council appears to have committed himself to insisting on the removal of the offenders. . .

5.   Debates followed in both the Chamber and the Senate; they were of no special interest, save for Professor Iorga's speech, the National Liberals and National Peasants maintaining that my colleagues had clearly been guilty of a grave indiscretion in participating in a political demonstration, while supporters of the extreme Right asserted that in view of the attitude of the Government up to and on the day of the funeral there was no reason to regard the presence of diplomats at that ceremony as objectionable.

6.   Professor Iorga's speech met with universal approval. He had already won the sympathy of the house by taking the wind out of the sails of M. Manoilescu (of the extreme Right) who had embarked on a tirade about M. Seba's peccant book. He declared his abhorrence of Bolshevism as being destructive of civilization and of belief in God, and, as a free man who could not live in an atmosphere where thought was suffocated, he was opposed to any sort of dictatorship. To an old man who had taken part in the education of many successive generations, nothing made a stronger appeal than an act of courage and of self-sacrifice, and he felt profound admiration and affection for these young men who had died fighting against communism. But death should not be treated as a public spectacle and the commemoration of the dead should not be used by interested parties as an incitement to civil war. As for the international aspect of the matter, Roumania was neutral in the Spanish civil war and persons accredited to the Roumanian Government should respect that neutrality.

7.   I understand that neither the Italians nor the Germans are prepared to express disapproval of the action of their Ministers, who have defended their action by asserting that their presence at the service in church and their abstention from any participation in the actual procession render the charge of interference in internal politics baseless. Apparently my German colleague, who is perhaps not a very ardent Nazi, was in a position of some difficulty as his Counsellor, supported by the leader of the Nazis here, wished him to attend the proceedings accompanied by his whole staff and also wished a delegation of Germans to take a formal part in Nazi uniform. . .

10.   The Iron Guard is becoming a serious menace and must therefore be dealt with. [Tatarescu] may well have decided that the easiest way to prick the bubble of its growing popularity is to appeal to national susceptibilities and brand it as an organization dependent on and guided by foreign influences. . .

12.   It is not easy to decide how formidable a task the Government have undertaken; Dr. Costinesco, with whom I had a talk yesterday, appeared perfectly confident that though there is a good deal of sympathy in

society for the movement it has little hold on the masses of the population and can easily be suppressed. Other people, however, regard it as firmly established in parts of Roumania such as the Bucovina and. . . assert that it is fear for their individual safety that has deterred the Government from acting, and suggest that fear will continue to inform their conduct.

13. It is easy in a country which produces a new rumour every half hour to fall into exaggeration, but I have a fear that, if the Government draw back now, we are at the beginning of a Nazi movement which will gather an irresistible impetus, driven by a fanatical spirit similar to that which so frequently produces a tragedy in Japan.

A. D. E. Gascoigne to A. Eden
No. 24(36/7/37)
(R 1533/987/21)

BUDAPEST, *February 26, 1937*

(Excerpts)

I have the honour to refer to the letter which the Southern Department of the Foreign Office addressed to the Chancery of His Majesty's Legation. . ., concerning an article published by the "Pravda" of Moscow on the 2nd instant regarding anti-Soviet tendencies in Hungary.

2.   As a result of the verbal enquiries which I have made of Baron Bessenyey, the acting Political Director of the Hungarian Ministry for Foreign Affairs, I have the honour to report as follows:

Baron Bessenyey has assured me that no agreement of the kind mentioned by the "Pravda" had been concluded between Dr. Kozma, the Hungarian Minister of the Interior, and Dr. Frick, or any other German authority. He stated, however, that Dr. Kozma had, during his recent visit to Berlin, made some verbal representations to Dr. Frick on the question of national-socialist propaganda in Hungary. As regards this propaganda, Baron Bessenyey was good enough to explain to me how matters stood at the present time.

3.   National-socialist propaganda in Hungary, he said, was known to be conducted through two different channels, which were, (a) certain members of the German Colony and German minority, and (b) German students, and particularly women students, who paid visits to Hungary for periods of varying lengths. The Hungarian Government were not particularly disturbed by this propaganda, as they did not believe that the Magyar mentality and temperament provided fertile soil for the planting of such a creed — the Hungarian was far too fond of his individual liberty to become enamoured with the "Prussian" principles of national-socialism — but they felt that it was desirable that the German Government's attention should be directed, "verbally and informally", to it, and Dr. Kozma's journey to Berlin provided a suitable opporunity for this to be done.

4.   With regard to Dr. Frick's reaction to Dr. Kozma's verbal representations, Baron Bessenyey further informed me that, while not, of course, admitting that any propaganda had in fact been made in Hungary,

Dr. Frick had promised to do what was possible to cause a control to be exercised over German male and female students wishing to proceed to this country. Thus, Dr. Frick had undertaken to see that students should be warned against permitting their natural feelings of admiration for the Nazi régime to become too effervescent during their stay on Hungarian soil. Dr. Kozma had been fairly satisfied with the attitude of accommodation displayed by Dr. Frick in this matter, but of course it was realized that only time would show whether the Germans really meant to desist from their endeavours to spread their gospel in Hungary. . .

6. . . . The fact, therefore, that Dr. Kozma found it necessary to make even these verbal representations at Berlin seems to show that the Hungarian Government are more perturbed regarding the national-socialist activities in this country than was admitted to me by Baron Bessenyey.

No.35

Sir G. Knox to A. Eden
No.28(R 1827/844/21)

BUDAPEST, *March 11, 1937*

(Excerpts)

As reported in my telegram No. 7 of March 8, there began early this month to circulate in Budapest rumours of an impending *coup d'état* by elements of the extreme Right. These generally took the form that a plot was afoot among the more advanced members of the Government Party, who had suffered something of an eclipse with the death of General Gombos, to march on Budapest under the leadership of M. Marton and M. Mecser and to seize power with the help of the "Crossed-Arrow" movement and other groups of a definitely Nazi character. Rumour added that the plot was being encouraged and financed from Germany. From March 5 onwards veiled allusions to the proposed *coup d'état* were made in a large part of the Hungarian press and attention was drawn to the fact that as soon as the public had begun to get wind of the affair, Herr von Mackensen, the German Minister, and Baron Hahn, the head of the "Deutsches Nachrichten Buro" had suddenly left Budapest. There was, in fact, nothing abnormal about Herr von Mackensen's movements who, before these rumours began to circulate, had arranged to take three weeks' leave in Greece. . .

2.   As the rumours of a plot grew in strength M. Eckhardt, leader of the Small Farmers' Party, took it upon himself on March 6 to warn the Prime Minister that strong measures must be taken to maintain order. M. Daranyi thereupon sought an audience of the Regent and afterwards conferred with the Ministers of War and Industry, after which the press was informed that the Government had become aware of certain rumours, which had no foundation and that the necessary measures had been taken for the maintenance of public order. This statement was followed on March 9, by the communiqué declaring that "The Government had investigated the rumours which had disturbed public opinion during the previous week, and it had been established that nothing had happened in Hungary which endangered public order, the internal safety of the country or the economic life of the country. There had been no kind of armed organisation and no attempt had been made which might be classed as treason. The Public Prosecutor had received instructions from the

Minister of Justice to take the most severe action against any person or persons held responsible for using slogans or spreading rumours which would endanger peace and the economic life of the country."

4. It is impossible to estimate what element of fact may have lain behind this spate of rumours, but it is still widely believed here that the "Marton group" were at least playing with the idea of a theatrical coup. This same group, which includes the closest associates of the late Prime Minister, had actively intrigued against M. Daranyi when he formed his Government in October. . . Foiled on this occasion, they had since turned their attention to agitation in the provinces by exploiting, hand in hand with more avowedly Nazi elements, the economic distress of the agricultural labourer, and it is more than probable that there has been much wild talk in their inner councils.

5. The opportunity thus offered was eagerly seized upon by a very large part of Hungarian opinion to inveigh against the German propaganda which is so actively deployed in this country. That the Government delayed so long in putting an end to this campaign is, to my mind, sufficiently explained by the desire to allow Germany to appreciate how strongly Hungarian public opinion feels on the matter – a method more likely to be effective than any official protest from a small State situated towards Germany as Hungary is. The answer given to the Military Attaché to this Legation by the Honvéd Ministry to an enquiry whether there was anything behind the public rumours then current would seem to show that the Prime Minister's disclaimer of any knowledge of attempts by a foreign Power to exercise an influence on Hungarian internal politics, was no more than a necessary, if belated, gesture of appeasement. Major Benfield was informed by Colonel Juhasz that the reports of an attempted *putsch* by extreme National Socialist elements were a gross exaggeration. Nothing even remotely resembling such a danger had ever existed. It was a fact that National Socialist influences had been at work throughout Hungary. They were of German origin and the German Legation was directly implicated. Ever since the death of General Gömbös Hitlerism had lost ground among the better classes and it was in order to make good this lost ground that the importers of Hitlerism had turned to the lower orders in Hungary as the most promising field for their activities. Sixty per cent of the present day followers of Hungarian Hitlerism were the people who, after the war, had followed Bela Kuhn. (sic!) The Government had first been made aware of these German activities by the Jews who, of course, greatly exaggerated the real situation. At the same time the Government had no illusions about the danger of this kind of propaganda. They realised that the setting up of a Hitler State in Hungary would only be the first step towards the eventual incorporation of this country in the Reich.

From the purely military point of view, Hungary's policy was towards a close co-operation with the military might of Germany. In fact, there already existed the closest liaison, but that did not mean that Hungary had bound herself body and soul to Germany. She was determined to maintain her own independence and she would not brook any interference in that respect. Finally, not a single officer or man of the Honvéd had been implicated in this affair.

6.   German propaganda in Hungary, to which attention has been drawn in reports from this Legation during the past year, has followed a systematic and effective line. It first gained a firm footing by a strongly anti-Czech tone and a fanciful development of the menace to Hungary arising from the Russo-Czech agreement, it then passed to the theme – ever welcome in Hungary – of the Communist danger and has now turned in a more definitely Nazi strain to the exploitation, with the usual catch-words, of the unsatisfactory conditions of labour both agricultural and industrial, and of the poor prospects for educated Hungarian youth, by the intensification of an already indigenous anti-semitism. Simultaneously pan-German propaganda is conducted, largely by German students and tourists, among the Swabian population and the budding Nazi parties such as the "Crossed-Arrows" are carefully wet-nursed from Germany. It was recently stated in this connection, in a case in the Hungarian Courts, by a high official of this party that all the material for the programme of the party came from Germany.

7.   This propaganda has inevitably had some effect, and much of the ground lends itself to it. The recent strike in the coal mines at Pécs, ... has shown how poor is the lot of the industrial worker in this country. That of the agricultural labourer is in many cases still worse, while before the majority of the students who pass through the universities, lies little prospect of an adequate career. The Hungarian Government in recent years have done much to improve the financial and economic situation of the country, but on the social side very little progress has been made. That the politicians of the country are growing conscious of these shortcomings was shown in a remarkable debate in Parliament on the subject of the Pécs strike in which members of all parties spoke emphatically in favour of the workmen. This unanimity might perhaps have been lacking had not the company owning the mines been a foreign one, but in any event this new manifestation of interest in the condition of the working classes is a healthy symptom as it is clearly in social reform that the best defence against extreme doctrines lies. . . .

Minutes

The responsibility of Berlin for this coup seems to have been indirect.

That is was nevertheless a real one is attested by the fright it is alleged to have given to Signor Mussolini and the nervousness of the Gov[ernmen]t at Vienna. . .

Particularly significant is this sentence in the latter part of para 5 that "Sixty per cent of the present day followers of Hungarian Hitlerism were the people, who after the war, had followed Bela Kuhn" (sic!)

C. BRAMWELL, 19/3

Sir R. Hoare to A. Eden
No. 141 (12/30/37)
(R 2220/162/37)

BUCHAREST, *March 26, 1937*

I have the honour to transmit herewith a summary, prepared by Mr. Coulson, of a book entitled "For the Legionaries" produced last year by M. Codreanu, the leader of the Iron Guard Movement.

2. ... It is noteworthy that unlike the Nazis M. Codreanu bases his anti-semitism not on ethnic prejudice but on the theory that the Jews have stolen land which is the inalienable property of the original inhabitants of a country. Apart from anti-semitism the religious fervour enjoined by M. Codreanu is the most striking feature of the book, and he shows that before embarking on any enterprise his adherents are at pains to obtain the blessing of the Church.

3. It is difficult to judge from M. Codreanu's book what his own estimate is of the strength of his movement. Such strength as it has lies possibly in the astonishing vagueness of his doctrines which do little more than enjoin a nationalism of a nebulous nature. In this connection he lays great stress on the fact that at no time has he accepted financial assistance from any foreign source, maintaining that a movement which fails to maintain itself can have no enduring vitality.

4. M. Codreanu states that a second volume is to appear, containing "considerations on social and state problems in Roumania and on the new man — the legionary".

5. Since the enactment of the measures reported in my telegram No. 18 of March 2nd M. Codreanu has given no sign of life, and it is believed that he intends to confine his activities for the present to strengthening his influence amongst the peasant population by engaging in useful social work.

6. It is perhaps worth recording, though I cannot vouch for the story, that M. Codreanu recently addressed a second minatory letter . . . to King Carol in the sense that as it was certain that the measures taken against his movement by the Government must have the approval of the Sovereign he wished formally to notify His Majesty that the Iron Guard movement would in future be developed without any special regard for the future of the dynasty.,. .

Remark by Ross 6/4)

"Roumania being among the number of the 'Haves', the Iron Guard movement is deprived of one of the stalking-horses of nationalism and derives its strength in the main from hatred of Jewry and of the 'politicians'.

Sir Reginald Hoare draws attention to a point of dissimilarities between the movement and German National Socialism. On the whole I think the resemblance is to the Croix de Feu."

No.37

Sir R. Hoare to A. Eden
No. 162 (R 2583/162/37)

BUCHAREST, *April 9, 1937*

(Excerpts)

[Reports on a talk with Gregoire Filipescu, Conservative Senator]

8.   I told M. Filipescu that I was much interested at what he said about the King's absolute unwillingness to form a Government from the Extreme Right, as I always had in mind a forcible remark of M. Titulescu's reported in my telegram No.50 Saving of November 7th, 1935: "even it the King told you himself that he was going to form an Extreme Right Government, I should advise you to tell the Foreign Office that 'I don't believe it'."

Sir G. Knox to A. Eden
(R 2721/1644/21)

BUDAPEST, *April 16, 1937*

[Reports on Hungary's relations with Austria and the Little Entente]

(Excerpts)

12.　The smooth solution of last winter's Constitutional crisis in England, the impressive scale of British rearmament and the evident honesty of our foreign policy have done much to restore the waning credit of democracy and to rob dictatorship of some of its glamour. The ubiquitous mendacity of Count Ciano's diplomacy is beginning to inspire distrust: the recent papal encyclical has made a deep impression and reasonable opinion is seriously perturbed by the extent of German propaganda and political intrigue in Hungary. Though this last sentiment is daily voiced to me, I was yet surprised when recently the Archduke Joseph, a Field Marshal of the Empire and a man of quiet and moderate views, said to me without preamble "We are being rapidly strangled by Germany, will England help us?" Leaders of the Christian Party and many other Hungarians of influence have spoken to me in equally emphatic terms, while Monsieur Eckhardt, the most active figure of the opposition, is publicly fulminating against German propaganda and interference in Hungary's internal affairs.
13.　However propitious the moment may thus be for an improvement in this country's relations with Czechoslovakia, the obstacles that stand in the way are imposing. The greatest of these is that territorial revision, thanks largely to irresponsible encouragement from England, has become the indispensable first article in the creed of the Hungarian politician. A political rapprochement to be of any value must entail at least a damping down of this note. The Hungarian Government is to-day faced with an internal problem of some magnitude – that of the extreme right wing which it inherited from General Gömbös and which is now leaning on Germany and, in alliance with the local Nazi parties, assumes a monopoly of patriotism and exploits the economic distress of the rural population. That the Government has not yet thrown off this embarrassing appendix is probably due, in the main, to the fact that it formerly controlled the electoral machinery of the whole party. It would be a bold act indeed for the Government to give to the active and unscrupulous extremists who

claim to have inherited the pure doctrine of General Gömbös, the opportunity to dub them renegades and traitors to Hungary's cause. Herr Hitler, at least, when he put an abrupt end to revisionist propaganda against Poland gave his orders to a country which was already fettered and dumb. . . .

Minutes

. . . . I think it is all to the good that it should be known in Danubian States that we are not going to acquiesce silently in the establishment of an Italo-German protectorate, and that we have ideas of our own as to how the Danubian States ought to defend their independence.

O. SARGENT, May 4, 37

No.39

Telegram (Draft) from the Foreign Office
to Sir R. Hoare
No.107 (R 2670/26/27)

FOREIGN OFFICE, *April 17, 1937*

(Excerpts)

[M. Grigorcea, Romanian Minister in London, expressed the following views in the Foreign Office:]
". . . Insofar as Roumania's position was concerned it was important to do nothing which would give the Iron Guard an excuse to indict the Government for pro-Russian leanings. That would be very clumsy." In reply to a question the Minister stated his view that the Iron Guard was not as yet very formidable. It was a Fascist organisation, strongly antisemitic. In his view the Government had not dealt with it sufficiently seriously in the past and now they were beginning to alter their attitude towards it. It was high time they did so, for the movement was showing itself anti-monarchist as well as anti-democratic and anti-semitic.

No.40

Sir R. Hoare to A. Eden
No.229
(R 3718/770/67)

BUCHAREST, *May 19, 1937*

[Reports on a conversation with King Carol]

(Excerpts)

2.   His Majesty observed that the great difference between Britain and Continental thought was that we were more impressed by the Nazi than by the Communist danger. I agreed, and to illustrate the issue I told him that my Polish colleague had recently remarked to me that as between the utterly distasteful alternatives Poland would sooner see Czechoslovakia conquered by Germany than victoriously defended against Germany by the Soviets. The King and I realized that from the Polish point of view this was fairly natural. His Majesty said incidentally that he did not believe any European war could be localised. . .
3.   . . . [Concerning Czechoslovakia] probably the Germans would demand more than the Czechs could give but none the less the Czechs ought to put the issue to the test. . .
9.   This discussion naturally led on to the Jewish question, and His Majesty expressed his hope that there would be no decrease in emigration to Palestine, which relieved the pressure of a most difficult problem. There was, he said, no doubt that a considerable number of Jewish immigrants obtained Roumanian citizenship by fraud, and he was not sure that it might not become necessary to turn them out of the country. I made a wry face and said that I felt that any such decision would give rise to much administrative abuse. . .

No.41

Memorandum on Autonomy of Subcarpathian Russia
prepared by T. H. Kadlčik (Czech translator
of the British Legation in Prague)
(R 3703/154/12)

Enclosure in PRAGUE *despatch No.133, May 20, 1937*

(Excerpts)

This autonomy has not so far been put into operation, and the delay has always been excused by pointing out the lack of education (or rather political responsibility) of the Ruthenians. In fact, however, the holding of independent elections (as guaranteed under the Treaty of St. German [sic] and the Czechoslovak Constitution) immediately after the annexation of the Ruthene territories would have been most favourable for the Czechoslovak State idea, since at that time the Czechs were considered as "liberators" from the Hungarian yoke, and from Jewish profiteering. If these elections had taken place, there would not exist at present over 200 Czech schools, mostly frequented by Jewish children, and the number of Ruthenian civil servants would be much higher. These 200 schools have failed however to turn Ruthenian Jews into Czechs; instead, the confidence in the Czechs and in their policy (which very often depends on Jews, and even on Hungarians) has been badly shaken.

No.42

B. C. Newton to A. Eden
No. 163 (R4021/188/12)

PRAGUE, *June 8, 1937*

(Excerpts)

... For some months past there have been spasmodic mutterings in Agrarian newspapers with regard to the necessity of checking political propaganda carried on by such refugees, who are labelled, for party purposes, as Communists. In "championing the cause of democracy against the encroachments of Communism" the Agrarian Party is in point of fact using a popular cry for the purpose of weakening its opponents in the coalition – and particularly the Socialists – whom it suspects of anti-Agrarian activities in country districts. These opponents, Agrarians hint, are "left-minded" and supporting the German refugees; thereby promoting the plans of Moscow and poisoning Czechoslovak-German relations. On both sides, however, the accusations and counter-accusations are more a matter of party politics than of conviction.

No.43

Intelligence Report on Roumania
(R 4703/2982/67)

BUCHAREST, *July 2, 1937*

(Excerpts)

Aims. A considerable body of opinion consisting of Right Parties in Roumania looks with sympathy on National Socialism in Germany. But the advent of these parties to power would by no means necessarily imply a change in Roumania's foreign policy. Her chief interest would and always must remain the preservation of her recently acquired territories . . . The politcal situation is largely coloured by the considerable number of Jews in Roumania. This fact has given rise to outbursts of anti-Semitism, although never carried to such lengths as in Germany, and has caused the rift between Right and Left to become wider. The Liberal Government which has been in power since the beginning of 1934 and King Carol have in the past shown considerable weakness in dealing with the disorderly elements of the Right, due largely to their fear of Communism. Lately, however, they have shown signs of taking the situation firmly in hand and the strong measures taken by them against extremist students and forbidden organisations such as the Iron Guard at the beginning of 1937 have not given rise to any active opposition.

In foreign policy there is little difference of opinion on fundamental issues between the various parties, and if only the extremists of either side can be held firmly in check, there is no real reason why internal stability should not be maintained, all the more so, since the King has slowly but unostentatiously established for himself a position of autocracy – a regime which seems to suit this country, in its present state of political development, somewhat better than a weak and corrupt democracy.

Foreign Office Memorandum
(R 5969/853/37)

FOREIGN OFFICE, *July 7, 1937*

Jews in Roumania

There are between 800,000 and 1,000,000 Jews in Roumania out of a total population of 19½ millions. Competition between the Jews and the "ethnic" Roumanians is keen, especially in the legal profession and in small retail businesses. Anti-Semitism has recently increased owing to the rise in popularity of German National Socialism, and "patriotic" Roumanians, especially students, have been led to believe that Jewish competition ought in their own interests and that of their own country to be circumscribed. There has, therefore, been a constant agitation for proportionate ethnic admission to the Universities and to the professions, and a certain amount of beating up of Jews. In view of the proximity of Soviet Russia the terms Jew and Communist are largely regarded as synonymous. This confusion of ideas has done much to increase anti-semitism. The movement is noisily championed by the newspaper "Universul" which is controlled by the nationalist fanatic Stelian Popescu. A violent press campaign waged last summer between "Universul" and "Dimineata" the newspaper which championed Anna Pauker, who was accused of receiving instructions and money from Moscow, was carried into the streets.

The most important incident in the anti-semite campaign this year has been the tabling of a draft law which would have discriminated against the employment of members of the minorities in Roumania to the extent of fixing a compulsory minimum of 75% of employees of so called "ethnic" Roumanian origin. The draft law was, however, pronounced illegal by the Legislative Council and was dropped. There have also been meetings and resolutions by the various Roumanian bars in defence of the *numerus clausus* or *numerus nullus* as regards "non-Roumanian" members of the legal profession.

The Foreign Office are frequently approached by the Secretary of the Joint Foreign Committee, Mr. Brotmann, who asks for the latest information on the trend of anti-semitism in Roumania. By arrangement between the Department and His Majesty's Legation at Bucharest these enquiries are forwarded to His Majesty's Minister who furnishes his observations at his discretion.

No.45

A. D. F. Gascoigne to A. Eden
(R 4992/1681/21)

BUDAPEST, *July 16, 1937*

[Reports on a conversation with Baron Apor, Secretary General in the Hungarian Ministry for Foreign Affairs about the "dissemination of National-Socialism in Hungary and pan-German propaganda"]

(Excerpts)

[Baron Apor said that] the Government and the major portion of public opinion in Hungary are averse to the importation into their country of an ideology which is not compatible with the Magyar temperament. That the Hungarian Government are, however, much on the alert as regards disturbances from the Right is shewn by a long statement which Herr Szell, the Minister of the Interior, found it opportune to make recently to a representative of the Budapest vernacular newspaper "Az Est". . . Herr Szell stresses with great emphasis and severity his determination to preserve the peace at any price. . . The wearing of green shirts by members of the Crossed Arrow Party (the Hungarian Nazi Party) did not in itself constitute an infraction of the law whereby "home made" uniforms were illegal; but if these individuals chose to band themselves together and march about in groups the police would immediately take action. The concludent sentences of this statement were as follows:

"We are prepared for all eventualities, and we do not fear surprises from any quarter. Turbulent and fanatical extremists certainly exist, whose aim it is to implement their nefarious policy by exaggerated methods. We are resolved to take proceedings against these fanatics; but only when we are in possession of concrete charges. As soon as we discover any suspicious or disquieting symptoms we shall strike and strike again. . ."

No.46

H. L. Farquhar to A. Eden
No. 314(R 5355/162/37)

BUCHAREST, *July 30, 1937*

[Reports on political situation as to communal elections.]

(Excerpts)

5.   The general opinion seems to be that the King favours a continuance in power of the team of Ministers with whom he himself has stated he *can* work, but that if M. Tatarescu insists on going into opposition for a time on the basis of "reculer pour mieux sauter", he will reluctantly fall back on a National Peasant Government under M. Mihalache. In this connexion it is perhaps of interest that M. Maniu, whose violent hostility to the King has always been a source of disruption and weakness in the Party, is alleged to have said that if this chief was summoned to power he would take up a position of splendid isolation and not interfere in any way.

6.   As far as the foreign policy of the National Peasant Party is concerned, there has of late been a dearth of any pronouncements or speeches of importance by leading members of the Party, and the opinion expressed in the last paragraph of my despatch No.216 of the 3rd July, 1936, that the advent of the National Peasant Party to power would appear to leave Roumania's foreign policy unaltered, probably still holds good. As far as the Right parties are concerned, the "Shirt" movement has been in abeyance ever since the Government's firm handling of the situation brought about by the excesses of the Iron Guard, but fears have been expressed in certain circles of the possible advent to power of the National Christians (Blue Shirts) under the leadership of Professor Cuza and M. Goga, or a combination with other parties of the Roumanian Front Party (Black Shirts) under Dr. Vaida Voievod with consequent manifestations of extreme nationalism in its more obnoxious forms and a disquieting increase in German and Italian influence. Such an eventuality seems less likely to occur than six months ago. . .

R. H. Hadow to A. Eden
No.218 (R 5359/154/12)

PRAGUE, *August 3, 1937*

(Excerpts)

2. ... It is not, I believe, true to say that the Right-Wing Agrarians were collaborating with the Henlein Party, but their detestation and fear of Communism led them privily to demand a revision of the foreign policy of this country in the direction of greater tenderness towards Berlin and less towards Moscow.

Minutes by C. Bramwell (August 3, 1937)

... The points to note are that there exists a strong movement among the Right-wing Agrarians in favour of closer relations with Berlin and less closer relations with Moscow; but also that this does not imply any desire to become "vassals" of Germany. ...

No.48

R. H. Hadow to A. Eden
No.225 (R 5657/217/12)

PRAGUE, *August 10, 1937*

(Excerpts)

4. ... For some time past it has been apparent that there are two conflicting trends of opinion within the Cabinet with regard to this country's foreign policy. On the one hand the Agrarians, whose natural instinct it is to fight shy of radicalism and particularly of the doctrines of Moscow, have repeatedly been reported as urging the importance of better relations with Germany... As the most powerful party in one coalition Government after another, the Agrarian party is...constantly seeking to obtain control of the Ministry for Foreign Affairs.

5. ... It is now none the less clear that the Agrarian party – with the exception of Dr. Hodza whom I regard as balancing perilously between the two camps – regard Dr. Benes with sulky enmity as the lion in their path. They have labelled him...the protagonist of Moscow; and been answered by an effective riposte in the shape of accusations that they are "selling the country to Germany."

No.49

Telegram to Sir R. Hoare
No.12 Saving
(R 6314/130/37)

FOREIGN OFFICE, *October 5, 1937*

When the Roumanian Patriarch was over here a year ago, the Archbishop of Canterbury hinted to him that he was suspected of heading or at least countenancing the anti-Semitic movement in his country. His Holiness denied the imputation but said that he had sometimes been led away to praise the leaders of this movement, though for other reasons, and that he would take greater care in the future.

The Archbishop is now being urged by certain British Jews to remind the Patriarch of his undertaking. This His Grace is very unwilling to do unless there is some real foundation for the accusation of renewed activity or indiscretions.

I shall be grateful for your observations both on the facts and on the advisability of any further informal action by Dr. Lang.

As you are aware, Dr. Nussbaum and Dr. Rushbrooke are convinced that the Patriarch is behind Roumanian Gov[ernmen]t's present attitude to religious minorities.

Minutes by Ross on September 24, 1937

I have seen nothing from Bucharest linking the name of the Patriarch with the anti-semite movement. . . I believe however that it is generally held by persons who make a study of religious persecution, e.g. Dr. Nussbaum, that the Patriarch who is said by the same persons to be the éminence grise of the Tatarescu Government is largely responsible for the somewhat intolerant attitude of the authorities at present towards religious minorities in Roumania. . .

No.50

Sir R. Hoare to A. Eden
(R 7169/162/37)

[Reports that by Royal Decree there has been brought into existence the "Straja Tarii" youth organization.]

(Excerpts)

The wide powers granted in the Decree to the "Straja Tarii" and the fact that its head will rank for all practical purposes in importance as a cabinet minister and that the King himself will be President of the Executive Committee, make it difficult to exaggerate the importance of the part which the "Straja Tarii" is intended to play. But the reflection that the Roumanian temperament does not take kindly to discipline leads me to doubt whether this attempt to organise the youth of the country will yield results in any way proportionate to those obtained by the Hitler movement in Germany or the Ballila in Italy. There appears, however, to be no doubt that the present measure marks a further step towards the consolidation of the King's personal authority and I presume that he has personally decided that by this means he can steal the thunder of the Iron Guard. It is, therefore, not irrelevant to report that the "Times" correspondent has just had a conversation with M. Codreano, who announced that he was now 90% a business man and 10% a politician, and went on to explain that he had made a successful attack on the monopoly of the scrap iron trade hitherto held by Jewish merchants, that he had opened two restaurants in Bucharest, that he was anxious to take a share in the import trade (British cloth was one of the lines which particularly interested him) and that his motto to-day was "few legionaries but many sympathisers".

No.51

Sir R. Hoare to the Foreign Office
No.384 (R 6872/130/37)

(Excerpts)

[Transmits press summary of statement made by Roumanian Patriarch to Israelite World Alliance (as published in *Universul* of 20th August, 1937)]

". . . most of the Jews, he [the Patriarch] declared, lived in easy circumstances, monopolising all the riches of the country, commerce, industry, houses, towns, etc. With the acme of refinement they instigated and cultivated the germ of social corruption and other ills; and had acquired the monopoly of the press which, with obviously foreign aid carried out a sinister campaign against the very soul of Roumania.

. . . Large numbers of Jews . . . came over like a flood during the war and after it, and had thus begun to endanger the very existence of all Roumanians and Christians. . . The fate of the poor Roumanian people from which the Jews squeezed out even the marrow from the bones made one weep with pity. To defend themselves was a national and patriotic duty and was not anti-semitism. Failure to react and to escape from this danger would be the mark of a cowardly and indolent people and would be tantamount to digging one's own grave. . . Where was it written that only Jews had the privilege of living on other peoples and on Roumanians like parasites?. . .

The Patriarch went on to say that through their powerful organisations the Jews should look for a country and colonise and work the land like others, instead of exploiting others. He did not know enough geography to say where they could find this land, but thought that there ought to be a free place somewhere in Africa, Australia, Asia or in the islands etc."

No.52

Telegram from Sir R. Hoare to the Foreign Office
No. 45 (Saving)
(R 6887/130/37)

BUCHAREST, *October 12, 1937*

(Excerpts)

Position is that when in London the Patriarch gave a statement to Israelite World Alliance. . . strongly hostile to Jews in Roumania.

In July last Curentul was canvassing desirability of urging Roumanian Government to take representations to His Majesty's Government regarding immigration into Palestine and eventually invited the Patriarch's help, who in reply handed to Curentul through his secretary copy of statement mentioned above. . .

It cannot therefore be said that the Patriarch has kept his promise and I think there is therefore amply justification for envisaged action.

I feel a certain diffidence in advising on a matter of this nature but if it is true, as I imagine, that Church opinion in the United Kingdom would be strongly opposed to further development of relations with Orthodox Church if the Patriarch's anti-Semitism became a matter of notoriety, this fact would be all-sufficient reason for action by the Archbishop. . .

As regards effect on the Patriarch I think his anti-Semitism is partly at any rate prompted by desire for popularity but that he is like everyone else in Roumania anxious to stand well with us and would therefore accept a brotherly remonstrance from the Archbishop. . .

Minutes

I had rather hoped that accounts had been exaggerated, and that we could ask the Archbishop to maintain silence: but I really think he ought to be in possession of the fact, and of the rather wicked statement in R. 6872.*

SIR S. GASELEE (October 18, 1937)

*See Doc.No.51.

Enclosure to No. 52

Sir S. Gaselee to the Bishop of Lincoln (Draft)

FOREIGN OFFICE, *October 21, 1937*

(Excerpts)

You will remember that when we met on September 20th you asked me whether we had any evidence here of renewed activities or indiscretions of an anti-Semitic character by the Roumanian Patriarch. You made this inquiry. . .at the instigation of the Archbishop of Canterbury, who had been asked by Mr. Neville Laski and other British Jews to remind the Patriarch of an undertaking given to His Grace on the subject. . . You will remember that the Archbishop had then hinted to the Patriarch that he was suspected of heading, or at least countenancing the anti-Semitic movement in his own country, but that His Holiness had denied the imputation. . .

As a result of enquiries. . . we learn that. . . the Patriarch gave a statement to the Israelite World Alliance. . .that is very strongly hostile to Roumanian Jews. . .

Last July [the Patriarch]. . . handed to "Curentul" . . . a copy of the statement of which I am now sending you a summary. The statement was published in the "Universul" newspaper. . .as well as the "Curentul" and some press controversy not unnaturally ensued.

I am afraid therefore that it is impossible to agree with the Bishop in Jerusalem that the Patriarch's anti-Semitism is more apparent than real; and in these circumstances we think that His Grace would be amply justified in reminding the Patriarch of the undertaking he gave last year. . .

No.53

Sir R. Hoare to A. Eden
No.397 (R 7213/162/37)

BUCHAREST, *October 20, 1937*

[Reports on conversation with Minister for
Foreign Affairs]

(Excerpts)

3. I. . . asked whether it was the intention of the Roumanian Government to push on the conversations with Hungary, and was told that of course nothing definite could be done until the King had taken a decision whether or not to retain the Tatarescu Cabinet, but that contact would be maintained. I remarked that I had just read . . . an announcement by M. Mihalache to the effect that important political developments would occur in about three weeks' time and that the National Peasant Party would play a prominent part in them. Did this mean that a definite decision had been taken? M. Antonesco replied that consultations would undoubtedly take place in the near future and that of course the National Peasants would take part in them, but that most certainly the King had reached no decision. The position was one of some complexity. If the result of recent elections was examined it would be seen, if the parties of the Right were counted as one entity, that there were three groups of more or less equal strength, the Liberals being slightly the strongest. As a matter of fact the parties of the Right were not a single entity and it might be regarded as certain that they would not be called to take office. I interjected that, as I reported to you at the time, M. Titulescu had once told me that even if the King told me himself that he proposed to form a Right Government I should be wise to inform you that I did not believe it. M. Antonesco went on to say that the National Peasants are in the same boat as the parties of the Right as they certainly received the votes of persons holding socialist or even communistic views. Moreover the parties of the Right were far more strongly opposed to the National Peasants than to the Liberals. If, therefore, the former were called to office they would be definitely a minority Government.

4. All this appears to indicate that the King is having considerable difficulty in making up his mind and does not intend to give any sign until the last moment. Some people outside politics think that he will solve the problem by summoning a non-party Government to hold the elections and

will then decide what the complexion of the next administration shall be.

6. I have reported once or twice that I have tried in vain to obtain a satisfactory explanation of the objections, which are certainly regarded as very grave, to the Liberal Party remaining in office for another legislature. It has now been suggested to me that if they did so M. Mihalache would probably resign the leadership of the National Peasant Party, which would then be assumed by M. Maniu, who would develop an active and bitter opposition on constitutional grounds to the manner in which the administration is now conducted. This seems to be fairly plausible.

7. Since I began to write this despatch it has become a matter of common knowledge that the King has been making strenuous efforts to persuade M. Mihalache to go into partnership with M. Vaida Voevod for the formation of a Government. The general opinion appears to be that while M. Vaida might be willing to drop the violent anti-semitism and nationalism which had been his principal plank since he left the National Peasant Party in 1935, M. Mihalache could not risk the disruption of the National Peasant Party which any alliance with M. Vaida would render probable. . .

No.54

Sir G. Knox to A. Eden
No. 139 (58/19/37)
(R 7208/844/21)

BUDAPEST, *October 20, 1937*

(Excerpts)

1. .... the season of internal politics opened on October 10 with a joint meeting of the leaders of all the more important Opposition parties at Körmend. Those represented were the Small Farmers Party, by M. Tibor Eckhardt, the United Christian Party, by Count János Zichy, the Legitimist Party, by Count Antal Sigray and the Independent Opposition, by M. Charles Rassay.

2. The speeches delivered were mainly devoted to two topics. Count Sigray and Count János Zichy, emphasized the growing importance of making provision for the settlement of the Kingship question and the urgent necessity for the Government to adopt a firm attitude against any, and all, elements which aimed at the introduction of a dictatorship or foreign form of government; both speakers maintained that the political needs of the nation were fully met by the existing Hungarian Constitution.

3. M. Charles Rassay, in his speech, particularly attacked those groups which set out to undermine the present administration. None of these, he said, had ever taken any constructive step towards the tranquil progress of the nation; their whole doctrine was drawn from "Mein Kampf" and the pamphlets published in Hungarian by the Fichtebund, and their Christianity was that of Ludendorff and Rosenberg. He complained that whilst they trampled upon the flag of "God, King and Country" they stood stiffly to attention whenever a German agitator passed through the country in a car flying the Nazi flag. In conclusion M. Rassay called upon the Government to put down this "terror" stating that he was convinced that his opinion was shared by ninety per cent of both Houses of Parliament.

6. M. Eckhardt, whom I met on October 14 at a dinner given in Honour of M. Paul Reynaud, told me that his monarchist "profession de foi" – although fully representing his inner convictions – was made on this occasion merely as a tactical move. He realised that any attempt at restoration in the present state of Europe would be extremely dangerous to Hungary and fatal to Austria. What he set out to do was to bring about

240

a truce between legitimist and elective monarchists, which would not commit either group to action against its own convictions when restoration eventually became a matter of practical politics, but which, in the meantime, would allow both to unite, without internal dissensions, in the pursuit of the one immediate aim of all opposition parties – the suppression of Nazi agitation in Hungary.

7.   On October 18, a few days after his return to Hungary from a long absence in South America, the Archduke Albrecht made a declaration to the press in which he stated that his name had been mentioned in connection with various unconstitutional movements and agitations: he stood now as in the past for the Christian and national conception of the State and, as a member of the Upper House, was loyal to the Constitution. He considered every tendency to undermine the Constitution, from whatever side it might come, as dangerous: he had taken and would take no part in such movements nor give them either material or moral support.

9.   The only visible reaction on the part of the Hungarian Government to the widespread outcry against extremist agitation has, so far, been a declaration by the Minister of the Interior to the press. M. Széll affirmed that the Government was showing no weakness in this matter. It was entirely untrue to state that the Minister had been hampered from above in his efforts to put an end to the agitation of the extreme parties: had any restraint been put upon him in such matters he would immediately have resigned. The public should recognize that he was no dictator but a constitutional Minister and that Hungary enjoyed freedom of opinion, of speech and of the press. At the same time he assumed the full responsibility that no seditious movement would come to fruition: the foolish plans of the extremists of both sides were fully known to the authorities who were in complete readiness to act should the moment for action come. At the same time the Minister recognized that the old established legislation in regard to the rights of assembly and speech was perhaps not entirely adapted to the political hysteria of to-day; if this proved to be so the Government would not hesitate to enact adequate measures.

10.   A striking comment on M. Szell's declaration is offered by the outcome to-day of the trial of the leaders of a Hungarian National-Socialist group on a charge of subservise conspiracy. The Court of First Instance found the accused guilty and sentenced the three principal conspirators to terms of two years' penal servitude. I can recall no example in my experience of Hungary of the imposition of so severe a sentence on a political charge, except in the case of offences connected with Communism, and it will be interesting to see whether it is confirmed by the Court of Appeal. . .

No.55

Letter from
Sir G. Knox to Sir O. Sargent
(R 7542/1644/21)

BUDAPEST, *November 4, 1937*

(Excerpts)

[The] fear of Germany has two sides, the foreign and the internal. The first is that, once the Prussian is established in Vienna, he will inevitably become a very undesirable over-lord in Budapest. The second, that every effort is being made by the "party" in Germany to exploit the deplorable situation of much of the agricultural population in Hungary by preaching to them in the Nazi interest ideas which differ in little or nothing from the gospel of Bela Kun. .,. All I have to add to them for the moment is that the Chief of the Political Police recently told Redward very confidentially that the police would be taking drastic measures against extremist agitation about the middle of the month. I do not much fear for the present a serious development of the Nazi movement here; the temperament of the people is opposed to it and leaders are lacking, but the ground is propitious as the poverty of the labouring classes is extreme. At the same time, the encouragement given from Germany to what is, in fact, a subversive movement works against that country's influence in foreign affairs.

No.56

Sir R. Hoare to A. Eden
No.451 (R 8194/162/37)

BUCHAREST, *December 2, 1937*

[Reports on Codreanu's manifesto concerning the "non-agression pact" signed with the Georgist Liberals and the National Peasants' Party]

(Excerpts)
(Quotations from Codreanu's manifesto)

6. "In internal policy M. Maniu is for democracy. I am of an exactly opposite opinion. I am against democracy, just as I am against dictatorships. Tomorrow will be another system, new and hardly known at present, and for this system I stand. Dr. Maniu says that his party will introduce justice and tolerance for the minorities. I am for justice without tolerance, because we have tolerated so much that we are now on our death bed. The Legionary Movement will establish justice for Roumanians. I speak of this justice denied through the centuries to the Roman people, I speak of those millenial rights of the Roumanians which they must reconquer.

7. "I finish with a declaration. I speak about M. Titulescu. The youth of the Roumanian Legion, whose liberty has been stolen from them, who were pitilessly tortured in 1933/34, will combat with the greatest violence every list on which M. Titulescu appears. The entire youth of Roumania will be present in every district in which he is a candidate and will oppose with all their power the re-entry of this man into the politics of the country. With M. Titulescu we will conclude only a pact of aggression."

8. It may have been these references to the totalitarian states in M. Codreanu's manifesto which induced M. Maniu, in a speech at Cluj on November 30th, to make somewhat similar eulogies of the virtues of nationalism, as at present exemplified in Germany and Italy. M. Maniu said: "My point of view is not an abstraction, but a great reality which, even if the masses do not understand they feel. I believe that in following this path we shall let loose a movement which will protect the truest aspirations of our soul. I cite two examples to illustrate this case. By exploiting this sentimental force Mussolini has become the leader of Italy and Hitler has become the leader of Germany. After the unification of Italy Mussolini, seeing that certain elements in the nation endangered the

243

results of the war and threatened Italy with dissolution, said to himself: 'Let us unite into a body – a fascio – to protect against materialist tendencies the unity of Italy which has been won by the war and by so much sacrifice'. In Germany the socialists and communists were masters. They had millions of votes but they tried to satisfy only material interests. They were not able to touch the sentimental side of the German people. By exploiting this side Hitler became ruler of Germany. His watchword was 'The peace which has been signed insults our national dignity. We wish to be the equals of other nations'. On these lines and by exploiting the economic resources of his country, the Leader has conquered not only Germany but the attention of the whole world which is obliged to take him into account because he has been able to mobilize into a formidable force the sentimental force of the race and the national dignity. We are of the opinion that we, the Roumanian people, must do the same. We must not only look after our material interests but must take care that our national dignity does not suffer a humiliation. To-day it has been placed in a humiliating position."

9.   It is regrettable that one of the parties essential to the maintenance of the democratic principle should have fallen on such evil days.

No.57

Sir R. Hoare to A. Eden
No.455 (R 8195/162/37)

BUCHAREST, *December 3, 1937*

[Reports on political situation in Rumania]
[Informs about a conversation with Gregoire Filipescu,
Conservative leader]

(Excerpts)

8.   At one point in the conversation M. Filipesco said something that
reminded me that in the last few days a vague rumour had reached me to
the effect that the King's entourage believed opinion in England to have
recently swung sharply to the Right so that a dash of dictatorship here
would not meet with our strong disapproval. M. Filipescu answered that in
his opinion the truth was rather that the successes of the dictatorial
powers ever since the failure of sanctions against Italy had induced a
frame of mind here which took less account of the approval or disapproval
of the Great Democracies than in the past. The mention of Italy, sanctions
and M. Laval started M. Filipesco off on a long disquisition which
rendered it difficult to pursue further the question of a swing to the
Right.
9.   I then reverted to the impending pact between the National Peasants
and the Iron Guard; and said that I presumed it would be for the purpose
of the defeat of the Liberals at the elections and of the present tendency
towards autocratic government, and did not mean that the two Parties
would endeavour to formulate a common constructive policy. . .
15.   I am reporting in a separate despatch the election manifestoes of M.
Maniu and M. Codreanu. The former contains little of any special interest,
while the latter promises, the moment the Party is in power, to join the
Berlin-Rome axis. I am inclined to imagine that M. Codreanu's levity will
be worth a number of votes to the Government.
16.   As a small indication that the Government are not altogether happy,
I report, however, that M. Titulescu, whose impending arrival had been
frequently reported throughout the last few weeks, actually reached
Bucharest on November 29th and was greeted with considerable
enthusiasm by a crowd, mostly recruited from amongst the National
Peasant Party. The Government had sent three cars to a suburban station

and attempted to persuade him to leave the train there, alleging that they could not be responsible for his safety if he arrived in the normal way. M. Titulescu, whom Dr. Lupu had gone to meet further up the line, in order to inform him of the welcome which awaited him, is alleged to have replied to the Government's emissary that a man can die but once and that the Bucharest station was as good a place to die as any other. . .

17.   I went to see the President of the Council of Ministers yesterday. M. Tataresco explained that circumstances had rendered it inevitable for the Liberal Party, against its wishes, once again to hold office. His Government would resume its task with redoubled energy and would put through measures which would add immensely to the welfare of the country. Having listened patiently to this exordium, I invited His Excellency to tell me, as objectively as possible, full objectivity being impossible when one is directly interested, whether his electoral pact with M. Vaida would do his party harm in the country. He was quite clear it would not; on the contrary, it had been a masterstroke of political strategy as it had effectively broken up the parties of the Right who might have been quite a nuisance, though not a danger. In the new Chamber the Vaidists would be the second strongest party and as leader of the Opposition M. Vaida would drop a lot of the ultra nationalistic nonsense which he had been preaching of late. M. Tataresco looked a little unhappy when I suggested that M. Vaida might have compromised himself with his supporters, but he welcomed with enthusiasm my question whether M. Maniu had not seriously damaged his party by concluding a pact with the Iron Guard, and he went on to say that the National Peasants were so much upset by M. Codreanu's idiotic manifesto that at the present moment M. Mihalache and M. Titulescu were likely to inform M. Maniu that he must either cancel the pact or resign the leadership of the party. . .

No.58

Sir G. Knox to A. Eden
No.159 (58/23/37)
(R 8185/844/21)

BUDAPEST, *December 4, 1937*

Following upon the trial and conviction of M. Böszömény, a minor National-Socialist leader, for conspiracy against the State, on which I had the honour to report in my despatch No. 139 of October 20, judicial proceedings have now been taken on a similar charge against Major Szálasi, a more important figure in the same movement.

2.   At the conclusion of the trial Major Szálasi was sentenced to ten months "State-imprisonment" – a penalty which is usually reserved for duellists and entails no moral stigma. In pronouncing sentence the judge stated that the heroic war service of the accused had been taken into consideration, but, at the same time, it had to be remembered that the activities of Major Szálasi during the present period of uncertainty and discontent, might prove disastrous to the nation. Both the Public Prosecutor and Major Szálasi have lodged appeals.

3.   It is interesting to compare this sentence with that imposed on M. Böszömény in October for activities which would appear to be far less dangerous or serious than those of Major Szálasi. M. Böszömény, who is looked upon as a harmless fanatic, endeavoured to persuade a crowd of uneducated peasants to join him in an attempt to overthrow the Government; he had no followers among the intellectual classes, nor any support from influential quarters; nevertheless, he was sentenced to two years penal servitude. Major Szálasi, on the other hand, is generally recognised as the most dangerous of the Nazi agitators in Hungary. He is a popular swashbuckler with a brilliant war record and ready eloquence: he is also a virulent anti-Semite and is believed to enjoy the sympathy, if not the support, of exalted quarters. One will be better able to judge the value of this sympathy when the case comes up on appeal.

4.   For the present there appears to have been no attempt by the Hungarian Government to implement their recent promises of measures against extremist agitation. . . Proceedings against M. Böszömény and Major Szálasi had been instituted before these promises were made, and the opinion is growing that the indulgence shown by the Government towards extreme movements by the Right is inspired by the sympathy which is tacitly shown towards them by the Regent, by officers of his Household,

247

by some of the senior military commanders and by the Right Wing of the Government Party.

5.   Although there is no indication to lead one to expect in the near future a dangerous development of the Nazi movement, the principles of which are, in general, incompatible with the national temperament and traditions of Hungary, yet there are considerations, such as the extreme poverty of the working classes, the preponderance of Jews, and the wide extension of German propaganda which render the soil by no means unfruitful to such doctrines. . .

Telegram from Sir R. Hoare to the Foreign Office
No. 103 (R 8788/162/37)

BUCHAREST, *December 29, 1937*

(Excerpts)

All Monsieur Goga's past naturally suggests intention to abandon French connexion in favour of Germany whilst reconciliation with General Antonescu whom Monsieur Titulescu used to describe as the only man in Roumania, can readily be construed as intention to establish some form of dictatorship but my surmise that King's manoeuvre is mainly directed against Iron Guard is partly confirmed by statement recently made to one of my colleagues by one of the leaders of that party to the effect that establishment of a National Christian Government was the only thing it had seriously to fear. I therefore do not exclude possiblity that the King intends to give the country "a hair from the dog that bit it" as a surest means of counteracting rapid growth of Iron Guard Movement. Some support for this theory lies in fact that such violence as took place during elections was mainly between National Christians and Iron Guard members.

For the moment my main anxiety is lest French press aggravate the situation by denouncing "betrayal" possibly under influence of Jews who are naturally dismayed. . .

Minutes by Sir O. Sargent (1st January 1938)

(Excerpts)

This surprising move on the part of King Carol is certainly difficult to understand, but perhaps the most plausible explanation is that given in yesterday's "Times" and more or less endorsed by Sir. R. Hoare in this telegram, to the effect that he has appointed M. Goga in order to steal the thunder of the Iron Guard, just as Hindenburg appointed von Papen in the hopes of out-manoeuvring Hitler. If so, the precedent is not a very encouraging one. In any case Goga is unlikely to be able to get together any sort of majority in Parliament, and will therefore presumably be compelled to resort to a more or less dictatorial form of government. And this, in itself, is calculated to prepare the way for the Iron Guard, on the ground that if the country is to have a dictatorship, it is better to have the most efficient form available.

Meanwhile, the only ostensible policy up till now advocated by Goga has been violent anti-Semitism, and his first acts as Prime Minister have been in this direction. With Mme. Lupescu still the power behind the throne it is difficult to imagine that King Carol can have much sympathy with a violent anti-Semite policy, and it may therefore be supposed that he will try to keep Goga's persecuting activities within bounds. But having once allowed the ball to start rolling he may not be able to stop it. . .

But what is more important than Goga's probable ephemeral appearance on the political stage is the growing strength of the Iron Guard − a purely Nazi Party in Roumania. This, I fear, is symptomatic of a general trend in the Danubian countries away from parliamentary democracy, and I have no doubt that it is being hastened by the growing fear that Germany's domination of the Danubian Basin is now inevitable. If the Danubian States begin now to put on the Nazi garb, it will be because imitation is the sincerest form of flattery and because they want to ingratiate themselves in time with their future master. We may expect the same tendency in Yugoslavia, for Stoyadinovitch's present policy of balance can hardly become a permanency in present conditions. In this connection I would quote the following passage from Sir R. Campbell's despatch No.255 of December 17th: ". . . I am inclined now to think that the spectacle of the Duce and the Führer dealing so simply and effectively with every form of obstruction is beginning to tell on a man who is constantly hampered by an opposition which employs means, fair and foul, to supplant him, and who has not the qualities of character that would deter him from changing his coat. The transformation is not complete, but I think it has begun. He is, for instance, engaged in enrolling young men in a kind of SS. formation and would have issued them with a coloured shirt of some hue had he not been restrained by Prince Paul. The movement is not proving a success, but the fact that he started it shows perhaps the way in which his mind is working."

In Hungary, conditions are not unfavourable for a similar evolution, and as for Austria, we are of course always being told that a Nazi revolution may happen at any moment with a little pressure from across the border. This leaves only M. Benes, and he may soon be standing in Prague, like the boy on the burning deck, whence all but he had fled. But will even he stand for very long, when once he feels himself completely abandoned by his Little Entente allies?

As for us. . . the only thing which might stop it [the "German flood"] would be to put new courage into the democratic elements of Central

Europe by showing them that the great democracies of the West are resolved to prevent the Nazi flood from breaking through the present weak and weakening dyke, which is Austria; and this the great democracies are definitely not prepared to do.

Meanwhile this foretaste of what we may expect when Hitler is established at Vienna. . . may be useful as giving us time to adapt ourselves to the effects which this reorientation of the Danubian States is going to produce in European politics. . .

Minutes by Sir Alexander Cadogan, January 3rd 1938

It certainly seems that an "authoritarian" wave is beginning to surge through the countries of Central and Eastern Europe. The trend is away from "democracy" which is represented as clogging and inefficient for dealing effectively with the successive shocks to which the world is subjected. I quite agree with Sir O. Sargent that there is no good that we can do in the way of diplomatic lectures and advice. We can only hope that the Western democracies may one day, by their firm action give the lie to all the stories of this "effeteness".

Meanwhile on one point I am not clear: if these countries admire the German (or Italian) system of Gov[ernmen]t, they may adopt it and we can't stop them. That is an "ideological" point. But would that make them love Germany any the more or be any more yielding to her? Neither Nazism nor Fascism, so far as I am aware, includes among its tenets the idea of giving away anything to any other nation. I should have thought they were both in essence violently nationalistic. It would be logical, if Roumania went genuinely Nazi that she sh[oul]d go violently Roumanian. But perhaps I am wrong. . .

Annual Report, 1937
Hungary
Sir G. Knox to A. Eden
(R 549/549/21)

BUDAPEST, *January 1, 1938*

(Excerpts)

III *Internal Political Situation*

75.   In March, rumours were current in Budapest of an impending *coup d'Etat* by members of Right extremist movements. The leaders of these groups included M. Marton and M. Mecsér, of the extreme Right of the Government party, Major Francis Szálasi and other Hungarian National Socialists. They had, it was alleged, planned to march upon Budapest and take over the administration and run the country upon dictatorial lines. Although the rumours, which had been prevalent for some weeks prior to the 1st March, assumed substantial proportions, the Government seemed reluctant to take any definite steps to appease public opinion. . . Eventually, an official statement was published to the effect that the Government had investigated the rumours and were convinced that public order had not been endangered;. . .As it turned out, this "Putsch" was still-born, but it seems possible that something serious was afoot and, judging by various remarks alleged to have been made by the Ministers of National Defence, Education and others, the Government was more than a little embarrassed.

76.   In the course of a speech which M. Darányi made in April, he referred to the activities of extremist groups and affirmed that dictatorship was not in itself a solution. . .

IV *Hungarian National Socialism*

80.   A review of internal politics would be incomplete if it included no reference to the progress of national socialism in Hungary. There exists as yet no unified National Socialist party. . .but six or seven groups, having different titles and leaders, actively propagate a doctrine closely allied to that of German national socialism, and employ the same catch-words and methods. They are represented in the Chamber by two deputies, Count Alexander Festetich and M. Balogh, and enjoy the support of some members of the right wing of the Government party. No other leader of

252

any importance has yet emerged except, perhaps, Major Francis Szálasi, who is reputed to be a good organiser and forceful speaker. He was, in December, sentenced to ten months' "State imprisonment"...for subversive activities...

81. Although not yet centralised nor under capable direction, the propagation of the National Socialist idea in Hungary is nevertheless widespread, and its catch-words find a ready echo among the labouring classes whose poverty is extreme, and among the educated youth who see in the future little prospect of settled employment. As has previously been mentioned, the Prime Minister and other prominent politicians have openly deprecated the aims and methods of the Hungarian National Socialists, but the Government have not taken active measures to suppress the movement....It has been more or less openly alleged that the reason for the Government's lethargy was the sympathy shown towards the movement by the Regent himself, who is violently anti-Semitic in his views. Although the leaders of the movement have declared that it is distinctly Magyar, and that they are not supporters of an ideology which is foreign and incompatible with the Hungarian temperament, nevertheless, there is no reasonable doubt that its branches are closely connected with the active German Nazi programme which is carried out in this country by German students and various "Vereine" scattered in the provinces. The future will...reveal the attitude of the Government towards the movement, and it is possible that more effective action may be taken to suppress it. During the year, however, it seems to have gained ground, although, as stated in the second chapter of this report, the Government seemed optimistic as a result of an arrangement alleged to have been reached with Germany in November, that German propaganda in Hungary would be damped down.

No.61

Annual Report, 1937
Roumania
Sir R. Hoare to A. Eden
(R 3554/3554/37)

(Excerpts)

117.   In the last annual report it was stated that King Carol had unostentatiously established for himself a position of autocracy. In the course of the year under review he for all practical purposes became his own Prime Minister and after his dismissal of M. Titulescu he took a more active part in the direction of foreign affairs. As far as the army is concerned, his popularity can certainly be said to have increased, in spite of the counter-attraction excercised by the Iron Guard.

129.   ...the Liberal party issued a statement severely criticising the weakness of the Government towards the Iron Guard, whilst the situation was aggravated by an admission extracted from the Minister for the Interior that a member of a Liberal organisation amongst the students had been kidnapped on the 6th January by Iron Guardists and severely beaten.

130.   The diplomatic embarrassments which ensued have already been dealt with. . . and the reasons which induced the Government to take this line were almost certainly that, realising at last that the Iron Guard was becoming a serious menace, they considered that the easiest way to deal with the problem was to lay emphasis on the participation of these foreign diplomats in an internal political demonstration and turn it into a question of national prestige, thereby appealing to the spirit of nationalism and branding the movement as an organisation dependent on, and guided by, foreign influence.

132.   It was not long before a further indication was given of the danger of the Iron Guard movement in the country. At the end of March a murderous attack was made on the rector of the University of Jassy. . . . During the course of the next month or so the Government did, in effect, pass a series of measures putting some of these good intentions into effect. . . .

136.   At the end of the month (April) the Iron Guard once more came into prominence when they issued a circular championing Prince Nicholas and alleging that the real reason for the disgrace of a Prince. . . .was that he had never been willing to bow before Mme. Lupescu. Although Prince Nicholas denied that he had any contact with any political group,

representatives of the Iron Guard were active in his support. In view of the subsequent electoral pact between the Iron Guardists and the National Peasant party it is of interest that on this occasion the Iron Guard's activities had the approval of M. Maniu, whose antagonism to the King is notorious.

141.   On the 13th November, the King, after consultation with the leaders of all political parties, except the Iron Guard, requested M. Mihalache to form a new Ministry. The next day M. Mihalache issued a statement to the effect that he was unable to accept the mandate in view of the condition which had been placed by the King for collaboration with M. Vaida Voevod, a former National Peasant Prime Minister and now the leader of the Roumanian Front party. . . .

151.   Bucharest gasped, and. . .the constitution of a Government of this nature had not been regarded by a single soul as a possibility. (It will be remembered that some two years ago M. Titulescu said to His Majesty's Minister: "If the King should ever tell you that he intends forming a Government from the extreme Right, I would advise you in reporting his statement home to add that you do not believe it.")

Anti-Semitism.

159.   The success of the Iron Guard's extreme nationalism found its natural counterpart in the growth of anti-Semitism which first manifested itself in measures taken against lawyers of Jewish origin. Thus, on the 7th February, the Association of Roumanian Christian Advocates held a meeting to discuss "the means by which the Roumanian Bar could acquire the ethnic character to which it had the right". . . .

160.   At the end of June the election of seven representatives of the Ilfov Bar to the General Union of Roumanian Barristers was due to take place. The Government had been warned that serious disturbances were likely to occur owing to the determination of the Extreme Right and nationalistic parties to ensure the election of their nominees, and the law courts were surrounded on the day fixed for the elections by cordons of gendarmes and troops. . . .

No.62

Minutes by A. D. M. Ross
(New Roumanian Government)
(To a telegram by Sir E. Phipps,
No.1. Saving) Paris, January 1, 1938
(R 34/9/37)

FOREIGN OFFICE, *January 3, 1938*

The French Gov[ernmen]t and Sir R. Hoare are inclined to regard the establishment of the National Christian Party in power as a prophylactic inoculation against the greater evil of the Iron Guard. The efficacy of this treatment depends on the strength of the more virulent germ. It was powerless when Herr von Papen was put up to keep Herr Hitler out. But the Iron Guard cannot compare, from the point of view of strength and appeal, with the N.S.D.A.P..

No. 63

Telegram from Sir R. Hoare to the Foreign Office
No. 4 (R 109/9/37)

BUCHAREST, *January 4, 1938*

I had a very frank discussion this morning with Minister for Foreign Affairs. Essence of his views is that Jews have morally vitiated minority treaty by enlisting outside support for a minority which consistently refused to be loyal citizens. As you are aware I have some sympathy with this view but I retorted that it was open to Roumanian Government to ventilate their views either formally or informally at Geneva and I asserted that I entirely shared M. Titulescu's view that you cannot wisely pick and choose what treaty you will respect and expect others to respect and what treaty you will disregard. Anyhow there would be trouble for Roumanian Government at Geneva unless it acted with circumspection. He replied that Government must proceed with its measures or play straight into the hands of the Iron Guard. I then said that though it was not my strict business I was alarmed at President of Council's statement that there were hundreds of thousands of Jews in the country who had no right to be here having obtained false papers by bribery. Minister for Foreign Affairs replied that there were in fact 500,000, a figure which I said was quite incredible.

Prime Minister this afternoon held similar language though he appeared to say that none of the measures which he would take would be violation of treaty as they would only be aimed against Jews who would be shown to have no right to citizenship. He admitted that I had made a point when I said that distinction between the two categories of Jews did not appear in this preliminary measures. He looked rather shaken when I said that the thought of the volume of corruption which would result from revision of identity papers appalled me. I knew what I was talking about in view of endless bother over residence permits. When I asked what he *would* do next supposing he did establish his thesis he answered that he would appeal to the League to find a solution. And then he reverted to real point that something must be done lest the Iron Guard prevail.

Minutes by A. D. M. Ross, 6/1

M. Micescu's preoccupation is evidently to take the wind out of the

257

Iron Guard's sails. There will be reprisals not only against Jews but against the "corrupt" members of the bureaucracy who have given Jews a leg up.

Minutes by P. N. Nichols, 6/1

It looks very much as though the present Roumanian Government were going to use the Iron Guard as a threat with which to blackmail foreign Powers into acquiescing in a policy which is in itself reprehensible. But the whole position still remains somewhat obscure, and more particularly the part played by the King and likely to be played by the King in the future.

Meanwhile from the last paragraph of this telegram it would seem that we may have the curious spectacle of the Roumanian Government rather than the afflicted Minorities appealing to the League. We know that in a general way the Secretary of State is very anxious that the League should be given some opportunity for positive action, though whether the case of the Jews in Roumania would be likely to serve the purpose which the Secretary of State has in mind seems very doubtful. I have had a word with Mr. Makins on the subject, who points out that little credit is likely to accrue to the League unless they can tackle the problem successfully. Their capacity to deal with Jews (sic) refugees is already being tested to the utmost, and another half million would of course be beyond their powers.

We do not, of course, know whether the present Roumanian Government seriously intend to dispossess half a million Jews of their naturalisation papers or whether, on the other hand, M. Micescu is merely talking big. Meanwhile it seems not at all impossible that the Roumanian Jews themselves may enter a petition to the League, and if both sides – the Minorities and the Government – were to appeal to the League before any irrevocable steps were taken by the Government, I think this fact might possibly redound to the credit and eventual advantage of Geneva.

No.64

Telegram from Sir R. Hoare to the Foreign Office
No. 2 (Saving)
(R 270/153/37)

BUCHAREST, *January 5, 1938*

(Excerpts)

Chief impression made on me by the Prime Minister during long and rambling conversation was that he is already realizing practical difficulties of doing anything radical in Jewish problems without simultaneously doing grave injury to national economy, but that he is convinced that he must make an attempt to accomplish something, not only because he is prisoner of his past, but because he believes rightly or wrongly that only way to defeat the Iron Guard is to steal its thunder in which considerable element is of course anti-Semitism. . . .

Yesterday French Minister read me . . . telegram drafted, he thought, by Monsieur Delbos which contained threatening phrase in sense that the French Government expected from the Roumanian Government at an early date "deeds and not merely words". On the strength of this telegram my French colleague had spoken with vehemence to the Prime Minister and the Minister for Foreign Affairs both of whom had impressed him most unfavourably. It is not obvious to me that it will be impossible to work with them however vigorously it may be necessary to differ openly over Jewish problem.

N. Chamberlain to Sir R. Hoare
No.12 (R 8788/162/37)

FOREIGN OFFICE, *January 6, 1938*

In your telegram No. 103 of the 29th December last regarding the political situation in Roumania, you suggested that King Carol's object in calling M. Goga to power might be to combat the infection of the Iron Guard movement by injections of a similar but less virulent germ. While I am inclined to agree with this suggestion, I notice that you do not regard the introduction of some measure of dictatorial government by M. Goga as out of the question. Indeed, if the figures of the recent elections are any guide, it appears unlikely that M. Goga will be able to command a majority in Parliament, and, pending fresh elections, he may therefore be compelled to set up a more or less "authoritarian" régime. This in turn may merely provoke the Iron Guard to work for a coup d'Etat, which might result in the establishment of a frankly "authoritarian" regime along Fascist or Nazi lines. Thus there seems to be a distinct possibility that King Carol's prophylactic methods may end by precipitating the very outcome which they were designed to avoid. It seems necessary, therefore, to consider in advance the possible implications of the establishment of a dictatorial régime in Roumania.

2.   For some time past a trend away from parliamentary democracy has been noticeable in most of the countries of the Danubian Basin and the Balkan Peninsula (with the noticeable exception of Czechoslovakia). But the recent occurrences in Roumania may be symptomatic of a more positive development in the direction of authoritarian government on the model of Germany or Italy. If and where this tendency towards authoritarian government does exist, it is of considerable interest to know what constitutes the motive force behind it. Is it merely due to the feeling that temporarily during the period of political and economic abnormality through which Europe is passing, a stronger and more efficient form of administration is needed than in a more peaceful and settled period? Or is the real impulse due to the influence of Germany's example, combined with the fear that Germany's domination in Central and South-Eastern Europe is now inevitable? In that case, how far does admiration for, and imitation of, the German system of government in itself denote in these States a disposition to yield to German advances? Imitation may be the sincerest form of flattery, but flattery can be symptomatic of fear as well

as of affection. It may be felt that the only way to combat the threat of German domination in the Danube Basin is, so to speak, to set a thief to catch a thief. The "authoritarian" ideology, whether Nazi or Fascist, is inherently nationalistic and acquisitive, and it would be only logical that the policy of Roumania, for example, in the event of that country embracing these principles wholeheartedly, should become violently Roumanian, and should resent dependence on or the intrusion of outsiders, particularly of outsiders having the international reputations of the present German Government. On the other hand, it is equally easy to argue that, realising the inevitability of eventual German domination, public opinion in these countries is beginning to feel that imitation of the totalitarian regime is the surest way of currying favour with the future overlord.

3.   From the foregoing it would appear that this veering away from democracy and towards an "authoritarian" regime among the States of Central and South-East Europe, may theoretically at any rate, either presage a disposition to fortify themselves for resistance against German encroachment or else denote a determination, proceeding from a conviction that German dominance is merely a matter of time, to compound with the inevitable, and by ingratiating themselves stave off the worst effects of that domination when it eventuates.

4.   I shall be glad if you will, as soon as you conveniently can, furnish me with your observations, from the Roumanian standpoint, on the considerations advanced in this despatch. Similar requests are being addressed to His Majesty's Ministers at Belgrade, Budapest, Sofia and Athens. . .

No.66

Letter from Sir R. Hoare to E. M. B. Ingram
(R 457/153/37)

BUCHAREST, *January 11, 1938*

(Excerpts)

... I am inclined to think that if we could arrange a "symbolical" absorption of Jews from here into some part of the Empire it would have a good effect both on nationalistic Roumanian opinion and on the Jews who, feeling that there was a possible way of escape, would be less panicky than they are now.

Robertson knows all about the regulations governing immigration into the principal Dominions, and our present impression is that they present almost insuperable difficulties to mass, or even group, immigration. But I remember reading the report of the Commission that went to have a look at British Guiana as a possible home for the Assyrians (sic). My recollection is that the Commission was quite favourably impressed by both the climatic and physical conditions, though I do not remember why the scheme broke down.

... in my despatch No. 267 of August 29th, 1936, on the Jewish question here, I wrote:

> There is in Roumania a collection of political rag-tag and bobtail who aspire to office largely on an anti-Semitic platform. I cannot imagine them in office but it may well be that some of the Jews can. I think that these fears should be borne in mind because fear is the father of folly, and that, if it be decided to restrict immigration into Palestine, authority should be reserved to relax those restrictive measures in the event of unexpected or dramatic developments in countries such as Roumania where there is an important Jewish minority.

Any relation of restrictive measures on immigration into Palestine has now become out of question. I believe that in these circumstances it would be of very serious value to make a definite effort to find some other safety valve. The knowledge that we were looking would help to tide this over whereas if we all refuse to look for one there may be an unpleasant explosion.

I should add that Robertson's two visitors, who appeared to him to be eminently respectable and serious people, say that they have nothing to do, and wish to have nothing to do, with Zionism.

Minutes by A. D. Ross, 19/1

This is an invitation to us to work out a scheme for the settlement of the Jews who are assumedly about to be expelled from Roumania somewhere in the British Empire. . .

But before approaching any other Dept. of H.M.G. or before considering whether we should or should not work only with the League, we have to make up our minds as to whether we want to take any initiative. I am inclined to think if the nationalist element in Roumania got mind of any attempt by H.M.G. to find room for Jews in the British Empire they would only be the more encouraged to clamour for the ejection of more Jews. Moreover I don't think that those people in Roumania & elsewhere who have expressed disapproval of your "interference" so far would take a more sympathetic view of our action if we volunteered to take the Jews to our bosom. On the other hand if the result of the petitions by the Jewish organisations to the League includes a request from the Council to examine the possibility of finding a place for the Jews who have to leave Roumania to settle, we shall obviously have to face our responsibilities.

Minutes by G. W. Rendell 21st January, 1938

(Excerpts)

It would be admirable if we could find any room for Jews in either the Dominion or the Colonial Empire. We have assumed a number of obligations towards the Jews, which, though ill-defined and the subject of much controversy, are nevertheless real. We have in fact obtained a good deal of value for our money, but the genuineness of that money has hitherto been open to question, since up till now, we have always tried to fulfil our obligations towards the Jews at the expense of third parties. If we could now do something in the direction of fulfilling those obligations at our own expense instead of at the expense of others, it would go a very long way towards (a) giving real and *effective* help to the persecuted Jews of Central Europe, (b) convincing our critics at Geneva, and in the United States, of the sincerity of our sympathy for the Jews and of our professed desire to help them, and (c) providing a real solution of the Palestine problem.

My own feeling is that we are under a strong moral obligation to do something for the Jews within the Dominion or Colonial Empire, and that it would be quite possible to do it if the question were faced frankly and courageously. It has, however, been difficult for the Eastern Department to raise the question hitherto, without drawing a red herring across the track of the far more immediate and dangerous problem of Palestine. There are obvious disadvantages in raising two controversial questions simultaneously. It will be difficult enough to get the Palestine problem considered objectively and solved rapidly and effectively on equitable and practicable lines. Too many interests and prejudices are involved; and all those interests and prejudices would be likely to come into play if the question of doing something for the Jews within the Empire were raised at this stage. . .

I am not sure whether it is appropriate for me to have written this minute on this paper, since my minute deals with the general question of Jewish settlement within the Empire, while the present paper is mainly concerned with the situation inside Roumania. But this Roumanian situation corresponds so closely to that existing in Poland and in certain other countries that it is impossible to deal with it in isolation. Moreover, anything connected with the resettlement of Jews anywhere inevitably involves Palestine, and will continue to do so until the Palestine problem is disposed of.

Query: Bring up in a year.

Sir G. Knox to A. Eden
No.11 (R 628/99/21)
[Printed as R 618/112/7]

BUDAPEST, *January 13, 1938*

I HAVE the honour to acknowledge receipt of your despatch No. 6 of the 6th instant inviting my observations on the considerations raised in your despatch No. 12 of the 6th instant to His Majesty's Minister at Bucharest regarding the trend towards authoritarian government in Central and South-East Europe.

2.   Since the reign of St. Stephen Hungary may be said to have enjoyed a Constitution of her own making, of which she is consciously proud. The origins of this Constitution date back to the semi-legendary blood pacts of the steepe (sic), and her parliamentary institutions are the result of a gradual historical development over a period of more than a thousand years. The Crown of St. Stephen and the Golden Bull, the Hungarian National Charter of 1222, are anchored firmly in the hearts of this romantic people, and, so far as can be foreseen at present, are likely to oppose a formidable moral barrier to any attempt to set up an authoritarian régime.

3.   It is a fact that during General Gombos's tenure of office (1933–36) fears became increasingly widespread lest his ambitions might result in the setting up of a dictatorship on German lines. With his death, however, these fears for the immediate future have passed, and I have no doubt that, for the present, the great majority of Hungarians remain in favour of a constitutional parliamentary government, albeit of the feudal complexion traditional in this curiously unmodern country.

4.   Nevertheless, there exists in Hungary a considerable "right extremist" movement, represented by six different political organisations, all of which draw their inspiration from Nazi philosophy, but are divided on the most delicate of all points — that of the "Leader". It cannot, moreover, be denied that in many quarters this doctrine exercises a considerable appeal; its current catch-words strike the imagination of industrial and agricultural workers, who suffer from a deplorably low standard of living and of wages; the promise of spoliation of the Jews and the system's offer of an infinite range of minor dictatorships arouse new hopes in the yearly glut of educated youth, which sees little prospect for the future in already overcrowded liberal professions, while to the more politically minded the

possibilities inherent in the authoritarian régime of rapid action and radical solutions, the ease with which public opinion is formed and guided and the seemingly infinite spending power which appears, under this system, to be the corollary of national bankruptcy, have an undoubted attraction.

5.   Such agitation, however, and such sentiments, which are fairly widespread among the younger generation and are sedulously exploited from Germany, do not, to my mind, suffice to constitute as yet a trend away from parliamentary government (democracy is perhaps too strong a term to apply to Hungary). Even if they do in the future show more cohesion and take on a wider extension than to-day, they are in themselves entirely foreign to this country and are unlikely to overcome without a far severer struggle than there has been seen elsewhere a constitutionalism that is founded in age-old tradition and national pride. . .

No.68

Telegram from Sir R. Hoare to the Foreign Office
No.12 (R 473/153/37)

BUCHAREST, *January 17, 1938*

(Excerpts)

... I have this morning received very confidential record made by Jewish delegation of interview with Prime Minister on January 4th during which delegation was categorically informed by him that reports which had appeared in papers on this subject were untruths [grp.undec.] therefore be presumed that extremists have gained the victory, their most effective argument having from time to time been the Iron Guard bogey. . . and it is natural to conclude that they will press for further measures. It appears to me quite possible that if not checked they will create atmosphere which will render it undesirable for the King's visit to England to take place. . .

... Prime Minister* has been profuse and, I have thought, sincere in his assurances to me and to others including Jewish section that he will countenance no excesses. It is therefore possible that a very plain statement of impression which his government is making on public opinion in Great Britain will lead him to check his extremists before it is too late.

I still think though with less confidence than before that we should endeavour to keep on friendly terms with government and do nothing to bring about its downfall. I therefore suggest that we should not seek either French or American support for such representations as you may desire to make and that you instruct me when speaking to Prime Minister to say that so far as we are concerned, we shall endeavour to withhold from the press the fact that His Majesty's Government are seriously preoccupied by a terribly grave incitement to race-hatred.*

*Sir R. Hoare informed O. Goga about possible shock in England because of anti-semitic excesses in Romania.
**In his telegram No.9 of 16 January 1938 (R 417/153/37) Sir R. Hoare transmits order of Minister of Labour forbidding Jews to employ Gentile women under 40 years of age.

No.69

Sir R. Hoare to A. Eden
No.22 (R 679/9/37)

BUCHAREST, *January 19, 1938*

(Excerpts)

[Reports on a conversation with King Carol]

. . . His Majesty appeared to me rather preoccupied by the Jewish and Iron Guard problems. With regard to the latter. . . he was quite clear that it must be combated and that the only way to do so was to adopt part of its programme. To use force against it and so create martyrs was not the way to handle the situation, though if force became unavoidable, he would not hesitate to use it.

2. With regard to the Jews, some measures must be taken to relieve the pressure and His Majesty mentioned various parts of the world where Jews might perhaps be admitted. The ideal thing would, of course, be an independent Jewish state and he regretted that His Majesty's Government had not originally tackled the Palestine problem from that aspect. . . . Before we left this subject I said that I was inclined to think that a small symbolical emigration of Jews from this country would very possibly constitute a satisfactory solution of the problem. . .

Remark by A. D. M. Ross, January 25, 1938

. . . The King's marked concern in the matter of the Jewish and the Iron Guard problems suggests that he would be particularly receptive of "advice" from His Majesty's Minister.

No.70

Letter from Frank Walters (League of Nations)
to R. C. S. Stevenson (Foreign Office)
(R 605/9/37)

GENEVA, *January 19, 1938*

[Reports on a conversation with I. Micescu, Roumanian Foreign Minister]

(Excerpts)

[Micescu] pointed out once more that the country was in a very excited state, that the Iron Guard was expecting to increase its vote very much, and that the anti-Semite policy of the Government was absolutely necessary to enable it to prevent the Iron Guard from coming into power, the results of which would be a complete volte face in foreign policy and a complete catastrophe for the Jews in the country. This was the main object of the Government, which was in no sense a fascist or totalitarian one. . .

No.71

A. D. F. Gascoigne to A. Eden
No.16 (R 1016/126/21)

BUDAPEST, *January 19, 1938*

(Excerpts)

2.   As you are aware, the bulk of the private commercial and financial enterprises in this country are in the hands of the Jews. Statistics show that some 75 per cent of the business houses, banks, etc. of Pest are owned and staffed by Jews. . .

4.   During the past two years the feeling in this country against the Jews has been inflamed by the sedulous anti-Semitic propaganda put about by the extremist organisations. Moreover, there is no doubt that considerable indirect pressure is exerted by the Hungarian authorities to induce Jewish firms to employ Christians in preference to their co-religionists, and I am informed that the leaders of the Jewish community in Budapest are substantially perturbed by the general situation and outlook.

5.   In my despatch No. 60 of May 21, 1937, I had the honour to inform you of a speech delivered by Count Stephen Bethlen. . . he deprecated the methods employed by Nazi Germany to eradicate the Jews, and suggested that a solution might be found by the introduction of a progressive programme destined to assist Christians to win back their position in the economic sphere. Those hot heads in the ranks of the extremists who are in favour of drastic action against the Jews similar to that adopted by the German Nazis, would do well to take Count Bethlen's counsel to heart. For any change in the existing situation must be brought about very gradually since, apart from other considerations, it is a fact that there is no class in Hungary to-day capable of replacing the Jews in the commercial and industrial life of the nation. . . .

No.72

Telegram from Sir R. Hoare to the Foreign Office
No.19 (R 661/9/37)

BUCHAREST, *January 24, 1938*

[Reports on a conversation with the Roumanian Minister of Air and Marine]

(Excerpts)

He is uneasy and he asserts that growth of Iron Guard can probably only be checked by formation of non-party Government of men of known integrity with primary task of stamping out "system of protections and intervention" which has in his opinion been enormously extended under the late Government and revolt against which has found expression in support of Iron Guard. He appears to think that a Government so formed could obtain sufficient support from Chamber to pass the budget and to carry on for a year during which Iron Guard would lose momentum. . . . Minister for Foreign Affairs is strongly opposed to the Iron Guard and I suggest opportunity be found to speak to him in general sense of this telegram. Minister of Air should not be quoted.

No.73

Foreign Office Memorandum on
Political Situation in Roumania
(R 733/9/37)

FOREIGN OFFICE, *(Southern Department)*,
January 24, 1938

(Excerpts)

The present Government* in Roumania is in a difficult position. It is only a stopgap Government representing about ten per cent of the electorate and probably transitory. We know from Monsieur Micescu that the forthcoming elections (first week of March) will be fought on the anti-Semite issue. If the present Government take a moderate line they play straight into the hands of the extremists of the Iron Guard. If they themselves take a strong line against the Jews they will rouse great resentment abroad. . . and foreign opinion will move against them. From our point of view the advent of the Iron Guard to power is a development which we would wish most earnestly to avoid because it is pledged to ally itself with the Berlin-Rome axis, which in its turn meant breaking with the Little Entente, France and Russia. If therefore it is true that the present Government must put forward a fairly strong anti-Semitic programme if they are to beat the Iron Guard, then this is possibly the lesser evil of the two.

Sir R. Hoare . . . quotes the Minister of Air and Marine as holding that the Iron Guard can probably only be checked by the formation of a non-party Government. The only alternative method in the view of the Minister. . . would be the suspension of all pretence of Parliamentary Government, i.e. an undisguised dictatorship. The formation of another dictatorship would not suit His Majesty's Government for many reasons: it might also mean the disappearance of Parliamentary Government in Roumania for a very long time.

The outline therefore, is gloomy and it looks as though some pretty frank speech with the Roumanian Minister of Foreign Affairs is called for.

Monsieur Micescu would be aware of the interest Great Britain has always taken in the question of minorities. . . and any violent anti-Semitic measures that might be embarked on by the Roumanian Government were

*The Goga Government

272

bound to have very unfortunate repercussions in the United Kingdom. At the same time, however, we quite understood the difficulties the Roumanian Government were placed in owing to the position off-stage of the Iron Guard. The rise to office of a party pledged to ally themselves with Germany and Italy would cause great apprehension in England and France. [The Secretary of State] had been turning the situation over in his mind and though, of course, he had no wish whatever to intervene in what was a matter of internal Roumanian politics he wondered whether at this moment a non-party Government might not serve Roumanian and European interests best, always assuming that the present Government did not, as he hoped they would, obtain sufficient support at the polls to enable them to carry on in power. . .

No.74

Telegram from Sir R. Hoare to the Foreign Office
No.23 (R 716/9/39)

BUCHAREST, *January 24, 1938*

(Excerpts)

It is becoming daily more certain to my mind that only feasible solution of present situation is suspension of parliamentary life even if Government manages by foul means to secure majority. My main reasons for this conclusion are that anti-semitic agitation must be stopped, a task which this Government, which is already believed to be disunited over Jewish question, is obviously unfitted to undertake... in the new Parliament there will be no possible alternative Government which could secure support of a Parliamentary majority; therefore a third phase would constitutionally be inevitable but fresh elections would be culminating catastrophy and only serve to strengthen the Iron Guard.

I think effort will be made to convince the King that suspension of Parliament is the only solution and that peasants would welcome it, being disgusted with politics.

I feel sure that in any case no final decision will be taken until after the visit to London.* It has been put to me that genuine dictatorship would be definitely preferable to "bastard" one which has grown up under late Government. Political blunders of the last few weeks resulting in present situation incline me to agree.

*King Carol's visit.

Telegram from Sir R. Hoare
to the Foreign Office
No.24 (R 822/9/37)

BUCHAREST, *January 28, 1938*

Your telegram No. 1 from Geneva.

1.   I fear it would be quite impossible to suggest postponement of elections as postponement would be regarded as definite confirmation of widespread rumours that they will in fact not take place. I am sure that intention both of the King and President of the Council is to hold them on March 4th as announced.

2.   You can take it as certain that there is no possibility of formation as a result of elections of a Government which will promptly announce accession to Berlin-Rome axis. Such a danger would only exist if Iron Guard obtained absolute majority which is out of the question. In that event I fancy the King would immediately suspend Parliament even at the risk of revolutionary disturbances.

3.   I still think far the most probable result of elections will be renewal of stalemate in which case I imagine the King will work for the formation of a Government either on lines indicated in my telegram No. 19 or for some form of coalition which would undoubtedly be short lived but would manage to pass budget in April.

4.   If Government should obtain a majority I anticipate that President of the Council's prestige will be so far enhanced that he will have no serious difficulty in carrying out what will certainly be the King's emphatic wish to damp down anti-Jewish agitation at any rate until after visit to London.

5.   I fully realize all the latent unpleasantness in present situation and that realization was in large measure the reason of the rather alarmist tone of my Saving telegram No. 12.

6.   If situation deteriorates further it will be a matter for consideration whether I should not receive your instructions to speak to the King as well as Prime Minister on lines suggested in that telegram.

7.   Since drafting above I have had conversation with the Palace dignitary who is the King's right hand man. He maintains that Government has good chance of winning elections without doing anything too outrageous, his argument being that spectre of Iron Guard coupled with knowledge that Government will deal firmly with any excesses of propaganda will influence many voters. These factors are no doubt of some importance

and Government prospects are improved by acute dissensions which have developed in Liberal Party and by effective use which dissident National Peasants in Government seem to be making of inept leadership of Monsieur Maniu.

8.   Monsieur Urdariano went on to say that anti-semitic agitation had of course gone too far. It would be checked after elections. To check it before would be to play into the hands of the Iron Guard. I admit this to be true but I repeat that I fully realize possibility of unpleasant reactions at our end. It is some comfort to learn from your telegram No. 13 that I have tended to exaggerate sensitiveness of British reactions.

9.   Dominant factor in my opinion remains the King's conviction of the value of British connexion. . .

No.76

British Delegation (Geneva) to Sir R. Hoare
Telegram No. 10 (Saving)
(R 830/9/37)

GENEVA, *January 29, 1938*

(Excerpts)

1.   My interviews here about the Jewish question with Monsieur Micesco have been most unsatisfactory as he has not shown the slightest desire to be helpful. He was prepared to give an undertaking that no further anti-Jewish legislation would be passed before the elections, but he declined to give any pledge to suspend either action under the decrees etc. already issued, or administrative action against the Jews. He intimated, moreover, that if the urgency procedure were applied to the Jewish petitions, Roumania would follow Poland's example and withdraw from participation in the minorities procedure.

2.   After consultation with the French, we agreed, though not on account of this threat, that to apply the urgency procedure would in the circumstances present no advantages and might further prejudice the position of the Jews. The petitions will therefore be sent to the Roumanian Government in the ordinary way for their observations, and it is understood that they will submit some.

4.   Monsieur Micesco has been taking the line that the Jewish petitions constitute an insult to His Majesty, but he could hardly suggest that this would apply to the exercise by His Majesty's Government of the rights conferred upon them by the Treaty.

No. 77

Record of an interview of Lord Cranborne
with Prince Antoine Bibesco (on January 30, 1938)
(R 914/153/37)

UNITED KINGDOM DELEGATION,
GENEVA, *January 31, 1938*

(Excerpts)

[Bibesco said that Micesco, the Roumanian Foreign Minister] ... had derived the impression that Great Britain and France were anxious to score a spectacular political victory over Roumania. I told Prince Bibesco that, as I am sure he himself already knew, this was a fantastic suggestion. We had no reason for wishing to score a victory over Roumania. . .

Prince Bibesco asked me whether I could give him any advice as to action which the Roumanian Government might take in order to meet the wishes of the League. I told him that the best thing they could do would be to refrain from giving effect to any decrees or laws regarding the Jews until the Minorities Committee had had an opportunity of considering the subject and the reply given by the Roumanian Government. He said that this would be very difficult. I must remember that elections were impending. If the present Gov[ernmen]t delayed action on decrees which had been already passed the impression would be given that they were influenced by international Jewry and this might be enough to throw them out of power and bring in the Iron Guard which would be very much worse. . .

... He asked me, speaking personally, to transmit a message to the Secretary of State to the effect that he thought that it would be of great assistance if Sir Reginald Hoare could speak to His Majesty. Roumania was a semi-dictatorship and a personal approach of this kind might be of use.

CRANBORNE

No. 78

*Record of a conversation between
A. Eden and the French Ambassador in London
(A. D. M. Ross)
(R 926/9/37)*

FOREIGN OFFICE, *February 1, 1938*

(Excerpts)

The French draft instructions to Mr. Thierry are intended to bring home to King Carol beyond all possibility of doubt the repercussions which the denunciation by Roumania of her obligations under the Minorities Treaty would have on Franco-Roumanian relations. . .the French draft. . . goes much further than the Secretary of State's telegram to Sir R. Hoare and a detailed examination of the two documents will make the differences between the French and the British positions abundantly clear. . .

His Majesty's Government have. . . a potent weapon in the shape of the official visit of King Carol to London. . . The cancellation of the visit. . . would have such an effect on the King that he would exert all his influence to ensure the adoption of a policy which would restore him to favour with His Majesty's Government. The dangers of such a weapon however are great. The cancellation of the state visit now would. . . destroy our influence over Roumanian policy in which. . . His Majesty is the one stable factor; it would give the Fascist Powers a golden opportunity to denounce the Western democracies as meddlers and would play into the hands of our detractor in Roumania with whom the King might in desperation be forced to throw in his lot. . .

It appears. . . that we cannot join the French démarche on the terms which their draft suggests. . .It should be noted that Sir R. Hoare may feel obliged to point out the dangers which even such a démarche [the British] would entail for the Roumanian Government which. . . can only survive the elections by pandering to the anti-Semitism of the people. . .

Telegram from Sir R. Hoare
to the Foreign Office
No. 26 (R 924/9/37)

BUCHAREST, *February 1, 1938*

(Excerpts)

Addressed to Geneva telegram No. 1 of February 1st for Secretary of State.

Your telegram No. 2 from Geneva and my telegram No. 24.

From the beginning of this trouble* I have felt that there are five factors of approximately equal importance.

1.   Roumania's foreign orientation threatened by the rise of Iron Guard.
2.   Confused internal political situation in which "down with the Jews" is almost as potent a slogan as "hang the Kaiser" or "Chinese slavery".
3.   The King's position which has been impaired by the recent political blunders.
4.   Necessity for good atmosphere for London visit.
5.   Fears of treaty obligations.

As I see the picture in the light of these factors I am convinced that we must abstain from threats which would in actual practice even in the unlikely event of the government pretending to yield to them, do little to ease matters for the Jews. Knowledge that threats had been uttered would weaken the government and might provoke a crisis even before the elections and in those circumstances I think it possible that extreme anti-Semites might provoke outrages which would be ascribed to the popular story of foreign interference. Were it not for the atmosphere which has been created, actual measures taken so far would be of little practical importance apart from the treaty aspect and I feel strongly that we have nothing to gain and the Jews something to lose by daring the Roumanian Government to follow the Polish example, as if it were followed such a declaration of independence would be in the eyes of many Roumanians a most effective piece of electioneering. I dislike urging that we swallow our principles for the time being and should perhaps not do so if I thought that a vehement representation today would ease pressure on the Jews and therefore on national economy which is a matter

*The political crisis leading to Goga's dismissal on 10 February, 1938

of grave moment but I am sure that any attempt to check the present fever by drastic means would fail and perhaps create a situation of even greater delicacy for which we should be regarded as responsible.

There is another aspect which is that the Jews of the old kingdom are inclined to dissociate themselves from those of Transylvania etc. and still more the "invaders". Please see letter from my legal adviser to Mr. Laski which will reach England with covering letter from me on Wednesday. I hope you will not send me any categorical instructions until you have given this letter full consideration. Ethically I disagree with much of it but its ethics are not altogether my business. Practically it gives us a fairly good reason for not rushing matters and its general tenour inclines me to believe that whatever the Minister for Foreign Affairs or President of the Council may say to you or me the Roumanian Government will in some measure be influenced and guided by our representations. I should not wish my French colleague to be associated in any formal representation which you may wish me to make after a full examination of all conflicting factors of an entirely abnormal situation. President of the Council has told me recently in a short dinner party conversation that he regarded the French Govenment as Jew ridden. Minister of Education (?) was a young Jew in the early thirties. I replied that I did not quite follow his train of thought and that to the best of my knowledge Secretary of State for War was a Jew. Goga's answer was that in England a Jew attains high office because of his personal attainments whereas in France he is imposed on the government by Jews because he is a Jew. It would be a pure waste of time to try and convince Goga that he is talking nonsense. For the time being if they are wise the French will leave the *entire* conduct of our joint relations with Roumania to us. There are rumours that they are contemplating suspension of armaments deliveries shortly.

Let us be quite clear.

If the situation becomes yet more difficult you and your Minister here and not the French must find solution. It may not be palatable to the French but it is a quite undeniable fact that there is greater desire to stand well with us than with anyone else.

Concluding paragraphs of your telegram and indeed its entire tenour suggests to me that the Roumanian Minister for Foreign Affairs is being dishonest especially when he talks about "insult to His Majesty" and I have suspicion that in mentioning His Majesty he may have wished to provoke you into bringing His Majesty directly into controversy. . .

No.80

Cabinet 3 (38) Conclusions 2.

February 2, 1938

FOREIGN AFFAIRS, *Roumania*

(Excerpts)

The Secretary of State had not formed a good impression of the new Foreign Minister of Roumania, who had suggested that after the elections Roumania might denounce the Minorities Treaty. These Treaties were part of the arrangement by which somewhat exaggerated boundaries had been granted to Roumania by the Peace Conference, and in the circumstances he had felt constrained to speak rather strongly to M. Micescu. The situation was rendered awkward owing to the forthcoming state visit to London of King Carol. He proposed to send a telegram on the subject to Bucharest. The French also had sent a surprisingly stiff telegram hinting that they would not be able to maintain the alliance unless the Roumanian Government modified their attitude. . .

No.81

Minutes by Sir O. Sargent
on conversation with P. Cambon,
French Ambassador in London
(R 1161/153/37)

FOREIGN OFFICE, *February 3, 1938*

[Sir O. Sargent discussed with P. Cambon the French instructions to the French Minister in Bucharest concerning the Jewish question.]

(Excerpts)

. . . for the rest, I told M. Cambon that Sir R. Hoare had warned us very strongly that in dealing with Roumania in her present state the dangers to be avoided were:

(a)   weakening the position of the King, who is the only moderating influence on whom reliance can be placed now or in the immediate future, as his opposition to the Iron Guard is well known and thought to be quite genuine;

(b)   badgering the Roumanian Government to an extent which would give the present Government and the Iron Guard the election cry for foreign interference in the internal affairs of Roumania. . .

No.82

Telegram from the Foreign Office
to Sir R. Hoare
No. 17 (R924/9/37)

FOREIGN OFFICE, *February 4, 1938*

My telegram No. 2 and your telegrams Nos 24 and 26 (of January 29th, January 28th and February 1st respectively: political situation in Roumania).

I fully appreciate your arguments, but in view of what took place at Geneva and of the impression produced on M. Delbos and myself by the policy enunciated by M. Micescu, I feel bound to address some form of communication to the Roumanian Government.

You will realise, however, that positions of His Majesty's Government and French Government are different and that it is impossible for me to follow line of instructions which are being sent to your French colleague who, I gather from your telegram No. 28, has already apprised you of their gist. I am anxious therefore that the matter and timing of what you say to the Prime Minister should not convey to the latter the idea that you and your French colleague have received identic or joint instructions or are acting simultaneously. I am equally conscious of the danger of saying anything which could be interpreted or exploited as interference in Roumanian internal affairs. It is therefore the League aspect of Roumanian policy and its effect on British opinion that I wish to stress perhaps even more than the nature of the anti-Semite measures being adopted or in contemplation.

Bearing the above in mind you should therefore seek an interview with the Prime Minister and inform him of the concern with which I had heard of the policy of the Roumanian Government regarding Minorities as interpreted by M. Micescu at Geneva, more particularly in so far as I understood him to intimate that Roumania might find herself constrained to withdraw from participation in the Minorities procedure. You should leave M. Goga under no illusion as to the reaction on British public opinion if a wave of anti-Semitism is encouraged either by the measure or the propaganda of the Roumanian Government, particularly if these measures involve a violation of Roumanian treaty obligations. You should further point out to His Excellency that given the circumstances of the case, everything possible was done in the procedure adopted at Geneva to avoid additional embarrassment to the Roumanian Government while

284

ensuring serious examination of the petitions in accordance with the ordinary procedure. If, however, the Roumanian Government were to carry out the threats adumbrated by M. Micescu, the situation would be as set forth in paragraph 3 of my telegram No. 2 from Geneva.

Since drafting the above I have received your telegram No. 29, in which I am amazed to read of the Minister for Foreign Affairs' account to the press of his conversations with myself and M. Delbos. You should inform M. Goga that this account is a travesty of what passed between us, as reported in paragraph 1 and 3 of my telegram No. 2 from Geneva, the gist of which (less the first sentence of paragraph 1) you may convey to His Excellency. You may add that I resent such misrepresentation of fact.

Enclosure to No.82

*Telegram from the Foreign Office
to Sir R. Hoare
No. 21*

February 10, 1938

French Embassy have been informed of instructions sent to you. . . It had previously been explained why we felt unable to send you instructions similar to those which French Government contemplated sending to M. Thierry.* . . .M. Cambon was informed that you had warned us very strongly that in dealing with Roumania in her present state the dangers to be avoided were (a) weakening the position of the King, (b) pressing the Roumanian Government to an extent which would give them and the Iron Guard the election cry for foreign interference.

*French Minister in Bucharest

Telegram from Sir R. Hoare to the Foreign Office
No.31 (R 1085/9/37)

BUCHAREST, *February 5, 1938*

(Excerpts)

During the last few days a general realization that the country is moving towards a grave crisis has begun to show itself and people are saying frankly that this anti-Semitism is folly. I learn. . . that Bratiano will today present to the King memorial on behalf of entire constitutional opposition urging that elections be postponed because of dangerous state of mind created by anti-Semitic propaganda of Government and by the Iron Guard campaign which in many respects is hard to distinguish from Communism.

Minutes by P. B. B. Nichols, February 9, 1938

The situation in Roumania is. . . a rapidly developing one and we must now take it that Sir R. Hoare. . . is of the opinion that elections early in March would be a definite mistake. We may share this opinion and the hope that a non-party Government of all the talents may be brought into office; but to share this hope and this opinion is one thing, to tender advice and to work for its realisation quite another. There is, too, the further consideration that if the elections are postponed we have no means of telling when elections will ever again be held. . . — it seems quite possible that they will disappear from the scene for years to come — and if we take any active hand in the game. . .might we not be held pretty responsible for the disappearance of democratic institutions and methods in Roumania, and would this suit our book?

Minutes by Sir O. Sargent, February 10, 1938

I don't at all like the idea of Sir R. Hoare expressing any opinion, however unofficially, as regards the postponement of elections and the constitution

286

of a new non party government. A Minister gets on to very dangerous ground once he begins to express opinions in matters of internal politics in an independent country. I would propose therefore to cut out the passages which I have bracketed in the draft telegram.

Remark by Sir A. Cadogan: "I agree with Sir O. Sargent" (February 10, 1938)

Sir R. Hoare to A. Eden
No. 43 (R 1423/9/37)

BUCHAREST, *February 7, 1938*

[Reports on a conversation with Armand Călinescu, Minister of the Interior]

(Excerpts)

[Călinescu affirmed that] Codreanu's party contained many strange elements and there was not a shadow of doubt that since the Communist party had been declared illegal in Roumania the vast majority of its members professed Iron Guard sympathies.

3.   His Excellency then expressed the view that at the forthcoming elections the Iron Guard would do more than maintain its position. It was natural. . . that at the last elections many persons should have voted for the extreme Right, not only because they were tired to death of the Liberal Government but also because the extreme Right was the most prominent representative of nationalistic sentiment. Today things were very different with a Government of the Right in power and obviously taking into account the state of public feeling. . .

No. 85

Telegram from Sir R. Hoare to the Foreign Office
No. 39 (R 1224/9/37)

BUCHAREST, *February 9, 1938*

May I say frankly that but for the fact that it was evident French Government was determined to use threatening language I should have begged you not to insist on instructions in your telegram.

I happened to go this morning to Ministry of Foreign Affairs and met the Minister in the hall. He asked me to go and see him. In the circumstances it would have been obviously discourteous not to tell him of communication which I was about to make to Prime Minister. We then had a good natured wrangle in the course of which he maintained that having accepted non urgency of the procedure we and French Government were for all practical purposes engaged in trying to impose it. I said what I thought we required to know was that petitions would be taken into proper consideration by Roumanian Government and answered. To this he did not demur. At one point he maintained that in pressing Jewish issue we were mainly concerned with Roumanian foreign relations and that we were in some respects going the wrong way about it. If anything could drive Roumania into the German camp, which would certainly not occur during his tenure of office, it would be the impression that our only interest in Roumania was Jewish question about which feeling ran high. I replied that I did not think there had been more than six Jewish petitions to the League, during the time that I had been here and that feeling which he spoke had been in a large measure worked up by the present Government. If public opinion in England were roused by the numerous reports of brutalities against members of the Bar or reports of students it was inevitable that public opinion would react. He said that he supposed I had in mind King Carol's visit to London and I said that I was not thinking of it but that I supposed I might possibly have reason to do so some time.

I had a similar conversation with President of the Council this afternoon. He said that my French colleague had been to see him and had rather dramatized matters. He was sometimes appalled at the susceptibility of the French e.g. in an interview he was reported to have said that he hoped to widen the circle of Roumania's friends without "profoundly" affecting existing relations. He really did not know whether he had used word "profoundly" but French had attached desperately sinister meaning to his words.

I then spoke of brutality committed against Jewish lawyers and medical students. He said he was aware of them and deplored them but nationalism which here was bound to be anti-foreign semi-officially could not be dispensed in strictly medical doses. I would however be glad to learn that he had issued a most categorical circular to the Prefects that they would be held personally responsible for any ill-treatment of Jews during election campaign. Jews were not the only lien. He had established electoral pact with Germans and was on the point of concluding one with Hungarians which he hoped would be the precursor of general improvement of relations with Hungary. . .

No.86

Telegram from Sir R. Hoare to the Foreign Office
No. 43 (R 1242/9/37)

BUCHAREST, *February 11, 1938*

[Reports on a conversation with Prof. N. Iorga]

(Excerpts)

He [Iorga] was quite clear that drastic action was necessary as in Agrarian parts of the country the peasants are entirely out of hand as result of reckless promises made by the Government perhaps even more than by the Iron Guard. . .
He was. . . anxious that it should be made clear to the country that dictatorial régime was a phase between two constitutional periods. . .
[Concerning the King's visit to England] I [Hoare] had been beginning to wonder, whether in view of anti-Semitic excesses which naturally aroused much attention in Great Britain it was propitious moment for the visit.

Enclosure: Draft of a telegram from Sir A. Cadogan
to Sir R. Hoare
(No.23, February 14, 1938)

(Excerpts)

. . .If the new Government modifies the anti-Semitic policy of its predecessors and shows respect for Roumania's obligations under the Minorities Treaty, there would be no longer any reason why Royal visit should not take place. Could you not put this to the King and obtain the necessary assurances from him?

No.87

Letter from
Sir G. Knox to E. M. B. Ingram
(R 1504/99/21)

BUDAPEST, *February 12, 1938*

(Excerpts)

I had the other evening a long talk with Bethlen about the Right extremist movement in Hungary. His views corresponded exactly with those expressed in my despatch No.11 of Jan.13 last.

The remedy, in his view as in mine, is social reform, and proposals for this on as extensive a scale as the financial situation will allow are, I understand, shortly to be put forward. In the meantime Bethlen also holds the opinion. . . . that the Government should take stronger police measure against such agitation than have hitherto done.

Foreign Office telegram to Sir R. Hoare
No. 24 (R 1378/9/37)

FOREIGN OFFICE, *February 16, 1938*

(Out file)

(Excerpts)

2.   You should inform His Majesty that you have been instructed to have a frank talk with him regarding the forthcoming State visit. While we have every sympathy with His Majesty's difficulties it remains true that in the event of His Majesty's new Government continuing the anti-Semitic measures of their predecessor there can be little doubt but that British opinion will be aroused, more particularly as owing to recent developments the policy of the King's Government can not be divorced from his person pending the promulgation of a new Constitution. If his Majesty can give you an assurance that his new Government will not proceed with any anti-Semitic measures, and will do their best to suppress persecution of the Jews then there is reason to believe that the visit could take place without the danger of its being marred by untoward incidents. (For your own information we are bound to envisage the possibility that if King Carol is the victim of hostile demonstrations, King George VI. may fortuitously be associated with them.)

3.   Should His Majesty the King be unable to give you the requisite assurance you should then suggest to him that the question of postponing the visit to a more suitable occasion must in those circumstances inevitably arise.

5.   The following is for your own guidance:

We are in a position of some embarrassment about this visit. We certainly do not wish to make King Carol's position in Roumania more difficult. Indeed he seems to us to be on the whole the best element in a very unstable situation. . .At the same time, it will neither do him nor His Majesty's Government any good if he pays a State visit here and that visit is a failure. Unless it can be made reasonably apparent to the British public that anti-Semitic measures have been damped down, such a failure is to be anticipated. If, on the other hand, it came to be appreciated that the King himself stood for tolerance in Roumania and for genuine friendship with the democracies, then the success of the visit would be much easier to assure.

Foreign Office Memorandum (Southern Department)
Political Situation in Roumania
(Prepared for Lord Plymouth for the House of Lords)
(R 1603/9/47)

FOREIGN OFFICE, *February 21, 1938*

(Excerpts)

. . .it is believed that M. Goga was called to power by King Carol solely in order to counteract the growing influence of the extremist Iron Guard.

2.　Among its internal measures the Goga Government had included a number of anti-Semitic measures, some of which it had already enacted. When these measures were first announced His Majesty's Minister at Bucharest was instructed to remind the Government of the interest which His Majesty's Government had always taken in the Minorities Treaty and in the minorities procedure generally. Similar instructions were sent to the French Minister at Bucharest. Several petitions were presented to the League of Nations by Jewish organisations and are at present under consideration.

4.　His Majesty's Government were disposed from the outset to believe that collaboration with the Goga Government would not be impossible. Assurances had been given that foreign policy, which would remain under the personal direction of the King would be unchanged. The attitude of the late Foreign Minister, however, when the Jewish petitions were discussed with him by the Secretary of State and M. Delbos, and the manner in which he misrepresented those discussions to the public on his return to Geneva, gave reason to doubt whether this belief was justified. Nevertheless, the views of His Majesty's Government as to the serious situation which might arise if the Roumanians were unreasonable in the matter of the petitions were expressed with reserve and in terms more moderate than those employed by the French Government.

5.　The policy of the late Government caused considerable disturbance in public confidence and the financial position of the country was adversely affected. M. Goga, who had little ability as a leader and whose colleagues were of widely differing sentiments and calibre, had to compete not only with those saner elements which realised the folly of his policy but with the Iron Guard extremists who had sworn enmity to the Government. The shooting of two members of the Iron Guard apparently by the Police may well have given rise to the fear that a period of violence was about to begin.

6.   The immediate cause of M. Goga's resignation is not yet known for certain, but there is little doubt that he was dismissed by King Carol on his own initiative. It is widely held in Roumania and also in certain quarters here and in France that a démarche said to have been made to King Carol by His Majesty's Minister at Bucharest was responsible for the King's decision. It is alleged that Sir R. Hoare gave His Majesty to understand that the Royal visit which was fixed for March 22 could not take place if the situation continued to develop on present lines. There is no truth in this allegation. . .

8.   So far as is at present known the new Government will pursue approximately the same policy as its predecessor but will proceed more gradually.

Remark by A. D. M. Ross (26/2)

A copy of Secretary of State's reply to Colonel Wedgwood of February 7th regarding the Jewish petitions is attached *à toutes fins utiles.*

No.90

Telegram from Sir R. Hoare to the Foreign Office
No. 58 (R 1756/9/37)

BUCHAREST, *February 23, 1938*

(Excerpts)

The King received me today and after he had asked me whether I had any special news to which I replied in the negative he enquired about London visit. I replied that during late Government anxiety was felt lest anti-Semitic movement here have repercussions in London and render immediate visit inopportune. . . I then asked him what his own view was both from internal and external point of view. He replied he was quite satisfied with situation in the country and saw no reason why he should not go abroad unless tomorrow's plebiscite yielded results which he did not at all expect. As regards external aspect he strongly deprecated postponement of visit as postponement would be prejudicial to his policy of establishing closer relations with Great Britain. . . His Majesty then asked what sort of incidents had been regarded as possible. I replied that perhaps small groups might gather at strategic points in streets and boo. The King then said that replacement of Jews must and would continue. Would that be regarded as an anti-Jewish measure? I replied that I thought educated opinion would have regarded it as a perfectly reasonable one if taken nineteen years ago. Now it would be regarded as a submission to popular clamour which could yield no practical results. His Majesty did not demur.

2. His Majesty then said that he thought that we were discussing past history and that he believed that there had been considerable improvement in feeling abroad since present Government came in. I replied that I had no information and had not felt it would have served any useful purpose to have consulted His Majesty's Government during last few days and when he said no further measures had been or would be taken against the Jews I mentioned suppression of Jewish papers. .,. He replied that there were far too many papers in the country and affirmed that whereas there were before the war under twenty papers in Transylvania there were now well over one hundred. . .

3. I then asked His Majesty whether he had any comment regarding feeling in France and said that I had been interested by Monsieur Goga's complaint that France tended to dramatize things. . . His Majesty replied a

296

little sourly that the French dramatized one thing and we dramatized another and said there was some danger lest we create impression that only interest we took in Roumania was in the Jews thereof. I said that this was hardly fair so far as my experience went. . .

No.91

Sir R. Hoare to A. Eden
No. 70 (R 2058/153/37)

BUCHAREST, *February 24, 1938*

(Excerpts)

I have the honour to report that I called on the Patriarch on February 17th, and as the Greek Minister had told me His Beatitude had given him a most interesting account of recent political developments I was considerably disappointed to find that nothing would induce him to talk about anything but the Jewish problem. What he had to say on the subject was of no great interest but he unfortunately believes that the Jews have almost literally sucked the blood of the Roumanians and that a drastic remedy must be found. The rights of genuinely established Jews would be respected but after the revision of the papers of Jews had been completed the Roumanian Government would probably appeal to the League of Nations to find a solution, i.e., a home for those who had no right to be here.

2. M. Tataresco said the same thing when I saw him on February 16th, so that I imagine that the Roumanian Government is seriously contemplating something of the sort.

3. The Patriarch made one suggestion, which was that a detached and impartial Englishman should come out and conduct an unobtrusive but thorough investigation of the Jewish problem, rather on the lines on which, he said, Mr. Seton-Watson had conducted an investigation into the racial problem of the Austro-Hungarian Empire immediately after the war. I said I would report this home but did not think the proposal would be received with favour, if only because a tour of inspection would almost inevitably give rise to hopes that His Majesty's Government were prepared to take an active part in solving the Jewish issue, and therefore to great disappointment if it proved that they were unable to do so.

4. I then called on General Antonesco, who told me a number of interesting things. He assured me that the situation was much calmer now and that he had the army thoroughly in hand. I asked him whether it was true that it was largely owing to his influence that M. Codreanu issued his statement after the recent encounter between guardists and gendarmes, that he was giving up all electoral propaganda. . . He replied that it was quite true that he had given Codreanu advice in this sense and had told

him frankly that the country was drifting towards civil war and he was determined that there should be no civil war and was fully resolved to use any measure of force necessary to prevent it.

5.   He said that he had greatly disliked entering the Goga Government but as in the past he had been accused of conspiring against the King he felt that to refuse to do so would lend some colour to charges of this nature. He had from the outset been convinced that it was impossible in the existing state of the country to hold elections. I then told him that since leaving office the Liberals were inclined to tell me that evidence was pouring in to the effect that the Codreanu organisation and funds were derived from Germany. What did he think about it? He replied that when he had no evidence he was not prepared to make accusations, but he could tell me that he had warned Codreanu that these things were being said and had received from him a positive assurance that "my hands are as clean as yours". As for the Iron Guard movement, it was partly a revolt against the malpractice of party politicians and partly a mysticism. It could not be dealt with by force but he hoped that as older and wiser men joined the movement it could be weaned from its more obnoxious aspects. I tried, but failed, as I have failed on other occasions, to get some explanation of M. Codreanu's passion for the Berlin-Rome axis. All that General Antonesco would say on the subject was that this passion was the origin of the charges made that the movement is subsidized by Germany. The General then told me that he had spoken very seriously to M. Codreanu about the presence of communists in his movement. The reply had been that they were all converted, and the General had said that this was nonsense as it had not been a matter of individual adhesions but whole groups joining with their organisation intact. . .

8.   Since these conversations took place much has happened, the country has been given a new Constitution, which considerably enlarges the King's powers and foreshadows a corporative Chamber; the Iron Guard has been dissolved by "The Captain" and first impressions are that the people, wearied to death of politicians and graft, "love to have it so". If first impressions are right the durability of that love depends on the success of the widely-advertised attempt to cleanse the administration. Whether that is possible in a country where many officials receive salaries which would barely keep a moderate smoker in cigarettes is one which I am not prepared to answer.

Minutes by A. D. M. Ross (March 7)

Sir R. Hoare rightly deprecates any attempt to constitute HMG as the protector, official or unofficial, of Roumanian Jewry.

299

. . . If the Iron Guard could be weaned from its affection for the Rome-Berlin axis and from its violent anti-Semitism, it might be a force of which even the King would be glad in the interests of the country to make use. Perhaps if someone else were to pay the Iron Guard they would change their tune. . .

Minutes by A. N. Noble (March 8)

But if the Iron Guard were to change that much it would cease to be the Iron Guard. I think General Antonescu is shutting his eyes to past events when he talks of older and wiser men curbing the Guard. Roumania may be a case apart but the history of Germany, Italy and Russia all tends to show that older and wiser men cannot moderate the views of these extremist movements. I should have thought that in Roumania it could best be done by firmness and well ordered Government – as Gen[eral] Antonescu himself suggests. . .

Remark by Sir O. Sargent (March 11)

Roumania is bound to go Nazi, and that will automatically settle the Jewish question.

No.92

Sir G. Knox to Lord Halifax
No. 40 (R 2044/99/21)

BUDAPEST, *February 27, 1938*

(Excerpts)

I have the honour to report, with reference to my despatch No. 11 of January 13 last, that in recent weeks there have been some further signs of activity among Hungarian extremists of the Right.

2.   On January 11 M. Ladislas Endre a former magistrate of Gödöllö and now the leader of one of the National Socialist groups of a particularly marked anti-Semite character, was, to the general surprise, elected to the post of "Vize-Gespann". . . of the county of Pest.

3.   A dinner given in his honour was attended by M. Homan, the Minister of Education, and M. Sztranyavsky, the Speaker of the Lower House, the latter of whom used the occasion for a somewhat truculent speech. M. Sztranyavszky declared that the election of M. Endre . . . was an event of great significance for all Christian Hungarians. It was not true to say that the Right extremist movement had been smuggled in from abroad. On the contrary, it was deeply rooted in the soul of the Hungarian people, and it was the ideas of liberalism, democracy and freemasonry which had been imported. He considered that the future of the nation was bound up with the Hungarian Right extremist policy. The success of this policy was extending over the whole world and could not be restrained by any power. . . Many people criticized the Hungarian Right extremist movement because it sympathized with similar movements abroad. Naturally it did so and it was justified in hoping that it would receive from foreign Governments of the Right protection for its own national feelings, aspirations and justified demands.

4.   These utterances appear strange in the mouth of a Speaker. . .

5.   On the other side of the picture the Hungarian Government has at last undertaken more vigorous police measures against the extremist movement of the Right. On the 21st instant the police raided the Budapest headquarters of the Hungarian National Socialist party and its other premises; confiscated documents and arrested all the members of the party who were found in the party premises.

Among the arrested people were the leader, Major Szalasi, on whose activities I reported in my despatch No. 159 of December 4 last, and who had been released from the arrest pending appeal against his recent sentence... A communiqué was issued in the press of the 22nd instant. It was stated... that many of the members of an already dissolved political party (The Will of the People's party) had joined the Hungarian National Socialist party and that many aimed at taking over the administration of the country by non-Constitutional means.

6.   In some quarters it is thought that this action was inspired by the shock which the Berchtesgaden meeting with its promise of more rapid German penetration in Austria had given to the Hungarian Government. Others hold, however, that it was taken in order to reassure the Jews so as not to compromise the success of an internal loan, if this should become necessary.

No.93

Sir G. Knox to Lord Halifax
No. 47 (R 2913/99/21)

BUDAPEST, *March 10, 1938*

(Excerpts)

... During a speech which he made at Gyor*... on the 5th instant the Hungarian Prime Minister, M. Darany,** dealt with the question of Extremist movements coming either from the Right or from the Left.
2. ...It must not be forgotten, he said, that Communism was often proved to conceal its subversive movements under cloaks of a democratic, liberal or even Nazi character. Such masked movements would not be tolerated and none of Bolshevism's "piratical standards" would be respected...
3. ...The realisation of the Government's policy of social relief, he said, might be menaced by the senseless exaggeration of extremists. Subversive movements should be strangled at birth.

*Correctly: 'Györ'
**Correctly: 'Darányi'

No. 94

Sir R. Hoare to Lord Halifax
No. 87 (R 2874/9/37)

BUCHAREST, *March 11, 1938*

IN his despatch No. 12 of the 6th January last Mr. Chamberlain requested me to examine the political situation in Roumania from the following points of views:—

1) Is there the possibility of the establishment of a frankly authoritarian régime along Fascist or Nazi lines?

2) If so, what constitutes the motive force behind the movement; (a) is it due to a feeling that for the time being a more efficient form of administration is needed, or (b) is the real impulse due to the influence of Germany's example? In that case, is this flattering imitation caused by fear or by affection?

2. Before attempting to express an opinion on these points, I should point out that the situation has been completely changed since this despatch was written, and that King Carol, finding that the Goga-Cuza régime was rapidly leading the country towards economic disaster and to a state which might even have ended in civil war, has brought off a bloodless revolution and has introduced a Constitution which foreshadows the establishment of a corporative régime.

3. Up to the time of the parliamentary impasse resulting from the failure of the Tataresco Government to secure a majority in the December elections, it may be said that there was one organisation definitely aiming at the establishment of a totalitarian State. This movement was, of course, M. Codreanu's Iron Guard. The beginnings of that movement and its growth down to 1933 are described in the memorandum enclosed in my despatch No. 141 of the 26th March, 1937. It began as a purely anti-Semitic movement organised by M. Codreanu in his student days at Jassy nineteen years ago. It passed through many vicissitudes and experienced many ups and downs. Thus, there appears to be no mention of the movement whatsoever in the Legation archives of 1932, but the annual report for 1933 shows that the movement was largely, if indirectly, responsible for the fall of the National Peasant Government in the autumn of that year, and that it had sufficient adherents to put forward sixty-eight candidates for the elections, for which they were prevented from standing by a decree dissolving the organisation.

4.   It had for long been believed that, in spite of harshly repressive measures of the Government, of which abundant instances are given in M. Codreanu's book summarised in the memorandum enclosed in my despatch referred to above, the King afforded the movement a measure of support, and even after the sensational murder of M. Duca it is almost certain that he maintained contact with it through M. Inculet, then Minister of the Interior.

5.   From 1933 until recent events the activities of the Iron Guard were mainly confined to strengthening their position in the country districts by useful social work, and shortly before the last elections it returned to official life under the designation of "All for the Country".

6.   Apart from anti-semitism and a contempt for democracy, the movement has never evolved any political programme whatsoever, but it has been successful in attracting to itself all the malcontents in the country, including even Communist organisations, and recently it has in a large measure been the expression of a widespread dissatisfaction with the ineffectiveness of Parliament and the cupidity of politicians. It remains to be seen whether it has been destroyed by King Carol's coup d'Etat or not.

7.   As stated above, King Carol maintained contact with the Iron Guard over a number of years. It would be fruitless to attempt to indicate what his motives were. It seems certain, however, that he decided, after the impressive demonstration organised by it on the occasion of the funeral, in February 1937 of two legionaries who lost their lives in Spain, that the movement constituted a danger, rather than a support, for the Crown, and fear of the Iron Guard is undoubtedly one of the reasons which led to the recent coup d'Etat.

8.   It remains to examine briefly King Carol's policy and to try to determine in some degree to what extent he has deliberately worked for the situation which now exists, or has been forced by circumstances to take a grave political risk.

9.   His enemies maintain that ever since his return to Roumania King Carol has worked with diabolical skill to break up the two big parties and thus automatically to create such an excess of demagogy as to render a drastic change inevitable. In my introduction to last year's annual report I stated: "King Carol has unostentatiously established for himself a position of autocracy." It is obvious that all this tendency is toward autocracy, but I do not consider the charge of deliberately conspiring for a dictatorship is proved. Thus we find that the National Peasant Government of 1932 fell. . . owing to the dissensions between the Prime Minister and M. Maniu, and a little further on in the same report we find that the King, "who has

had sufficent cause in the past to dislike and distrust the Liberal party," did, after one or two manoeuvres, consent to the formation of a purely Liberal Government.

10. On the other hand, King Carol told me shortly after his coup d'Etat that he had for some time past been anxious to bring about a modification of the Constitution and the establishment of parliamentary life on a corporative basis, but the opportunity had not presented itself. This cannot, however, be held to mean that he foresaw and worked for the political impasse which resulted from the December elections and deliberately faced the very real risks of internal disorders.

11. In my opinion King Carol would have been prepared to allow parliamentary life to continue as in the past had M. Maniu not been determined to exact from him conditions regarding both his private life and his share in the government of the country which he definitely knew were quite inacceptable, and I imagine that after a spell of National Peasant government the King would have sought to introduce modifications in the Constitution by the constitutional means provided.

12. As regards the future, I am inclined to think that it is of relatively little importance whether the new corporative Parliament proves to be a serious body or as ineffective as the hitherto democratically elected chambers, and that all turns on whether under the new dispensation the Administration is more efficient and less corrupt than it has been in the past. In fact, on whether a serious attempt is made to "depolicianise". For the moment there appears to be no shadow of doubt that in the villages, where life has become seriously disturbed by political feuds, there is a very great sense of relief. If the present experiment proves a failure, I should be inclined to say that a National Peasant revolution, which would mean the substitution of a strictly controlled King Mihail for an autocratic King Carol, would be more likely than the establishment of an Iron Guard dictatorship, though the issue would, of course, be greatly influenced by general developments in Europe.

Minutes by A. Noble, March 23, 1938

Sir R. Hoare's conclusions would appear to be that fear of or affection for Germany does not weigh as a considerable factor; that the Roumanian swing away from democratic government has its roots in purely local soil, discontent with the corruption and inefficiency of politicians and that the trend is towards autocratic dictatorship rather than to totalitarian dictatorship, partly perhaps because the country's ills spring from maladministration rather than from a clash of ideologies.

No.95

British Legation to the Southern Department
Foreign Office
(37/12/38)
(R 3978/126/21)

BUDAPEST, *April 9, 1938*

(Excerpts)

We think that it may interest you to see a letter of the 8th instant which Gascoigne received from Bruce, the Adviser to the Hungarian National Bank, containing a note which the latter drew up at the request of the President of the National Bank, Dr. Imrédy, explaining and commenting upon the Jewish Bill.

We are inclined to agree generally with the view expressed in this note. It is, of course, much too early to prophesy the effect which the bill (should it become law in its present form) will have upon the Right extremists, and upon the economic life of the country.

Minutes

I am not altogether convinced by Mr. Bruce's apologia.

At present the Jews occupy a predominant position in commerce and the intellectual professions, because they are abler than the Hungarians who incline to disinterest themselves in such things. Now a considerable number of Jews are to be forced out of their jobs to make room for Hungarians and this will particularly hit the better class Jews. It may be true that the law under consideration is better than the iniquitous system in force in Germany but that does not make it anything but a wicked law. One can understand that the Jews in Hungary might be prepared to accept this measure of restriction, if they had some guarantee that it was final for all time; but is there really any ground for supposing that it will "take the wind out of the sails of the extremists"? If, as is only too likely, M. Daranyi is succeeded in the near future by someone more extreme, will not this law – assuming it is passed – be replaced by something more severe.

I fear this is the beginning and not the end of a drive against the Jews in Hungary and that they will ultimately be lucky if the are left with a right to 5% of the plums. . .

A. M. NOBLE, 22nd April, 1938

307

No. 96

A. D. F. Gascoigne to Lord Halifax
No. 62 (R 3979/99/21)

BUDAPEST, *April 11, 1938*

(Excerpts)

I have had the honour during the past two years to make mention in my despatches to Your Lordship's predecessor of the activities of the Right extremists in this country.

2. The Anschluss. . . has undoubtedly given a vigorous, but possibly only an ephemeral, fillip to the Hungarian Nazi movement. . . there is a substantial amount of poverty in Hungary in the industurial, agricultural, and professional spheres of the country's life, and the standard of living of the masses is low. It is not perhaps surprising, therefore, that many members of the middle and lower strata of the population should be impressed, generally with the efficiency of German methods, and in particular with the extraordinarily rapid implementation of such methods in a country which now marches with Hungary. While it is not possible at the present time to estimate the numerical strength of the Hungarian National Socialist movement, it seems clear that its ranks have become appreciably swollen since the Anschluss. Precise details regarding the extremists' programme. . . are not available. The Press Attache to this Legation, however, who has for many years been a close personal friend of Major Szalasi's chief lieutenant, gathers that its main plans, which would, of course, be put into force by unconstitutional means, are (a) the complete eradication of the Jewish element from Hungary's financial economic cultural and official life (sic), (b) agrarian reform, (c) redistribution of capital, and (d) intense economic development of the country on German lines.

3. It is extremely difficult to assess the number of persons in Hungary who would actually welcome a German Nazi administration, involving some form of subordination to the Reich. The majority of Hungarians of all classes who vaunt National Socialist ideas. . . refute any idea of domination by Berlin. . . and refer vaguely to a system parallel to that of Herr Hitler but purely Hungarian in character. . . My information leads me to believe that the leaders of the various extremist movements are not in favour of a German hegemony, and would be loath to submit to any form of German regimentation.

4. ... At the end of March I was moved by the echoes which reached me from responsible quarters, and by the severe criticism levelled against the Government by deputies of all colours, for its apparent inability to deal firmly with the situation... The unrest amongst the Jews which had amounted almost to a state of panic may be said to have reached its peak on March 31; but the speech pronounced by the Prime Minister of April 1 and, in particular, the address ... by the Regent... on April 3... have gone far towards tranquillizing public opinion...

5. At the time of writing it is difficult to predict as to the future. In so far as can be foreseen, however, the Prime Minister's policy of dealing with the extremists will be to endeavour to clip their wings by the gradual adoption, by constitutional means, of a programme similar but substantially less drastic, than their own. Thus a start has been made by the implementation of the Government's new schemes for social reform... and by the tabling of a Bill destined to restrict the activities of the Jews. It is too early to forecast whether this new orientation of Hungary's internal policy will have the effect of stemming the tide of extremism. At any rate something concrete is now being done to counter it, although it still remains to be seen whether the "New Deal" and the anti-Jewish measures contemplated will go far enough to satisfy the predatory exigencies of the Nazis.

No.97

Sir R. Hoare to Lord Halifax
No. 146 (4/101/38)

BUCHAREST, *April 14, 1938*

(Excerpts)

In continuation of my telegram No. 93 of to-day's date I have the honour to report that the Minister for Foreign Affairs spoke to me to-day with passionate earnestness on the subject of the Jewish problem. He said that in the course of the next two or three months the Roumanian Government would know how many of the Jews resident in Roumania had no rights of citizenship. Quite clearly it would be impossible to induce Soviet Russia, Poland, Hungary or Germany to allow them to return to their original homes even if they were prepared to go. Roumania would be certainly unwilling to give them the rights of citizenship but to keep them in the country as *staatslosen* would be to create an element susceptible to any revolutionary propaganda. A home must be found for them and quite obviously Palestine was entirely inadequate for that purpose. A radical and at the same time humane and statesmanlike solution of the Jewish problem in Central Europe was a matter of urgency and of world wide importance.

2.   He had, with the approval of the King, asked the American Minister whether the American Government would not be prepared to extend the scope of their recent proposals respecting political refugees from Austria and Jewish emigrants from the whole of Central and Eastern Europe. He hoped that under a Commissioner General of international repute it should be possible to float an international loan and he thought that the Roumanian Government should be able to devote a reasonable annual sum towards Jewish emigration, and that an organisation could be built up to acquire land in some of the empty spaces of the world including the British Empire where the Jews could settle in a real national home. It was in his view, as a citizen of the world and a good Christian, the great tragedy of history that for centuries Jews had been almost all over the world aliens in the country of their birth or residence. For countries with an excessive percentage of Jewish population such as Roumania and Poland there could be no real peace, and there was danger of serious trouble which admonitions from the League of Nations could do nothing to prevent, until some safety valve had been found.

3. I asked M. Comnen what my American colleague appeared to think of his proposals and he replied that he was interested and promised to report to the State Department. I have since learnt from Mr. Gunther that he has reported M. Comnen's request to Washington for favourable consideration, adding that he entirely shared the view that the Jewish problem should be tackled as a major international issue.

4. In a letter to Mr. Ingram of January 11th I urged the importance of indicating a readiness to cooperate in any serious emigration scheme that might be put forward and I still feel strongly that even if the number of Jews who eventually emigrated were only an infinitesimal percentage of the Jewish population of the country the psychological effect would be very valuable.

5. I have nothing very substantial to go on but I think the general impression is that the Iron Guard has not been appreciably weakened by the events of the last ten weeks. If this is so, and if the present Government fails to make even a beginning of a solution of the Jewish problem, I have an uncomfortable feeling that at a not very distant date serious trouble from the Iron Guard is to be expected. M. Comnen naturally did not give me any indication that such a thought was in his mind or in that of King Carol, but it would be natural if some such thought were present.

6. I recently received a visit from a Mr. Short who has been examining the Jewish problem on behalf of Chatham House. I gathered from him that, in his opinion, the Jewish problem is becoming desperately acute in Poland, and I am inclined to think that it is almost certain to become equally acute here. I would therefore urge that any proposals which the Roumanian Government may make with a view to a solution should not lightly be rejected because of obvious practical difficulties.

No.98

Foreign Office Memorandum on
Situation in Central and South Eastern Europe
(Prepared by Ph. Nichols)
(R 4141/1737/67)

FOREIGN OFFICE, *April 21, 1938*

(Excerpts)

[Germany] will attempt to extend her influence and make her will predominant by means of (a) the organisation of Nazi (or its equivalent in the idiom of the country concerned) cells or parties within the country itself and (b) by economic pressure. As regards (a) the circumstances vary of course in the different countries. In Czechoslovakia the Sudetendeutsch, who have accepted the *Führerprinzip* and are closely allied to National Socialist Party in Germany, already represent the biggest problem in the country. In the case of Roumania, the Iron Guard has been in existence for some time and constitutes the nucleus of a formidable party organised something on the lines of the Nazi and Fascist parties in Germany and Italy. In Hungary those in favour of totalitarian government represent so far only a small minority but active Nazi propaganda is being carried on with the help of German subsidies.

Yugoslavia and Greece are already virtually military dictatorships, and Bulgaria, though engaged in re-erecting a facade of parliamentary institutions, still enjoys what is in essence an authoritarian régime. The seed of Nazi doctrine, therefore, falls on fertile ground.

As regards (b), it is only necessary to say that Germany already has a predominant share in the trade of most of those countries, and that with the absorption of Austria this share will necessarily increase.

Sir G. Knox to Lord Halifax
No. 69 (R 4322/99/21)

BUDAPEST, *April 24, 1938*

(Excerpts)

The trend towards national socialist doctrine among the public and more particularly in the army becomes more marked, and I noticed for the first time the somewhat ominous symptom that public attention is beginning to concentrate on a particular one of the half-dozen groups which represent this ideology and on a particular leader — Szálasi,

2. For the moment at least Germany does not appear to be giving any open support to the movement, and, indeed, information reaches me from the Nazi camp to the effect that both Festetich, the leader of the Crossed Arrow Party, and an envoy of Major Szálasi, recently visited Herr Bürckel in Vienna only to be told Hungarian National Socialism was not welcome in Germany. I cannot, of course, vouch for the truth of this story. . On the whole. . . I am inclined to believe that it is true, since it is natural enough that the Germans should not wish to indispose a Hungarian Government which appears to be sufficiently subservient to them, by any encouragement of a subversive movement that must inevitably come to that Government's knowledge.

3. Meanwhile the Hungarian Government have done nothing to implement the recent assurances of the Regent and the Prime Minister that they would vigorously suppress subversive activities. Major Szálasi, it is true, remains, pending appeal, in domiciliary arrest, whence he conducts his agitation with the same energy and with a more romantic background than before. As for M. Boszormény. ,. who had also been released pending appeal, his case came up two days ago when the Court of second instance increased the sentence. . . passed on him. . . .

4. In general the Hungarian Government seems to be bent on placating their right wing by stealing the thunders of the extremists and re-emitting them as stage noises, a policy which does not inspire much confidence and of which the recent examples that occur to one, such as the Papen Government in Germany in 1932 and the Goga Government in Roumania last winter are not encouraging. The Government, it is true, have had to face an unfortunate combination of circumstances since they decided, in my opinion rightly, to counter an extremist movement which throve on

the great poverty of the working classes by the introduction of a large-scale plan for capital expenditure and social reform.

5.   Most unluckily the announcement of this plan was almost immediately followed by the Anschluss, which gave a further impetus to the Hungarian extremist movement, correspondingly frightened the Jews, weakened the Stock Exchange and thus went far to compromise in advance of the Capital Levy on which the plan is founded. The tabling of the Bill to restrict the normal activities of the Jews has further advanced this process and weakened the position of the Government.

Minutes (A. D. M. Ross, 29/4)

With all respect, I don't think the story in para 2 can be entirely true. Germany can perfectly well countenance and encourage the spread of Hungarian Nazism and at the same time prevent it from discomfiting the subservient Gov[ernmen]t at Budapest.

The Hungarian Gov[ernmen]t's policy against the Nazis. . . is proving ineffective. But even an effective policy against the Nazis w[oul]d not release Hungary from the German embrace. . .

No.100

Letter from Montagu Norman to Lord Halifax
Notes on a discussion with B. Imrédy,
Governor of the Hungarian National Bank
(R 4496/99/21)

April 26, 1938

(Excerpts)

The young men of Hungary, and not only those without employment, are infected, to an overwhelming majority, with National Socialist and notably anti-Jewish, ideas. More serious still, these ideas are rampant among the officers. It goes without saying that these ideas, which date from well before the 11th March and were even among the causes which impelled Imrédy to draw up, some six months ago, his economic programme, have received a considerable impetus from the Anschluss. Although Dr. Eckhardt. . . emphatically asserts that the extremist movement is being encouraged and financed from Germany, it is not believed in more authoritative circles that this is the case. Indeed it would seem reasonable to suppose that the coming into power of a dilettante National Socialist Government in Hungary, resulting in economic chaos and ending perhaps with an appeal, à la Seyss-Inquart, for German intervention would greatly embarrass the Germans.

But, with or without German support, the movement exists, and in spite of a perceptible tendency in Government circles to belittle its importance, in spite . . . of such measures as the economic programme and the anti-Jewish Law, it is fast gaining in momentum. . .

As far as the economic programme is concerned, it is Imrédy's firm intention that it should go on, though of course, until confidence is restored, there can be no question of an internal loan, and the Government will have to proceed by some other means, such, for instance, as drawing on its giro account with the National Bank or on other funds – e.g., the agrarian fund – at its disposal.

At the bottom of all this crise de confiance are, only too naturally, the Jews. They would have welcomed, and indeed many of the more far-sighted, on the principle of half a loaf being better than no bread, actually solicited the sacrifices imposed upon them by the economic programme and even by the anti-Jewish Law, had those measures been accompanied by firm action on the part of the Government to put a stop to extremist agitation. But such action has not been taken. Speeches have been made, a few ladylike arrests have been carried out, officers guilty of observations perilously approaching high treason have been told not to be naughty boys, but no real examples, visible for all to see, have been made.

It is easy to criticise; much more difficult to make a concrete proposal as to what should be done. Excessive leniency has been shown to lead nowhere; the making of martyrs would lead in the wrong direction. Probably the middle way and the wisest would take two directions; firstly to clear the army of politics with a firm and demonstrative hand; secondly to try, by centrally directed propaganda, to point out to the youth of the country that their way is the path of eventual but sure destruction, individual and national. Such a policy, however, requires for its success a leader with a hard fist and with the power to inspire men with enthusiasm. Unfortunately, the present Prime Minister, honourable and able politician though he is, has neither of these qualifications, and so long as he remains in office there is unlikely to be any return of confidence sufficient to set the wheels of the machine turning again.

There is in fact only one man in Hungary who possesses these two gifts and to whom all the better elements in Hungary turn for salvation, and that is Imrédy. Eckhardt has asserted that he will never rest till Daranyi leaves office and Imredy takes his place. The Regent is alleged by Eckhardt to be in favour of Imredy's becoming Prime Minister but to be unwilling himself to provoke the crisis. Eckhardt is consequently in favour of Imredy doing so by going to the Regent and refusing responsibility for the economic programme unless confidence is restored. This of course Imredy refuses to do. He would be willing, if the appointment were made "before things get too bad" to take over the Government, but he will himself do nothing to provoke the crisis. He says Eckhardt and the Jews are "supporting him to death". . . .

No.101

Telegram from Sir R. Hoare to the Foreign Office
No. 98 (R)
(R 4366/4032/67)

BUCHAREST, *April 28, 1938*

Minister for Foreign Affairs begs you will not press for observations on Jewish petitions stating fact that observations had been submitted would certainly be known and would be regarded here as defeat of Roumanian Government by International Jewry and abandonment of position successfully maintained by M. Micescu. It would produce a storm just at the moment when the Government was being eminently successful in restoring confidence of Jewish population. He said he would give me particulars of message from prominent Jews here to the world Jewish congress urging that petitions be at any rate suspended. I told him we had always [grp. omitted]* (though it is not very categorically stated in telegram No. 2 to me from Geneva) that observations would be furnished in ordinary way and Minister for Foreign Affairs replied that M. Micescu had certainly not reported [grp. undec.] He went on to beg while maintaining as he fully understood we must, our obligations under minorities treaty we mark time and he felt positively sure that by the autumn improvement in minority situation would be apparent to all. He begged you to remember that Roumanian Government were still engaged in critical struggle with a dangerous movement of extreme right and in that struggle Jewish issue played an important even though [grp. omitted]** part.

Nothing that he said was to be taken to mean that he would not be more than willing to discuss with yourself or your experts any aspects of Jewish problem which you might wish to raise but he repeated that if the League insisted on procedure laid down in minorities treaty being strictly followed at present time the task of appeasement which the Government had successfully initiated would be rendered infinitely more difficult. I then told Minister for Foreign Affairs that he had presumably noticed before the recess a number of Parliamentary Questions had been addressed to His Majesty's Government on the subject of the Jewish question and you anticipated there would be more and you had therefore asked me to

*?supposed? (Marginal note added by an official in the Foreign Office)
**?unpleasant? (Marginal note)

317

furnish you with concrete evidence that the situation of the Jews had materially improved. I had no difficulty in telling you that general atmosphere was definitely better but I was far from being sure what position was at the Universities especially in faculties of the law and medicine and whether Jewish lawyers were free to exercise their profession.

Minister for Foreign Affairs said he would look into these points and let me know.

Minutes by A. D. M. Ross (April 30, 1938)

It should be remembered (a) that the Iron Guard, which lives largely on anti-Semitism, has recently received a number of fairly serious blows the effect of which would be considerably lessened if it were possible for them to indulge in an orgy of anti-Semite exaltation, (b) that the better Jews in Roumania, for example of the old Kingdom, deplore the action of so-called representative bodies at Geneva, Paris and London (we knew this in the days of the Goga Government). (c) If in addition M. Comnen keeps his promise and supplies Sir R. Hoare with informations as to the position of the Jews in the universities and the professions we should have a fair amount of justification in soft pedalling at Geneva.

No.102

British Attitude Towards Roumanian Jewish Policy
Cabinet 22(38)10.
May 4, 1938
(Conclusions)

The Secretary of State for Foreign Affairs said that he had seen Roumanian Minister who reported that his Government was adopting a better attitude towards the Jews and that there was a considerable *détente* in Roumania on this question. The Minister had added that nothing could be more detrimental than pressure from Geneva. He himself had told the Minister that if Roumanian Government had a case to make on these lines it would be as well that they should make it at Geneva. It would, however, be a great mistake on their part not to answer the questions put to them by the League.

No. 103

Memorandum by Royall Tylor,
the League of Nations financial adviser to
Hungarian Government on situation in Hungary
(Transmitted by the United Kingdom Delegation, Geneva)
No. 61 (R 4851/99/21)

GENEVA, May 14, 1938

(Excerpts)

3.   Such, roughly speaking, is the prevalent view in the circles that have governed Hungary, and are still governing today, and of the majority of Hungarians who have a stake in the country, including the mass of peasant proprietors. It is not certain, however, that these circles will continue to govern. There is much discontent in the country, much criticism of the Government on the ground that it does nothing on a sufficiently big scale, that it is afraid to deal with the Jewish question, afraid of industry, finance and the big landowners, and that its fidelity to Hungarian Parliamentary tradition is a fatal handicap at a time when a Government cannot afford to be hampered by hindrances to rapid and efficient action. These criticisms are made by numerous malcontents, by young men turned out by the Universities and technical schools, many of whom cannot in present circumstances hope to find employment in the branches for which they have been trained. Similar doctrines are being preached to the agrarian proletariat, not without effect. And in this connexion it is important to remember that no one can safely call himself a communist in Hungary to-day, but many hold communist opinions, and find in the Nazi doctrine enough to their liking to make them willing to join forces and to improve the new opportunities for agitation conferred on them by a label which is not taboo. Further, the army, and in particular the general staff, has long considered that national defence was being starved by a Government composed of politicians, hidebound in their prejudices in favour of the country's ancient Parliamentary tradition, of individual freedom, of budgetary stability and other such obsolete fetishes. There is thus a large body of opinion in Hungary, representing several strata of society, which regards it as a necessary condition of progress to break with the past, to put the conduct of affairs into the hands of men who are uncorrupted by wealth or by the political game. Its leaders would not hesitate to appeal to Germany for guidance, and indeed for a general staff

to make order after the Nazi pattern. The watchword would be to take finance and industry out of the hands of the Jews, thus providing jobs for the educated unemployed, split up the big estates and give land to the landless peasant, and make rearmament the cardinal point in the Government's programme, all under German management.

4.   It is difficult to estimate Nazidom's chances of prevailing in Hungary, but few who know the country well would deny that it is gaining ground. It appears not to have thrown up, so far, any outstanding leader. Major Szalasi (sic), who for a time looked like becoming one, has lately suffered from the revelation that he is of Armenian origin, and that his war record is not an impressive one. But evidence of its spread is beginning to show even in the attitude of certain prominent members of the party supporting the Government. At present an active, confident and irresponsible minority is agitating for a Nazi solution, while the Government itself, having made its bid with its one milliard pengo public works and rearmament programme and with its bill curtailing the employment of Jews, waits for the hoped-for response, and so far waits in vain. . .

No.104

B. C. Newton to Lord Halifax
No.160 (C 4632/2319/12)

PRAGUE, May 16, 1938

[Transmits Memorandum by "a reliable British subject" on future of the Slovak policy, noting: "I am in general agreement with the views expressed therein."]

(Excerpts)

24. . . . .The Slovaks would never be willingly led, whether by Sidor or by anyone else, into open treachery to the republic. They might be misled into it. *Sidor* has stony cards in his hand now: Slovakia has a new, nationally conscious and under-employed intelligentsia and *Hlinka* has led this intelligentsia part of the way towards rapprochement with their former rulers. If and when the Czechoslovak Government is compelled by Hitler to accede to extravagant Sudetic German demands, *Sidor* will have a stronger case in his hands. For, if the Germans are worthy of complete autonomy, how much more worthy are the Slovaks. . .

The Jews are believed to be not averse from lending a hand to Hungarian intrigues, and the financial power of the Jews in Slovakia is great.

25. Many Jews in Bratislava are already beginning to look around for some other country in which to settle. But there are many more who realise that their hope of getting out is small; and they tend to take the Hungarian or German rather than the Czech side. There is one reason for this in the fact that the Slovak Jews generally have relatives in Hungary, and that, it is said, these relatives are liable to painful pressure from the Hungarian authorities if the Slovak branch of the family does not show itself pro-Hungarian in spirit. There is one reason for this in the fact that many Slovak Jews believe the Czechoslovak state to be doomed and, as one Jew said to me, "would become Turks tomorrow if we could ensure our safety that way."

26. . . . .Since . . . the other provinces are in an unsettled state, and since this state seems likely to be intensified in the near future, the possibility of Slovak defection – even if it is no more than a possibility – should perhaps be taken into account.

No. 105

Sir G. Knox to Lord Halifax
No. 83 (R 5163/99/21)

BUDAPEST, *May 21, 1938*

(Excerpts)

2.   . . . . It has become increasingly clear both in Parliament and on the Stock Exchange that neither moderate political opinion nor the monied classes — consisting mainly of the Jews — were prepared to stomach both the Capital Levy and the legal restrictions which it was sought to impose on the Jews unless the Government could on their side give good ground to hope that these measures would be final and not only the prelude to a campaign of spoliation, by taking proper steps to suppress extremist and anti-Semitic agitation — a task, which it had long been evident, was beyond either the powers or the will of the Daranyi Government.

3.   [The new Government, formed by B. Imredy]. . .presented his bills for the suppression of subversive activities [and] has smoothed the passage through the Upper House of the bill imposing restrictions on the Jews. . .At the same time some concern is felt in the Hungarian National Socialist camp where, it is said, Major Szalasi intends for the time being to abandon his subterranean activities and to harness himself to the political party of M. Hubay.

4.   . . .though I personally believe that, had the authorities six months ago meted out to a few adventurers of the Right the same justice as is reserved for those accused of Communism, their movement, which in Hungary is fundamentally alien, would by now have been extinct, I do not feel that this treatment could be applied with the same confidence today. With long impunity, with tacit and even sometimes overt encouragement from above and with the impetus of the Anschluss National-Socialism has spread widely in the Army and even in the Police force so that to send Major Szalasi and his compeers to penal servitude might no longer offer a solution — and it is on a solution of this question that the ultimate success or failure of the Imredy Government will depend.

No.106

Remarks by R. H. Hadow on P. W. Scarlett's letter
to R. M. Marins (from Riga, June 30, 1938)
(C 6873/1667/62)

FOREIGN OFFICE, *July 14, 1948*

(Excerpts)

With regard to the remark. . . that "there is no anti-Semitic feeling among the Czechs", this is quite incorrect. Mr. Short cannot possibly have talked to the Jews of Prague whose constant complaint is that they are disliked by both sides: by the German-speaking (Henlein) minority as anti-Germans, by the Czechs as "Germans" because they speak and use that language for business purposes, support the German (and not the Czech) opera as giving more scope for music, (in the Czech Opera House only Czech music is given) and must – in order to live – trade with Germany.

Their gradual "occupation" of such professions as medicine, law (these two especially) and their hold over business have – as in Vienna – earned them the most unfortunate dislike of Czech and Sudeten students alike.

In fact in Czechoslovakia as in the other countries mentioned there is a deep-seated *popular* prejudice against them due largely to their success and "encroachment" upon restricted fields of activity. Of this prejudice they are only too well aware and it is a source of great anxiety to them. The Czechoslovak Government does not on the other hand discriminate against them as elsewhere; but they are not liked by the Agrarian or "National Alliance" political parties because of their trade-and-loan profession in the villages.

No.107

A. D. F. Gascoigne to Lord Halifax
No. 139 (R 7062/99/21)

BUDAPEST, *August 15, 1938*

(Excerpts)

2.   . . . the Right extremist movement in Hungary is not a united one but is carried on by some seven parties each other under their own leader. . . At the beginning of the present month the Hungarian National-Socialists belonging to the party under the leadership of Count Alexander Festetich decided to throw in their lot with Major Szalasi. The number of registered members in Count Festetich's party amounts. . . to some thirty thousand, and now that this fusion has taken place, Major Szalasi will have a total of some ninety thousand registered followers. In this connection I would further mention that the Press Attaché to His Majesty's Legation has been informed. . . that there were some fifty thousand more applications for entry to the party which had not yet been dealt with. . .

3.   . . . Anti-Semitism in the country districts is, I understand, on the increase, but this is not as yet conducted as a racial question, and the peasants apparently have confined themselves up to now to marking down such Jews who have in their estimation treated them badly in the past. Thus, a certain amount of discretion is being used and the Jews who are not considered to have done harm are not molested.

6.   While the Prime Minister is relentlessly pushing forward his plans in economic, financial, and cultural fields for exterminating the National-Socialist disease, I have learnt . . . that Dr. Imredy remains somewhat apprehensive of the danger which may assail him from this quarter. . .

No.108

B. C. Newton to Lord Halifax
No. 294 (C 8458/2319/12)

PRAGUE, *August 15, 1938*

[Transmits record of a conversation between Lieutenant-Colonel H. C. T. Strange, Military Attaché, and Count Eszterházy, leader of the Hungarian minority in Czechoslovakia]

(Excerpts)

Count Eszterházy. . . referred briefly to the present situation in Hungary. He said that Nazism was gaining ground rapidly because the people, especially the peasants, were dissatisfied with their lot and saw in Nazism a remedy for most of their ills. Young Hungarians who had been to Germany came back vastly impressed with what they had seen and spread the doctrine. The land, a considerable portion of which was in the hands of a few large landowners – he cited incidentally his brothers' big estates – would have to be more fairly distributed and that would probably come about under a Nazi régime. There would also be less unemployment and better markets for produce. . .

No.109

Letter from A. D. F. Gascoigne to P. B. B. Nichols
(17/55/38) (R 7393/99/21)

BUDAPEST, August 20, 1938

[On conversation between Count Mycielski, Polish Minister in Budapest and F. Szálasi]

(Excerpts)

My Polish colleague, an intelligent young man who has served here for several years, gave me recently an interesting description of a conversation which he held with Major Szálási some two months ago, before the latter was sent to prison.

Count Mycielski, while he found Major Szálási fairly practical in his outlook, did not consider that he had the makings of a "Führer" either physically or mentally. He did not think that he possessed the attributes which are necessary for a leader.

Major Szálási spoke at length to Count Mycielski on the subject of the internal and external programme. He prefaced his conversation, and repeated this at short intervals, that one of the chief aims of the Hungarian Nazis if they came into power would be to avoid German domination, The Nazi movement was a purely Hungarian one and would remain so. As to external policy, Major Szálási would favour a Warsaw-Budapest-Rome axis (Sir G. Knox's despatch No. 100, para 10, of June 4) which would form a protective barrier against Germany. He was also in favour of an "economic" axis running from Berlin to Bucharest via Budapest and Belgrade. While he admitted that Hungary was to all intents and purposes at Germany's mercy economically, much could be done to mitigate this by the formation of the political North to South axis above-mentioned. He further spoke most pretentiously of regaining Hungary's pre-war territories by force of arms!

As regards the internal programme, he explained more or less the same policy as Mr. Hubay, the Nazi Deputy, expounded in his speech at Szombathély (my despatch No. 139, para 4, of August 15), and stressed that he was fully aware of the danger, to the economic life of Hungary, of any drastic agrarian reform.

Speaking generally Count Mycielski agreed with me that, although the internal atmosphere was less charged than it had been, the Nazi danger was still something to be reckoned with. He further agreed that if anything happened to the Prime Minister, Dr. Imredy, the situation might become extremely dangerous, as there seemed to be no one else fitted to tackle the very serious position in which Hungary now finds herself both internally and externally. But, given a fair wind, however, we both thought that the present Government had an excellent chance to exterminate the Nazi disease from Hungarian politics. . . .

No.110

A. D. F. Gascoigne to Lord Halifax
No. 147 (R 7394/99/21)

BUDAPEST, *August 25, 1938*

[Reports on Szálasi being sentenced to penal servitude for aiming at seizing power by force:]

(Excerpts)

3. The firm attitude adopted by Dr. Imredy's Government against refractory extremist elements has reassured public opinion. . . the confirmation of Major Szalasi's sentence has, contrary to popular expectation, been taken quietly by his party, and no violent reaction appears to be imminent. But this does not, of course, necessarily imply that the present leaders of the party are resting on their oars, or that the party is losing ground.

Minutes by A. N. Noble (7/9)

But the battle has hardly even begun yet.

Minutes by G. L. McDermott (7/9)

It is not surprising that a young Nazi party in Hungary sh[oul]d stress its support of Hungarian independence and nationalism. But as it has probably been fostered partly by German funds it is questionable whether these affirmations w[oul]d be realised in practice if the Nazis were to come into power in Hungary.

Minutes by A. N. Noble (7th Sept., 1938)

It is obviously impossible to forecast the policy of a Nazi Government in Hungary. The fact that it came to power with German support would not necessarily make it pro-German in the long run; gratitude is rare in international affairs and such movements tend to be nationalistic. But common aims, particularly in regard to Czechoslovakia, would tend to draw Hungary and Germany together under any circumstances and a similarity of ideologies would of course strengthen this tendency.

No.111

Sir Neville Henderson to Lord Halifax
[Transmits record of a conversation between
S. Horthy, elder son of Admiral Horthy and
F. N. Mason-MacFarlane, Military Attaché;
record by F. N. Mason-MacFarlane]
No. 905 (203/59/38), copy of despatch from
Berlin, August 26, 1938
(R 7305/719/21)

BERLIN, *August 26, 1938*

(Excerpts)

2.   We discussed the *NAZI* situation in Hungary and he admitted that the whole question had assumed serious proportions. He thought however that the Government had the matter well in hand, as the movement was not united and lacked efficient leaders. Adequate disciplinary action was being taken against these. The most disquieting feature of the situation was the fact that the Hungarian NAZIs are very well provided with funds. I asked if these funds were of German origin, and he replied without having definite knowledge of the sources from which the Hungarian NAZIs obtained their money it was only possible to guess, but that the conclusion he had come to was the obvious one.

No.112

Foreign Office Minutes by I. Mallet
on political situation in Hungary
(C 12627/2319/12)

FOREIGN OFFICE, *October 12, 1938*

Sir A. Salter said that he did not share the view held in certain quarters to the effect that Hungary had irretrievably fallen under German domination. He felt sure that neither M. Imredy nor Count Teleki wished their country to be completely under German domination. . . The second point Sir Arthur made was that M. Imredy and Count Teleki were probably the best bulwarks which there could be against Hungarian Nazism. He, however, felt it essential that if Nazism were to be prevented in Hungary — and if Nazism came Hungary would be definitely lost to Germany — the present Government should be enabled to show a reasonable measure of success in foreign policy, viz. in the minority question in Slovakia and Ruthenia.

No.113

Foreign Office Minutes
by Davis Stephens
(R 8335/99/21)

FOREIGN OFFICE, *October 17, 1938*

[Records conversation with Mr. Bruce, Adviser to the National Bank of Hungary and Imrédy's friend.]

(Excerpts)

3.   The alternative to the present god-fearing and civilised Government in Hungary was an even more vicious form of Nazism than at present existed in Germany. If Imredy's Government fell it would be replaced by a régime that would be distinguished by all the barbarities and none of the efficiency of the Nazis in Germany.

4.   Would it not, asked Mr. Bruce, be possible for His Majesty's Government to take a little more friendly interest in the question of Hungarian claims. . . . ? This friendly interest need not go to the length of backing the Hungarian claims, some of which were justified and some not, but it would go far to dispel the Hungarian *déception* if we came forward from time to time with advice, thus showing. . . that it did matter to us whether a civilised Government was maintained in Hungary or not.

Minutes

. . . There is a certain amount of evidence to show that if Hungary does not soon get what she regards as reasonable satisfaction from Czechoslovakia, the moderate M. Imredy will be driven from power by the extreme Nazis. Hungary is still an independent state and she may not yet feel compelled to do everything that Germany might wish her to do, but she can do nothing that Germany does not wish. . . It is worth our while to do what little we can to help M. Imredy to retain some slight freedom of manoeuvre if only because Hungary may under certain circumstances form the battleground in a clash of German and Italian interests; but we must not flatter ourselves that we can do very much.

A. N. NOBLE, 19.X.1938

And we must be careful not to do anything which will enable M. Imredy to play us off against Hitler.

O. G. SARGENT, Oct.20 (1938)

No.114

Letter from B. C. Newton to W. Strang*
(C 12946/2475/12)

PRAGUE, *October 22, 1938*

(Excerpts)

2.   I said in my telegram No. 985 of the 18th October that my impression was that Czechs had not yet taken all their new bearings. While I was thinking chiefly of their international position, the same applies, I think, to the internal position. . . This is not to say that the ordinary peasant feels greatly affected by the recent upheavals. . . the contrary is indeed the case, and his chief feeling is probably one of relief that he was not called upon to spill his blood. I am not suggesting that he would not have done his duty if called upon to do so, but that is quite a different thing. He had no great use for the politicians of the past régime, whom he regarded largely as a band of robbers feathering their own work. . .

3.   But it is not, of course, the ordinary peasant who makes history. The Czech *political* world is still wondering where it stands or is moving. The dominant party in Bohemia today is that of the Agrarians, who have always been renowned for political opportunism, and were in the past more favourable to co-operation with Germany than any other of the coalition parties. It may safely be assumed that they stand today for co-operation with Germany and have persuaded a majority in the Government that that is the only possible policy. The more leftward parties, who were loyal supporters of Benes, and violently anti-German in outlook, are now of course discredited and feel entirely at sea. Their intellectual home lay in the west (sic!) which has now deserted them, and Russia, the big Slav brother, is a long way off. The feeling of spiritual brotherhood with Russia may go deep, but I doubt if it has any great political importance at the moment. You will have had a glimpse of the state of confusion from my saving telegrams Nos. 509 and 510 of October 17th, showing how Benes' old party (or at any rate its two leading papers) turned pro-German almost overnight, and the Social Democrats severed their connection with international socialism. . . Now they are talking of changing their name into the Working People's Party.

*Published in Documents on British Foreign Policy, Third Series, III, No.219

4. ...The authoritarian trend is clearly visible and, as the left is discredited and German influence an obvious if unpleasant necessity, it means a drift to the Right and not the Left form of authoritarianism. The Communist Party for example has been eliminated, labour camps being formed, and I hear that legislation is being discussed to restrict the activities of Jews. I am also told that the new Ministry of Propaganda is staffed with officials who hold views very much to the Right. The same tendency is appearing in all the Government departments.

5. In Slovakia. . . the People's Party. . .is going ahead on fascist lines far more openly and obviously than the Central Government. It seems already to have eliminated all Slovak opposition. . .

It is indeed a misfortune that the protestants, who are probably the most civilized people in Slovakia and the most inclined to co-operate with the Czechs, should not be able to participate in organising the country at this time of stress. I fear we must look forward to a period of very crude Slovak nationalism and no doubt corruption. One result will be that the Czech officials will be turned out – the process has begun already – thus adding to the refugee problem. Another will be a more or less acute anti-Jewish policy.

Minutes

The main tendency seems clear i.e. a steady trend towards national-socialism. Meanwhile particularist feeling seems likely to become increasingly strong among the various national groups, with Germany encouraging local differences in order to weaken the Central Gov[ern-men]t's authority and establish her stranglehold on the country all the more firmly.

R. G. A. ETHERINGTON-SMITH, October 31, 1938

A new point we shall have to keep an eye on is the likelihood of anti-Jewish legislation.

R. SPEAR HUDSON, November 2, 1938

No.115

Telegram from B. C. Newton* to the Foreign Office
No. 999 (C12773/11896/12)

PRAGUE, *October 22, 1938*

(Excerpts)

... The last thing Czechoslovakia wanted today was an addition to her Jewish population. Nor would it be beneficial to the Jews themselves as feeling against them in the country was rising. It was asked at the same time whether representations could not be made in Berlin to stop German authorities dumping these unwanted Jews of occupied territories into what remained of Czechoslovakia.

I am sure you will agree that these arguments and requests are reasonable. . . Even though these refugees may be Czechoslovak citizens their living room has been taken over by the Reich and living room left for the real Czechs is likely to be seriously overcrowded. While too accommodation of extra Jews may be an inconvenience for other countries it may for the Czechs be not only an economic but a political danger. There is already evidence of this in continuance of anti-Jewish campaign in Czech broadcast from Germany. Further point is that many Jews expelled from occupied areas are said to be persons of means whose property has if I am rightly informed, been seized by German authorities. It seems indefensible that cost of maintaining such persons and sending them to new homes should fall either upon Czechoslovak Government and upon £10,000,000 especially if the latter is to be a loan and not a gift.

Enclosure in No.115

Foreign Office Tel. No. 513 to Sir N. Henderson

FOREIGN OFFICE, *October 26, 1938*

(Excerpts)

... German authorities in Sudeten areas are expelling Jews. . . [Czech Government] are refusing to admit them, and Jews are squatting in

*Published in DBFP, III, No.219

335

deplorable conditions in no man's land between Czech and German lines. Czech Government state that Czech Red Cross are arranging to supply food and clothing to these people, but the practice of expelling Jews in this manner is not only inhumane, but also contrary to the intentions of the Munich Agreement, Article 7, which provides for the right of option into and out of the transferred territories but contemplates the making of proper arrangements to assist optants and protect their property rights. Nor can the Czech Government be altogether blamed for refusing to admit refugees created in such a manner.

Please therefore approach German Government in your capacity as a member of the International Commission and in accordance with the supplementary declaration of the Munich Agreement, and urge them to refrain from such expulsions.

No.116

B. C. Newton to Lord Halifax
No. 365 (C13112/2475/12)

PRAGUE, *October 26, 1938*

(Excerpts)

2. .... There is a tendency to attribute to the short-sighted and selfish policy of the parties, in pursuing their own rather than national interests, a considerable share of the blame for the country's recent misfortunes, and all shades of political opinion seem agreed that the former party system must be radically reformed and simplified to meet the new situation. It is moreover pointed out by many papers that a mere reduction in the number of parties will not be sufficient unless they are animated by a new spirit and are prepared to put nation before party.

3. The organ of the Agrarian Party, the "Venkov", recently published an article advocating the formation of a national party on a wide basis. The article said that a dictatorship would not be suitable for a fundamentally democratic nation like Czechoslovakia. The alternative was to create an authoritative and disciplined democracy, free from corruption, and a new party system which would serve the State and not the parties. The Social Democrats had refused to unite with Communists and were negotiating with the National Socialists to form a Labour Party. Nor were the Agrarian party being active. The middle class section of the population must unite in a great national party to serve the nation. The party would be based on the groups which represented agriculture, trade and industry, the intellectuals and those elements of the labouring classes who were genuinely nationalist and repudiated the idea of the class struggle.

No.117

B. C. Newton to Lord Halifax
No. 366 (C 13068/1667/62)

PRAGUE, *October 26, 1938*

For some weeks past it has been apparent that feeling against the Jews is on the increase not only in Slovakia, where the Slovak People's Party have long been making party capital out of it, but also in Bohemia which has sometimes been regarded as a kind of haven for the chosen race.

2.   An indication of the new trend of feeling was given in a resolution approved on the 23rd October at a committee meeting at the Sokol organisations. The resolution dealt with many aspects of national reconstruction, and contained a paragraph which read as follows:

> "The Jewish question should on national and social grounds be so resolved that those who have immigrated into the country since 1914 should return to their original homes. Of the remaining Jews those who have acquired Czechoslovak nationality since 1930 might gradually be incorporated in the social structure of our nation in proportion to their number. The remainder might then return to the lands of those nationalities which they voluntarily professed in 1930" (i.e. at the time of the last census).

3.   While the precise proposal of the Sokol organisations is not clear, no room for doubt is left as to its general spirit.

*B. C. Newton to Lord Halifax**
No. 377 (C 13469/2475/12)

PRAGUE, *November 1, 1938*

(Excerpts)

3.   There can be little doubt that the democratic system as it has developed in this country during the past twenty years has not been a wholly unmixed blessing, even for the Czechs by whom and for whom it was elaborated. Under it quick and clear decisions were difficult to come by, and party considerations were only too often given pride of place over national. Moreover, it is hardly an exaggeration to say that all public appointments, even down to that of crossing sweeper, depended upon possession of the necessary party ticket, so that each party became almost a State within the State. To-day there is a natural tendency to say goodbye to all that and one of the constant themes in the press is that public life and the social services must be cleansed of patronage and the misuse of political influence. Criticism is heard not only of the quality but of the quantity of officials in the Civil Service. . . .

4.   It is being found easier, however, to diagnose the disease than to find a remedy. The reform and simplification of the party system to which I referred in my despatch No. 635 of the 24th October appears to be meeting with difficulties. A great manifesto was to have been published . . . to inaugurate the new national party which the Agrarian leader, Monsieur Beran, has been endeavouring to organise. No such manifesto appeared, but only an announcement by the Traders' party, which was to have formed part of the bloc, that though ready to co-operate with other parties, it was determined to maintain its independent existence. The Clericals made a similar pronouncement. . . It is suggested that a greater measure of unity is being shown on the Left, and the new National party of the Working People, under which title the Social Democrats are now appearing, did indeed publish a manifesto. . . appealing to all honest citizens of whatever class, profession or party to join its ranks. . . The National Socialists held a meeting two days later and passed a resolution which, while recognizing the need for closing the political ranks, added

*Published in DBFP, III, No.245

that there must be no mechanical fusion of parties and groups of interests. . .

5.   There is thus nothing to show as yet that the confusion into which the political world fell a month ago is at an end. The press utters warnings against adventures, dictatorship and other undesirable possibilities, but gives little positive lead. There are nevertheless indications that things are moving in what is commonly described as a Fascist direction. General Syrovy's broadcast with its warning against 'politics' was significant in that respect. On the same day the unofficial Czechoslovak National Council published a manifesto pleading for the reconstruction of a "true National State" (that rock on which the Sudeten issue foundered), free of all unhealthy elements. Reference has been made in previous communications to the new anti-semitic trend, and anti-semite demonstrations have even taken place in Prague. Again the Communist party . . . has been dissolved. Meanwhile. . . . economic measures are being taken of an increasingly authoritarian nature. There are some who suggest that the Czechs are going Fascist as hard as they can in order to spite the French and English, against whom their bitterness has little abated. Whether or not this be the case, there are many other reasons which would naturally lead the Czechs to change their whole political outlook. In the first place it seems clear that they have no option now but to do Germany's bidding. That in itself would incline them to follow Germany's political example. Secondly, the paths of democracy have led them but to the grave, and it is only natural that they should turn elsewhere in their efforts at reconstruction. Thirdly, the problems to be solved are of too urgent a character to permit of the slow processes of decision hitherto in use. Finally, though the Czechs like to think of themselves as democrats by nature (and far be it from me to question the claim), nevertheless they were accustomed for three hundred years to a very different system, and a tradition of authoritative rule dies hard. Altogether, there is no need to search for reasons why this country should adopt a more authoritarian system. The difficulty may be to find the men to work it, as the politicians of the old régime are largely discredited and there are no new names that leap to the mind. . . .

8.   . . . Having at last won their independence, the Slovaks are now proceeding to enjoy it with more enthusiasm than responsibility. . . According to Dr. Tiso the party system must give place to the corporative. . . The Slovak Government, again, were the first to dissolve the Communist party. Freemasons also came under the ban, and the Jews, who have always been an important element in the towns, must be feeling anxiety as to their future. Deputy Sidor, for example, . . . published a violent anti-Jewish article. . . saying that the country must be swept clean

and the Aryan clause proclaimed. Fascist ideals and practices seem clearly to be the order of the day in the new Slovakia, to which must be added a primitive clericalism. . .

Minutes by J. K. Roberts (9/11)

An interesting despatch, showing the state of confusion throughout Czechoslovakia. As the previous democratic régime and its leaders are so clearly discredited by the turn of events, and drastic remedies will be needed, evolution towards an authoritarian régime seems inevitable.

No.119

Sir G. Knox to Lord Halifax
No. 173 (R 8919/33/21)

BUDAPEST, *November 2, 1938*

(Excerpts)

5. ...One has constantly heard it affirmed during the past month that M. Imrédy's Government had to take action that appeared unnecessary or out of place because they were forced to do so by pressure from the extreme Right or popular passions... I have seen no evidence of any such pressure, but have had the constant impression that the Government were running away from their own shadow and giving encouragement to the National Socialists by displaying an unreasonable fear.

Minutes by A. N. Noble (14/11)

Sir G. Knox has been consistently pessimistic about the internal situation in Hungary and about her subservience to Germany. He may well be right on both points, but many other competent observers disagree.... Recent history seems to show that a determined minority will always succeed in fighting their way to power unless firmly jumped on at the beginning of the movement. It is impossible to assess the strength of the Hungarian Nazi movement, in the face of the conflicting opinions we hear about it; but it does seem clear that it must be jumped on *now*; otherwise, weak or strong, it will be a formidable weapon in German hands...

NOBLE, 14 November, 1938

No.120

Sir G. Knox to Lord Halifax
No. 175 (R 8921/626/21)

BUDAPEST, *November 5, 1938*

(Excerpts)

9.   There still appears to persist in certain circles in England a belief fostered by unofficial agents of the Hungarian Government that, if His Majesty's Government would only make wide but unspecified economic and financial concessions to Hungary, this country would be able to remain outside the German orbit, and to avoid the establishment of a National Socialist Government. I am afraid I can lend no encouragement to these illusions. Whether Hungary is to have a totalitarian Government or not will depend here, as elsewhere, on the power of the constitutional authorities to govern, and not on any largesse received from outside. There is, of course, the possibility of a National-Socialist Government being imposed from abroad, but I have no ground whatsoever to believe that there is, for the present, any likelihood of this, nor, if there were, could any concessions from us prevent it. I am therefore, of opinion that we should do what we can to develop our trade with Hungary on purely economic lines of mutual benefit, free of all political considerations.
10.   As to the possibility of Hungary keeping outside the German orbit, or standing in the way of German progress to the South-East, I agree entirely with Count Ciano's simile of the single strand of wire in front of an elephant. I am afraid that those who play with these ideas fail to appreciate the simple historical truth that the only period of effective independence which Hungary has enjoyed since the medieval kingdom was destroyed at Mohacs in 1526, has been the twenty years during which Austria was a negligible quantity after the armistice of 1918. . .

Minutes

The basis of all Sir G. Knox's arguments is that Hungary is, must be and always will be in any foreseeable future utterly and entirely dependent on Nazi Germany and that we should therefore be foolish to waste on Hungary any effort that can be usefully employed elsewhere. We cannot say that Sir G. Knox is wrong; on the contrary, events may very well prove him to be right, but it is not the view taken in this Dep[artmen]t. . .

So far as we are concerned the moral seems to be that we should not waste too much effort on Hungary, because we cannot hope to achieve very much, but that we should nevertheless do whatever we conveniently can, because Hungary under Imredy, with all its weaknesses, suits us better than would Hungary under a Nazi regime. And with due respect to Sir G. Knox, I think that history does show on the contrary that extreme Governments may come to birth at least partly because foreign powers fail to give encouragement and support to the moderate regimes which went before.

NOBLE, 24th November, 1938

. . . Without wishing to be impertinent, one might say that a kind of surface logic seems to have a fatal attraction for Sir G. Knox. This species of logic has the same attraction for the French, and we know where it has landed them — the whole of their carefully planned edifice in Europe has collapsed.

S. NICHOLS, November 25, 1938

Letter from J. M. Troutbeck to W. Strang
(C 13800/2475/12)

PRAGUE, *November 8, 1938*

(Excerpts)

...Negotiations* are meanwhile still going on with the object of simplifying the party system, but they don't seem to have got anywhere yet. The Clerical party's organ asks today why the big four – Beran (Agrarian), Sramek (Clerical), Hampl (Social Democrat), and Klapka (National Socialist) – could not form a kind of directorate to organise one single party for the whole State. This is an odd suggestion from the Clericals who have hitherto been the most insistent on their independence. Others are talking of a two-party system, and others again of three parties. The Agrarians are saying that "authoritarian democracy", which is their recipe for salvation, doesn't mean totalitarianism. I may mention that I had a talk yesterday with Masaryk... He is now Chvalkovsky's private secretary... He said it was quite wrong to think that this country was going fascist. His chief fear arose from the Jewish problem, which he suggested it was for those to solve who had brought Czechoslovakia into her present situation...

The Slovaks are being as Slovak as ever. They have now invented the original slogan "One God, one Party, one Nation". The Social Democrat party is dissolved, and the Slovak branches of the Clerical and Agrarian parties are to amalgamate with the Hlinka party. The Government press commissioner has stated that the entire press in Slovakia is to be reformed and must place itself at the service of the Christian idea. Anti-semitic feeling shows no sign of abatement. .It was reported on the 5th November that the Slovak Government had taken energetic measures against the hostile Jewish elements which had worked against the State particularly at the time of the negotiations with Hungary...

I inquired the other day at the Ministry for Foreign Affairs precisely what the Hlinka Guard amounted to. I received no very clear reply. The idea is of course copied from Germany. The members are recruited largely from the Orel organisation (a Catholic gymnastic body) and wear armlets bearing the Christian cross...

*Between representatives of four parties (Agrarian, Clerical, Social Democrat and National Socialist)

No.122

Memorandum by R. J. Stopford
on Refugees in Czechoslovakia
(C 1437/118896/12)

PRAGUE, *November 14, 1938*

(Excerpts)

... There is no doubt that feeling in this country at the present moment is extremely anti-Semitic and the Jews are much frightened, although Dr. Engliš remarked to me today that he hoped that the result of the recent pogroms in Germany would be to cause a reaction here among the people from the extreme anti-Jewish policy. It is clear, however, that the possibility must be faced of a wholesale expulsion of Jews from this country. The census figure for racial Jews in the remaining territory is about 150,000; but there are probably many more who would be regarded as Jews in such a case. I have received from a Jewish source a total figure of 250,000.

No.123

Letter from Sir G. Knox to E. M. B. Ingram
(R 9394/99/21)

BUDAPEST, *November 15, 1938*

(Excerpts)

.... Incidentally the new steps foreshadowed against the Jews... are generally said to have been brought to the fore, because the Prime Minister did not feel himself strong enough to carry through a reasonable measure of agrarian reform and hoped to divert public attention in this manner. It is generally feared that these measures are to be sweeping — there is talk of reducing the permissible percentage of Jews in business from 20 per cent to 3 per cent. The Hungarian Government will certainly be sensitive to any manifestation of British opinion in this matter — particularly in the "Times", because of their fears of reactions in the City. The "Times" are not likely to have anything to use from their correspondent here who is a former Hungarian diplomatist, now the Editor of the "Pester Lloyd" and entirely servile to the Axis.

If you wish to do anything to forestall the possibility of intensified Jewish emigration from here a little attention in the British press would be useful.

Minutes (A. N. Noble, November 26, 1938)

There is a considerable danger of an anti-Jewish hunt in Hungary; whether remarks about it in the British press would really help, it is difficult to say. It has not helped in Germany or Italy, but Hungary may be more amenable to reason. I can't help feeling that if the Hungarians are such fools as to attack the Jews, no press warning will deter them.

Remark by P. B. B. Nichols (28/XI)

But this is not Sir G. Knox's view, & I think the best we can do is to pass the hint on to the "Times" & perhaps the "Daily Telegraph" as well.

Remark by E. M. B. Ingram (28/XI)

I am rather sceptical about turning the Press as to this prospective menace to the Jews in Hungary. They will get on to it soon enough when the first symptoms occur: to instigate a campaign in advance. . . .

Remark by Ch. Bramwell (28/XI)

I agree with Mr. Ingram. I am increasingly apprehensive about the incipient anti-Semitism in this country & abroad (apart from Germany & Italy). . . . I fear action in the sense suggested by Mr. Nichols might merely serve to increase it without assisting the Jews in Hungary.

No.124

J. M. Troutbeck to Lord Halifax
No. 397 (C 14188/2475/12)

PRAGUE, *November 15, 1938*

(Excerpts)

I have the honour to transmit to you herewith an interesting record of a conversation between Mr. Stopford and Count Kinsky on political prospects in this country...

9. ... German influence is making headway in Slovakia. Everything indeed points in that direction. The members of the new Slovak Government are mostly very young men to whom the pomp and circumstance of Nazi display make a strong appeal. They have already adopted the single party system, the party guard and even, I am told, the Hitler salute...

10. An unpleasant feature of the new regime in Slovakia is the strong anti-Semitic trend, ... There have been widespread reports of anti-Jewish hooliganism in Bratislava... Then again there are the stories... that before the Hungarians entered their new territory, several thousand Jews were driven into it in a practically penniless condition. Now there are reports that the Hungarians are terrorising the local population in the Schutt Island, who are fleeing into Slovakia. Needless to say Jews feature among the refugees. In fact it must be confessed that the outlook for Jews, not only in Slovakia but throughout this country, is not a rosy one...

Enclosure in No. 124

Record of a conversation between
Count Rat Kinsky and R. J. Stopford
(Sd. R. J. Stopford, November 14, 1938)

Count Rat Kinsky came to see me yesterday, November 13th, and said that he had just had two hours' talk with Chvalkovsky... The new Government's policy will include the turning out of all representatives of the old system and their replacement by younger men more in touch with the new outlook. If this can be done and the results of the elections reflect the new outlook of the people, the independence of the State will be preserved and the danger avoided that the people, feeling hopeless of removing the old order, would invite Germany to come in. . .

.... Count Kinsky referred to the very strong anti-Jewish feeling which had come to the surface and said he had asked Chvalkovsky about it. Chvalkovsky had replied that the Jewish problem must be settled. Although the Germans were pressing for action to be taken against the Jews, there must be no pogroms before January or February as nothing must be done to interfere with the possibility of obtaining a further Anglo-French loan. On the other hand they hoped in the meantime that all the Jews in the country would have decided that they must emigrate. . .

Minute by F. K. Roberts (November 22, 1938)

. . . In his conversation with Count Kinsky M. Chwalkovsky was very cynical about the future of the Jews and the Anglo-French loan.

No.125

J. M. Troutbeck to Lord Halifax
No. 398 (12/12/38)
(C 14177/1667/62)

(Excerpts)

Under cover of my despatch No. 397 of to-day's date I had the honour to transmit to you a copy of record of conversation between Mr. Stopford and Count Kinsky in which the latter had informed him of a talk he had had with Monsieur Chvalkovsky, the present Minister for Foreign Affairs and the prospective President of the Republic.

2.   You will no doubt have been struck by the following excerpt from Mr. Stopford's record:

"Count Kinsky referred to the very strong anti-Jewish feeling which had come to the surface and said that he had asked Chvalkovsky about it. Chvalkovsky had replied that the Jewish problem must be settled. Although the Germans were pressing for action to be taken against the Jews, there must be no pogroms before January or February as nothing must be done to interfere with the possibility of obtaining a further Anglo-French loan. On the other hand they hoped in the meantime that all the Jews in the country would have decided that they must emigrate."

3.   There is no great reason to doubt the general accuracy of Count Kinsky's account and the cynicism of Monsieur Chvalkovsky's remarks on the Jewish question is, to say the least, disturbing. No objection can be taken to the desire of the Czechoslovak Government to avoid increasing their Jewish population. Nor could, to my mind, serious objection be taken to their introducing restrictions such as have been made in other countries to the number of Jews permitted in the various professions, for this country has suffered grievously in the last month or so and the problem of finding employment for Czechs, and particularly educated Czechs, is a real one. But a deliberate policy of driving the Jews to the wall is another matter. A virulent and new-born anti-Semitism in Czechoslovakia would indeed be an unfortunate offshoot of the policy of appeasement inaugurated at Munich.

4.   The question remains what action if any is open to His Majesty's Government to prevent such a situation arising. It is indeed not easy to suggest any action that can be assured of success, for in this case natural

desire will be encouraged by urgent promptings from an all-powerful neighbour. As against this there is of course the effect which will be produced on British public opinion and I am inclined to think that British opinion may still count for more in this country than the pessimists would admit. There is also public opinion in the United States of America to be reckoned with. But the only practical, as opposed to psychological, hold we would seem to possess lies in the financial and economic fields. The "Národni Politika" put the matter candidly in a recent article in which it said that what Czechoslovakia now needed is peace and money. Peace would be obtained by good relations with Germany and Italy and all her neighbours; financial assistance could be obtained from England and France. . .

5.   The financial card can, however, only be played so long as the Czechoslovak Government still hope to obtain from us more than the ten million pounds already advanced, and Dr. Chvalkovsky's idea appears to be to wait till he has got all he can out of us financially before getting down in earnest to an anti-Jewish campaign. Once we have come to the limits of the financial assistance we are prepared to offer, there will only remain the economic lever, consisting in the fact that Czechoslovakia still wishes to sell her goods to us. But the application of such a lever, even if practicable, would only drive Czechoslovakia still further into German arms, which would hardly be encouraging to the Jews.

6.   I will bring the matter to the notice of His Majesty's Minister immediately on his return in a week's time. In the meanwhile you will doubtless be considering whether you think it desirable to send him any instructions in the matter. Subject to his views, I think that a frank word in good time might prove useful. In the meantime Mr. Stopford is considering what useful action he for his part may be able to take. . .

Minutes by R. M. Makins (November 24, 1938)

. . . The question of the loan is greatly complicated by the prospect that the new Czechoslovak Government will be Nazi in spirit and is likely to pursue anti-Semitic measures, and I think we must do what we can to extract assurances from the Czechs in connexion with the loan negotiations. Unfortunately, the whole of the £10 million has been placed at the disposal of the Czech Government and we cannot now withold any portion of this advance. . .

Remark by Sir O. Sargent (November 25, 1938)

I agree.

Enclosure to No. 125
Copy of a letter from R. M. Makins to S. D. Waley

FOREIGN OFFICE, *November 26, 1938*

(Excerpts)

With reference to my letter of November 22nd about the Czechoslovak loan negotiations, we think that we must do what we can to extract assurances from the Czechs in connexion with these negotiations that they will abstain from anti-Jewish measures.

Memorandum by John Keyser on Situation in Hungary
(October 1938)
(R 9340/1022/21)

[At the request of the Secretary of State, John Keyser called
on R. A. Butler and left a memorandum on a visit to Budapest]

(Excerpts)

a) *The Internal Position*

The so-called "Nazi" movement in Hungary is now seen in a much clearer
light than at the time of the Anschluss. In the first place, "Nazi", in the
sense which that word generally implies, is something of a misnoma. A
more correct definition would be "social revolution". This has its roots
primarily in the youth of the country... Since 1932, the aristocracy has
been largely replaced by the gentry and officials class (sic), represented
successively by Gombos, Daranyi and Imredy. The first two of
these... were essentially weak, the latter so much so that, had it not been
for the energetic action of a number of members of parliament, a Nazi
government was almost certain to have been introduced at the time of the
Anschluss...

The youth of the country, largely victimised by the restriction of
opportunity in post-war Hungary, chagrined by the lack of resolve of
successive governments, obviously influenced by the apparently better
situation of their brothers in the dictator States and now encouraged by
signs of real intention on the part of the present government to proceed to
social reforms, is clamouring for action. In a rather natural way the more
extreme elements look towards Germany as being a land flowing with
milk and honey. One or two youth organisations are distinctly
"German-Nazi" in appearance, as for instance the one called "Turul
Szovetseg" and the group under the leadership of Mr. Rayniss, one of the
Nazi chiefs. On the other hand, it is interesting to note that within the last
fortnight a fairly important youth movement has burst into life. It calls
itself "Fiatal Magyarsag" (Young Hungary) and its slogan is "Order and
discipline". Its basis is a fiery Hungarian nationalism and its goal the
maintenance of Hungarian independence...

Apart from youth, the present unrest can be ascribed to three distinct
movements. First, a national movement to regain lost territory...

secondly, a middle class movement which aims at occupying the positions held by the capitalists; and, thirdly a movement of the masses – both urban and rural – which seeks to destroy capitalism. Both the second and the third are, of course, included in the first and share an expression of their aims in a common anti-semitism.

It would be extremely difficult to assess the degree of pro-German Nazism which exists among these various movements. On the whole it is probable that there is comparatively little. Nationalism and individualism are far too strongly developed in the Hungarian character to permit a wholesale submission to foreign ideas and rule. Moreover, there is an absolute absence of competent leaders in the real Nazi party. Neither Major Szalasi. . . nor M. Hubay. . . are men of substance. Their arguments are futile and their mouths are full of words which probably neither they nor certainly anyone in Hungary really understand. Their party is badly organised and lacks cohesion and consists of various factions among whom is a large measure of disagreement. The common basis is anti-semitism. In fact this platform unites all the extremist movements in Hungary and is becoming increasingly fierce.

Apart from this Nazi party (whose members talk in terms of Hungarian National-Socialism or "Hungarism" rather than Nazism), there is only one direction in which Nazism has won a decided hold. That is in the army which is computed to be between 80 and 90 per cent Nazi, or in this case pro-German. This is especially so among the young officers. The reason is not hard to find. They are mesmerised by the glory of the German army. . . The situation with regard to the army is peculiarly dangerous and unless energetic measures are taken to counteract its present tendency, it may lead to evil consequences.

In general, therefore, apart from the army and certain student organisations, the "Nazism" which exists in Hungary is mostly of a domestic brew. It is entirely erroneous to regard Hungary as being won completely over to German Nazism and anyone who does so renders an ill service both to Hungary and to Europe. . . It is obvious that the dynamic forces. . . will not put up with a static position of the government and therefore, rather than let this dynamism run riot, the intention is to guide it into well-defined channels. A number of important social reforms are planned such as, the distribution of land to the peasants, the introduction of minimum wage levels and family allowances. Whether these will actually take place and whether. . . they will be sufficient to satisfy the demands of the people, are questions which no one can satisfactorily answer at present. . . It should be added that this programme of "taking the wind out of the sails" of the extremists is somewhat dangerous, for it may play straight into their hands.

355

Fundamentally, it matters little whether the State is governed by Hungarian "Nazis" or pro-German Nazis, for the former is a rich pasture on which the latter can feed. The most important thing is to avoid all forms of extremism or centralisation and it is uncertain whether the present Hungarian Government is of this opinion. . .

Foreign Office Minutes
by A. N. Noble
(R 9340/1022/21)

FOREIGN OFFICE, *November 28, 1938*

[Comments on a memorandum by John Keyser on political
situation in Hungary and Anglo-Hungarian relations]

(Excerpts)

Mr. Keyser's memorandum is interesting and his picture of the underlying political and social conditions in Hungary strikes me as being fairly accurate; I am less sure of the conclusions that he draws. The present strength of the Nazi movement in Hungary (I do not think that Mr. Keyser's objection to the use of the term "Nazi" is very important) is the subject of considerable argument. I think it probable that the movement at present is comparatively weak on account of the lack of effective leadership, to which Mr. Keyser rightly draws attention; it is potentially strong because it can make appeal, as did Fascism in Italy and Nazism in Germany, to a large class of young people who are thoroughly dissatisfied with the present state of affairs. Again there is considerable argument as to how far Hungary is pro-German. In this connexion Mr. Keyser's remarks about the pro-German sympathies of the Hungarian Army are important and rather weaken the strength of his statement that there is comparatively little pro-German Nazism in Hungary. Mr. Keyser's comment that either Hungarian Nazis or pro-German Nazism would be equally under German influence is certainly true. I also agree with his comment that M. Imredy's policy of adopting a right-wards policy in order to take the wind out of the sails of the Nazis is dangerous; it is a game that might be played successfully by a bold and skilful politician, but it has yet to be shown that M. Imredy is such a man; there are reasons for thinking he is not. Mr. Keyser suggests at the foot of page 4 that M. Imredy's Government are themselves playing with the idea of a Government on dictatorial lines; a good many Hungarian politicians think so too and this has been the cause of the recent crisis. M. Imredy remains in power and it is to be hoped that he has learnt his lesson. . .

Mr. Keyser's conclusion is in the main sound, i.e. that M. Imredy must deal firmly now with the extremists and push through a comprehensive scheme of social reform. I think he greatly exaggerates the possible effects of anything that we could do for Hungary (there is not very much), though I do not altogether accept Sir G. Knox's contention that nothing we can do will make the slightest difference and that Hungary is already and will always be completely subservient to Germany. I think our policy should be to do what little we can to help provided that it will not cost us valuable effort which could be better employed elsewhere, e.g. in Greece, Roumania, Bulgaria or Yugoslavia.

No. 128

Telegram from B. C. Newton to the Foreign Office
No. 1066
(C 15022/2475/12)

PRAGUE, *December 5, 1938*

(Excerpts)

So far as loan is concerned I would suggest that even though Czechoslovakia is now in the German orbit it may better serve our interests on the long view to assist her towards economic reconstruction than to see her stagnate or collapse in a state of economic misery. The fact that Germany may benefit is surely not in itself a bar. There is also the consideration whether having been one of this state, as well as in its recent organisation we have not some moral responsibility in assisting to re-create its economic existence.

The decision to grant a loan was not taken as a matter of business but I presume in recognition of the above consideration and also of the fact that Great Britain as well as Czechoslovakia had benefited from the preservation of peace for which the heavy price had been paid by Czechoslovakia alone. Nevertheless some delay in loan negotiations may not be amiss as a means of making the new Czechoslovak Government realise that we still count, and that in particular attention should continue to be paid to our views in regard to the Jewish and refugee questions.

Minutes by J. K. Roberts (7/12)

... In all the circ[umstance]s it would be extremely difficult to draw back from the loan, but it is clearly advisable to make the Czechs realise that any further financial favours depend upon Czech policy, particularly as regards the Jews and refugees.

J. K. ROBERTS, 7/12

No.129

B. C. Newton to Lord Halifax*
No. 430 (C 15240/2475/12)

PRAGUE, *December 5, 1938*

(Excerpts)

6.   The President of the Council [Beran] said that the recent changes had made the State more homogeneous from a national point of view. The "national purity" must be safeguarded and a number of measures were necessary to this end. The question of foreign immigrants would be energetically solved. . . The national life and education would be inspired by a Christian spirit and by the tradition of St. Wenzel. Foreign models would not be blindly copied. . .
8.   With reference to the Jews, [Hacha] said that their number was relatively small in Bohemia and Moravia, and that the Jewish problem was not, therefore, the same as in Slovakia. A way must be found to limit the rôle of the Jews in national life. . .

*Published in DBFP, III, No.401

No.130

Telegram from Sir R. Hoare to the Foreign Office
No. 99 (Saving)
(R 9891/9/37)

BUCHAREST, *December 8, 1938*

(Excerpts)

I had some conversation with the Minister for Foreign Affairs. . . on the subject of recrudescence of Iron Guard acts of violence and His Excellency said that while opinions differed as to whether or not there had been direct participations or intrigues there could not be the slightest doubt that recent German excesses against Jews had given strong fillip to anti-Semitism here. Government had taken immediate and energetic measures to prevent violence but the problem of a national home for the Jews was becoming more and more urgent and he hoped in the near future to communicate to His Majesty's Government the written views of Roumanian Government on this subject.

B. C. Newton to Lord Halifax*
No. 434 (C 15338/2475/12)

PRAGUE, *December 8, 1938*

(Excerpts)

12.   Meanwhile German intellectual or propaganda influence is making its impression. It is to be doubted if at bottom the feelings of the Czechs have greatly altered towards Germany as a result of the crisis . . . But willy nilly the Czechs have now to adapt themselves to the new situation and it is possible that they are more pliable than they at first sight appear. However that may be, it is apparent that those noted for their anti-German sentiments are being ousted from public life and influence. It is disillusioning to see how low the stock of Dr. Benes and even Dr. Masaryk has fallen in the country to which they devoted their lives and energies, and their busts are being removed from schools and public places. Agitation has not ceased for a public enquiry to be made into Dr. Benes' responsibility for the débâcle. . .
The old leftward papers are either disappearing or changing their colour. A film by Karel Capek was prohibited the other day. . . The new party of Working People, though officially the opposition, is despondent as to its future, and it looks as though parliamentary democracy may soon be replaced by a more or less authoritarian Government. The Party of National Unity is said to be chiefly notable for its internal dissensions but the Government has already prepared a Full Powers Act which should enable it to ignore if necessary the party politicians. . .
13.   But it is over the Jewish question that German influence is being most actively pressed. It seems that, not content with exterminating the Jews in their own country, the Germans are determined to carry the campaign into that of their neighbour, realising no doubt that Jewish influence is bound to be hostile to them and should therefore be eradicated wherever possible. The Czechs thus find themselves between two fires, being urged by the Germans to destroy the Jews and by ourselves to protect them. I fear there is little doubt which advice will be the more strongly heeded, nor in which direction the sentiments of the Czechs themselves are now turning. There are already a number of

*Published in DBFP, III, No.413

individual cases of persecution in the professions and by students at the University. Even the more decent-minded have a feeling of helplessness in the matter, and one of them recently remarked to a member of my staff: "We were never in our history anti-Semitic, but the world is forcing us to become so".

14. ... all visitors to Slovakia bring back tales of the inhabitants' enthusiasm for Germany. It is no doubt fanned in some measure by the peculiar dislike felt by the Slovaks just now for the Czechs. "Slovakia for the Slovaks", the slogan goes, "Palestine for the Jews, the Danube for the Czechs". In their eagerness to be rid of Czech ideas, the Slovaks therefore turn with increased alacrity to German methods. The single party system is already installed... The trade unions are being organised in a single body. Jews are being deliberately oppressed. The first concentration camp will soon be open. The Hlinka Guard struts about in its new black uniform, which is remarkably similar to that of the Reich S.S. ...

15. It is strange that pro-German feeling seems to have been so little damped by the Nazi treatment of the Roman Catholic religion or by the slight regard paid to Slovak interests on the German side.

18. ... The Ruthenian Government have established on their side a "S.A." formation under the name of "Sic". Ruthenia has a special importance for Germany in that it contains a Ukrainian population and could be made a focus of intrigue and starting point for adventures in both Polish and Russian Ukraine...

Minutes by Sir O. G. Sargent, December 16, 1938

... After reading this Desp[atch] one begins to wonder what purpose will be served by our guaranteeing this vassal state — and for whose benefit we shall be giving our guarantee and against whom it is likely to be invoked. It is as though Germany were to guarantee Egypt!

Minutes by F. K. Roberts, December 23, 1938

It is true that Czechoslovakia is now a "vassal state". But we are at least partly responsible for that. And though it is true that there is nothing now left to guarantee, the argument that we should now recede from our promise does not lie well in *our* mouths. It would come better from the enslaved.

No.132

B. C. Newton to Lord Halifax
No. 448 (C 15720/2475/12)

PRAGUE, *December 20, 1938*

[Reports on the Government's Full Powers Bill
approved by Chamber of Deputies on 14 December]

(Excerpts)

4. A reference to the Jews was made by an independent Deputy, Dr. Rasin, who said that he welcomed the fact that the President of the Council had not given way to "gutter demagogy" in this question. The result of anti-Jewish excesses would only be that markets would be closed to Czecho-Slovakia's export trade, the promotion of which was the chief task of the Government. For economic reasons the Jewish concerns and the Jews themselves must be given legal security again as soon as possible.
5. The Full Powers Bill was yesterday discussed and voted by the Senate. During this debate criticisms were again directed at the behaviour of the Slovaks by representatives of the National Party of the Working People, one of whose speakers stated that opinion abroad was reacting unfavourably to the anti-Jewish proceedings in Slovakia. A member of the Party of Slovak Unity made a statement on Slovak policy...He declared...the time had passed when the Jews could clothe their egoistic capitalism in the red garments of Marxist internationalism and provoke class war. The Jews would now have either to subordinate themselves to the national community or disappear. . . .

No.133

Telegram from Sir G. Knox to the Foreign Office
No. 61 (Saving) (C 5/5/62)

BUDAPEST, *December 24, 1938*

My telegram No 59 Saving.

Bill as an instrument of persecution goes far beyond existing law which already violates principles of article 58 of the Treaty of Trianon: it is moreover unlikely that once the Hungarian Government have reached this point of a slippery slope they will stop there. If the Bill becomes law it will provoke further Jewish emigration and will offer a deplorable example to the rest of South Eastern Europe.

If we are obliged on this occasion to take steps similar to those taken a year ago in connexion with Monsieur Goga's legislation, I can hope for little result from these with an Hungarian Government which would quite possibly welcome an opportunity to leave the League of Nations with eclat, and I think indirect action would have more chance of proving effective.

There will probably be considerable opposition to the Bill in the Parliament which would seek to base itself on public opinion that may express itself coherently. The following would be the most effective lines:

1.   Hungary by her treatment of this minority is stultifying her claim for better treatment of her own minorities elsewere.

2.   Hungary derives the greater part of free devisen which are indispensable to her economy from a very favourable payments-agreement with Great Britain who had concluded that agreement with a State which was then both derelict and (independent). (sic!)

3.   The Hungarian has never shown the capacity nor the inclination to occupy the positions from which the Jew is being ousted. The result is that the Jew will be replaced not by the Magyar but by the Magyarized German.

My recent reports will have made it clear that I consider that our influence on Hungary by precept and example has sunk to nothing; our "nuisance value" however both in the financial domain and as one of the principal factors of world opinion is very great. The present is, I think, an occasion on which we should use it.

No.134

Annual Report for 1938
Hungary
(C 730/730/21)
[Submitted by Sir G. Knox]

BUDAPEST, *January 1, 1939*

(Excerpts)

Hungarian National Socialism

113. The thread of Hungarian national socialism has been closely interwoven with the internal situation throughout the year. Although many responsible and sober-minded Hungarians are prone to make light of this movement, it is doubtful whether, in view of the constant manifestations of National Socialist activity in the country, there is any justification for this view. During the year M. Daranyi, the Former Prime Minister, and M. Imredy, the present Prime Minister, gave repeated and constant warnings that extremist agitation would under no circumstances be tolerated. In April the Regent broadcast an address. . . ostensibly with the idea of appealing to all classes to support the Government's programme of reconstruction and development, but there is no doubt that, although his words directed against extremist agitation sounded forceful enough, . . . the general public was not reassured and belief persisted in many quarters that the Regent himself and members of his immediate entourage sympathised inwardly with the movement. . .

115. The above indicates the negative side of the picture of Hungarian national socialism during the twelve months under review, but on the other side must be placed the election of a prominent member of the party to the post of "sous-préfet" of the County of Budapest . . . In February another National Socialist was elected to Parliament as the official representative of the Party and the spreading of national socialism became apparent in the army, police force and civil service. The leaders of the party maintained at the end of the year that they had the majority of the masses behind them.

116. In July it became apparent that the newly-elected National Socialist Deputy, M. Coloman Hubay . . . had automatically assumed a leading rôle *vis-à-vis* the various National Socialist groups in Hungary. The supporters of M. Hubay described themselves as "Hungarists", thus

366

endeavouring to demonstrate that they dissociated their movement from German nazism... An early champion of national socialism in Hungary, Count Alexander Festetich, voluntarily resigned his leadership to M. Hubay; thus the ranks of the main party were increased by some 30,000 members. Previously six different groups had existed, but the action of Count Festetich eventually resulted in consolidating the movement, and towards the end of the year most of the minor parties had been fused into one group.

117.   The movement has thus taken on a more Hungarian complexion and signs are not wanting that it has lost the German support and encouragement which it formerly enjoyed.

118.   It is difficult to estimate how strongly the "Hungarist" movement has taken root in the country; it is true that the very low standard of wages and of living prevailing in Hungary must tend to make men seek a remedy in extremist doctrines, and, since any "leftward" agitation has been ruthlessly and effectively suppressed by the police, the forces of discontent inevitably tend to the extreme Right. Leaders, however, are lacking, and, if the movement has, as it is affirmed, great numbers behind it, these numbers are not yet conscious of their strength or they would not have stood by, inactive, during the drastic measures which were taken against the party this year.

No.135

Annual Report for 1938,
Czechoslovakia
B. C. Newton to Lord Halifax
(C 1720/1720/12)

PRAGUE, *January 14, 1939*

(Excerpts)

(xxi) *Reorganisation of the Party System.*

64.   The Munich settlement left the Czechs confused and dispirited. The Prague press reflected bitter disappointment at the manner in which Czecho-Slovakia's friends and allies had enthusiastically purchased peace at her expense. Disillusioned at the results of their previous policy of co-operation with the Western democracies, it seemed to the Czechs that they must endeavour to rebuild their country on Nationalist, but more authoritarian, lines, a task to which they applied themselves with commendable energy and courage. One of the results of this revulsion of public opinion was that the Agrarian party, which had in the past been more favourable to co-operation with Germany than any other of the coalition parties, became the dominant political force. The left wing parties, which had been loyal supporters of President Benes and violently anti-German in outlook, were, on the other hand, discredited. Some of them showed an almost indecent haste in repudiating their former leaders and ideals. President Benes's departure was followed by a good deal of public washing of dirty political linen and the institution of an enquiry into responsibilities for the *débâcle* was canvassed in the press. A considerable share of the blame for the country's misfortunes was atributed to the short-sighted selfish policy of the parties in pursuing their own rather than national interests, and all shades of political opinion were agreed that the former party system must be radically reformed and simplified so as to be capable of dealing with the urgent problems of reconstruction facing the nation. . .
65.   The Agrarian party took the lead in capitalising this movement of public opinion, inviting other parties to join it in the formation of a great national party which should form the basis of an authoritarian and disciplined democracy, free from corruption and putting the service of the State before party interests. By the middle of November the National

Socialist party, the Traders' party, the National Alliance party, the Clerical party and the National League had joined the Agrarian party in the formation of the new "Party of National Unity," which announced that it had assumed responsibility for the leadership of the new State. This party could count on the support of nearly half the 228 Deputies in the Chamber. The chief other parties were the party of Slovak Unity (see paragraph 176), the Communists (who were threatened with dissolution) and the National Party of the Working People. The latter party was chiefly composed of the old Social Democratic party (which had a month previously broken off relations with the Second International) and constituted the official Czech "Opposition."

. . . The new Government was formed by M. Rudolf Beran, who had been leader of the Agrarian party and largely responsible for the formation of the Party of National Unity. . .In December the Slovaks were persuaded to agree to the Government's Full Powers Bill authorising the Government to reform the Constitution and to legislate by decree provisions being included to safeguard Slovak autonomy. The enactment of this measure in the middle of December marked a further step away from parliamentary democracy towards authoritarianism.

67. In a statement of the Government's programme in Parliament in December M. Beran gave a sketch of the tasks to which his Government intended to apply itself in the new year. He stated that the country's foreign policy had been completely transformed, and the Government's first concern was to establish friendly relations with all neighbouring States, and particularly with Germany. In internal affairs the interests of the State must come first. No fresh political disintegration would be permitted, and political life, the public administration and all associations and organisations would be reorganised in accordance with the principle of service to the State. Healthy and numerous families were proclaimed to be essential to the welfare of the State. The educational system must be reformed and more regard paid to Christian principles. Whilst promising liberal treatment to the national minorities remaining in the new State, M. Beran emphasised that energetic steps would be taken to solve the questions of the Jews and of the German immigrants from the Sudeten areas.. . .

FOREIGN RELATIONS

Roumania

153. The turn of events in Roumania at the beginning of the year caused some uneasiness in Czecho-Slovakia. Already, in 1937, Czecho-Slovakia

had watched with anxiety the growing Roumanian distaste for "Dr. Benes's Soviet policy," and the results of the December elections and the assumption of office by M. Goga did nothing to reassure public opinion in Czecho-Slovakia. In the latter's increasing isolation the possibility that the development of the influence of the Iron Guard might drive Roumanian policy into the German orbit was particularly unwelcome. Everything was therefore done to make a success of the visit of M. Micesco, the Minister for Foreign Affairs in M. Goga's Government, to Prague in January on his way to Belgrade and Geneva, and Czecho-Slovak public opinion eagerly seized on the visit as a token that all was yet well with Roumania's foreign policy, and that she would not desert her old friends. That an undercurrent of uneasiness remained was, however, evident from the relief with which the Czech press received the news of the fall of M. Goga's Government and of the disgrace of the Iron Guard, which it was hoped marked the end of Roumania's flirtations with a policy of closer relations with the Rome-Berlin Axis.

176. The Slovaks were now at liberty to give free rein to the clerical and authoritarian ideals which appealed to a backward and fervently Catholic peasant people. The Slovak People's party quickly eliminated all opposition and proceeded to make use of its predominant position with more enthusiasm than discretion. Significant of the new spirit were the honours paid to Dr. Tuka, who had been condemned ten years previously to a long term of imprisonment for high treason. Encouraged by daily broadcasts on the German wireless, the Slovaks showed no hesitation in copying Fascist methods; concentration camps were set up, M. Sidor formed the "Hlinka Guard," which was entrusted with the security services and recognised as the sole para-military organisation in Slovakia. The Communist party was dissolved and the various other parties were obliged to group themselves together with the Slovak People's party in the "Party of Slovak Unity," it being announced that the party system must give place to the corporative. Czech officials were turned out, and agitation began against the Jews, who had hitherto been a powerful factor in the Slovak community. This crude Slovak nationalism was, however, tempered by a liberal policy towards the other minorities. State secretaries were appointed to look ater the affairs of the Germans and the Hungarians, and Deputy Karmasin, the German State Secretary and the head of the German party (as the Slovak branch of the Sudeten German party was now called), was given full assurances that he would be allowed to organise the German minority on National Socialist lines. In short, the Slovaks, thoroughly disillusioned by Poland, who, despite all her former professions of friendship, was supporting Hungarian territorial claims and demanding parts of North-West Slovakia for herself, out of temper with

the Hungarians for the ruthless manner in which they had pressed their territorial demands, and unwilling, for reasons of *amour-propre,* to put themselves under any great obligation to the Czechs, turned increasingly to Germany for political inspiration and the economic assistance which they so badly needed to reorganise their mutilated country.

178.   Despite Parliament's acceptance of this law and the inclusion of a Slovak representative in the person of M. Sidor in the Central Government, when M. Beran formed his Cabinet at the beginning of December, co-operation between the Czechs and the Slovaks remained far from easy. For instance, the Slovaks persisted in their opposition to a Full Powers Bill which the Government had tabled at the middle of November, and it took a full month of arduous negotiations before a compromise could be reached and the Bill be made law. M. Sidor began his career as a Cabinet Minister by explaining to his Slovak followers that he had accepted the post in order to "liquidate the Centralist régime all along the line." He declared that in foreign affairs a policy must be pursued whereby all races which fought Jewish bolshevism were "our brothers." As regards defence, it would be his aim that the Hlinka Guard should soon be armed and defend the interests of the Slovak people as a Slovak army.

No.136

Annual Report, 1938,
Roumania
(R 5290/2832/37)

BUCHAREST, *June 20, 1939*

(Excerpts)

79.   The announcement of these decisions (the general election was suspended, martial law was proclaimed and the King formed a new Government* was accompanied by the issue of a proclamation in which the King stated his reasons for departing from constitutional practice. . . The new constitution. . .was published on the 21st February and accepted by the country in a plebiscite three days later with almost Hitlerian

*On 10th February, after Goga's dismissal

unanimity. Meanwhile, on the 22nd February, Codreanu had announced the dissolution of the Iron Guard.

87. The international crisis of September left little time for the consideration of domestic problems, but towards the end of October rumours began to circulate that a rising of the Iron Guard was imminent. There were student agitations. . .and reports of anti-semitic outbreaks in Transylvania. . .

88. Early on the morning of the 30th November, Codreanu and thirteen of his fellow prisoners were shot dead, ostensibly while "attempting to escape" . . . horror was soon followed by a sense of finality and relief, for there is no lack of oriental fatalism in Roumania, although life itself may be somewhat less cheap than in some other Balkan countries.

89. In the closing days of the year, the Government announced the formation of the National Renaissance Front, a political organism of corporative structure and totalitarian complexion, whereby the King, no doubt, intends ultimately to restore some measure of normal contact between the Government and his people.

Anti-Semitism

90. Anti-semitism being one of the salient features of M. Goga's programme, vigorous measures against the Jews were taken early in the New Year immediately after the Government's assumption of office. . .By February matters had reached a climax. . . a proposal was made, but promptly dropped when it was indicated that British public opinion would be revolted, that no maid servant under forty should be allowed to serve in Jewish households, and the Government declared its intention of carrying through a revision of the citizenship of Jews resident in the country, ostensibly with a view to deporting a number of Jewish immigrants, variously computed at between 200,000 and 800,000, who were said to have entered the country illegally since the war. These measures began to have an immediate effect upon the national economy. The leu** began rapidly to fall, extravagant prices were paid for sterling on the Black market, agricultural prices also slumped, and it soon became obvious not only that the country was about to face a first-class financial crisis, but also that the Jewish element was an essential factor in the national economy. . .

92. Immediately after the formation of the Patriarch's*** second Government, however, and the establishment of an authoritarian regime,

**Romanian currency
***Miron Cristea

matters began rapidly to improve. While no change of policy was officially proclaimed, it became obvious that the more stringent Jewish measures would be allowed to lapse or would not be applied with excessive severity. . . By the autumn, confidence had begun to return and economic conditions had readjusted themselves. A solution was found for the liquidation of Jewish provincial banks, and anti-Semitism, particularly after the suppression of the Iron Guard, ceased to be an actual problem.

Foreign Office Memorandum (By J. K. Roberts)
Concerning the Position of Jews in Czechoslovakia since Munich
(C 399/5/62)

FOREIGN OFFICE, *January 4, 1939*

The following summary of our information regarding the position of Jews in Czechoslovakia since the Munich Agreement may be found useful in view of the suggestion that anti-Jewish measures are only being delayed until the conclusion of the loan negotiations.

The rise of anti-Jewish feeling is instanced by the following pieces of information:—

1. On the 23rd October the Committee of the Sokol organisation passed a resolution suggesting that Jewish immigrants since 1914 should return to their original homes and that those who acquired Czech nationality since 1930 might gradually be incorporated in the social structure of the nation in proportion to their numbers.

2. In the first half of November Mr. Stopford was informed by Count Kinsky that Dr. Chvalkovsky, the Minister for Foreign Affairs, had told him that the Jewish problem was to be settled but that although the Germans were pressing for action against the Jews there must be no pogroms before January or February in view of the possibility of an Anglo-French loan. The Government hoped, however, that in the meantime all the Jews in Czechoslovakia would have decided to emigrate.

3. The Legal Adviser to H.M. Legation at Prague, himself a Jew, informed the Legation early in December that Jews were suffering from all sorts of restrictions, arising not from any legislation, but from police regulations and other forms of practical obstruction, and this was in his opinion the way in which an anti-Semitic policy would be pursued.

4. Towards the end of December the Youth organisation of the Party of National Unity (The Government Party) published a programme stating that the Jews would be regarded as a foreign minority and their legal position would be regulated by State law. They would be excluded from State employment and from influencing education. In other fields their activity would be regulated in accordance with the principle of proportionality.

5. Reports were published in "The Times" on December 23rd and 24th emanating from their Prague correspondent that Jewish Professors and teachers at German Universities and schools would be pensioned off on January 1st, that several high Jews (sic) Civil Servants would also be

pensioned off on January 1st, and that the Government contemplated the introduction of a *numerus clausus* for the learned professions and various other restrictions on Jewish activities. These reports were based upon reports in the Prague press which went further in stating that all Jewish school teachers would be dismissed as from January 1st.

It will be noted that only the 5th item suggests any definite Government measures against the Jews. Mr. Newton, however, made enquiries in this connexion and was informed on January 2nd by the chief permanent official at the Ministry of Foreign Affairs that he knew nothing of the introduction of a *numerus clausus* or of any discrimination against the Jews. It was added that the Youth organisation mentioned in 4. above was not in a position to commit the Government. On January 3rd, Mr. Newton was informed that there was no foundation for the "Times" reports of December 23rd and 24th and he was officially assured that the Czechoslovak Government, so far from having taken any decisions on these lines, had not even considered taking action.

In reply to any enquiry from the Department of Overseas Trade regarding anti-Jewish feeling in Czechoslovakia, the Commercial Secretary at H.M. Legation in Prague on December 13th stated that there were not in his opinion any grounds for such anxiety. In Slovakia anti-Semitic agitation had been fairly troublesome, but even there anti-Jewish feeling for several weeks past had shown no signs of growing worse. In Bohemia the movement was merely an irresponsible under-current. There were no outward signs of official sympathy for such agitation and although the Jews of Czechoslovakia were naturally nervous, it was they themselves who were mainly responsible for suggestions that the Czechoslovak Government would be pressed by Germany to introduce anti-Jewish legislation. The Commercial Secretary was in touch with many Jewish agents of British firms who were known to be working without any difficulties and the Commercial Secretary recommended that British firms with Jewish agents should continue on the basis of their present arrangements.

It is perhaps worth noting that Sir. E. Phipps reported on the 10th December that he understood from the French Government that their information did not cause them any anxiety with regard to Jews in Czechoslovakia.

The conclusion to be drawn from our information would therefore appear to be that no definite anti-Semitic measures have yet been introduced in Czechoslovakia, although Jews have certainly suffered from the excesses of anti-Semitic agitators during recent disorders in Slovakia. On the other hand there is sufficient evidence to justify Jewish fears regarding the future, particularly in view of the stranglehold which Germany now possesses over Czechoslovakia.

Financial Assistance to Czechoslovakia
Foreign Office Minutes on a letter
from M. Waley (Treasury) to W. Strang (January 2, 1939)
(C 95/3/12)

Minutes by W. Strang (January 5th, 1939)

(Excerpts)

I think that matters have gone too far for any reversal to be possible of the decision taken by H. M. G. to increase the amount of the financial assistance to be afforded by H. M. G. to Czechoslovakia. The extra money is required in order to secure from the Czechoslovak Government assurances – (a) that money will be found for the maintenance and settlement and immigration of refugees; and (b) that there will be no discrimination in any part of Czechoslovakia against any person on account of his religious beliefs, political opinions, or racial origin. Without these assurances in hand, the position of H. M. G. will be more difficult when they approach the House of Commons to pass the necessary legislation.

Looking back, it was probably a mistake on the part of H. M. G. to make this financial provision for Czechoslovakia at all. If that is so, it is equally a mistake now to increase the amount.

It is becoming increasingly clear that Czechoslovakia is in a state of vassalage to Germany, and it will be seen from Mr. Newton's letter to me of January 3rd. . .that there is some confirmation of the opinion held in Germany that the object of the Nazi régime is to reduce Czechoslovakia to such a state that she will eventually ask for incorporation in the Reich. . .

There is the further point that in asking the Czechs to give the required assurances about non-discrimination on account of religious beliefs, political opinions, or racial origin. . .we are asking the Czechs to promise something which it is as certain as anything can be that they will not be in a position to fulfil. There are signs already of anti-Semitic feeling, and indeed indications of anti-Semitic action, in Czechoslovakia, as will be seen from Mr. Roberts' memorandum of January 4th. . . The stronger German influence in Czechoslovakia grows, the greater will be the degree of anti-Semitic action. . .

Minutes by Sir Orme G. Sargent (January 5, 1939)

(Excerpts)

I do not quite understand from the Cabinet Conclusions – see C 16040 – why it is now found necessary to offer the Czech Government another £2 million, when we had made up our minds previously that the £10 million which they have already received, plus the £4 million which the French are contributing by way of taking over the service of the Czech debt, was all that was necessary or reasonable to give to Czechoslovakia in the very altered circumstances of to-day.

It looks as though the difficulty were that the Treasury fear that the Czech negotiators will not give us satisfactory assurances: (a) to devote an adequate part of the money to the relief and settlement of refugees; (b) not to introduce anti-Semite legislation, and that in order to obtain these assurances the Czechs may have to be given another £2 million as a bribe. . .

As regards the second assurance, i.e. that there will be no anti-Semite legislation, it is surely unfair even to ask the Czechoslovak Government to give such an undertaking and to accompany it with a bribe of £2 million. In such circumstances they will naturally be tempted to give the undertaking, pocket the money, and the proceed to argue, quite truthfully, that they were unable to honour their undertaking because circumstances which they could not resist compelled them to introduce anti-Semite legislation. . .

No.139

Foreigh Office Minutes,
Central Department (G. Jebb)
(C 395/3/12)

FOREIGN OFFICE, *January 6, 1939*

[Notes on a conversation with Dr. Papirnik, after his return from the Carpatho-Ukraine]

(Excerpts)

2.   He fully confirmed our reports about anti-Semitism in Czechoslovakia and said that even if this sentiment could not be excused, it was perfectly comprehensible in the circumstances. The immigrant Jews could only speak German, for instance, and were regarded by the Czech peasants and workers as parasites who were taking the bread out of their mouths.

No.140

B. C. Newton to W. Strang
(7/4/39)
(C 764/7/12)

PRAGUE, *January 12, 1939*

I have referred on more than one occasion recently to the activities of the National Youth Movement and I have been trying meanwhile to gather information as to what is the standing and position of this organisation.

Nobody seems to know, or to be willing to say, much about it but I think you may care to have what little information we have been able to glean.

The National Youth Movement is composed of the youth of the Party of National Unity: "youth" being apparently in this case a somewhat elastic term as I was told by Krno that it contained men up to thirty. But I gather that the unity is more outward than inward and that in fact there are different groups in the Movement, the chief of which are Agrarians and the former National Democrats, to whom the President, Dr. Lukavsky, belongs. A Fascist group is alleged to be small numerically but to possess, by reason of its radical views, an importance out of proportion to its size.

I think that the aims of the Movement have been sufficiently clearly brought out in my telegrams not to need elaboration here; but it may be of interest to note that, whilst the parent Party of National Unity has adopted a grey shirt as a uniform, it has given the Movement permission to clothe its "Ordner" (stewards) in a panoply resembling that of the Hlinka Guard (which was itself inspired by the uniform of the German S.S.). Its present and future importance are difficult to gauge but there is no doubt an impression that it may be a shadow cast by coming events.

Minutes by J. K. Roberts (24/1)

The National Youth Movement is a sort of "ginger group" behind the Gov[ernmen]t Party. It advances extreme views on such questions as the future of the Jews and is then disowned by officials.

No.141

Meeting between
Sir F. Leith Ross (Treasury) and Dr. Pospisil
(C 545/3/12)

LONDON, *January 12, 1939*

[Sir F. Leith Ross transmits record of conversation with Dr. Pospisil]

(Excerpts)

The position of his [the Czech] Government was that if the loan could be increased to £10 millions they were prepared to agree that the £4 millions free grant should be allocated and distributed exactly as the British Government wished; they would have no objection to its being placed in a special account and all the expenditure supervised.

As regards the general assurances which we wanted about no discrimination on racial grounds, the Czech Government was in difficulty. They were anxious not to adopt anti-semitic measures, and Mr. Beran's statement was intended to reassure at least the Jews who had long been settled in Czecho-Slovakia. But in many of the frontier districts the German Jews represented 60 per cent or 80 per cent of the doctors, lawyers and other professional men and there was growing agitation in the country for some limitation. The popular movement was not directed against those men only as Jews, but as German Jews. Meanwhile, the German Government had been doing everything to foment anti-Jewish movements by their broadcasts and had criticized Beran for not going far enough. They were placing large orders in Czechoslovakia, but had informed the Czechs that they would not place such orders with any firm which was controlled by Jews. In these circumstances it was very difficult for the Czecho-Slovak Government to fix their policy until the negotiations with Germany were completed. The Czech Government would certainly not go further than they could help, but they were being treated like a conquered country and they could not guarantee that they might not be pressed to take more drastic action than they would like to take themselves. If the assurances could be kept secret it would be easier to find a formula which the Czech Government would be able to give us.

No.142

Letter from Sir G. Knox to Sir Orme Sargent
(2/3/39) (C 821/129/21)

BUDAPEST, January 12, 1939

(Excerpts)

In my telegram No. 12 of January 12 I let you know how far the Regent had travelled from his primitive anti-Semitism under the influence of neighbourship with Germany.

For the rest he used this occasion of the Nuncio's luncheon for an almost embarrassing display of his present feelings. From the end of the meal until he left he talked only to Montgomery (my American colleague) and myself, to the neglect of half a dozen other Chefs-de-Mission. After his remarks about the Jewish Bill* which I have reported, his conversation was nothing but a sustained diatribe aginst Germany – some of it within earshot of my Italian and Polish colleagues. He complained of Germany's dog-in-the-manger attitude about Ruthenia** but most bitterly of the breach of her promise not to touch former Hungarian territories, by seizing Ligetfalu and Deveny. (He did not say when this promise, of which I was ignorant, was given.)

He expressed the belief that Germany would attempt to break up Russia in the Spring in which case all possibility of any balance of power would be gone; when discussing the possible lines of such an attack, Montgomery asked him point blank what would happen if German troops were to advance across Hungary. "We would fight them to the last ditch and start a European war" said the Regent – quite unconscious that he was echoing exactly those sentiments which his own Press had scornfully attributed to Benes only four months ago.

It was a pathetic occasion; and made the more so by his intense niceness and sincerity. I can quite well imagine him going out against eighty millions on his white horse, but I cannot see the Hungarian Government that would follow him. . . I hope the Regent may never recall his "ich spreche nur theoretisch."

---

*Passed by the two Houses of Parliament in the summer of 1938
**The Germans objected to Ruthenia's annexation to Hungary. Ruthenia was occupied and annexed by Hungary, March 16-17, 1939

Incidentally, the Regent, speaking of German instability. . . said to us "If anyone were to kill Hitler the whole thing would break up." For one Head of a State to speak thus of another to two representatives of Foreign Powers, seems a little odd even in the world of today.

No.143

Telegram from J. M. Troutbeck to the Foreign Office
No. 18 (C 1002/3/12)

PRAGUE, *January 26, 1939*

IMPORTANT

I informed Dr. Masarik last night that I feared information he had given me regarding Czechoslovak Government's intentions in respect of limiting professional [gp. undec.] s of Jews might have unpleasant repercussions on loan negotiations more particularly in view of assurances contained in Mr. Newton's telegram No. 4.

He replied he had since our talk made further enquiries and discovered that this point had been dropped out of proposed programme which was now limited to liquidating émigrés and revising nationality [gp. undec.]. He added that these latter measures would not be designed specifically against the Jews.

I am inclined to doubt whether introduction of numerus clausus is more than postponed but I gather from your telegram No. 559 that its postponement is your chief preoccupation. Dr. Pospisil's reaction to draft letter contained in your despatch No. 835 may provide some clearer indication of possible subsequent intentions though it must be remembered that Czechs are past masters in legal quibbling and may well argue that if any measures such as the numerus clausus are applied to all races in the country there will be discrimination against none.

Minutes by J. K. Roberts (26/1)

Clearly the Czechs will find great difficulty in avoiding anti-Jewish measures, but they have hitherto put up a good fight.

No.144

Sir G. Knox to Lord Halifax
No. 12 (C 1397/166/21)

BUDAPEST, *January 27, 1939*

(Excerpts)

... The Hungarian Prime Minister had inaugurated a new movement in Hungary styled "The Hungarian Life" movement... Although it has reawakened a certain amount of hostile activity in the Opposition parties, it is hoped that it will be successful in rallying substantial numbers of the masses to the Government side, and thus weaken the ranks of Hungarian National-Socialists...

The Minister for Foreign Affairs told me today, that although the recent wave of anti-German feeling in Hungary had caused him grave embarrassment, it had had the inestimable advantage of eradicating finally National-Socialist spirit from the Hungarian Army.

No.145

Memorandum on Political Situation in
Slovakia
(P. Pares, Consul)
No. 65 (60/5/39)
(C 1872/7/12)

BRATISLAVA, *February 3, 1939*

(Excerpts)

10. The more sensible elements who were inclined to congratulate themselves last December that the Slovaks' past friendly and unprejudiced attitude towards Germany had proved them wiser than the Czechs, are now asking themselves why they should continue to be so friendly. Only the extremists of the Hlinka Guard, like Murgas, the chief of staff, and admirer of Fascism and author of a book of Fascist Italy, continue to be fascinated by the powerful and energetic Reich. They seem to feel that they at least are in her good books so that they have nothing to worry about.

11. Whilst Slovakia's foreign relations have been taking definite shape the realities of the economic situation at home have begun to make themselves felt. The undisciplined and even riotous period of internal politics appears to have ended fairly soon. At any rate it was already a thing of the past by the middle of last December. The atmosphere is now much calmer. Administrative difficulties are beginning to become apparent.

12. In addition to all these problems the considerable migration of Jewish capital from Slovak to Prague banks is reckoned a serious source of weakness to the Slovak financial position. The amount estimated to have been transferred runs into milliards of crowns.

13. In anticipation of discriminatory measures the Jews in Slovakia are endeavouring to emigrate. The extent of this movement can be particularly well assessed at a British Consulate where numerous callers enquire every day regarding immigration into the British dominions and colonies.

14. The result of all these factors combined must inevitably be the economic stagnation of Slovakia and might even mean a disastrous impoverishment. Dr. Tiso, who, though he can have little understanding of economics, is nevertheless a level-headed man, is beginning to be worried

about the future and his recent speeches have contained statements to the effect that capital from outside whether Czech or foreign is welcome here. His references to the Jewish problem are not radical and though he says he intends to arrange a final solution of it he will see that this is carried out without damaging Slovak economic interests.

15. At the present time the Slovak government contemplates sending a commission to Prague to arrange for the emigration of Jews from Slovakia. They will be allowed to take with them their capital which will be converted into foreign currency at a rate equivalent to 300 crowns to the pound. The government hopes to gain by restricting the scope of the black market and the Jews themselves will profit by obtaining a better rate than the 400-500 crowns they are paying now. Many Jews, according to my informant, have been selling their property to Germans from the Reich and the government considers it far more dangerous, he said, that these properties should fall into the hands of Reich Germans than that they should remain under Jewish ownership. The government's plan is intended to remove this risk.

No.146

J. M. Troutbeck to Lord Halifax
No. 63 (C 1868/5/62)

PRAGUE, *February 9, 1939*

I have the honour to report that on the 7th February I had a long conversation with the Legal Adviser to the Consulate on the question of the decrees for the revision of Czecho-Slovak citizenship and the residence of immigrants in the Republic...

2. Dr. Feygl is himself a Jew but by chance of circumstances an old-established Czech Jew... Dr Feygl himself inherited his father's "Heimatsrecht" and so became automatically a Czecho-Slovak citizen in 1918 and did not have to acquire his citizenship by naturalisation. In this way he escapes being affected by the decrees in question. But he explained to me how great a matter of chance this was. Every citizen of the old Austrian Empire had to possess "Heimatsrecht" in some community within its boundaries. But "Heimatsrecht" was passed down from father to son, and those who changed their place of residence inside the Empire never troubled to change their "Heimatsrecht", which in fact never came into consideration unless a person became a pauper. The Succession States nevertheless followed the old Empire in making "Heimatsrecht" the basis of nationality, so that it was not the *residents* within the new State of Czecho-Slovakia who became automatically Czecho-Slovak citizens in 1918 but those who had their "Heimatsrecht" therein. Those who resided there but had their "Heimatsrecht" in another part of the old Empire could only become Czecho-Slovak citizens by naturalisation, and they and their children now fall under the axe of decree No. 15.

3. The foregoing gives some indication of the complexity of the question and of the difficulty of assessing the number of persons who will, under decree No. 15, have to report to the Provincial authorities in order to have their citizenship re-examined. Dr. Feygl thought the number could hardly be less than 100,000 not including the 150,000 odd Russian émigrés who had been allowed to acquire Czecho-Slovak nationality and who, he felt sure, would in fact be allowed to continue their lives here undisturbed. For, while both the new decrees were careful never to mention the word "Jew", it was obviously against the Jews that they were designed.

4. And they will be affected, he pointed out, in the most cruel way. For

387

while those persons whose citizenship has to be re-examined must report to the Provincial authorities not later than April 30th next, no date is specified by which the Provincial authorities must give their decision. This will mean that the wretched Jews will never know from day to day whether they will not receive a notification that their citizenship is not confirmed and that they must leave the country within a stated period. Apart from the effect of such suspense on the moral of the persons affected, it will prevent their being able to make any proper plans for their lives, whether in business, renting houses, educating their children or in any other way. Dr. Feygl expressed his conviction that the Czecho-Slovak authorities would do their utmost not to enforce the new decrees against the Jews, but he was equally convinced that pressure would be brought to bear upon them by the German Government, who would make such enforcement a test of their goodwill.

5.   . . . there is a diversity of view among unprejudiced persons as to how far anti-Jewish measures are being forced upon the Czechs from Germany and how far the Czechs are merely alleging German pressure as an excuse for taking action which they themselves desire. Dr. Feygl is a firm adherent of the German pressure school. He admits that there are Czechs of the younger generation, particularly in the liberal professions, who beat the anti-Semitic drum — they are indeed being particularly active in his own legal profession. But he considers anti-Semitism in general to be foreign to the Czech temperament.

6.   However that may be, it seems clear that anti-Semitism is making headway. I am informed that Jews in the public service are receiving notice that their services are no longer required. A particularly hard case is that of Dr. Friedman, the head of the Economic Section of the Ministry for Foreign Affairs, who has done his country inestimable service and is in addition very difficult to replace. His services are now to be brought to an end. . .

Jewish doctors are, I hear, being turned out of the public hospitals, the leading Czech club of Prague is getting rid of its Jewish members. . . .

P. Pares to J. M. Troutbeck
No. 3 (C 1968/5/62)

BRATISLAVA, *February 10, 1939*

I have the honour to report that during the past week public interest in Slovakia, aroused by the fiery outbursts of Sano Mach and Karol Murgas at Risnovec last Sunday, has been occupying itself with the Jewish question. Today's "Slovak" contains a long front page article giving the answers of Father Rudolf Mikus, Provincial of the Jesuit Order in Slovakia, to certain questions put to him by the newspaper's correspondent. The answers are very conservative for although Father Mikus considers that the Church is in favour of a rapid solution of the Jewish question and always has been, and although he recommends the complete exclusion of Jews from public and commercial life to limit their evil moral and material influence (he refers specifically the professions of advocate, doctor and judge) he insists nevertheless that the solution must be just. He evidently excepts Jews who are Christians from the segregation which he recommends and is considering only Jews who have not been baptized. Further, he not only declares that the Church cannot withhold baptism, i.e. salvation from Jews who become converted to Christianity but maintains the doctrine that it is against the will of God for a state to prohibit marriages on grounds of race or nationality alone. He realizes that the rapidity with which the proposed solution can be carried out depends on the supply of christians available to take the place of the Jews in business, government administration etc.
2.   In the same issue of Slovak but in a modest place on the third page appears a report of Dr. Tiso's interview with a Jewish journalist. The prime minister observed that the government still has to determine the extent to which Jews shall be allowed to participate in the economic life of Slovakia. The coming Jewish law, he said, would remove uncertainty and would eliminate the possibility that Jews might find themselves with surprises. The solution, which would apply to the whole of Czecho-Slovakia would be just, social and humane. Emigrant Jews would either be sent home to their own countries or would be assigned a place of residence here.
3.   An example of how the official attitude works out in practice is given by the recent dispute over the allotment of a contract by the Bratislava Town Commissioner, who since October has been discharging the

functions of the Mayor. A Jewish firm competed for the contract and since their tender was by far the lowest they were successful. The local German newspaper "Grenzbote" in particular raised an outcry but the award was not cancelled. Last Wednesday the paper printed a sarcastic report that the commissioner had reacted to complaints on this head by announcing that "as soon as regulations regarding Jews have been issued, he will observe them strictly". "Slovak", however, the principal organ of the government party, printed the same report without comment.

Telegram from P. Pares to the
Chargé d'Affaires in Prague
No. 2 (Saving) (P 2320/7/12)

B R A T I S L A V A, *February 12, 1939*

(Copy)
(Excerpts)

On February 12th Sano Mach, chief of the Slovak Government's propaganda bureau, made a speech at Piestany in the presence of several thousands of Hlinka Guards and a small detachment of Ing. Karmasin's Freiwilliges Schutzkorps (FS). The speech is reported in to-day's "Slovak". The need of cooperation of Slovaks against attacks at home and abroad was stressed first of all and the general theme of the speech, which was much more moderate than last week's, was the importance of unity and discipline. We know, he said, with whose money these attacks are being made; we know how many millions Benes took with him when he fled and how with this money and with that of Jews and freemasons some statesmen and foreign newspapers are being misled. He attacked a recent unfavourable article on Slovakia published in the French paper, "La Croix". The Hlinka Guard exists, he said, to keep order and hinder the work of those profiteers who still want to lead the nation back to the position where it was before October 6th and grow fat on the labours of the poor Slovak people. He went on to say that certain people want to be more catholic than the Pope but only in order to create chaos and disorder. We must carefully examine those people who now wish to expel every Czech and Jew from Slovakia. They want to make Slovakia empty all at once and so produce chaos in the nation. . .

A. D. F. Gascoigne to Lord Halifax
No. 18 (C 1989/166/21)

BUDAPEST, *February 12, 1939*

(Excerpts)

. . . internal politics in Hungary have, for the past fortnight, concentrated mainly upon the Bill destined to curtail the economic and cultural activities of the Jews. In his telegram No. 15 of February 2 Sir G. Knox informed Your Lordship that the Hungarian Prime Minister, in view of his disinclination to modify the more drastic articles of the Bill in accordance with Admiral Horthy's wishes, had tendered his resignation, but that this had been refused. Since that date certain amendments to the Bill have been announced by the Government. . . and it seems likely that more will be introduced before it becomes law. Meanwhile the tussle which is taking place behind the scenes between M. Imredy and the Regent, a tussle over M. Imredy's dictatorial tendencies in general, and this anti-Semitic legislation in particular, seems likely to continue. Although it is not possible to foresee the turn of events when the Jewish Bill comes up for discussion in Parliament it is clear that the Regent and the majority of the deputies . . . are anxious that M. Imredy's Government should not fall over this question. For if, as seems possible, no satisfactory successor to M. Imredy were available, the Regent would find himself constrained to dissolve Parliament, and in this country, where anti-Semitic feelings run high, the dangers inherent in the holding of a general election with the Jewish question as the main issue are abundantly clear. . .
2. The autocratic methods of the Prime Minister are becoming increasingly marked. The introduction of "Standrecht" which followed a bomb outrage outside a Budapest synagogue on February 3 . . . does not seem to have been entirely warranted by this isolated incident. . .

As regards the emergency legislation. . . I have been informed on good authority that M. Imredy introduced it because he feared that the Hungarists might stage similar incidents throughout the country and bring about a general upheaval. At the same time he was anxious to impress public opinion in foreign countries that he was master in his own house . . .
4. As regards the progress of the Hungarist movement it is worthy of note that, although in two recent by-elections the Hungarist repre-

sentatives were defeated by the Government candidates, the former succeeded in polling a considerable proportion of the votes despite the "persuasive" measures which, I am informed, were taken to ensure the return of the Government's nominees. Owing, however, to the imprisonment of their leader, the annexation by the Government of the main planks of their programme and last but not least the hatred which is now entertained by all classes in this country towards Germany, the star of the Hungarists does not at present seem to be ascendant.

No.150

Letter from Count Pál Teleki to J. A. Keyser
About anti-semitism in Hungary
(C 2478/166/21)

BUDAPEST, *February 13, 1939.*

(Excerpts)

Dear Mr Keyser,
... I think Western-Europe gets and has a false opinion of the antisemitic movement and measures in Hungary. They do think that all this is the consequence of German influence, and nothing else, – and that German pressure, governmental or other, is pushing the Hungarian Government to go farther and farther.

The German influence, of course, is true in a certain respect. There was hardly any strong mental, social, economic or other movement or ideology in Europe which would not have spread from one country to the other, especially in a direction from the West to the East, like Christianity itself, later the Revival of Cluny, still later the Reformation and Counter-Reformation, Humanism and Renascence, the different styles of Art, Gothic and others; the Chivalry, the foundation and system of Universities, the change from the absolute monarchy to democracy, socialism, – I need not mention more. It is but natural that a movement and ideology so strong as the German antisemitism must influence the mind of peoples living in the neighbourhood and especially of peoples living to the East of Germany. Antisemitism is not a new movement and a new feeling in Hungary. It was general as a feeling even in the age of Liberalism. The restoration after the communism in 1919 was characterised also by a very strong anti-semitism, since the communism in Hungary was made and led by Jewish propagandists. There was even what one called the white terrorism but which was mild, since the Hungarian is by nature not cruel and not a terrorist, surely much less than most European nations (like Spaniards, Germans, Belgians, Balkan people etc). The very strong antisemitic feeling of 1919 could not express itself with the vigour which was inherent in it, – it could not because Hungary is too small and is too weak to start a European movement or even to maintain it inside its frontiers, in the midst of a different, uninterested Europe or Europe opposed to such ideas. The only law which was a consequence of this period's feelings was the numerus clausus on the Universities, and this law was attenuated a few years later much to the anger of broad masses of Christian public opinion.

Now it is only natural that in a country where anti-semitism is age-old as a feeling, and where there was a strong revival of this feeling in the recent past, antisemitism had to come to a strong expansion as soon as the European atmosphere, surrounding us, got favourable to it. It was easy for the antisemitic feeling to cross the frontier from Germany to Hungary. The growth of German power and the repeated political successes of Hitler played of course their part. Many people were of course so much influenced that they got enthusiastic admirers of Germany and of Hitler's system. There is nothing astonishing in it; every expansive idea, every successful leader has enthusiasts. There are still thousands of people who keep a portrait of Napoleon in their room.

Nevertheless, Hungarian antisemitism is not simply a copy and surely not a revival-copy of German antisemitism, and surely it will never be a copy because it will never grow to such cruelty, even if the Hungarian Law would be made as severe as the German or even more severe. It would not grow to such cruelty in consequence of our temperament, — I would like to say, our happily Oriental temperament.

For a development and growth of antisemitism in Hungary there was no need of a German example or influence. On the contrary, there is probably no country in which the situation would be more propitious for antisemitism. I would like to quote a part of the explanation which the Government presented with the draft of the Law to the Parliament. These lines, which I have inserted in this explanation, explain clearly the peculiar situation of Hungary, of which situation, as I was astonished to see, not only foreigners but even competent Hungarians had not a vivid knowledge. . . .

"Hungary lies on the borderland between the East and the West. As a result she became the first station of the Eastern Jews on their route to westernization. Hungary gave a proportionate amount of her cultural and economic possessions to these Jews who had scarcely, or not yet at all, begun to discard their Eastern character. She gave them the same privileges as the Western countries and Western social conditions could afford to grant, though the majority of these Jews not only retained their Eastern character, but the influx of such large numbers, caused the percentage of Jews in Hungary to approach that of the more Eastern countries."

"In addition we should bear in mind that Hungary, which apart from the small and geographically separate town of Fiume had no harbour, was the most continental country in Europe. Furthermore until quite recent times Hungary was unable to make up for the devastation caused by the

395

Turkish wars. In consequence of this, Hungarian commercial life could only develop very slowly and therefore no rich, selfconsciously commercial class, having its own traditions, could come into existence as was the case in Western countries. All this goes to show that the Jewish problem in Hungary is quite different from that of Western countries." . . . .

You are mistaken when writing that our Jews and their ancestors have resided for many centuries in this country. There are of course such Jews. And I tried everything to carry through a discrimination of this autochtonous Jewry from the bulk of Eastern Jews who came into the country in the last 50–80 years. The Law in its last form provides such discrimination. It was in 1919 or 1920 when I told some Jewish leaders of our public life: "You are Jews and you are Magyars. There is a conflict between the Christian Magyars and between the Oriental Jews who came in great masses to our country in the last half-century, and the continual infiltration of which did not stop and does not stop. You have to choose your place in this conflict because it is an earnest conflict, it is a problem of life and death for the Hungarian people. You must choose between your Magyar compatriots and between your Oriental co-religionists." Unhappily the greatest part of Hungarian Jews did choose the latter. They help the Oriental Jew with money, by the way of adoption and by giving them work, to come into the land, to get here a footing, to stay and to fight his life in competition with the autochtonous Christian people.

It is so that the danger grew so high that it may be too late for Hungary to save herself. The flux would have had to be stopped fifty years ago but that was the climax of the period of liberalism. To-day we have more than 6% Jews in the country and the radius of their ideology makes the number far greater. By intermarriages, by mixing in common work, their ideology is adapted by several Christians, and converts or baptised Jews keep their special mentality, especially in connection with this great number of Jews for generations. In the towns and in the intellectual classes the percentage is still greater. . . .

Just a few words about the solution and the draft of the Law. You think this step is stupid and highly dangerous. Well, the situation is dangerous with and without the Jewish Law. It would not be worthwhile to write down in a letter the history of the last twenty years. Neither would it be of use to criticise backwards and make recriminations. The result was a year ago that we were in a situation which could have led easily to a revolution. A revolution of extremists, it is true, but a revolution which would have had especially as to its ideology the sympathy of the overwhelming majority of the Christian public opinion. I have probably more connections with most different circles of people

396

than many parliamentary politicians. And I know quite well, how public opinion wishes a very radical solution of the Jewish problem. They are of course not aware of all the dangers, but their feelings are very decided. So dangers would not be avoided by dropping this Law or another one which would lead more or less to the same result or which would have the same goal. I do not say that this Law is the best law but I could imagine. We could have made, if we would have had more time to think it over soundly, a better one. Probably the Law is also much too complicated but I do not think this is to what you object, but something of the kind had and has to be made. Certainly it is a dangerous operation but it is like an appendicitis operation you make in the last moment. If nothing would be made, I do not know if anybody could maintain the inward peace. And we live in a much too dangerous surrounding to give the opportunity to any neighbour and especially the big one to interfere. And as to the cleverness of the measures, I do agree, the Law could be wiser, simpler and better in its details, but it is exceedingly difficult to make something cleverer. To think something cleverer is easier because while thinking you are playing with rational elements; when acting you must play with irrational elements to a great extent. You are right when thinking that the burden of my responsibility is great. But do believe, it would not be smaller by doing the contrary of what the Government is doing now. I meditated much, discussed these problems with clever men of the opposite opinion. Being without a party and without political ambitions, I could more easily compare opinions, though it is not easier for anybody who goes his own way instead of going the way of parties, but I came to the conclusion that of the different evils we had to choose this one. I see since long years the bad influence, the Jewish mentality has on the big part of our society; I see how the middle class and the aristocracy who were real values in the maintenance of our land, our character and in political leadership, are intoxicated with ideas and the morality strange to the Hungarian character. There is a deep ditch between our leading class and the great bulk of the people of our small towns and villages, and the growing-up youth imbued with the strong social feeling; I see the danger in the schools. I am sorrily convinced that, if things would go the way they were going since half a century, it would cost the life of the Hungarian people. As I told already, my only fear is that it is too late. There were four big dangers which menaced in the course of Hungarian history our land and people: the Mongols, the Turks, the Jews and the Germans. And I must say the Mongols were the best of the four because they came from very far and went back quickly. And the next best were the Turks who had the quietness, laziness and gentleness of the Oriental . . . .

(Signed) Paul Teleki

397

Copy of a letter from R. A. Butler to J. A. Keyser

FOREIGN OFFICE, *March 10, 1939*

(Excerpts)

I have now had a chance of studying in more details the letter from Count Teleki about anti-Semitism in Hungary. It has also been examined carefully by the department which deals with Hungary.

We are much interested in Count Teleki's views — the more so since he has in the meantime become Prime Minister — and his letter will be valuable in helping us to understand the point of view of the Hungarian Government in this tragic Jewish question.

Minutes by R. L. Speaight (March 4, 1939)

(Excerpts)

The first thing that strikes one is that Count Teleki has an uneasy conscience in the matter. The pages of justification. . .from a man in his position is in itself a sign that he does not feel very sure of his ground. Moreover, these ten pages do not, to my mind, contain a single really convincing argument to justify the anti-Jewish Bill.

He talks all the time of the need for protecting the purity of Hungarian life from Jewish influences, and suggests that the Hungarians are in imminent danger of losing, on account of the Jewish element in their midst, all the qualities which made them a great race in the past. Actually I should have thought that the opposite was nearer the truth. Hungary. . .owes a very great deal to the Jews, who have been largely responsible for building up its industries and have generally provided the country with an indispensable business and professional middle class which it is unlikely the Magyars themselves would ever have succeeded in building up. It is true that this middle class has been created by the assimilable westernised Jews, but despite what Count Teleki says, these surely form by far the most important part of the Jewish community in Hungary. The oriental ghetto Jew of the type so common in Poland is virtually non-existent in Budapest and, I think, present in large numbers only in the newly annexed territories. . .

No.151

P. Pares to J. M. Troutbeck
No. 6
(C 2332/7/12)

BRATISLAVA, *February 14, 1939*

(Copy, transmitted to the Foreign Office)

[Reports on a talk with Sano Mach]

(Excerpts)

5. He [Šano Mach] took great pains to convince me that the treatment of Jews in the refugee camps in Bratislava is humane. He insisted that excellent relations exist between the inmates of the camp and the warders who are members of the Hlinka Guard. An English refugee worker had already told me this but it is worth nothing that the local Jewish organization which provides food and clothing is also expected to pay the warders fifty crowns a day each. On such terms the warders ought to be able to show good humour. Mach said that the government does not expect to solve the Jewish problem immediately. Licences to keep hotels, inns etc. will in future be limited to Christians and Mach added that the withdrawal of licences from Jews can be effected within a month. He suggested that in professions where Jews are at present indispensable, such as the medical profession, restrictions on a proportional basis will be introduced. This part of the Jewish problem, he said, can only be solved in four or five years.

6. Mach declared that public opinion in the villages, always strongly anti-Semitic and in recent months fanned by fiery speeches and newspaper articles, is now complaining that the government is proceeding too slowly in the solution of the Jewish problem. Reports have been coming in, he said, from the organizations of the Hlinka Guard in the country recommending that something should be done to ally the rising discontent. Hence Mach's lively speech in Risnovec on February 5th. Since the Hlinka Guard are themselves responsible for the increase in anti-semitic feeling it is rather odd that they should now lay the blame on the people. However Slovaks are simple people and it is just possible that after shouting themselves hoarse for several months the Hlinka Guard are genuinely perturbed to find that somebody has been listening to them.

The Vienna broadcasts which are said to be controlled by the minister Durčiansky is [sic] according to Šano Mach, responsible for a great deal of the anti-semitic agitation on account of its daily denunciations of individual Jews in this or that village. I asked Mach whether, in view of the fact that the government was having its hand forced by these broadcasts, any steps had been taken to moderate their tone. He replied at once that steps have been taken. Perhaps this is the truth but it is difficult for me to judge.

7.   Shrewd observers believe that the government are trying, so to speak, to blackmail Prague. Knowing that the Czechs need Slovakia, the Slovaks are blustering about independence and threatening to take capital from the Jews unless the Czechs supply it. In a trial of nerves it is certain that the Czechs will hold out longest and as one might have expected the negotiations for a loan between the government and the local branches of some Czech banks have been suspended. . .

B. C. Newton to Lord Halifax
No. 73 (60/8/39)
(C 1967/7/12)

PRAGUE, *February 14, 1939*

(Excerpts)

2.   A further indication of a more moderate trend in Slovak opinion may perhaps be found in two reports in to-day's press. It is stated in the first place that the resignation of Monsieur Mach, the head of the Slovak Propaganda Office, is under consideration. Elsewhere there is a report of a speech made by Monsieur Mach to the Hlinka Guard which for him is surprisingly moderate in its tone, both towards Czechs and Jews. . . . , Monsieur Mach has been extremely active of late and his activities have been far from helpful in promoting good relations with the Czechs. Indeed, it has been his great boast that the ultimate aim of the Slovaks is complete independence. In the meantime he has been making such embarrassing proposals as severance from the League of Nations and accession to the Anti-Comintern pact, while the elimination of all Czechs from the province is evidently dear to his heart. The cause of Czech-Slovak friendship would certainly be helped were he either removed from his office or forced to restrain his language.
3.   A still more extreme protagonist of Slovak nationalism is Professor Tuka. His violence is perhaps natural in view of the many years he spent in Czech prison for high treason. Unfortunately there has been no indication hitherto that the Slovak Government are proposing to push him into the background. On the contrary, they appear to have gone out of their way to do him honour. His return to the province towards the end of last year was made a public occasion. Subsequently he was made honorary head of the Hlinka Guard. Now he is, according to the press, to be made head of an organisation entitled the "Rodobrana", which is a revival of an old semi-military body of the same name and would seem to be designed in its reincarnation to bear much the same relation to the Hlinka Guard as the S.S. does to the S.A. Dr. Tuka's speeches have been becoming so irresponsible that last week some organs of the Czech press were moved to protest. This had two results. Their further circulation in Slovakia was prohibited and Monsieur Mach made a speech stoutly defending Dr. Tuka and declaring that all the Slovak leaders were agreed with regard to his activities.

4.   I had an interesting conversation not long ago with the Italian Consul at Bratislava on the Slovak situation. If he is to be believed, Monsieur Mach is only stating the truth when he says that the ultimate aim of the Slovaks is complete independence. In the Consul's view, that is undoubtedly their ideal, though the more responsible realise that economic difficulties may make it at the moment impracticable. He was inclined to be sceptical as to the reality of a moderate and extreme section of Slovak opinion and to think that all the Slovak leaders were pretty well hand in glove, a moderate or extremist being put up to speak as occasion demanded. He mentioned the intense bitterness felt in Slovakia against the Czechs, saying that they are regarded with even greater dislike than the Jews. For this he thinks the Czechs largely to blame for having never taken the Slovaks seriously and having imagined that they could always buy them off if necessity demanded it. But such bribes, he said, had never done any good, for as soon as they were paid the Slovaks became more intransigent than ever.

No.153

J. M. Troutbeck to Lord Halifax
No. 93 (C 2373/7/12)

PRAGUE, *February 22, 1939*

I have the honour to inform you that the second session of the Slovak Diet was held on the 21st February. A speech was made by Dr. Tiso, the head of the Slovak Government, of which the following is a summary.

2. Dr. Tiso said that the Diet's first task would be to work out a provincial constitution. In public administration account would be taken of the results of the census of the 31st December, 1938, which had shown that Slovakia had 2,709,000 inhabitants, of whom 128,000 were Germans, 76,000 Hungarians and 70,000 Ruthenians. He announced that the Slovak labour market would be protected from foreigners and immigrés. The Government would assist the emigration of Jewish elements and would enlist the help of Jews at home and abroad to this end, care being taken not to destroy industrial enterprises in Slovakia.

3. In the field of education and cultural matters, said Dr. Tiso, the Christian and national idea would be in the foreground. In localities where there were large groups of Jews, Jewish classes would be established in the State schools. Christian teachers would instruct in Christian schools and Jewish teachers in Jewish schools. Religion would be a compulsory subject in all schools, and, in general, State laws and regulations would be in harmony with the teachings of the Church.

No. 154

P. Pares to the British Legation in Prague
No. 8 (C 2550/7/12)

BRATISLAVA, *February 27, 1939*

[Reports on debate in Slovak Parliament on political programme of
the Government]

(Excerpts)

5.   Dr. Tiso's theories regarding the political role of the corporations or professional groups (in german – Stände –) were aired again but no precise plan of action was formulated. He said that the natural divisions of the nation in estates or professional groups will be reconciled and united under the representation of one party. They will be organized from the lowest foundations in the communes up to the supreme central organs.

6.   The representative of the united national will in the political sphere is to be the single party which is now more of an organ of the state than a representative of a certain group of people and each member of the party irrespective of the political group to which he may have belonged in the past will be considered a deputy for the whole people and will adjust the interests of his group to those of the nation.

7.   Turning to foreign affairs the prime minister indicated that Slovakia will have its own diplomatic representation, though on a modest scale. He conceives Slovakia's foreign policy as one of neutrality. "We shall not join with any world powers" he said, "which provoke the hostility of others" (presumably he was referring to the Soviets) "nor shall we join with any power which is foreign to us in its political ideology". (This seems to exclude Germany and the fascist countries whose ideology seems to be different from the purely Christian ideology described by Dr. Tiso in another passage as being that of the Slovaks.)

9.   . . . In any consideration of the future of Slovakia the Hlinka Guard cannot be overlooked. It will be an important organ for setting the new political and philosophical standard among the mass of the people. . .

In their speeches Sidor, Murgas and other leaders of the Guard emphasise that now that "freedom" has been obtained not dreams and illusions are wanted but the recognition of facts and hard work. No one has the right to enjoy the good things of the Slovak table who does not work and, it is already being implied, belong to the Hlinka organisation.

The Czech and Jewish problems are to be settled according to their "rights"...

Most of the members are young officials and clerks in private or semi-State employ. Their attitude towards the Czechs or to anyone who stood in their way, was at first overbearing, an expression one was told of "being master in one's own house", but is now beginning to calm down. *The active anti-Semitism of the early days of November has been only rarely repeated.*

The official attitude of the Church towards the Hlinka Guard, a matter of supreme importance in so Catholic a land, was during the first days hostile but is now on the whole favourable. Some individual priests remain reserved, but others are members, even officers of the Guard...

10. The manner in which the Jewish question is to be solved will apparently be quite moderate. The announcement of the solution is now a matter of days. Dr. Tiso declared that Slovakia will not imitate any other country but in evolving her own plan must consider the consequences for her national life.

No.155

A. D. F. Gascoigne to Lord Halifax
No. 26 (C 2539/166/21)

BUDAPEST, *February 27, 1939*

(Excerpts)

2. The fact that the outgoing Prime Minister, M. Imrédy, discovered that, despite his previous assertions. . . he had some Jewish blood in his veins, was only the final link in the chain of circumstances which led to his enforced resignation. The fundamental cause is I think to be found in the reactionary methods which he chose to employ for the implementation of his programme of reforms. . . . Imrédy, who, at the beginning of his period of office in May last year, was faced with the necessity of curbing the activities of the Hungarian Nazis (The Hungarists as they are now called) annexed a large part of their programme, and proceeded to move . . . towards the adoption of methods which were not on all fours with the customary tenets of Parliamentary government. He had, in fact, embarked upon a path which was leading him away from the Constitution towards an authoritarian régime, and there is no doubt that for several months past his methods have proved a thorn in the sides of the Regent, and of many of his Cabinet and Party colleagues.

3. Moreover, M. Imrédy has assumed a number of the personal characteristics of the modern dictator. I have it on the best authority that he would listen to no advice and that his general lack of prestige, and his unpopularity with almost all the prominent persons in the country, were rendering the conduct of State business well-nigh impossible. . .

8. Count Teleki's action in suppressing the Hungarist Party. . . has shewn that he intends to act firmly, and this has given him a good start. It has been announced that this step was taken as a direct consequence of the recent bomb outrage against the Jews. . . which it is alleged was proven to be the work of the Hungarists. The Minister of the Interior declared on February 24 through the medium of the Press that while the Government did not wish to prevent the existence of organizations which conformed with the Law and the Constitution, the Hungarist Party was a centre of illegal and anti-Constitutional action, and as such could not be permitted. Up to the present there has been no reaction on the part of the Hungarists who are seriously handicapped by the absence in prison of their chiefs and by the continued enforcement of Martial Law. . . But the situation

406

deserves closely watching. It is possible that, as happened once before when the same party, then known as the Hungarian National Socialist Party, was dissolved by M. Daranyi's Government in 1938... this extremist organization may rear its head again under some different guise. As to this, much will depend upon the success or otherwise which will attend Count Teleki's efforts to alleviate the economic distress which is so prevalent amongst the lower classes, both in Budapest and in the country at large.

9.   One of the first actions of Count Teleki on assuming office was to bring about the fusion of M. Imrédy's "Hungarian Life" Movement with the Party of National Unity, the Government Party. The resulting organization is to be known in future as the Hungarian Life Party. As far as can be foreseen at present the theatrical activities in connection with the Hungarian Life Movement, which were undertaken by M. Imrédy, will not be continued by Count Teleki. At any rate I hear that the emblem of the movement, a large embroidered representation of the Mythical Stag, which is said to have led the Magyar hordes from the Mongolian Plain to their European home, and which accompanied M. Imrédy and his satellites on their canvassing tours, has been relegated to the Archives Department where it seems destined to remain.

10.   Count Teleki has declared that in so far as Hungary's external relations are concerned he intends to follow in the footsteps of his predecessor, and in his maiden speech to the Chamber of Deputies he stressed, *inter alia*, Hungary's attachment to the Rome-Berlin axis...
Count Teleki is not regarded here as being enamoured of the methods of Nazi Germany, and his action in suppressing the Hungarist Movement, which, even if it was not materially assisted by the German Government was certainly smiled upon by the Nazi Party, will not be likely to enhance his popularity with Berlin. The information which is available to me here is that the present leaders of Germany do not trust him, and, from what I have been able to glean so far, the German Press have been somewhat luke-warm, to say the least of it, in commenting upon his appointment. . . .

No.156

Telegram from B. C. Newton to the Foreign Office
No. 56 (C 2913/5/62)

PRAGUE, *March 10, 1939*

I took an opportunity to say to the Minister for Foreign Affairs on March 10th that I was somewhat perturbed at his reference to Jews during rather hurried conversations which he had on March 8th. I appreciated the difficulty of his position but it would obviously have a bad effect in his country if the Jewish problem were further aggravated just when we were doing all in our power to alleviate it. Was there any foundation for rumours of specific and discriminatory legislation against the Jews?

Minister for Foreign Affairs assured me that no such legisation beyond the laws already issued... was in contemplation. Of course if the German Government exercise enough pressure the Czecho-Slovak Government would have no option but so far as they could they were trying to evade action and to justify themselves with the German Government by maintaining that Jewish question was an international problem in regard to which Czecho-Slovakia proposed to pursue the same policy as Roumania and Poland.

No.157

Sir G. Knox to Sir O. G. Sargent
(C 3339/166/21)

BUDAPEST, *March 13, 1939*

(Excerpts)

. . . there has been something almost pathological in Imredy's decline since the crisis and certainly the atmosphere he succeeded in creating of late was thoroughly unhealthy — clearly the mixture of innate German mysticism and inbred Hungarian romance is not a good one. It is a tragic case, if ever, of "capax imperii nisi imperasset." Though I have had a great liking for him personally and much respect for his intelligence I can now only hope, for Hungary's sake, that he and his white stag will remain in the wilderness.

[Paul Teleki]. . . both he and the Regent spoke with a new confidence of the internal situation, the latter emphasizing particularly that Germany's "betrayal" of Hungary had entirely extinguished any sparks of Nazism that there had been in the Honvéd.

No. 158

A. D. F. Gascoigne to Lord Halifax
No. 64 (C 6985/166/21

BUDAPEST, *May 6, 1939*

(Excerpts)

4.   The "Hungarists" or the "Hungarian Crossed Arrow Party" as they are now called, who might in the past have proved a serious menace to the Government at the elections, have not recovered from the action taken against them by Count Teleki last February. . .

. . . [Teleki] has shewn courage in suppressing the "Hungarists" (albeit this action was not wholly successful) and his handling of the highly controversial and difficult question of the anti-Jewish legislation has, at least, been tactful and correct.

No. 159

O. St. Clair O'Malley to Lord Halifax
No. 83 (C 8207/166/21)

BUDAPEST, *June 1, 1939*

[Comments on the Arrow Cross success in the May elections]

(Excerpts)

2. . . . It looks at first sight as if the increase in the Crossed Arrow party's vote should be taken to indicate a growing desire for ever more intimate relations with Germany, but this view is not held by most intelligent observers in Budapest who consider that the increased support given to that party is mainly attributable to public impatience with the slow progress of social legislation. This opinion is supported by the fact that many of the Hungarist candidates spoke openly against a German ascendancy. It is regrettable that the elected members of the Party are mostly persons who neither deserve nor enjoy the personal respects of their countrymen, and there are grounds for fearing that they may conduct themselves in the new chamber in a way likely to bring parliamentarism into disrepute.

411

No.160

Sir R. Hoare to Lord Halifax
No. 161 (R 5076/214/67)

BUCHAREST, *June 15, 1939*

With reference to Your Lordship's telegram No. 260 of the 8th June, I have the honour to report that Mr. Perlzweig called on me on the 13th June and that I arranged an interview for him with the President of the Council of Ministers.

2. Mr. Perlzweig has, at my request, furnished me with a record of the conversation of which I have the honour to enclose a copy. He tells me that he hopes that his visit here has done something to reduce the profound pessimism which he found prevailing amongst the Roumanian Jewish community, and that his conversation with M. Calinesco will yield some concrete results.

Enclosure to No.160

Mr. Perlzweig thanked Monsieur Calinescu warmly for his friendly reception and emphasised his full understanding of the difficulties which confronted the Government and expressed appreciation of what had already been achieved in relation to the suppression of subversive anti-Semitic violence. His own motive in coming to Roumania was, first, humanitarian. Jews who had lost the right to work were in great distress, and their appeals for help were producing uneasiness among British and American Jews, who already had the terrific burden of the German refugees to sustain. Secondly, he was anxious that nothing should happen which might embarrass the British Government at the present inter-national juncture. He believed that it was in the enduring interests of all the parties concerned that the problem should be solved on practical lines, and he had therefore cast all questions of theory and ideology aside and – in full agreement with Mr. Butler had come to offer his services in a friendly spirit and on a practical basis. Unhappily the Jews of Great Britain and America, as well as many of their non-Jewish friends, were disquieted at the course the régime was taking in reference to the Jews.

At this point Monsieur Calinescu broke in and said he would state the position very frankly. Neither he nor his Government was anti-Semitic. Their suppression of the Iron Guard had rapidly altered the situation and, incidentally, had been of great benefit to the Jews. But they had to take certain elements in the life of the country into account. No Government could ignore them, and certain measures had to be taken "pour calmer l'opinion publique". But it had all been carried through deliberately in a spirit of moderation. In the matter of the revision of nationality only a third of the cases examined had been struck off the list of citizens. The number ought strictly to have been greater, but many cases had been viewed with an "œil indulgent". Mr. Perlzweig broke in to say that the "œil indulgent" had evidently been closed on a number of occasions. He knew of cases of crippled ex-servicemen, whose fathers had fought in the War of Independence, but who had been struck off. Monsieur Calinescu said that this was impossible, but Mr. Perlzweig persisted and Monsieur Calinescu made a note of the point for further enquiry.

Mr. Perlzweig referred also to the unhappy situation in the Bukovina, where "mutilés", war widows and orphans had been deprived of licences to sell tobacco and alcohol. Monsieur Calinescu said that this was entirely due to motives of hygiene. Mr. Perlzweig asked whether it was not a rather extraordinary coincidence that all the Jews were bad and all the others good? To which Monsieur Calinescu replied that he had photographs. Mr. Perlzweig then pointed to the order compelling Jews — many among them the most orthodox in the world — to work on the Sabbath and to open their businesses on that day. It had caused a most painful impression abroad, and it was clearly not an act calculated to calm public opinion, especially as he knew that the non-Jews in the Bukovina were annoyed at having competition thrust upon them on one of their best days. Monsieur Calinescu denied strenuously that the order was still in force, but Mr. Perlzweig returned to the charge (knowing that it was) and at last Monsieur Calinescu undertook to have the matter investigated and settled.

Mr. Perlzweig said that there were other ways of calming public opinion. He had no plan, but the resumption of emigration on a normal scale might ease the tension as well as provide for those now in distress. Monsieur Calinescu said that démarches had been made in London without success in the hope that the Jewish question might be regulated by international action in this way. Mr. Perlzweig replied that he knew that Beck had not received satisfaction, and he was certain that no British Government, specially of view of what was happening in Germany, would do anything which might seem to encourage forcible emigration or reward oppression. A new and friendly atmosphere and the collaboration in a friendly spirit of the Roumanian Government might make all the difference. Monsieur Calinescu asked what was proposed, to which Mr. Perlzweig replied that the Roumanian Jews must be given an opportunity to organise themselves. It was urgently necessary to have a representative

413

committee, embracing all sections, and mentioned three names: Dr. Niemerover, the Chief Rabbi, Dr. Theodor Fischer and Dr. Fildermann. Monsieur Calinescu said he knew these gentlemen and added "By all means call them together and come back with the results". Mr. Perlzweig said that he did not want to do this as (a) he wanted to go home, and (b) it was bad in principle. He did not want to interpose himself between a Government and some of its citizens. These gentlemen represented all sections and wanted to work with the Government. Their loyalty was beyond dispute. They ranked in the estimation of the General Staff, as was well known, after all other minorities for their reliability. Why should they be rebuffed? Monsieur Calinescu confirmed the view of the General Staff and asked what Mr. Perlzweig would suggest. Mr. Perlzweig said that even in Germany, where the Government was certainly not philo-Semitic, there was a Reichsvertretung over Judaism, (sic) and these men should be allowed to be constituted as such a committee in Roumania. Monsieur Calinescu agreed and asked that these men should come to see him with their proposals. "Je vous autorise, je vous encourage", he added, to communicate this suggestion.

As the interview ended Monsieur Calinescu once again took up the Iron Guard question, and said that it had been difficult to suppress in view of the attitude of a foreign Government. Mr. Perlzweig said that the Jews duly realised this and acknowledged the friendliness of his reception. He asked whether he might write through Monsieur Tilea if necessary. Monsieur Calinescu said that he might write, by all means, and direct if he chose. He would be glad to see him again whenever he felt it necessary.

No.161

The British Vice Consulate (Prague)
to the Minister for Foreign Affairs
No. 52/39 (C 11116/5/62)

PRAGUE, *August 4, 1939*

(Excerpts)

The Budweis (Budejovice) branch of President Hácha's National Union Party has issued the following order to its members "in the interest of cooperation with the German nation":—

(1) No woman of Czech nationality under the age of 45 can be employed by Jewish citizens of the Protectorate;

(2) All Czech political and non political associations and clubs as well as commercial companies are ordered to dismiss forthwith the Jewish members;

(3) Social intercourse between Czechs and Jews, both in public and private, is considered to be undesirable and compromising.

2. The provisions of this order must be fulfilled not later than August 15. After this date all contrary actions will be regarded as breaches of party discipline and will be dealt with accordingly.

No.162

Foreign Office note about a
conversation between Sir A. Cadogan and the
Hungarian Minister in London (G. Barcza)
(C 11172/129/21)

FOREIGN OFFICE, *August 9, 1939*

The Hungarian Minister told me this morning that his Government had ascertained that shortly before the recent Hungarian elections the German Government had purchased quantities of Pengös* in Paris, Zurich and London with which they had financed the election campaign of the Nazi Party in Hungary... The Hungarian Government wished to proceed against the Nazi Party and if possible to break it up and it would greatly facilitate this action if they were able to show that the Party was subsidised from abroad. The Minister asked whether it was possible to ascertain by any means and inform him who where the purchasers of Pengös in London...

A. C(adogan)

*Pengö: Hungarian currency

No.163

Minute by Sir O. Sargent on Conversation
with the Hungarian Minister Barcza
(August 26, 1939)
Enclosure to Foreign Office Telegram No. 247
to O. St. C. O'Malley (Budapest), September 2, 1939
(C 12506/350/21)

FOREIGN OFFICE, *August 26, 1939*

(Excerpts)

[M. de Barcza stated that]
(V) The signature of the German-Soviet Treaty had completely demoralised the Hungarian Nazi Party, whose main plank had always been opposition to Communism, since the Hungarian people preserved a vivid recollection of the Communist régime of Bela Kun.* The Hungarian Nazi Party were now so weakened and disorganised that they no longer constituted any danger to the Hungarian State, and the possibility of their being able to organise a coup d'état in certain eventualities might now be ruled out.

*Correctly: Béla Kún

417

No. 164

Record of a conversation between
staff of British Legation and
members of Slovak trade delegation
(190/16/39)
(C 19060/7/12)

BUDAPEST, *November 14, 1939*

[Talk with two members of Slovak trade delegation,
senior officials from Slovak Ministry of Commerce,
and one Director of Slovak National Bank]

(Excerpts)

. . . They described the constitution of their country as being "authoritarian on a democratic basis." Candidates are put forward by one party only, the Hlinka party, but the Hlinka party is not identical with the Government and may become less so in future. All Slovaks are now obliged by law to join the party which, it is believed, will become as a result of this a harmless movement, so diluted as to have no political character. The object of this dilution is to prevent it from becoming a political club which would attempt to dominate the Government.

They declared that they would never have attacked Poland if Poland had not robbed them last November of territory that had been Slovak for centuries. They did not in any case, they alleged, actually fire on the Poles but merely followed the Germans. They minimize the extent of German interference in the affairs of their country and they do in effect appear to have a large measure of economic independence. They extended an invitation to visit their country in order to verify that there was no trace of German control, they admitted, however, on being questioned, that the Gestapo, if invisible, are nevertheless to be reckoned with.

They were not averse to some sort of Danubian Federation if this left their control of home affairs unimpaired. A federal union with the Czechs would, they say, have no purpose as the Czechs would not be strong enough to defend them. . .

The Hlinka party does claim to be identical with the state like the Nazi party in Germany and its influence is all powerful in the appointment of members of the executive, the government and the legislature. Its internal structure is also such as to place the leadership in the hands of a small

418

clique. That this had not yet been completely realised is due to the Slovak constitutional incapacity for conceiving or carrying out a thoroughgoing dictatorship.

The view of federal union with the Czechs is an interesting comment on the present efforts of the Czech exiles in Paris. Slovaks only lean on the Czechs now to the extent that they feel the need for some outside support. If the Czechs cannot provide it there is no likelihood of a revival of any joint state. This general view of the Slovaks was rather caustically put by Šano Mach who held and still holds the Office of Chief of Propaganda, when he declared some weeks before March 14 (referring to the subservient position of the Czechs in Central Europe after Munich) "We do not want to be the slaves of slaves."

Index of Names

Addison, Sir Joseph, British Minister in Prague, 75-6, 78, 81, 90-1, 161
Antonescu, General Ion, Chief of the Romanian General Staff, Minister for National
  Defence in the Goga Government and in M. Cristea's first Cabinet, dictator
  (1940-44), 39, 42, 52, 86
Antonescu, Victor, Romanian Minister for Foreign Affairs (1936-37), 26-7, 28, 39, 52,
  161, 193, 238, 298.
Apor, Baron Gabriel, Secretary-General of the Hungarian Ministry for Foreign Affairs,
  124, 229
Ashton-Gwatkin, Frank T. A., Counsellor in the Foreign Office, 1934-39, 122, 130, 162

Barcza, György, Hungarian Minister in London (1938-41), 140, 416-17
Bárdossy, Ladislas, Hungarian Minister in Bucharest, 1934-41, 140, 152
Beneš, Dr. Eduard, 5, 13, 75-81, 83-5, 89-91, 99, 101, 155, 168, 183-5, 194, 200-1, 206,
  232, 250, 333, 362, 368, 391
Bentinck, Sir Charles, British Minister and Consul-General in Prague, 1936-37, 77-8, 81,
  162
Beran, Rudolf, Chairman of the Czechoslovak Agrarian Party (from 1935); Prime
  Minister, December 1938 – March 1939, 77-8, 80, 83, 85-7, 100, 103-4, 106, 110,
  184, 339, 356, 360, 369, 380
Bessenyei, Baron, Political Director of the Hungarian Ministry for Foreign Affairs,
  123, 212-13
Bethlen, Count I., Former Hungarian Prime Minister, Life Member of the Upper House,
  118, 127, 144-6, 270, 292
Bibesco, Prince Antoine, Romanian delegate at the League of Nations, 41, 44, 163, 278
Böszörményi, Zoltán, Leader of the Scythe-Cross movement (Hungary), 10, 118-19, 125,
  247, 313
Bramwell, Ch., Foreign Office Staff member, 1935-38, 149, 154, 217, 231, 348
Brătianu, Constantin (Dinu), Leader of the Romanian National Liberal party, 42, 65,
  286
Brătianu, George, I., Leader of the dissident rightist Romanian Liberal party, 23-4, 33
Brotman, A. G., Leader of the Board of Deputies of British Jews, 226
Bruce Lockhart, Adviser to the Hungarian National Bank, 94, 146-7, 307, 332
Butler, R. A., Parliamentary Under-Secretary of State for Foreign Affairs, February
  1938–July 1941, 151, 354, 398, 412

421

Festetics, Count Alexander, Hungarian Nazi leader (from 1933), 10, 119, 135, 252, 325, 366
Fildermann, Wilhelm, A leader of Romanian Jewry, 414
Filipescu, Grigore, Romanian politician, leader of the Conservative party, 24, 220, 245
Florescu, Radu, Counsellor of Romanian Legation, London; acted as Chargé d'Affaires, 72

Gajda, General Rudolf, Chairman of the Fascist party, Czechoslovakia, 79, 85, 86
Gascoigne, A. D. F., 1st Secretary, British Legation, Budapest, 1936-39; acted as Chargé d'Affaires, 122-3, 124-6, 132-3, 138, 145-8, 162-5, 307
Gaselee, Sir Stephen, Librarian and Keeper of the Papers in the F.O., 237
Gayda, Dr. Virginio, Italian journalist and editor of *Giornale d'Italia*, 16, 150
Gigurtu, Ion, Romanian Prime Minister (1940), 51
Goga, Octavian, Leader of the Nationalist Christian party (Romania); Prime Minister (December 1937—February 1938), 3, 9, 23-5, 32, 33, 37-45, 55, 56, 58-64, 67, 68, 120, 126, 133, 173, 196, 197, 202, 230, 249, 260, 267, 280, 281, 294, 296, 365, 370, 372
Gömbös, General Gyula, Prime Minister of Hungary 1932-36, 11, 119, 121, 123-4, 145, 214, 222, 265, 354
Grigorcea, B., Romanian Minister in Rome, later in London, 31, 195-6, 223

Hacha, Dr. Emil, President of Czechoslovakia, November 1938—March 1939, 83, 87, 103, 360, 415
Hadow, R. H., British Chargé d'Affaires in Prague, 1935-37; Member of Northern Department of the F.O., 75, 76-7, 79, 90, 100, 161-2, 164
Halifax, 3rd Viscount, 13, 14, 16, 17, 50, 69, 132, 134, 163-5
Harvey, Sir Oliver, Private Secretary of Anthony Eden, 18, 44
Henlein, Konrad, Leader of Sudeten German party, 76, 168, 184, 231
Henderson, Sir Neville, British Ambassador in Berlin, 106, 164, 330, 335
Hitler, Adolf, 4, 38, 49, 59, 89, 95, 121-3, 129, 133, 140, 141, 143, 154, 156, 168, 174, 199, 205, 222, 244, 249, 251, 308, 322, 332, 382, 395
Hlinka, Mgr. Andrej, Chairman of Slovak People's party; died August 1938, 76, 81, 89-91, 95, 109, 120, 169, 322
Hoare, Sir Reginald H., British Minister in Bucharest, 1935-41, 25-33, 34-7, 40-2, 48, 50, 52, 56, 58, 60-5, 67-9, 71-2, 127, 133, 161-5, 249 ff., 283, 286, 295 ff.
Hodža, Dr. Milan, Prime Minister of Czechoslovakia, 1935-38, 89, 183, 201, 232
Horthy, Admiral M. de Nagybánya, Regent of Hungary, 1920-44, 3, 9, 86, 89, 119, 121, 126, 133, 138-9, 144, 151, 153, 174, 247, 313, 366, 381-2, 392
Hubay, Kálmán, Hungarian Nazi leader, 10, 132, 137, 323, 327, 355, 366
Hudson, R. S., Parliamentary Under-Secretary in the F.O., Department of Overseas Trade, 1937-40, 106, 334

Iamandi, Victor, Romanian politician, member of National Liberal governments, 26, 175, 204
Imrédy, Dr. Béla, Hungarian Prime Minister, 1938-39, 3, 122, 134-5, 137-8, 147, 148, 150, 162, 199, 307, 316, 323, 325, 328, 331, 332, 342, 344, 354, 357, 366, 392, 406-7, 409
Inculeţ, Ion, Romanian Minister of the Interior, 26, 172, 181, 187, 192, 305
Ingram, E. M. B., Counsellor in the F.O., Head of Southern Department, 62, 163, 311, 348
Iorga, Nicolae, Historian, Politician, Romanian Prime Minister, 24, 56, 210, 290

O'Malley, Owen St. Clair, Counsellor in the F.O.; Minister in Budapest 1939-41, 17, 139, 165, 190, 417

Ostrovsky, Soviet Minister in Bucharest, 34, 181

Pares, Peter, British Consul in Bratislava, 1938-39, 92-3, 111-13, 165

Pauker, Ana, Romanian Communist leader, 58, 191, 228

Perlzweig, Dr. M. L., Leader of World Jewish Congress (London), 70, 412-14

Phipps, Sir Eric, British Ambassador in Berlin, 1933-37, then in Paris 1937-39, 104, 256, 375

Popescu, Stelian, Owner of the rightist daily *Universul*, 58, 197-8, 228

Pospisil, Dr. Vilem, Governor of National Bank of Czechoslovakia, 165, 380, 383

Rendell, G. W., F.O. official, British Minister in Sofia, 1938-41, 63, 263

Ribbentrop, Joachim von, 18, 142

Roberts, F. K., Member of Central Department of the F.O., 85, 87, 341, 350, 359, 363, 376, 379, 383

Ross, A. D. M., F.O. official, 38, 72, 133, 148, 162, 233, 255, 256, 263, 268, 295, 299, 314, 318

Salter, Sir Arthur, M.P., Parliamentary Secretary, Ministry of Shipping 1939-41, 135, 331

Sargent, Sir Orme G., Assistant Under-Secretary of State for Foreign Affairs, 1934-39, 12-13, 15, 37, 41-2, 61, 64, 69, 72, 85, 103, 124, 154, 162, 165, 222, 242, 251, 283, 286, 353, 363, 377

Seton-Watson, Hugh, British historian, 42, 53, 140, 156, 298

Sidor, Karel, Slovak Minister without Portfolio in Czechoslovak Government, 1938-1939; Minister of the Interior of Republic of Slovakia, 1939, 93, 110, 322, 340, 370-1, 404

Sima, Horia, Leader of the Iron Guard, 51, 52

Speaight, R. L., F.O. official (Central Department), 152, 154, 398

Stopford, R. J., British liaison officer in Prague, 101, 110, 164, 349-52, 374

Strang, W., Counsellor in the F.O.; Head of Central Department, 1937-39, 102, 164-5, 376

Syrový, Jan, Czechoslovak Army General, Prime Minister, October–November 1938, 83, 85, 100, 103, 340

Szálasi, Ferenc, Leader of the Hungarian Arrow Cross Movement, 10, 119, 125, 131-3, 135-6, 138-9, 149, 152, 154, 247, 252-3, 301, 308, 313, 321, 323, 327-9, 355

Szekfü, Gyula, Hungarian historian, 156-7

Széll, Kálmán, Hungarian Minister of the Interior, 1937-38, 124-5, 229, 241

Tătărescu, G., Romanian Prime Minister, 1934-37, 1939-40, 11, 24, 26-9, 30, 31, 57, 71, 171, 176, 181, 186, 187, 191, 203-4, 210, 230, 233, 238, 246, 298, 304

Teleki, Count Pál, Hungarian Prime Minister, 1939-41, 136, 138, 139, 143, 151-3, 154, 165, 331, 372, 398, 406 ff.

Tiso, Josef, President of Council of Province of Slovakia, 1938-39; Prime Minister of Republic of Slovakia, 1939-45, 91-6, 109-13, 340, 385, 389, 403-5

Titulescu, N., Romanian Minister for Foreign Affairs, 1932-36, 24-6, 28, 31, 170, 176, 178, 187, 191, 193, 204, 220, 238, 243, 245-6, 249, 257

Troutbeck, J. M., 1st Secretary at the British Legation in Prague, 1937-39, 91-3, 102, 110, 164-5

Tuka, Vojtech (Béla), Deputy Prime Minister of Slovakia, 1939, 90, 94, 113, 370, 401

Tylor, Royall, British financial expert, 128, 134-5, 148, 164

Subject Index

427

LANC (Romania), *See* League of Christian National Defence
League of Christian National Defence (Romania), 9, 22
League of Nations, 41, 51, 64, 70, 93, 120, 148-9, 257, 269, 284, 289, 291, 294, 310, 319, 320-1, 365, 401
Legion of Archangel Michael, *See* Iron Guard

Minorities Treaties, *See* League of Nations

National Alliance (Czechoslovakia, Bohemia-Moravia), 76, 85, 100, 168, 324, 369
National Christian party (Romania), 5, 23, 25, 28-9, 32-3, 38-9, 43, 59, 167, 171, 175, 197, 202, 203, 204, 230, 249
National Fascist Community (Czechoslovakia), 79
National Liberal party (Romania), 8-9, 22-6, 29, 32-3, 43, 48-9, 56, 120, 171, 173, 175, 203, 210, 227, 238-9, 246, 254, 276, 288
National Peasant party (Romania), 8, 22, 24-5, 27, 29, 31-3, 48-9, 56, 167, 171, 175, 186, 188, 192, 195, 203, 210, 230, 238, 245, 255, 276, 304
National Renaissance Front (Romania), 50, 372
National Socialism in Czechoslovakia, 168, 194, 362, 364, 369
National Socialism in Hungary, 118-20, 122ff., 138, 141, 148, 182, 229, 241, 247, 252-3, 301-2, 308, 313, 315-16, 323, 325, 329, 342, 343, 354-5, 366-7, 394ff., 406-7
National Socialism in Romania, 227, 261
National Socialist party (Czechoslovakia), 76, 83, 168, 194, 337, 343, 345, 370
National Socialist party (Hungary), *See* Arrow Cross
National Unity party (Hungary), *See* Party of National Unity (Hungary)
Neo-Liberal party (Romania), 23, 33, 243
Nyilas (nyilaskeresztes), *See* Arrow Cross

Palestine (Jewish emigration to), 224, 262-4
Party of National Unity (Bohemia-Moravia), 85, 369, 374, 415
Party of National Unity (Hungary), 9, 10, 118, 122, 145, 407
Party of Slovak Unity (Slovakia), 92, 111, 364, 369-70
Popular Front (Spain), 26, 186

Romanian Front ("Frontul Românesc"), 23-4, 43-4, 56, 174, 203, 230, 246, 255
Royalist Dictatorship (Romania), 4, 32, 43, 47, 71, 190

Scythe Cross Movement (Hungary), 118-19, 247, 313
Slovak People's party, 4, 5, 76, 79, 81, 89-94, 95, 96, 99, 101, 109, 169, 334, 338, 345, 370, 418
Social Democratic party (Czechoslovakia), 76, 168, 333, 339, 345, 369
Sokol (Czechoslovakia), 101, 374
Straja Țării (Sentry of the Fatherland, Romania), 32, 234

Totul pentru Țară (Romania), *See* Iron Guard

Young Unity Movement (National Youth Movement, Bohemia-Moravia), 86, 374, 379

ROMANIA

Area

Before World War I:	139,000 km²
After World War I:	295,000 km²
After World War II:	237,500 km²

Population

Census of 29 December 1930:	17,793,252
Estimate for 1939:	19,934,000

The main political parties at the 1933 and 1937 elections

	1933			1937		
	votes	%	seats	votes	%	seats
National Liberal Party (nationalist, right wing)	1,518,864	51	300	1,103,353	35.9	152
National Peasant Party (democratic, centre)	414,685	13.9	29	626,612	20.4	86
Iron Guard (fascist)	—	—	—	478,378	15.6	66
League of National Christian Defence (anti-semitic, extreme right, led by A. C. Cuza)	133,205	4.5	9			
National Agrarian Party (anti-semitic, extreme right, led by O. Goga)	121,748	4.1	9			
National Christian Party (Goga and Cuza)				281,167	9.2	39
Neo-Liberal Party (pro-Fascist, led by George Bratianu)	147,665	4.9	10	119,361	3.9	16
Hungarian Party (right wing)	119,562	4.0	8	136,139	4.4	19
Radical Peasants Party (left wing, led by Grigore Iunian)	82,930	2.8	6	69,198	2.3	9
Peasants Party (democratic, led by Nicolae Lupu)	152,167	5.1	11	—	—	—

CZECHOSLOVAKIA

Area

140,000 km^2

Population

Census of February 1921:	13,374,364
Census of December 1930:	14,729,536
Czecho-Slovakia after Munich (estimate):	9,680,068

The main political parties at the 1935 elections

	seats	votes (%)
Republican Party of Agrarians (right centre)	46	14
Social Democratic Party	38	13
Communist Party	30	10
Czechoslovak National Socialist Party (democratic; centre)	28	9
Czechoslovak People's Party (centre)	20	7
Slovak People's Party (right wing)	20	7
Fascists	6	2
Sudetendeutsche Party (Henlein)	44	15

HUNGARY

Area

Before World War I: 325,000 km²
After World War I: 93,000 km²

Population

Census of 1930:   8,688,319
Census of January 1941*:   13,643,620

The main political parties at the 1935 and 1939 elections

	1935 seats	1939 seats
Party of National Unity (from February 1939: Party of Hungarian Life); right wing; anti-semitic	170†	180†
Independent Smallholders Party (democratic, centre)	25	14
Social Democratic Party	11	5
Christian Opposition	10	3
Liberal and Democratic Opposition	7	5
Arrow Cross (six National Socialist parties and groupings)	2‡	49

*Subsequent to the reincorporation of Slovak and Ruthene territory (November 1938 and March 1939) and of Northern Transylvania (August 1940)
†The number includes independent deputies and representatives of rightist groups which joined the Government party
‡Two small Nazi parties each achieved one seat